A Practical Approach
to Serials Cataloging

FOUNDATIONS IN LIBRARY AND
INFORMATION SCIENCE VOLUME 2

Editors: Hans H. Weber, *Assistant Director for Technical Services,*
University of Houston Libraries, and
Warren N. Boes, *Director of Libraries, University of Georgia*
Libraries

FOUNDATIONS IN LIBRARY AND INFORMATION SCIENCE

A Series of Monographs

Series Editors: Hans H. Weber, *Assistant Director for Technical Services, University of Houston Libraries*

Warren N. Boes, *Director of Libraries, University of Georgia Libraries*

Volume 1. The Mexican American: A Critical Guide to Research Aids
Barbara J. Robinson, *Bibliographer for Latin American and Mexican American Studies, University of California Library, Riverside, and* J. Cordell Robinson, *Associate Professor, Department of History, California State College, San Bernardino*

Volume 2. A Practical Approach to Serials Cataloging
Lynn S. Smith, *Head, Serials Department, University of California Library, Riverside*

Volume 3. The Microform Revolution in Libraries
Michael R. Gabriel, *Coordinator of Government Publications, Microforms and Serials, Mankato State University Library, and* William C. Roselle, *Director, University of Wisconsin Library, Milwaukee*

Volume 4. China in Books: A Basic Bibliography in Western Language
Norman E. Tanis, *Director,* David L. Perkins, *Chief Bibliographer, and* Justine Pinto, *all California State University Library, Northridge*

Volume 5. Budgetary Control in Academic Libraries
Murray S. Martin, *Associate Dean of Libraries, Pennsylvania State University Library, University Park*

Volume 6. Cost Analysis of Library Functions: A Total System Approach
Betty Jo Mitchell, *Associate Librarian,* Norman E. Tanis, *Director, and* Jack Jaffe, *all California State University Library, Northridge*

Volume 7. A Guide to Academic Library Instruction
Hannelore B. Rader, *Center of Educational Resources, Eastern Michigan University, Ypsilanti*

Volume 8. The Management of a Public Library
Harold R. Jenkins, *Director, Kansas City Public Library, Kansas City, Missouri*

Volume 9. Development and Organization of a Health Sciences Library
Charles W. Sargent, *Director, Texas Tech University Medical Library, Lubbock*

A Practical Approach to Serials Cataloging

by LYNN S. SMITH
Head, Serials Department
Library, University of California—Riverside

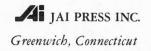 JAI PRESS INC.

Greenwich, Connecticut

Library of Congress Cataloging in Publication Data

Smith, Lynn S.
    A practical approach to serials cataloging.

    (Foundations of Library and information science; v. 2)
    Bibliography: p.
    1. Cataloging of serial publications.   I. Title.   II. Series.
Z695.7.S55   025.3'4'3   77-25282
ISBN 0-89232-007-9

*Dedicated
with Love
to my
Parents*

CONTENTS

LIST OF ILLUSTRATIONS

Preface

In the first volume of *Serial slants,* Louis Shores wrote an article entitled "Serials in the library school curriculum," in which he stressed that, since a new curriculum was emerging and standards for library schools were being rewritten, this was the time for the Serials Round Table of the American Library Association to fight for more attention to be paid to the preparation of serials workers. He sent out a questionnaire and solicited answers regarding serials in the curriculum and discovered that much more attention was being paid to these pesky publications in 1950 than had been paid in 1938. With respect to serials cataloging, Mr. Shores had this to say:

> There is usually a section devoted to the preparation of non-book materials that treats periodicals, newspapers, monographs, annuals, society and government publications, bringing in detailed attention to corporate entry.[1]

He went on to say that:

> . . .most library schools do not end their serial study with core courses. Elected advance courses frequently contain additional consideration of serials.[2]

However, it would seem from the experience of most serials librarians that the preparation received in library school is forgotten, if it is indeed as comprehensive as Mr. Shores seemed to think in his article. Surely this preparation is not always substantial, for all too many library schools would rather ignore the existence of serial problems, which can, in their opinion, usually be worked out in an on-the-job situation if necessary. Certainly serials are too difficult to discuss in most classes.

Another viewpoint would seem to give the situation more as it really is in the minds of most serials librarians:

> Most library school students are graduated without a glimmer of what serial problems are to be faced by them in their professional careers, regardless of the library department in which they come to be engaged. Other library departments come to be staffed with people simply unaware of the problems presented in making serials available.[3]

It also seems that serial publications are destined to be considered some kind of poor relation to the monograph. They are never really considered in their own right, but as problems deterent to the neat organization of the catalog and the orderly running of a neatly pigeonholed library. With such an attitude from those already in the profession, how can we expect better from neophytes?

> Large libraries were the first to feel the inadequacy of dealing with serials as though they were slightly variant monographs and . . . the Librarian of the British Museum wrote, in some exasperation:

> "There are two main reasons in favor of the separation of serials, periodicals, or whatever other name we may give the class. The theoretical reason is, that they are not like other books and that the rules for one will not apply to the other . . . it is a structural difference of the mode of composition.

> "The practical reason is, that you eliminate the chief disturbing elements of a catalogue. The catalogue of ordinary books, if well made in the first instance, requires little alteration and needs only additions; but the catalogue of serials by the very nature of its contents, wants continued change."[4]

This attitude unfortunately still exists all too widely. It would be nice to see library schools teaching students to become specialists in serials, as they teach them to become catalogers, reference people, children's librarians, and the like. Too many librarians cannot seem to see beyond the "book." This is too bad, for serials tend to scare people off and they may never discover the joy and exasperation of working with these publications.

> To many librarians the word "serials" immediately brings to mind spectres of difficulties and complexities which help defeat the simple ways to handle these publications before any action is taken. Just as the word "documents" raises ghosts, so serials have suffered over the years from the attitudes taken by many of those who handle them. I am not denying that both serials and documents raise problems, but so do corporate entries for separates, subject headings, and similar problems, which the librarian takes in stride, raising no mental block of fear to hinder solving the problem.[5]

Serials are much too important to be so ignored in libraries. In the light of coming revolutions in bibliographic control, as well as in the production of the publications to be controlled, adequate theory must be learned so that the principles of cataloging serials will not be lost and forgotten. The "fate of the serial, cared for by unskilled librarians"[6] is unthinkable. This book is to teach librarians to become skilled in work with serials, particularly in the cataloging thereof.

Serials need not be frightening. They are unorthodox, annoying and fun. They are a challenge to those who will accept the taunts they give. This book will attempt to teach those who would like to learn the principles which can guide the cataloger of serial publications.

It is the hope of this book, too, to offer some of the challenge to those who might never have the opportunity to be challenged by serials, in the hopes that they might seek out such an opportunity. It is also offered to those who have found themselves with such an opportunity and don't know what to do with it. Hopefully, those who have worked with serials will also benefit from what is contained herein.

I hope to build upon any expertise which you, the reader, might already have acquired in monographic cataloging and help to apply this knowledge to serials. This book should not be used in a vacuum, but as a companion to Andrew Osborn's monumental *Serial publications* and other articles and monographs which give a broader view of serials librarianship, cataloging and the professional spectrum in general. Serials cataloging is one of the most exciting aspects of our Renaissance-man-like existence as librarians.

In short, I hope to instill in you, dear Reader, some of the joy, exasperation, hate, fondness and — yes indeed — love I have for serials!

Riverside, California
September 1975   *lss*

FOOTNOTES
1. Louis Shores "Serials in the library school curriculum," *Serial slants* 1 (October, 1950):8.
2. *Ibid.*, p. 11.
3. John L. Moriarty "Let's tell each other about our serial problems," *Serial slants* 1 (July, 1950):2.
4. H. B. Wheatley, *How to catalogue a library,* London: Elliot Stock, p. 212, quoted in Edgar G. Simpkins, *A Study of serials processing,* M.S. in L.S. theses, Western Reserve University, 1951, p. 3.
5. Bella E. Shachtman, "Simplification of serials records work," *Serial slants* 3 (July, 1935):868.
6. J. Harris Gable "The new serials department," *Library journal* 60 (November 15, 1935):868.

Acknowledgements and Other Etceteras

First of all, I would like to thank all of the people who helped to make this work possible: Dick Anable, Deana Astle, Betty Baughman, Edward Blume, Judith Cannan, Phil Crocfer, Marian Davis, Margaret Ellis, Dorothy Glasby, Joseph Howard, Irene Hurlbert, Herb Linville, Seymour Lubetzky, Margaret McKinley, Norman McKinley, Marjorie Peregoy, Mary Sauer, Roberta Stevenson and Jean Wright. A very special thanks to Betty Cook and Neal Edgar and my deepest appreciation to my editor, Hans H. Weber. Thanks are also very much in order for Janice Tew, who typed the manuscript, and Toni Van Deusen, for some of the illustrations. My thanks also to the American Library Association and the International Federation of Library Associations for permission to quote from their publications.

And now for the "etceteras." For all of those of you who tend to get lost in the alphabet soup we have been inundated with, I have made a sincere effort to explain all of the acronyms and initialisms which appear in the text at the first point that they appear. If, however, you find yourself getting lost, turn to Appendix A for a glossary of "Acronyms and Initialisms Used in This Book."

Capitalization in this book has followed cataloging practices, as outlined in Appendix B. This means that not all words are capitalized as they would be in normal writing. The capitalization in quotations has not been changed, however.

Another brief note on style: the style of footnotes. All footnotes have been numbered with Arabic numerals. However, some of the sources quoted had very important footnotes which also had to be quoted in order to be discussed. In order to avoid confusion as to which was my footnote and which was the footnote in the source document, all source footnotes have been enclosed in parentheses.

As far as timeliness is concerned, it seemed best to try to codify what had been done to date in the world of serials cataloging. However, as this book shows, the changes are whirling by one ever more rapidly. Even as it goes to press, it is being outdated, although much of the concepts have not yet been toppled. When the dust clears above the rubble, perhaps it will be time to begin a new chronicle. Who can know yet what tomorrow brings?

Chapter I

By Way of Introduction: the Problem at Hand

Serials are a problem. This is probably one of the greatest understatements of all time, to which all who have ever had anything to do with serials will readily attest. They are hard to define, pin down and control. They are best handled by specialists, but such people are hard to come by, since serials are virtually ignored in most library schools. As a result, serials are usually given short shrift in libraries, particularly from a cataloging standpoint. This is truly unfortunate, since they are probably the most important and valuable assets any library can have.

First of all, let's see what we can do about defining the word "serial." Building such a definition is basic to any discussion of this genus of publication. This has always been a thorny problem. Here are some worthy attempts:

> A publication issued in successive parts, usually at regular intervals and continued indefinitely.
>
> Cutter, Charles Ammi, *Rules for a dictionary catalog,* 4th edition, Washington: Government Printing Office, 1904.

> A publication issued in successive parts, usually at regular intervals, and, as a rule, intended to be continued indefinitely. Serials include periodicals, annuals (reports, yearbooks, etc.).
>
> *Catalog rules; author and title entries,* American edition, compiled by committees of the American Library Association and the Library Association, Boston: ALA Publishing Board, 1908.

> A publication not issued by a government agency, appearing at regular or stated periods of less than a year, and including articles on various subjects.
>
> *Union List of serials in libraries of the United States and Canada,* edited by Winifred Gregory, 1st edition, New York: Wilson, 1927.

1

A publication which appears in successive parts or numbers usually at regular intervals and from which its character, auspices, or name, seems to carry assurance of indefinite appearance.

> Wyner, James I. *Reference work,* Chicago: American Library Association, 1930.

Publications issued in successive parts which are intended to be continued indefinitely, excluding all books issued in a limited number of parts. The term "serials," therefore, includes periodicals.

> Iowa State College Library. *A summary of reports, July 1, 1923 - June 30, 1933,* Ames, Iowa, 1933.

Any publication, whether issued at regular or irregular intervals, with some scheme for consecutive numbering, and intended to be continued indefinitely.

> Gable, J. Harris. *Manual of serials work,* Chicago: American Library Association, 1937.

Any publication issued serially or in successive parts more or less regularly.

> Shores, Louis. *Basic reference books,* Chicago: American Library Association, 1939.

A publication consisting of successive parts purposely related to each other by some common feature, in certain cases issued at regular intervals, and intended to be continued indefinitely. . . Serials. . include periodicals, annuals (reports, year-books, etc.), monographic or nonmonographic serial publications of societies and institutions, governmental bodies and other miscellaneous corporate bodies.

> Iskenderian, Yuchanik. *The extent and possibilities for cooperation in the cataloging of serial publications, based on a survey of libraries of over 350,000 volumes,* M.S. in L.S. thesis, Columbia University, 1942.

A publication issued in successive parts, usually at regular intervals, and, as a rule, intended to be continued indefinitely. Serials include periodicals, annuals (reports, year-books, etc.), and memoirs, proceedings, and transactions of societies.

> *A.L.A glossary of library terms,* Chicago: American Library Association, 1943.

Any publications in parts, appearing at intervals, usually regular ones. The term includes periodicals, annuals, and proceedings or memoirs of societies: e.g., Number 17, Part 7, Monographs 18, 42nd Annual Report.

> Sharp, H. A. *Cataloguing; a textbook for use in libraries,* 4th edition, London: Grafton, 1948.

Any title issued in parts which is incomplete in the collection.

> Shachtman, Bella E. "Simplification of serials records work," *Serial slants* 3 (July, 1952).

. . .The term serial should be considered as including all publications issued in successively numbered or dated parts, except newspapers, books issued in parts, looseleaf services, telephone directories, press releases, and comic books. . .not. . .U. S. Federal, state, and municipal serial documents unless they are publications of institutions such as libraries, museums, universities, etc. . . .not. . .United Nations documents unless they are publications of United Nations specialized agencies such as UNESCO, FAO, etc. [to be reported by the Library of Congress.]

Library of Congress. *Instructions for reporting serials for inclusion in New Serial Titles,* revised edition, Washington: Library of Congress, March 1959.

. . .Any publication, in any format, issued in parts for indeterminate periods at stated or unstated periods or intervals. [COSATI definition]

Information Dynamics Corporation. *A serials data program for science and technology; results of a feasibility study.* . ., Reading, Mass., 1965.

A publication issued in successive parts bearing numerical or chronological designations and intended to be continued indefinitely. Serials include periodicals, newspapers, annuals (reports, year-books, etc.), the journals, memoirs, proceedings, transactions, etc., of societies, and numbered monographic series.

Anglo-American cataloging rules. North American text, Chicago: American Library Association, 1967.

A publication issued in successive parts bearing numerical or chronological designations and intended to be continued indefinitely. Serials include periodicals (e.g., newspapers, journals, and the memoirs, proceedings, transactions, etc., of societies), annuals (reports, year-books, etc.), and numbered monographic series.

Anglo-American cataloguing rules. British text, London: Library Association, 1967.

. . .Publications (1) which appear in parts at intervals for an indefinite period of time and (2) which may successively be prepared by different authors, compilers or editors.

Dunkin, Paul S. *Cataloging U.S.A.,* Chicago: American Library Association, 1969.

Any publication issued in successive parts, appearing at intervals, usually regular ones, and, as a rule, intended to be continued indefinitely. The term includes periodicals, newspapers, annuals, numbered monographic series and the proceedings, transactions and memoirs of societies. Not to be confused with SERIES. . .(In the United States of America the term 'serial' is used to mean a periodical, regular or irregular.)

Harrod, Leonard Montague. *The librarians' glossary. . .and reference book,* 3rd edition, London: Deutsch, 1971.

A publication in successive parts bearing numerical or chronological designations and intended to be continued indefinitely.

Johnson, Donald W. *Toward a National Serials Data Project: final report of the National Serials Pilot Project,* Washington: Association of Research Libraries, 1972.

The definitions vary in their wording and in their inclusiveness, but some general patterns can be seen. Periodicity is expressed by means of dates, seasons, religious holidays (like Lady Day or Martinmas), months, or any other subdivisions of the year. The *Anglo-American cataloging rules* define periodicals as being issued more frequently than annually, so annuals and other publications issued at established frequencies of greater than a year (i.e., biennial, quinquennial, etc.) are technically not periodicals. They are serials, along with irregular publications which fit the other criteria of the definitions, such as bearing numerical or chronological designations. The term "serials," however, embraces all periodicals as well, although some libraries distinguish between the two and accord them different treatments. Serial publications can be further differentiated from nonserials by the following:

> By nature they are unlimited. They may be suspended, but they do not conclude. External circumstances, but scarcely exhaustion of the subject, bring about their end. A second difference lies in the number of their authors. Apart from collections and composite works, books possess more than one author only by way of exception. With periodicals, it is the reverse.[1]

Andrew Osborn makes elaborate attempts to define serials (and periodicals) in his book *Serial publications*. When he finally comes to the end, he drafts a very vague and very general, but also a very practical definition of a serial for library purposes.

> . . .A serial can be defined. . .as any item which lends itself to serial treatment in a library, that is, to listing in its checking records, whether they are manual or computerized; to cataloging and classifying as a serial; and to shelving in the current-periodical room or among the bound volumes of serials in the bookstacks.[2]

Osborn justifies his definition with what he calls "provisional serials" and "pseudoserials." Provisional serials are hybrid publications. They are basically monographs or closed monographic sets, updated by supplements which are serials in nature. The *Library of Congress/National Union catalogs* are examples of this type. *New serial titles* would also fall into this category, as would encyclopedias with annual supplements which update the basic contents. Some directories, catalogs, and legal publications also operate in this manner. It is better to give them serial treatment so that they will stand together on the shelves, so that they will be updated properly, and so that all pieces will be accounted for.

Osborn defines pseudoserials as publications which are frequently revised and updated. Examples are Burke's *Peerage* and *Periodicals for small and medium-sized libraries*. Often on the first go-around the publication is cataloged as a monograph. However, as the work continues to be revised and reissued, libraries, including the Library of Congress, which admits it does this often, although perhaps not consistently, tend to recatalog it as a serial with updated editions. Such was the fate of the title illustrated opposite:

Cattell, Jaques, 1904–   ed.
Directory of American scholars, a biographical directory, edited by Jaques Cattell. Lancaster, Pa., The Science press, 1942.

4 p. l., 928 p. 26ᶜᵐ.

1. Scholars, American—Direct. 2 Educators, American—Direct. 3. U. S.—Biog.   i. Title.

42–18822

Library of Congress   LA2311.C32

[5]   923.773

Directory of American scholars; a biographical directory.
[1st]–   ed.; 1942–
New York [etc.] R. R. Bowker Co. [etc.]
   v. 26–29 cm.
Editor: 1942–   J. Cattell.
1. Scholars, American—Direct.   i. Cattell, Jaques, 1904–   ed.
LA2311.C32   923.773   57–9125

Fig. 1-1. Title cataloged originally by LC as a monograph (top card) and recataloged as a serial (bottom card): a pseudoserial.

The *Anglo-American cataloging rules* allow for this in the introductory notes to serial rules, which state:

> Certain types of publications that are not true serials but that are issued frequently in new editions may be cataloged according to the rules of description for serials. These include certain directories, guidebooks, handbooks, etc., even though they may be of personal authorship.[3]

It is much more economical to treat the publication in this manner: there are fewer cards in the catalog, and less titles to be cataloged in the backlog; serial procedures can be instituted, such as claiming and the processing of superseding volumes. Osborn also hastens to point out that the volumes would get to the shelves faster than if they had been individually cataloged, and they would be easier to locate in the catalog. (After all, when looking for his *Peerage, Landed gentry* or other publications, who can remember Burke's first name?)

Another type of publication problem which serial catalogers come across from time to time is the conference publication. Various factors involved in the economy of cataloging and filing, as mentioned already, call for the elimination of useless added entries and duplication of card sets in the catalog for conferences. This tends to argue for serial treatment of publications of established and continuing conferences wherever possible. Unfortunately, regularity and uniformity are not notable characteristics of conferences, and successful serial handling requires that there be publications of two or more meetings issued with stable, or reasonably stable, titles and a stable conference name. Conference names, methods of numbering, names of related bodies, and forms of publication are subject to capricious change.[4] A really permanent and satisfactory entry cannot be assured until the series is concluded, as with many publications of a capricious serial-like nature, but at least some guidelines can be tentatively agreed upon when this so-called stability is reached. The Library of Congress has probably found the most tenable solution by cataloging these publications as monographs until they establish themselves adequately enough to be effectively cataloged as serials.

It is because of publications like these that the definition of "serial" becomes muddied in library practice. The treatment of monographic series, also a type of serial, also threatens what is not too clear anyway. For purposes of further discussion here, the AACR (*Anglo-American cataloging rules*) definition somewhat tempered by Osborn's, thus allowing somewhat for local customs, will be used. We shall allow for a "large measure of agreement in principle together with great latitude in practice,"[5] with, at the end of this book, hopefully a little less latitude in the latter, as well.

Now that we know what serials are, it would be hard to deny their importance in our libraries today. Serials are a relatively new form of publishing, but they have risen fast in their short history. Although some predecessors' existences have been chronicled, serial publications primarily came into being in the sixteenth century. Their importance has increased steadily since that time. Several witnesses will give their testimonials.

At the first meeting of the American Library Association, the importance of serials, as well as the problems they create, was described as follows:

> If railway companies, and coal companies, and hospitals, and colleges, and penitentiaries, and benevolent institutions of every sort—to say nothing of historical societies and library companies—keep publishing their annual reports for another century as they publish them now, may it not require the most active labor of the best librarian in America, to collect, to preserve, to bind, to arrange, and catalogue them all? Yet few books are more instructive as to special matters; few more often wanted by a large class of readers.[6]

The importance of serials grew. H. O. Severance, librarian of the University of Missouri, said in 1928:

> . . .Research work without immediate publication in a periodical is unthinkable. The periodical therefore is the handmaid to the researcher. . . The periodical is the main tool which the researcher uses in the field of the humanities. It is next in importance only to the microscope and the chemical reagents in the scientific laboratories.[7]

This point of view was furthered and amplified by J. Harris Gable, who said:

> The periodical today serves as a link between the newspaper and the book. The newspaper announces an event, the periodical follows it up with a more detailed account, but the book comes so much later that its treatment is really historical. Furthermore, much information is published in magazines on subjects about which no books have yet been written, even on subjects about which no books may ever be written.[8]

Margaret Hutchins remarked:

> It is no longer necessary to argue for the importance of periodicals and newspapers in reference work. From childhood up the present generation has read them and used them for information more than books. In view of the innumerable enthusiastic testimonials of reference librarians as to the supremacy of periodicals as reference materials it may become necessary to write an apologetic for books, lest the periodicals elbow them entirely out of libraries, and serials departments monopolize reference work.[9]

The Library of Congress began to notice the importance of serials and began to do something to better its bibliographic control of these publications. In 1946, LC pointed out the role of serials in the library:

In an age when the preponderance of publication is in serial form—newspapers, magazines, official and unofficial series of all kinds—it is obvious that upon a Library's control of its serials depends much of its ability to be of service.[10]

The following epoch-making statement came from the Library of Congress the next year regarding serials:

Serial publications (including newspapers, periodicals, bulletins, reports, most Government documents, and books in series), constitute perhaps 75 percent of all publications, an indispensible part from the viewpoint of research. It is in serial publications that advance information and discussion are found; in them are found also the detailed records which support most scientific, legal, and historical study. Attention to the acquisition and recording of serial publications is, therefore, of most importance to every large research library. Because the separate issues of serials cannot be treated individually as are books, but must be considered in conjunction with other issues, they represent the form of publication which is most difficult to control at all stages—acquisition, accessioning, processing, and service.[11]

And, last but not least, Miss E.M.R. Ditmas said:

. . .the literary, scientific or technical periodical has come to stay—more, it has won such an honoured place amongst the tools of research that it has attained the right to be treated *sui generis*, and not as a poor relation of the book.[12]

The latter part of Miss Ditmas' remark is very important. Serials have come a long way as far as their treatment in libraries is concerned. At first they were ignored or treated as variant monographs. As libraries became aware of the special problems which serials caused, special checking records were devised and acquisitions control attained top priority. Still, as far as cataloging was concerned, serials were forced into a mold evolved for monographic publications. Although the rules still seem to treat serials as a country cousin of monographs, this is changing. International standards are being set up solely with serial publications in mind. More attention is being paid to serials, formerly the stepchildren of the library, relegated to some obscure corner or basement. Serials are beginning to come into their own in the library as they have already in the academic world.

The movement forward into the light of day is moving slowly in some quarters, however. It has been pointed out by a number of librarians that there is a real lack of need to catalog serials for there are many guides and aids available. Bibliographies list the titles and indexes analyze their contents. What more can be desired? Besides, periodicals and serials are not stable and this makes them difficult to control. Wouldn't it be better just to forget the whole thing?

Absolutely not! Serials are much too important to be overlooked like that.

A[n]. . .essential to effective work with serials is adequate cataloging and classification. This is basic to a high standard in reference service to the users of the library.[13]

These publications [serials] are now so profuse and at the same time so significant for library purposes that librarians should have a good grasp of their nature and of the modes of controlling them.[14]

Bibliographic control can be defined as the process of uniquely identifying items of bibliographic information. Cataloging is an important aspect of bibliographic control. It is basic to all library work.

First of all, we need to define "cataloging." Kathyrn Luther Henderson lists the following as the functions performed by cataloging:

(1) Chooses an entry to serve as the main entry.
(2) Chooses added entries.
(3) Constructs headings for main entries and added entries.
(4) Provides a description of the physical item.
(5) Determines the subject of the publication for subject cataloging.
(6) Provides the necessary auxiliary entries such as references, information cards, etc.
(7) Provides an inventory record of the item cataloged.
(8) Prepares for the integration of all entries into an existing catalog.[15]

Heavy demand is made upon serials. They must be accessible, and this requires adequate records and prompt processing. Serials should be cataloged adequately to make this important material more readily available. You need to inform patrons that you have what they are looking for in your library, whether it be a specific title, a publication of a given organization, material on a special subject, or whatever. Whole issues and runs of issues need to be integrated into the library's collection and into the main library catalog. Proper coverage of access points in the catalog will provide the maximum of self-service to patrons who use the catalog.

Analytic cataloging — that is, the cataloging of individual articles or other specific parts for authors, titles, and subject content — may need to be done, especially if they do not appear in a bibliography or an index. There needs to be some access to the serials in any given library, no matter how sophisticated the method. This is cataloging.

Serials are being covered better and better in reference books, union lists, etc. There are more and more indexes, even on computers, which provide access. However, if the title being looked for as the result of reference searches is unfindable because it cannot be uniquely identifed in any given library as a single bibliographic entity, great problems and frustrations will occur. There would be no point in having spent money for purchase of a title if you cannot find it because there are ten others which are the same or similar. Even if you only have a list of holdings or a Kardex, the titles which appear on it have to be adequately identified. This is cataloging.

Cataloging doesn't necessarily refer to just representation of records in a public catalog, however; bibliographic control is even more important behind the scenes. Serials need to be cataloged for technical processing reasons, too. Serials need to be adequately identified for order and receipt purposes, especially if titles are identical or nearly so, or might be identified differently. When this is done, there will only be *one* primary location to look in for information on this title. There will be only one entry. Cataloging will supply essential data for check-in records, such as publisher, place, frequency, history statements, call number, etc. It will also produce a uniform medium for the arrangement of the charging system (i.e., entry or call number). It will provide a basis whereby shelving can be controlled. Serials will be bound under directives decided by a cataloger. The entry which the cataloger supplies, and its attendant bibliographic data, will control and direct the recording of serial issues so they won't backlog. Proper coverage of access points in the public catalog will serve most of the patron's needs. Without adequate cataloging, the library's serials will stack up on the floor with no hope of access exept by rooting through the mess. Serials need to be cataloged so that libraries can join in cooperative ventures like union lists, too. Adequate interlibrary loan cannot exist without cataloged serials. Whether a library follows the AACR or any other rules; whether it gives detailed cataloging, with complete classification, subject headings, and the whole gamut of auxiliary functions or not, the point is this: adequate bibliographic control of serials is an absolute must. Cataloging is the key to this bibliographic control. Without it, there is a naught but chaos.

Yuchanik Iskenderian outlined in her 1942 thesis[16] the following difficulties encountered in the cataloging of serial publications:

(1) The continuous nature of serial publication, resulting in changes of title, imprint, edition, size, frequency, and other bibliographic detail;
(2) The use of corporate entry as author or added entry and the problems involved in the establishing of such headings for constantly changing publications;
(3) The inadequacy of reference tools and bibliographies; and
(4) The inadequacy of the rules.

These difficulties are still being encountered, although not so much, nor as deeply as they once were. The cataloging rules have been revamped since Miss Iskendarian wrote. No longer do catalogers have to do the research unrealistically called for by the old rules. Description of serials still plays second fiddle to the rules for monographs, but these rules are also up for revision and perhaps things will change for the better. Corporate headings are still a problem, although the rules have been simplified enormously. It may even come to pass that this problem will not longer exist, at least as main entry for serials. Rules for hierarchical structures within corporate headings may also be simplified. This has always been a problem for serials catalogers, particularly ones who also do government documents. The number of bibliographic tools for serials cataloging has grown a great deal since her writing, *New serial titles* being the principal of these. Many cooperative undertakings on many levels, and even internationally, are making a great impact on the bibliographic control of serials. So, many of the difficulties mentioned in 1942 are being overcome. Still, her first and foremost remains. The nature of the pesky creature itself makes bibliographic "pinning down" a tough job indeed. It also makes it a fun job. Osborn said in 1955:

> The cataloging of monographs is comparatively straightforward; serials run the gamut from the straightforward to the wayward, if not the downright perverse.[17]

Osborn, in his famous article "The crisis in cataloging,"[18] described four theories or philosophies of cataloging: legalist, perfectionist, bibliographic and pragmatic. The legalist point of view calls for elaborate rules for each and every possible situation. This is what the 1949 code revision was to become. For serials there were rules for each particular kind. Seymour Lubetzky picked this code apart and, fortunately for all of us who are cataloging serials now, eased up on the legalistic pressures. Of course, the perfectionist approach cannot have anything to do with serials. A perfectionist cataloger would not touch a serial once because, with the everchanging nature of serials, he would have to touch it again (heaven forbid!). A perfectionist couldn't stand to do that. Backlogs would burgeon. The bibliographic cataloger would try to be much too detailed for serial work. Very rarely do serials really need to be described to the nth degree even if they are dead. Certainly, trying to pin one down while it is alive to painstakingly describe it, would be like trying to catch an elusive butterfly. It is also asking for trouble. Virtually meaningless detail in descriptive notes certainly doesn't serve any real function. The cataloger would feel obligated to chronicle the whims of a typographer, which would be madness. The card catalog would become a barrier between the patron and the material he desired, which is not exactly what the original makers of the catalog envisioned it to be. Osborn's answers to the problems listed here and in Miss Iskenderian's thesis is the last theory of cataloging: the pragmatic approach.

Libraries should conduct their cataloging practices along practical lines. The AACR helps in doing this, for it is by-and-large a practical code. Serials, certainly, demand a pragmatic outlook so that one doesn't get caught up in the tangles of meaningless trivia. The individual needs of each library and its users can be taken into consideration. The code is a standardizing factor, as are the

LC cards and other cataloging aids derived from it. Rules are there because they are necessary. The rules are fairly simple and the catalogers use their judgement. This is absolutely necessary in serials work where a precedent may be being set by the weird thing you have in your hand. The key guidelines in serials work are these: be as rigid as you can within the strictures of the rules of entry. It is here that uniformity is important. "Hang loose," as current jargon would have us do, in regards to description. In all work with serials, you need to know what is demanded of you and then you must rationally apply your knowledge to what you see. The biggest clue is this: use your head! Bella Shachtman summed it all up when she said:

> A direct, thoughtful, common-sense approach, bearing in mind the needs of the institution which you are serving, will help you find the best way to handle serial records for your library.[19]

This is probably the reasoning behind the very cursory treatment serials usually receive in library schools. Librarians, unless they are daring on their own, very rarely discover the headaches and delights of working with serials, a situation which serials librarians have been trying to rectify for a number of years now. Some guidelines can be put down for the edification of all. Then these guidelines can be bent and molded, if necessary, to fit the needs of a given library after a librarian gets on the job. But the principles need to be mastered first, particularly for those who may never get beyond the very basic basics and then go into other areas of librarianship where a knowledge of serials is useful, but total mastery not absolutely necessary.

This book hopes to set down some of these principles. It also proposes some guidelines, based upon experience (sometimes bitter), and observation. Deviations are always possible, but one must remember the implications of such deviations, especially in the light of the coming automated developments. The library's own policies need to be kept in mind, too. The library should tailor its needs, yes, but it should always remember its place in the library world as well. This book will attempt to offer some choices with some discussions of their implications. Consistency is a must. The patron should not be forgotten. And the material should be handled as well as possible.

The material is handled best by a small group of experts. Because library schools do not build these experts, they must band together and learn from each other in unified departments. Then, they must move around and, hopefully, influence others to do the same. All learn to set up central serial records as rallying points. Centralized and integrated serials departments, involving all functions, including cataloging, should come as a by-product of the central serial record. The most efficient set-up is one which includes the serial cataloger, for serials cataloging is part and parcel of the records-keeping operations of the serials department. This, too, will be explored here. The Library of Congress procedures will be discussed. Auxiliary functions to the actual cataloging operations will be discussed and a model routine will be set up. The rules will be covered in some depth with some application in the "real world." Automation will strongly influence the movement into the future, but hopefully will not compromise the principles set down here too much.

But enough of this! Let's get down to the real nitty-gritty — the practical approach to serials cataloging.

FOOTNOTES

1. Georg, Schneider *Handbuch der Bibliographie*, 4th ed. p. 369, (Leipzig: Hiersemann) Quoted in Andrew D. Osborn, pp. 5-6, *Serial Publications: their place and treatment in libraries*, 2d ed., rev. (Chicago: American Library Association , 1973).

2. Osborn, *Serial Publications*, 2d ed., p. 13.

3. *Anglo-American cataloging rules* North American Text (Chicago: American Library Association, 1967) p. 231. This and all following quotations from AACR are reprinted by permission of the American Library Association.

4. Joseph W. Rogers, "Miscellaneous rules including the entries for congresses, conferences, etc.," Chapter VII in Institute on Cataloging Code Revision, Stanford University, July 9-12, 1958. *Working papers* (Stanford, Calif., 1958) p. vii-3.

5. Osborn, *Serial publications*, 2d. ed. p. 19.

6. *Library journal* 1 (November 30, 1876), 94. Quoted in Fred B. Rothman and Sidney Ditzion "Prevailing practices in handling serials," *College and research libraries* 1 (March, 1940), 165, and elsewhere.

7. H. O. Severance, "How periodicals aid research," *Library Journal*, 53: (July 1928), 590-592. Quoted in Pearl Holland Clark *The problem presented by periodicals in college and university libraries* (Chicago: University of Chicago, 1930) p. 2.

8. J. Harris Gable "The new serials department," *Library journal* 60 (November 15, 1935):868.

9. Margaret Hutchins, *Introduction to reference work* (Chicago: American Library Association, 1944), *Serial publications*, 2d ed., p. 103. Quoted in Osborn, p. 42.

10. Library of Congress *Annual report of the Librarian of Congress* 1945 (1946) :31.

11. Library of Congress *Annual report of the Librarian of Congress* 1946, (1947): 400. Also quoted in Osborn *Serial publications*, [1st and 2d ed.].

12. David Grenfell, *Periodicals and serials; their treatment in special libraries* (London: Aslib, 1965) p. v, and elsewhere.

13. A. F. Kuhlman, "Administration of serial and document acquisition and preparation," in William M. Randall, ed., *The acquisition and cataloging of books; papers presented before the Library Institute at the University of Chicago, July 29 to August 9, 1940*, Chicago: University of Chicago Press, (1940) p. 105.

14. Andrew D. Osborn, *Serial publications; their place and treatment in libraries* (Chicago: American Library Association, 1955) p. vii.

15. Kathryn Luther Henderson, "Serial Cataloging revisited — a long search for a little theory and a lot of cooperation" in *Serial publications in large libraries*, edited by Walter C. Allen (London: Clive Bingley, 1971, c. 1970), p. 53.

16. Yuchanik Iskenderian, *The extent and possibilities for co-operation in the cataloging of serial publications, based on a survey of libraries of over 350,000 volumes.* M.S. in L.S. thesis, Columbia University, 1942. p. 6.

17. Osborn, *Serial publications,* p. 121.

18. Andrew D. Osborn, "The crisis in cataloging," *Library quarterly* 11 (October, 1941): 393-411.

19. Bella E. Shachtman, "Simplification of serials records work," *Serial slants* 3 (July, 1952): 6.

Chapter II

Serial Entry and Related Problems

Before any discussion on choice of main entry can really begin, it is necessary to discuss what a main entry is and what it can do.

The main entry in the past was the only place where information could be found in the catalog. All additional access points were references to the main entry. As techniques for card production advanced, the concept of the unit card was introduced. All unit cards are duplicates of the main entry and there is no longer the need for so many references. All cards give basically the same information. The concept of the main entry is diffused. The age of the computer is upon us. The computer can manipulate bibliographic data and provide access points where there were none before. The concept of the main entry is dead. Or is it?

According to the introduction to the Draft Code, the objectives of the catalog are as follows:

> First, to facilitate the location of a particular publication, i.e., of a particular edition of a work which is in the library.

> Second, to relate and display together the editions which a library has of a given work and the works it has of a given author.[1]

The function of the main entry should be to do these things. Therefore, its choice is most important. During the International Conference on Cataloguing Principles in Paris, a discussion took place regarding which of these functions was the more important. The two main protagonists were Seymour Lubetzky and Eva Verona—one favoring entry under one form of the name, and all works assembled there; and the other, entering under the title on the

15

publication. Dr. Verona agreed with Andrew Osborn's point that the catalog is basically for identification and that this is what the reader wants. Mr. Lubetzky argued that in many cases such an entry as Dr. Verona suggested would be confusing and chaotic. He stressed the systematic nature of the catalog. He felt that our "integrated national bibliographical economy" would suffer and our catalogs degenerate to mere finding lists if we did not pay attention to the second of his objectives, a position he has maintained since his Draft Code came out. However, as Leonard Jolley pointed out in his paper, which followed these two, the differences were really ones of emphasis, since both librarians recognized that both objectives are important. Both Lubetzky and Verona agreed that cataloging must be uniform and that this uniformity should be expressed by what is termed the main entry. The main entry is the catalog's medium of communication to the reader. It must be clear for the user.

The makers of the *Anglo-American cataloging rules* felt that the concept of main entry was still an important and viable one for cataloging today and had this to say:

Although the rules are oriented to multiple-entry catalogs, it has still been regarded as necessary to distinguish main entries from added entries. Since this distinction can be one of the most difficult operations in cataloging, it may be asked why it is necessary if all requisite entries are provided in the catalog and, when the unit-card system is used, the descriptive information on each entry is the same. The necessity persists because, for one thing, even in multiple-entry catalogs it sometimes happens that a work, other than the work being cataloged, must be identified by a single entry—e.g. a work about which the work in hand has been written, or a work on which the work in hand has been based. Beyond this requirement in the multiple-entry catalog itself is the manifest general need, permeating all library, bibliographical, and book-trade activities, for a standard mode of identifying bibliographical entities. Such standard identification is of great importance in single-entry bibliographies, book lists, order lists, bibliographical citations, and everyday communications referring to bibliographical entities. By prescribing what shall be the main entry, the rules respond to this necessity for a standard mode of identifying a work. They follow the principle, firmly established in modern cataloging and bibliography, that a work should be specified by its author and title, or if it lacks an author, by its title.[2]

The main entry for a serial is particularly important because of the functions based upon it. Serials need to be shelved in current periodicals reading rooms. This place needs to be a fairly stable one, not subject to the capriciousness of serial publishers. For this reason, "entry," rather than "title," is usually chosen. (This may not always be the same thing. See later on in this chapter and again in Chapter 4.) Serials are peculiar in the library situation because they have so many attendant records: order, receipt, claim, bindery, etc. In order to provide a system of complimentary records, with a minimum of duplication, the single bibliographic entity involved must be identified in a standard fashion. The entry chosen for order files must be chosen with particular care so that expensive duplications will not result. Serials need to be uniformly designated for indexing and abstracting services. Most libraries have some sort of serials list or catalog. This is almost always a single-access tool, although it may have some needed cross references in it. In some small or special libraries, the Kardex or other receipt record is the serial catalog. Because space is at a premium, few references are usually included.

It would seem that serials are most often involved in single-access files or catalogs. Some libraries still put holdings in their public catalogs. This information is most generally found only under the main entry because it is expensive to duplicate it elsewhere. Secondary entries then refer to the main entry for this information. In this way the main entry for a serial really is still the "main entry," as of old. The main entry is still important in terms of subject headings, too. The subarrangement under a given heading in a subject catalog really amounts to a single-access catalog under main entry. Patrons have to be able to find the material they are looking for with ease under the entry that is most logical for it. The heading which is most logical is that which best answers the fundamental objectives of the catalog. Even in the computer age the main entry is important for retrieval purposes. (Why not use the main entry for input into a computer catalog?) There is need for main entry to achieve consistency and maintain standards. The concept of main entry is still very much with us in cataloging today.

The concept of entry for serials has changed somewhat through the years. Under British Museum rule 17C, periodicals are entered under the form "PERIODICAL PUBLICATIONS," subdivided by place of publication. Corporate publications are put under the appropriate form heading for the academy, society or institution. Directories are under "DIRECTORIES," almanacs under "EPHEMERIDES," and the like. This put a great burden of geographic knowledge and specialized expertise on the shoulders of the user. Fortunately, this system never really caught on in the United States and is pretty much on the way out in Great Britain. The alternative left is some sort of entry based on the publication itself. For many serials, this alternative means title, for almost all serials have titles. Some may have authors as well, and this might be the choice. However, catalogers are to base their choice of main entry on the wording of the title-page, with the addition of other openly-expressed statements, if needed. This has simplified the role of the cataloger to some degree from the form headings of the British Museum.

The rule for choice of entry of serials in AACR is rule 6. It seems surprising to find a rule stated specifically for serials, since AACR is trying to get away from dependence upon special types of publications, a fault of its predecessor, the

ALA rules. However, serials present special bibliographic problems not adequately covered by the other rules. There is no real rule for changing authorship or editorship in AACR and this is covered in the main provision for serials, entry under title. Entry appears under corporate body, too, but this is determined more from the title than from other criteria, with some exceptions. There is a provision for personal author entry, but it is rarely used. Frequency is no longer a problem, as it once was. The rules are not particularized to the nth degree. They are pretty much compatible with monographic rules.

6. Serials

Preliminary note. These rules for serials apply also to the series added entries that are made for monographs in a series, whether the series is numbered or not.

A. Serials not issued by a corporate body and not of personal authorship. Enter a serial that is not issued by or under the authority of a corporate body and is not of personal authorship under its title.

Title page:
   The Atlantic
Main entry under title

Cover title:
   The Economist
Main entry under title

Caption title:
   Boston evening transcript
Main entry under title

If an added entry is required for a serial that is entered under title and if the title of the serial is identical with that of another serial entered under title, add in parentheses the city of publication. If this addition is insufficient, add also the years of publication.

I. International review (New York, 1874-83)
I. International review (New York, 1936-39)
I. International review (Zürich)

B. Serials issued by a corporate author

1. Enter a periodical, monographic series, or a serially published bibliography, index, directory, biographical dictionary, almanac, or yearbook,[8] issued by or under the authority of a corporate body, under its title with an added entry under the corporate body.[9] Exception: If the title (exclusive of the subtitle) includes the name or the abbreviation of the name of the corporate body,[10] or consists solely of a generic term that requires the name of the body for adequate identification of the serial, enter it under the body.

Entry under title:
Title page:
Law library journal. . .American Association of Law
Libraries

Entry under corporate body:
Title page:
Zeitschrift der Gesellschaft für Schleswig-Holsteinische
Geschichte
Title page:
. . . ALA bulletin. American Library Association
Title page:
University of London historical studies

2. Enter any other serial issued by or under the authority of a corporate body under the body. In case of doubt that the serial is covered by 1 above, enter under the body.

Title page:
Annual report of the Librarian of Congress for the fiscal year
. . . Library of Congress
Main entry under the heading for the library

Title page:
Interstate Commerce Commission. Bureau of Transport Economics and Statistics//Carload waybill statistics . . . Mileage block distribution; traffic and revenue by commodity class, territorial movement, and type of rate. Manufactures and miscellaneous and forwarder traffic

Main entry under the heading for the commission's bureau

C. Serials by a personal author. Enter a serial by a personal author under his name.

Title page:
New [year] ed. for preparing [year] returns. . ./ /J. K. Lasser's
Your income tax
Main entry under Lasser

[Rule 6 continues on with a section D, which is printed in the next chapter, where successive entry is discussed.]

(8)The term "yearbook" is to be understood to exclude a work the content of which is necessarily the expression of the corporate thought or activity of the body, such as a report of its management or a record of the results of its operations.

(9) If the serial is a monographic series that is not cataloged as an entity, substitute a reference for the added entry.

(10)The name is considered to be included in the title when it appears in direct conjunction with the other words of the title, including its appearance in a genitive connection such as ". . .of the [name]". When a part of the name appears in the title, do not construe it as an abbreviated form if 1) it consists of words used in their common meaning—e.g. *The National geographic magazine,* issued by the National Geographic Society, or 2) too incomplete to imply positively the body's involvement in the publication,—e.g. *Harvard business review,* issued by the Graduate School of Business Administration of Harvard University. Construe the presence in the title of the full name of a larger body, of which the responsible issuing body is a part and under which it would be entered as a subheading, as sufficient reason for not entering the serial under its title—e.g. *University of Detroit law journal,* issued by the Department of Law of the University of Detroit.

AACR/NA

The rationale for entry under title is fairly obvious. It is the most notable and memorable thing about the serial and is the logical choice. Serials are best known and most sought by title.

There are other reasons whereby title becomes the primary choice if one tries to draw parallels with monographic cataloging. Monographs having a great number of authors are entered under their titles. Serials usually have a great number of authors, or even editors, sponsors, etc. The serial usually outlives the humans who compile it, so no single person is responsible for it. A serial is, therefore, a work of complex or changing authorship. The title would be the most stable and long-lasting choice. The unifying factor in the run of a serial is its title. This makes it a kind of uniform heading. (Unless some person or corporate body is responsible for *all* of it.) The old British code, the Prussian Instructions, Cutter's *Rules,* and a number of other cataloging codes have considered serials to be anonymous works which would also put them under title. Serials basically fall into category 4 of the general principle outlined at the beginning of Chapter 1 of the AACR:

> 4)Entry should be under title in the case of other works whose authorship is diffuse, indeterminate, or unknown.[3]

The principle that serials should be entered under title is further reinforced by the Paris Principles, codified by the International Conference on Cataloguing Principles (ICCP), held October 9-18, 1961, under the sponsorship of IFLA. In section 11 of the Principles, "Works Entered Under Title," appears this subsection:

11.14 Works (including serials and periodicals) known primarily or conventionally by title rather than by the name of the author.

This principle is followed in the AACR by rule 6A.

There does not seem to be much of a problem with entry of serials under title. Most code writers have felt that it was a good thing and most librarians have agreed, especially public service librarians who have to explain things to the patrons, who also like title entry. There has been no real controversy about this rule, although the British text states it somewhat differently:

> 6.A. Entry under title. Enter a serial under its title, except when B or C below applies. If the serial is issued by or under the authority of a corporate body (other than one acting, in relation to the serial, solely as a commercial publisher), make an added *entry under* the corporate body.[9]
>
> [9] If the serial is a monographic series that is not cataloged as an entity, substitute a reference for the added entry.
>
> AACR/BT.

The problem comes with rule 6B. And when it comes, it comes with a vengeance. Rule 6B is, to put it bluntly, a bad rule. It is awkwardly worded, confusing, and hard to apply. Much of what is entered under this rule is actually entered under the "Exception," which is a little bit of a 'round-Robin-Hood's-barn approach. Rule 6B considers serials "issued by a corporate body."

Rule 6B in the North American version actually is based upon three premises. Rule 6B1 is based on the overriding desire at the ICCP to have entry under title. The titles in this case are "distinctive" and stand on their own, just as if they were not products in any way of corporate effort. However, rule 6B2 is based firmly upon the concept of corporate authorship. This is justified by Seymour Lubetzky as follows:

> Whenever we have an author, the basic principle requires us to enter the work under the author, it does not make any difference whether it is a serial or not. From the point of view of principles, there is not justification for making a decision between serial and nonserial publications.[4]

[He then goes on to explain that serials do present problems when they are of diffuse authorship, and, in this case, should be entered under their titles, as already mentioned. This is, of course, the basis for rule 6A.]

The third premise is that which underlies the Exception to 6B1, which requires that entry be under the corporate body if the corporate body's name or initials appear in the title, or if the title is a generic one requiring the name of the body for adequate identification. This rule tends to muddy the concept of corporate authorship for serials which could be so clear in rule 6B2 if this exception to rule 6B1 were left out.

The entry in this case is not one, necessarily, for a corporate author. It may be entry under a publisher or issuing agency, which may even have disavowed any responsibility for the contents of the contributions made to its journal. Nevertheless, "entry of serial works of diffuse authorship under corporate body when the body is named in the title"⁵ is listed as one of the exceptions to the general principles upon which AACR is based. This is justified as follows:

> . . .The [Catalog Code Revision] Committee held that the inclusion in the title of a serial of the name or part of the name of the issuing corporate body is too powerful a criterion to be nullified when, in unusual cases, no account of the activity of the body is included in the publication.⁶

The reference to the account of activities of the body refers to the corporate author definition which appeared in the Paris Principles.

The Paris Principles defined corporate authorship thusly:

9. Entry under Corporate Bodies

9.1 The main entry for a work should be made under the name of a corporate body (i.e. any institution, organized body or assembly of persons known by a corporate or collective name).

9.11 When the work is by its nature necessarily the expression of the collective thought or activity of the corporate body,⁽⁶⁾ even if signed by a person in the capacity of an officer or servant of the corporate body, or

9.12 when the wording of the title or title-page, taken in conjunction with the nature of the work, clearly implies that the corporate body is collectively responsible for the content of the work⁽⁷⁾

⁽⁶⁾e.g. official reports, rules and regulations, manifestoes, programmes and records of the results of collective work.

⁽⁷⁾e.g. serials whose titles consist of a generic term (Bulletin, Transactions etc.) preceded or followed by the name of a corporate body, and which include some account of the activities of the body.

The commentary in the *Statement of Principles* on this above principle lists a number of corporate bodies. It also states that the North American edition of the AACR tends to exclude commercial publishers from the list of corporate bodies, with exceptions made if the firm has produced the information·embodied in the works it publishes. This comes circuitously back to the question of corporate authorship raised by rule 6B2.

Further commentary on this section of the Principles should be studied, for it is most interesting. There were many complaints and criticisms, particularly regarding wording, but with practical ramifications. At the International Meeting of Cataloguing Experts in Copenhagen in 1969, the unsatisfactory nature of sections 9.11, 9.12, and footnote 7 were pointed out. No post-Paris code had been able to reconcile all of the problems and it was proposed that this be studied further. It is nice to know that, while the Anglo-Americans tripped and fell on their faces over this rule, they were not alone.

Eva Verona had this to say about corporate headings in AACR:

> AACR advocates a very broad use of corporate headings. Corporate authorship is recognized and is considered to be an extension of personal authorship, that is, the corporate author is responsible for the intellectual and artistic content of its work; in addition, the term corporate author embraces editors and compilers who are primarily responsible for the contents of a work. In spite of this definition, corporate headings are adopted in several cases where the principles of authorship cannot be applied and instead the principle of name most strongly associated with the publication is used.[7]

In 1958 Andrew Osborn had this to say:

> The expression "author and title entries" in *Catalog Rules* makes it clear that title entries were not considered to be author entries. Presumably, therefore, all nontitle entries represented the principle of authorship. However, the rules for government publications, which evolved at the Library of Congress under the influence of notable people in the field of document bibliography, introduced another principle which may or may not coincide with the principle of authorship, namely the principle of the issuing body. For checklists of government publications, the issuing body generally is the best medium of arrangement; but for library catalogs, which in theory at least are supposed to be based on the principle of authorship, the issuing body can only lead to confusion when that body is not at the same time the author.[8]

This has been continued over to nondocument serials in the exception to rule 6B1. Mr. Osborn's objections loom even larger.

The concept introduced in the exception to 6B1 is further explained in *Cataloging service bulletin* 96:

> If there is no evidence in the publication to the contrary, the presence of the name or abbreviation of the name of a corporate body in the title of a serial is to be taken as evidence that the serial is issued by the corporate body,—e.g. "Boston University papers in African history."[9]

Thus, the name of the corporate body being found in the title of a serial leads to an identification, in the mind of the catalog user, between the name of the corporate body and the serial. The corporate name becomes, therefore, the sought heading, irrespective of the actual nature of the serial.[10]

The corporate body is, thusly, represented as "author."

Rule 6B1 Exception is something of a deviation from footnote 7 of the Paris Principles, for there is no provision for reporting of activities of the body as a criterion for the entry in the rule. This is because such a rule would be difficult to follow. The cataloger would have to look beyond the title-page for information essential to entry. There would be the problem, too, of those serials which dropped the reports of activities somewhere along the line, yet retained the name of the organization in the title. Would this necessitate a change of entry? (Heaven forbid!) The user would be considerably perplexed, for how would he know where to look? A generic title serial which did not have reports of activities or business would be put under its title, which would not have been considered satisfactory by most of the makers of the code, and variant treatment for like-named serials would be very confusing to patrons, even though the author definition of the Paris Conference were in effect.

Serials with distinctive titles would probably be more likely to forsake their organizational links, or perhaps even search for others, than ones with corporate ties in their titles. This may be partially the basis for 6B1. Lubetzky points out that the *ALA bulletin* and the *Library Association record* cannot be divorced from the organizations which sponsor(ed) them, whereas the *Library journal*, which began as "official organ of the Library Associations of America and the United Kingdom," and became later organ of the ALA only, is now a private journal, and *Special libraries* dropped its affiliation with the Special Library Association in 1969.[11] For this reason, he felt that entry under the corporate body for serials with the name or initials of the body in the title, but entry under a distinctive title, even if an official organ, is rational and practical. Perhaps this deviation from the general principles of corporate authorship for serials with distinctive titles, but with corporate involvement, should be mentioned as a general exception in the rules, which it is not considered to be. Perhaps, however, this is because of the potential diffuseness of serial authorship, as exemplified by the *Library journal*.

The British rules lean much more toward title entries, for they disregard corporate authorship entirely when it comes to serials and provide for corporate entry only for the conveniences demanded by the name, part of the name, or initials in the title, or the need to further qualify generic terms. In other words, the British text only calls for corporate entry for names-most-associated-with-a-title. The British wording is as follows:

B. Entry under name of a corporate body. Enter a serial issued by or under the authority of a corporate body (other than one acting, in relation to the serial, solely as a commercial publisher) under the name of the body if the title of the serial (exclusive of any subtitle) 1) includes the name or an abbreviation of the name of the body,[10] or the title of an appropriate official, or 2) consists solely of a generic term or phrase which does not adequately identify the serial except when taken in conjunction with the name of the body. If the name included in the title of the serial, whether in full or in an abbreviated form, is that of a superior body to which the body responsible for issuing the serial is subordinate, enter under the name of the superior body, with an added entry under the subordinate body.

Title page:
University of Detroit law journal
(Issued by the School of Law of the University of Detroit)
Main entry under the heading for the university
Added entry under the heading for the school
Make an added entry or reference under the title of the serial unless this begins with the name of the corporate body used as heading for the main entry.

Title page:
Zeitschrift der Gesellschaft für Schleswig-Holsteinische Geschichte
Main entry under the society
Added entry or reference under title

Title Page:
University of London historical studies
Main entry under the university

[10]When a part of the name appears in the title, it should not be treated as an abbreviation of the name if 1) it consists of words used in their common meaning—e.g. *The National geographic magazine* (issued by the National Geographic Society), or 2) is too incomplete to identify the body definitely,— e.g. *Harvard business review* (issued by the Graduate School of Business Administration of Harvard University).

AACR/BT

The British rule for corporate entry is based entirely upon the relationship between the title of the serial and the name of the issuing body. The rule is considerably easier to apply, although it is not actually built upon the concept of authorship. The American rule tries to use authorship as a basis, but also confuses the issue with generic titles and the other exceptions. This makes it difficult to apply rule 6, although the results are pretty practical ones, in most cases. The British rule gets the cataloger "off the hook" when it comes to sticky decisions which the concept of authorship opens up. The reason for this discrepancy is that the British rules allow the Principle 11.14, "works known primarily or conventionally by title," to take prominence over Principle 9.11, which calls for corporate entry "when the work is by its nature necessarily the expression of the corporate body.'' The North American edition restricts this in favor of more corporate entry.

Publications which fall into the 6B2 group are actually being entered under corporate author, for the corporate author is responsible for the intellectual content of these works. The British rule does not have provisions for such cases as these, preferring title main entry. G. E. Hamilton spoke very negatively about this at the Nottingham Seminar,[12] much preferring the American text of the rule when it comes to statistical serials. The ALA rules called for corporate headings for these and they are really best put there. As Mr. Hamilton points out, monographic works would be entered under their corporate entries and the serials should be, too. The Board of Trade Library, where he worked, would find it a much better arrangement. Mr. Hamilton used the following examples to illustrate the difference in the two texts of 6B:

> Using the British rules:
> Fruit: a review of production and trade. . .1935 + London: H.M.S.O.
> 25 cm.
> Annually.
> Continues Fruit, issued by Empire Marketing Board.
> Compiled by Commonwealth Economic Committee 1935-64; by Commonwealth Secretariat 1965 + .
>
> Using the American rules:
> Commonwealth Economic Committee
> Fruit; a review of production and trade. . .1935-64. London: H.M.S.O.
> 21 v. 25 cm. annual.
> Set lacks 1936-37.
> Suspended 1939-48.
> Continues Fruit, issued by Empire Marketing Board, 1933.
> Superseded by the publication with the same name issued by the Commonwealth Secretariat.
>
> Commonwealth Secretariat
> Fruit; a review of production and trade. . . 1965 + London: H.M.S.O.
> v. 25 cm. annual.
> Supersedes the publication with the same title issued by the Commonwealth Economic Committee.[13]

The American rule 6B2 is very hard to interpret, partially because it does not state itself very clearly and the cataloger does not know what is being called for, and partially because many people are misled by the provisions of the exception just discussed, thinking that this actually calls for corporate *authorship* when it really is calling for corporate *heading*. The concept of corporate authorship for serials becomes confused and unclear. Actually, this rule does call for the provisions of footnote 6 of the Paris Principles, although this is never clarified.

(Footnote 6 makes no mention of the fact that it might cover serial publications either, although some of the examples listed might be serial in nature.) Annual reports of corporate bodies which have catchy titles, rather than generic ones, would fall into this category of material. (If the title is "Annual report," a generic title, this would throw it into the exception, which, fortunately, could yield the same result. This would be in keeping with footnote 7.) Statistical summaries like *Carload waybill statistics* are the actual "result of collective work," called for by footnote 6 of the Paris Principles, and are properly entered under corporate body as author, as Mr. Hamilton would prefer. The best way to interpret this part of the rule is to ask yourself, "What would I do if this publication were a monograph?" The answer would be: corporate entry. Then follow it.

Corporate entry was a new concept at the ICCP for many countries. Most of Europe followed the Prussian Instructions, which does not recognize corporate authorship, although it has been a part of Anglo-American cataloging for many years. In 1876, Cutter made a very strong statement indicating that societies and institutions were the authors of their publications. It was also Cutter's desire to bring together in one place the publications connected with a single corporate body under main entry, one of Seymour Lubetzky's primary functions of the catalog and the main entry. It is interesting to note that, although this had been a major bone of contention when earlier attempts were made to arrive at a uniform international cataloging code, many countries seriously considered the concept at the Paris Conference. Although not everyone was completely convinced, the principles of corporate authorship were adopted, as previously described. Unfortunately, they were not easy to incorporate into the AACR. C. Sumner Spalding tells us why:

> AA6, Serials was a problem rule. Schools of thought as to how serials should be entered ranged from the school that reasoned that serials should be entered according to the same criteria of authorship that control the entry of monographs to the school that would enter all serials under title regardless of other considerations. The Paris Principle for serials lies between these extremes, following the principle of authorship in most cases but specifying entry under title on the one hand, for a serial "known primarily or conventionally by title rather than by the name of the author" (11.14), and entry under corporate body, on the other hand, for a serial, such as a review or journal, consisting mainly of articles or papers by various authors, if the name of the corporate body occurs in the title and if some account of the activities of the body is included (9.12). The rule adopted by the Catalog Code Revision Committee is even more pragmatic than the Paris Principle. It yields very much the same result but avoids invoking either the vague criterion of whether or not the serial is known by its title or the consideration of whether or not a journal contains any account of the activity of the body named in the title.[14]

Specifically on corporate authorship of serials, Mr. Spalding had this to say:

> . . .It is very difficult to follow the principle of corporate authorship with serials, because if you do you are going to have unfortunate results, such as *Index Medicus* entered under the National Library of Medicine and the *Bibliography of Agriculture* under the National Agricultural Library. At least this would seem to me to be not too happy an outcome. We decided that if the corporate body's name is part of the title, either in full or in an abbreviated form, we would automatically enter under the corporate body, regardless of the nature of the publication. In other words, we felt that the pull of the appearance of the name of the body in the title was sufficient to warrant entry under the body (cf Paris Principle 9.12), at least it is a solid criterion, which can be explained not only to a cataloguer, but to a reader, and once it is understood it can be readily followed.[15]

Dunkin, in his working paper presented at the ICCP, questioned the use of the corporate author entry and indicated that, at best, it is a confused issue. Do people really care to find all of the publications of an organization in the card catalog, or would a bibliography serve these people just as well. Would the amassing of titles under generic terms like "Report" be as terrible as those long files under "Smith" or "U.S.?" These questions are still being asked today. He does sum up very well by saying that there should not be different rules for monographs and serials, just because of the form of publication. The principles of authorship should still apply. The desire to maintain some uniformity in the face of all odds won out.

The Catalog Code Revision Committee which worked on the AACR did the best they could, trying to juggle the concepts of authorship, constant and changing, personal and corporate, with the desire for title entry. Rule 6B was the result.

Spalding summed up by saying:

> It will probably strike you as a pretty arbitrary rule and it *is* arbitrary. The merits that I can claim for it are that I think that the results are satisfactory in most circumstances and that it will not be much trouble to follow. If we do have a serials rule that will not be much trouble to follow, we have really got something. We tried various ways of drafting a serials rule, and few of us were really happy with any of them. Finally we came up with this one, which, although it seems quite arbitrary, does produce entries that we think desirable in most cases.[16]

Apparently the critics of the rules have not found it so, for there is movement afoot to change the rule, as we shall see in the next chapter.

In both texts of the rules, rule 6C gives provisions for entry of serials under personal author.[17] This is considered a silly and unnecessary rule by many serials librarians who refuse to use it. Others prefer to use title entry for such serials because the red book did. Still others find it problematic for serials records and prefer entry under title, with added entries for the author. Nevertheless, the Library of Congress has imparted the following clarification to those who do use the rule, as LC does:

> If on the title page of a serial, or in another prominent position, a person is presented as *author* of the publication, rule AA6C is applicable. The type of publication, e.g. bibliography, index, dictionary, in such a case is not a factor. If the person is presented as editor, however, AA6C will not apply and the entry will be determined according to the provision of AA6A or 6B as applicable.[18]

This, of course, does not answer the question which is paramount in many librarians' minds when one tries to reconcile the definition of serials with personal authorship. Serials are, by definition, infinite. People are, by Divine Law, finite. Somehow this does not jibe.

It really can work, however. Here is a hypothetical example. If an individual puts out a series of Sunday School tracts every Sunday since his thirtieth birthday, this is a weekly publication. Let's say it is called *Lessons for a Sunday morning*. The publication continues until the man dies. It may stop then, and be a ceased serial like *The Tatler, The Spectator, Poor Richard's Almanack* and others of that ilk (even including ceased publications not of personal authorship). But, it does not have to stop, it has the potential of continuing. The man's wife continues it. Perhaps there is collaboration with their son, who then takes over on the death of his mother. The numbering is continuous and the title remains *Lessons for a Sunday morning*. Surely this is a serial. It is written by one or two people at a time, not more than three, even with the successive changes. Although the cataloging of such a publication by any library other than the local church or community library is unlikely, this situation does illustrate that personal authorship for a serial may indeed exist. Bigger and better examples may be found, such as the one below.

The fact that personal author entries for serials are very rare may serve to console those who hate them a little, but they really can and do exist.

The North American text of AACR does not mention alternative rules for entry for serials although the British text specifies rule 19 for serials that are supplements to other serials, and rules 26A and B for "certain legal serials." Rule 19 in the North American text makes no specific references to serials, except for special issues, extracts, and the like. Examples appearing on pages 42 and 43 of that book show entries for this type of material. Added entries rather than main entries are now given to such material and the rules for monographs are followed. The Library of Congress uses rules 20-26 for legal serials, although this is not specified as an alternative in the North American text of AACR.

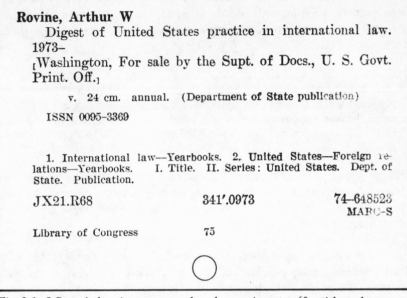

Rovine, Arthur W
   Digest of United States practice in international law.
1973–
   ₍Washington, For sale by the Supt. of Docs., U. S. Govt.
Print. Off.₎
      v. 24 cm. annual. (Department of State publication)
   ISSN 0095-3369

   1. International law—Yearbooks. 2. United States—Foreign relations—Yearbooks.   I. Title.   II. Series: United States. Dept. of
State. Publication.

JX21.R68   341'.0973   74-648523
                                                          MARC-S

Library of Congress   75

Fig. 2-1. LC card showing a personal author main entry (for title and corporate
entries see examples appearing in Chapter 6).

A meeting or a conference can be thought of as a corporate body if it regards
itself as such in the work to be cataloged, i.e., by a prominently displayed
name, continued existence and similar criteria.

It is not the aim of this book to go much beyond the choice of entry into
questions of forms of names for entries. That would be the subject of another
whole treatise in itself. It would behoove us briefly to consider a couple of points, primarily in the case of corporate names, however, because they affect both
discussions on choice of entry and cataloging recordkeeping. The primary
question is that of superimposition.

The Library of Congress looked over the rules when they first came out and
realized that many headings established under the old rules would have to be
changed. This would be a monumental task for LC to undertake, so it was not
undertaken. Instead, the Library adopted a plan which it termed "superimposition." This is announced and defined as follows:

The great size of the Library of Congress catalogs and of the catalogs of the research
libraries that depend on LC cataloging services, the continuing shortage of
trained cataloging personnel, and the emergence of centralized cataloging and
shared cataloging techniques have made it incumbent on the Library to approach

the new rules with due consideration of their effect upon the catalogs and cataloging activities of all American libraries. Accordingly, the Library of Congress has adopted a policy known as "Superimposition" in applying the new rules. This means that the rules for choice of entry will be applied only to works that are new to the Library and that the rules for headings will be applied only to persons and corporate bodies that are being established for the first time. New editions, etc., of works previously cataloged will be entered in the same way as the earlier editions (except for revised editions in which change of authorship is indicated). New works by previously established authors will appear under the same headings. If a new work is to be entered under a general form subheading according to the new rules (e.g. San Francisco. Ordinances, local laws, etc.), it will be entered under the established heading when there is one, even if it is in a different style (e.g. San Francisco. Ordinances, etc.). New subordinate units of previously established corporate bodies will be established according to the new rules so far as the questions of independent entry or direct or indirect subheading are concerned. If the unit should be treated as a subheading, the established heading for the main body will be used.

Exceptions to the policy of superimposition will be largely confined to instances where very few entries are involved and where it is judged that some decided improvement in entry or heading may be obtained by revising existing entries in accordance with new rules.

The Library will announce in future issues of these *Cataloging Service Bulletins* its decisions with regard to praticular entries or categories of entries when these decisions are likely to be of general interest.[19]

The principle differences between forms of corporate author names (the rarity of personal authors for serials makes discussion of changes of personal name forms fairly irrelevant) in AACR as opposed to ALA can be listed as follows:

1. There are no more distinctions between societies and institutions.
2. The name the body uses on its works is to be used; not necessarily the official name.
3. Successive entry, rather than latest, is to be used for bodies with name changes.
4. More subordinate bodies are entered directly under the new rules.
5. With the dropping of rules 98 and 99, for entry of local churches under place,[20] there is no longer any corporate entry under place.

These are where the discrepancies will lie between new headings and superimposed ones.

So far, superimposition has not been too much of a problem. Libraries have pretty much followed LC's lead, and catalogers have used LC copy as it was presented to them, even though the entry being established was a new one for their library. They used the old LC heading, based on the *ALA rules,* and made references as needed from the new forms. A few pioneering libraries did break away and actually used the new headings. Canadian libraries, following the lead of the National Library of Canada, did not superimpose, but changed their headings to the new ones. Now a problem has been caused as the CONSER Project for a cooperative conversion of serials and a resultant union list (see Chapter 18 for further details), gets under way. NLC will be in charge of establishing Canadian headings, which will not match with LC's. A problem! LC has decided to go over to the Canadian headings, which will be a reversal of its superimposition policy with reference to these headings only. This was announced in *Cataloging service bulletin* 114, (Summer, 1975) p. 3. LC will be in charge of establishing headings for the rest of the world for the project. The authority for the project will be the AACR, not the *ALA rules,* so LC will have to establish two forms, one for its catalogs, and one for CONSER. This will call for a lot of extra work, but it will also provide a useful tool in the form of the authority file to keep track of the forms used.

LC rocked the library world by announcing that it had coined another word: "desuperimpose." This meant it was thinking seriously of reversing its decision to keep its old headings and was going to switch over to new headings, established under AACR rules. There was no methodology decided upon, it was just decided to do it, because of CONSER and the pressure of other possible projects of a similar nature, requiring mergable headings. Libraries down in the grassroots worried about what they would do and rumors were rampant. Finally, LC decided that it would not consider desuperimposing its catalogs until all of its current cataloging is in machine-readable form and it has fully automated its authority file. Then, by a mere pushing of a button, (well, comparatively anyway!) the old headings will desuperimpose themselves. This will probably not happen until the beginning of the next decade. The desuperimposing of Canadian headings is the harbinger, however.

With the consideration to drop superimposition, things should sail a little smoother in the pond of corporate entry. One of the major criticisms of the old forms of entry was that you approached things in such a roundabout way, under places or inverted headings, or subordinate to something else. This was confusing and difficult to explain to the confused patron in an adequate manner. Differentiating between societies and institutions, especially foreign ones, was too fine a point for most people, including librarians, and especially patrons. Things are much more straightforward now. The clustering of entries around "University" is much better than the confusion of different groups of things — like museums, libraries, universities, etc. — clustered around and interfiled confusingly with municipal governments and organizations having the name of a city in their corporate names. Things will no longer be buried in obscure places. The burden of geographical or other specialized knowledge is not placed on the poor suffering patron any more. Perhaps, the corporate entry will not be such a critical problem area if things are simplified considerably and people won't be so afraid to use it, even as an added entry. Much of the onus will be lifted from corporate entry. Hopefully, things will be simplified even more if the present Catalog Code Revision Committee decides to use complete hierarchy of corporate names rather than leaving parts out. This is hard to interpret and explain, so any modification would be a step in the right direction!

According to rule 64 of the AACR, the language of a foreign society is to be preferred over English, unless the society is an international one with publications in many languages. A footnote to this rule indicates that, if desired, English can be used. This is a problem which very often comes up in the cataloging of serial publications. What do you do when you have the *Journal of the Mathematical Society of Japan*? Do you catalog under Mathematical Society of Japan or Nihon Sūgakkai? The latter is, of course, the society's name in Japanese. But the publication is in English, you say. Of course, but is it possible that you will ever get another publication from this organization, which might be in Japanese? Does your local library collect in Japanese? Is it a small university or college library that just happens to have this publication or is it a university or research library of fairly large size, wide interests, and room for expansion? Will you be networking with other research libraries, producing union catalogs and lists which will demand that you have entries which are standard with the norms created by the cataloging rules? Do you follow LC in its cataloging procedures? If you are a fairly good-sized library and your answer to all of the other questions is yes, you should choose Nihon Sūgakkai as your entry for this publication, just as you should choose Hebrew, Russian, Chinese, Korean and Arabic entries for corporate bodies that publish predominantly in these languages even if the body presents itself in the publication-in-hand as Academy of Sciences of the U.S.S.R. or Academia Sinica. References, or course, should be made from the form of the name not chosen, which is, in this case, the English form.

The clue to both of these problems above is an adequate authority file for corporate (and personal) names. All variant forms appearing in publications should be recorded in the authority file so that succeeding catalogers will be guided. References should appear in the public catalog and the serials list or catalog to guide patrons and public service librarians to the proper entry. Variant forms as the result of cataloging rules used should also be awarded references if the form used is not a direct one, as:

Los Angeles. University of Southern California.
    X University of Southern California, Los Angeles.

Variant romanizations should also receive references, especially if the variant appears in the piece being cataloged.

Page 34 is an example of an authority file card. The source is given for the corporate name being established. This may be from the LC or NUC catalog, a reference source, or the publication itself.

```
Nihon Sūgakkai.
 (Bulletin of the Mathematical Society of Japan)

        X  Mathematical Society of Japan


        LC  1968-72, 62:14




                        ◯
```

Fig. 2-2. Sample authority file card.

Here is a sample of a cross-reference card as it should appear in the public catalog or authority file.

```
            Mathematical Society of Japan

        see

    Nihon Sūgakkai.




                        ◯
```

Fig. 2-3. Cross-reference card.

There was some interesting discussion at the Paris Conference regarding title entries. The question raised was, "What should be the choice of entry word?" It was assumed that entry "under title" would mean "title as it stood on the publication." However, while some countries chose to disregard only articles, others chose to disregard other small words like prepositions. It was decided that this was not properly answered by the principles, since it related to an auxiliary function, that of internal arrangement of the catalog. A vote was to have been taken, but there was not sufficient time. Later, a brief poll was taken, with the results that the majority felt that entry should be under the first word, or the first word not an article. It has been the Anglo-American tradition to enter under the first word not an article.

This, however, brings up a problem that has never really been answered anywhere: "What really constitutes a serial title?" This seems like a very basic question, as it most certainly is. And, in most cases, it is a relatively easy one to answer, for the title may be very straightforward. But then there are the weird ones, and this is where the "rub" comes. How should one deal with over-printed titles, for example? And how should one deal with publications, particularly of the newsletter type, which have logos or printing devices next to the title bearing the initials or name of the corporate author? Then there are titles made up of initials or that have the name, perhaps with initials, of a person in them. Then there are funny titles made up of signs or symbols. And there are even serials that don't have titles. How should these be handled? These are questions that are not always easy to answer. There will be an attempt here to lay down some guidelines.

An example of a serial without a title is *List and Index Society,* a large folio publication published in Great Britain. Under the old rules a title was supplied, since the words which appear on the publication are obviously the name of a corporate author, and not a title. The title supplied was "Publications." This is in compliance with rule 133F, which appears in the discussion of description of separately-published monographs. The supplied title should describe the publication in a short but intelligible fashion. According to the ISDS *Guidelines* (see Chapter 18.), the corporate body, if it is all that appears on the piece, as in this case, would be the key title. Perhaps this will change the rule for supplying titles for serials, but this has not been worked out yet.

Titles made of signs or symbols are rare any more, but were quite popular in the nineteenth century with such titles as *The_____.* This should be transcribed as the title. Most filing rules call for such titles to be filed before the alphabet starts. Titles composed of numbers, such as the serial *1924,* would also be transcribed as on the title-page. Some filing rules call for numerals in titles to be filed as spoken, but this can cause a number of problems: is this "nineteen-twenty-four," "nineteen-hundred-and-twenty-four," etc.? The Library of Congress, in moving toward automated filing, has found an admirable solution, that of filing ciphers before the alphabet, in numerical sequence. These are specialized problems, but more of a filing nature than a cataloging nature.

Titles with the name or initials of a person in the title were the subject of a special rule (the last two paragraphs of 5C1), in the old *ALA cataloging rules for author and title entry*. Titles like *Justus Liebigs Annalen der Chemie* were to be entered under the first name in the title, with references (we would prefer added entries now), under *Liebigs Annalen der Chemie* and *Annalen der Chemie*. Titles like *A. Merritt's fantasy magazine* were not to be treated like this, however. Catalogers were told to enter under the first *word* of the title, rather than the initial, which was to be omitted. There was to be a reference from the actual title, as well as one from the title following the person's name, if distinctive. Although the reference, or preferably added entry, idea is a pretty good one, and probably should be retained, the main entry under a partial title, rather than the real one, is enough to curdle the blood of AACR-based catalogers. *A. Merritt's fantasy magazine* should be the entry — that is, entry under the actual title that appears on the piece.

Huibert Paul, in speaking out in favor of standardization among publishers of serials has this to say about a very sticky problem when it comes to the cataloging of serial publications:

> Then there are those numerous titles starting with initials. They are stumbling blocks to everyone and the number of man-hours wasted each year in each major library because of initials must be considerable. Take for instance *Massachusetts Studies in English*. Sometimes it is called as spelled out, at other times *MSE*. On the front cover the title is spelled out in rather small letters. *MSE* appears under it in big capital letters. Just what is the title? How many clerks across the nation will try to find the entry under *MSE* rather than under *Massachusetts Studies in English*? How many cross-references must have been made from coast to coast? How many added entries (under *MSE*) in card catalogs around the globe? Or take a similar case: *MT. Mechanical Translation*. Unlike *Massachusetts Studies in English* it has been entered under *MT. Mechanical Translation* in *New Serial Titles*. The bewildered clerk who thinks he has learned a lesson with *Massachusetts Studies in English* will go straight to *Mechanical Translation*, only to discover that the entry is under *MT. Mechanical Translation*. Then, too, agents may list the title as it is spelled out at one time and under the initials at another. No one but the publisher is to blame, especially when he puts initials in front of his title on some issues but not on others. And titles beginning with initials are easily misfiled, especially when the initials have vowels in strategic places. Titles like *LIT, NELPA News, NIPA Journal,* and *NATO Letter* are often filed as though they were words. Although librarians are usually aware of these pitfalls, clerks are easily misled and certainly through no fault of their own. And one should not forget that nonprofessionals handle serials almost exclusively. The only time librarians encounter them is when the publication is first established in the file, when it dies, or when something goes wrong. Of course things easily go wrong with initials. Yet even a medium-sized library has hundreds of these snares in its files.[21]

Although exception really should be taken to Mr. Paul's insinuations about the inability of clerks to cope with difficult material, absolutely no fault can be found with his basic complaint about the problems raised by titles with initials in them.

The Library of Congress offers the following as a solution to librarians having such a problem as Mr. Paul describes:

Titles Including Initialisms

1. Initialisms or acronyms are to be considered part of the title when visually or typographically presented as intended parts of the title.
2. In transcribing the title, the initialism or acronym and the rest of the title are not to be pieced together from different parts of the title page. For cases in which the title appears both as in initialism and in expanded form see "Abbreviated vs. Expanded Titles" below.
3. Initialisms or acronyms which appear on the title page as seals or logos are not to be considered part of the title.
4. In case of doubt, initialisms or acronyms are to be considered part of the title.

Abbreviated vs. Expanded Titles. If the title consists of a set of initials or acronyms prominently displayed and the expanded form is also present, both are to be considered part of the title proper and are to be separated by a comma. If the abbreviated form is not prominently displayed, the expanded form is to be considered the title proper. When in doubt as to prominence, the title proper should begin with the abbreviated form followed by the comma and the expanded form.

Examples:

> BPR, American book publishing record
> JOLA, Journal of library automation[22]

Note that this help from LC also answers the question brought up by logos or seals of corporate bodies. Mr. Paul brought up a question regarding filing: whether such initials as NIPA or NATO should be considered and filed as words. This, of course, is a question more related to filing than to cataloging, although the two are intertwined. Each local library will have to make a judgment about the use its clientele will make of the catalog and draft guidelines for acronyms and initialisms accordingly. The *LC catalogs,* of course, are a big help, as are dictionaries of acronyms and initialisms. The usage of the body in question may play a part in the decision, too, as well as common usage and the experiences of public librarians. NATO, one of Mr. Paul's examples, is used as a word now, and should be filed as such. This should not play a part in choice or form of entry, however.

The next peculiar problem is that of overprinted titles. Perhaps it is appropriate to call upon a science fiction example to illustrate this. The publication was called *Astounding science fiction* until January, 1960. The last number which bore this title was volume 64, no. 5. Then it changed its name on the cover with v. 64, no. 6, February, 1960, although the spine and masthead remained the same and did not change until August and September of 1960 (The spine changed in August but not the masthead, which changed in September.) The spine title in August said *Analog science fact & fiction,* a valuable clue. The periodical calmed down after the upheaval of its name change in October and became *Analog science fact & fiction* and was not much of a problem after that, but the stormy few months of its name change provided one of the real problems serials catalogers have to face, which is not covered adequately anywhere. You see, while the masthead remained the same, the cover title changed. The question was, "What did it change to?" A somewhat simple problem to solve, except that the title was not clear due to the overprinting and you could not tell what was really meant to be the title. The word "Astounding" appeared in bold type on the cover, with a slight shadow of outlined letters saying "Analog" behind/in front (?) of it. The rest of the words were clearly part of the title, but what did one do with the word "Analog" which seemed to be creeping in? As the months went on, this would get bolder and the word "Astounding" would fade out until it was really gone. What was the title, "Analog" or "Astounding?" Unable to find references, this cataloger put it under the title that appeared finally on the spine, which seemed to be the best answer. Added entries were made for the combined words, as a variant title with both orders of the words used. The overprinting was explained on the catalog cards so that both added entries were justified. Other variations were also covered with notes. The other choice was, of course, to consider the problem issues to be part of the first title, rather than the second. This was not chosen because of the change which appeared on the spine, before the masthead change. If the spine had not had such a change, the evidence might have been more strongly in favor of retention with the first title. This often happens as publishers try out new titles on their customers, wreaking havoc with library records. This actually puts this problem on the borderline between this chapter and the next one, which discusses changes-of-title. The cataloger used two entries for this title, which meant that the principle of successive entry cataloging was being followed, along with some latest entry cataloging for the "short duration" of the variant titles. However, the problem was included here because it also encompasses the concept of "what is a title?",

The following are some brief guidelines for coping with problems such as this last one, as well as some of the others mentioned previously. They are good procedures for any cataloger to get into when looking over serials publications, even if there are not real entry problems present: (1) Always see if you can verify the title elsewhere in the publication: the caption title perhaps, the spine, masthead, etc. The title may be formally presented in an introduction to the publication, or it might occur in some commentary within an article in one of the issues. Such a search will unearth variations that should be indicated in the cataloging and may help to reinforce the cataloger's choice of title. (2) if there is no answer in the publication, look outside the publication: ULS, NST, BUCOP, LC/NUC, etc. (3) If you must make the decision yourself, be as logical as you can and cover the other bases as well as you can with added entries or cross-references as appropriate.

According to rule 161, the title should be taken from the sources listed here: title-page, cover, caption, masthead, editorial pages, or other place. Such source is indicated if it is one of the last three. Differing titles need to be specified and clarified in notes, as later discussed in Chapter 6 of this book.

Although part of the rules of description, rule 162 deals with the recording of the title and, as such, bears quite directly upon choice of entry, particularly when entry is under title as it soon may be. This also ties in with the discussion which we have just been having and it is fitting, then, to discuss this rule here.

162. Recording of the title

A. A short title is generally used in cataloging serial publications if this makes it possible to disregard minor variations in the wording on various issues, especially if these occur in subtitles. Subtitles are omitted unless necessary for identification or for clarification of the scope of the publication. A long sub-title which is considered necessary may be presented in a note instead of following the title in the body of the entry.

AACR/NA.

This is a fairly straightforward rule explaining that, since serial titles can vary so much, the most stable part of the title should be picked. For serials entered under title, then, this becomes the entry. All of the problems discussed up to now, except titles with initials for corporate bodies in them (entered under body according to the exception to 6B1) are entered following this rule. The corporate initial titles follow this rule for recording of title.

Rule 162B is crucial to the discussion of entry. Rule 162B as printed in the 1967 AACR says:

B. When the title of a serial publication entered under a corporate body includes the name of the body or an abbreviation or the initials of the name (see 6B1, footnote 10), the name or its subtitle is omitted unless:

1) the name is written in non-alphabetic characters;
2) the name is given in a slightly different form from that in the heading and cannot be omitted without distorting the title (e.g. *Report of the Librarian of Congress* entered under U.S. *Library of Congress*);

3) the name appears at the beginning of the title in the form of initials or an abbreviation;
4) the remainder of the title is in an inflected form.

AACR/NA

Some further elaboration was made on this rule in *Cataloging service bulletin* 103:

162B. *The word "series" as the title of serial publications.* If the word "series" appears as the sole title of a serial publication and not in direct conjunction with the name of an issuing body or any other word or phrase, this word must necessarily stand as the title of the publication. If, however, the name of the issuing body does appear in direct conjunction with the word "series," in recording the title do not omit the name of the body according to AA162B if the resulting title would be simply the word "series." For example a publication entitled "Mysore Library Association series" would be cataloged as

Mysore Library Association.
Mysore Library Association series.

Not

Mysore Library Association.
Series.[23]

In a memorandum issued 14 December 1973, a revision of rule 162B was proposed by the Working Communications Subcommittee of the Ad Hoc Discussion Group on Serials Data Bases. It stated:

In the course of appraising the various entry fields for a serial record, it becomes apparent that the present MARC Serials Format, in order to comply with AACR rule 162B as presently construed, will require duplicative, confusing fields to record the variations.

The Ad Hoc Discussion Group on Serials Data Bases, Working Communications Subcommittee therefore strongly recommends that the Library of Congress and the National Library of Canada purpose [sic] to the ALA Descriptive Cataloguing Committee the revision of 162B, and that the text be changed to read as follows:

"When the title of a serial publication consists of a generic term, the title is to begin with that term, followed by the name of the issuing body, transcribed in the sequence and form given on the publication."

We further recommend that consideration be given to the use of the title as defined in revised rule 162 as the main access of a serial bibliographical record. This change in practice would simplify entry and linking fields and therefore would result in considerable economies in the maintenance of large serials data bases and of local serials control without sacrificing bibliographical integrity in any way.[24]

This memorandum has had a strong impact upon the cataloging of serials. The rule has been changed, as announced in *Cataloging service bulletins* 108 and 109. *Bulletin* 108 deleted rule 162B with the following:

> *Note:* With the deletion of rule 162B, the name of a corporate body or the abbreviation or initials of the name which is a part of the title of a serial will be included in the transcription of the title in all instances.[25]

For example, the title *Transactions of the American Philosophical Society* would have been truncated under the old rule to *Transactions,* entered, of course, under the heading for the Society. With the deletion of what Richard Anable, head of the Ad Hoc Discussion Group mentioned earlier (for more, see Chapter 18), calls the "butcher clause," the title would no longer be truncated, but would read as it does on the piece-in-hand: *Transactions of the American Philosophical Society.* Rule 6 for entry would not be affected, so entry would still be under the corporate name, according to rule 6B1, exception. Here is an LC card showing the new practice:

East African Academy.
  Proceedings of the East African Academy.

  ₍Nairobi₎ East African Literature Bureau

        v. 25 cm. (Proceedings of the annual symposium of the East African Academy)

      I. East African Literature Bureau.   II. Series: East African Academy. Proceedings of the symposium.

  AS625.E22   subser.   967'.08   74–647784
                                                      MARC–S

  Library of Congress   75

Fig. 2-4. LC card showing recording of generic title in full after the deletion of rule 162B.

Bulletin 109 brought further change to the rule. For "serials with generic titles," LC explains:

> To be able to input immediately into the MARC serials data base records which will be compatible in respect to title with records input after the adoption of the International Standard Bibliographic Description for Serials (ISBD(S)) the Library of Congress has adopted the following practice, prescribed by the ISBD(S): If the title of a serial consists solely of a generic term, that term is followed by the author statement. The two elements are separated by a space-hyphen-space (-). The author statement is transcribed as it appears on the publication, except that if the statement includes a corporate hierarchy, those parts of the hierarchy which are not necessary for the identification of the author are omitted. The parts of the hierarchy which are recorded are separated by commas.

The *Bulletin* goes on to give three examples:

> Information series - Geological Survey of Alabama.
>
> Bulletin - Commonwealth of Australia, Council for Scientific and Industrial Research.
>
> Publicacion - Universidad de Chile, Departmento de Geologia.[26]

This new rule has already affected monographic cataloging in the series area. Rule 142E3 of the new Chapter 6:

> If the title of a series consisting solely of a generic term is the title of a serial, the generic term is followed by the author statement. The two elements are separated by a space-hyphen-space (-). The author statement is transcribed as it appears on the publication, except that if that statement includes a corporate hierarchy, those parts of the hierarchy which are not necessary for the identification of the author are omitted. The parts of the hierarchy which are recorded are separated by commas.[27]

The rule goes on to give examples, some of which have already been given in *Cataloging service.* The new Chapter 6, however, explains a little more clearly how the hierarchy part of the rule works by indicating what appears on the publication. For example, in the third example already given, the publication actually has on it:

> Universidad de Chile, Facultad de Ciencias Fisicas y Matematicas, Departmento de Geologia.

For title recording, the "Facultad" has been eliminated from the statement as being unnecessary to the hierarchy.

Here is an example of an LC card using the generic title, followed by a space-hyphen-space and the corporate author:

United Reformed Church.
Year book—United Reformed Church. 1973/74–

London.
   v. illus. 21 cm. annual.

   1. United Reformed Church—Directories.

BX9890.U25U54a   285′.2   74–644755
                                                    MARC-S

Library of Congress   74 ₍2₎

Fig. 2-5. New method of title recording for titles which consist solely of a generic term.

LC gives further justification for such a change in *Cataloging service bulletin* 110.

> The Library of Congress anticipates that the American Library Association will adopt the ISBD(S): *International Standard Bibliographic Description for Serials* at an early date. It is highly desirable that serials entered in the MARC serials data base and in the pending CONSER data base be compatible with the provisions of ISBD(S) so far as the recording of the serial title is concerned. Therefore, the Library of Congress has on an interim basis adopted the following rule derived from standard 1.1.1.3 of the ISBD(S) for the recording of serials whose title consist solely of a generic term.

> [The same rule that appeared in *Bulletin* 109 was then repeated.]

> In the terminology of the ISBD(S), the construct of generic title plus author statement constitutes the "distinctive title."[28]

In order to show more clearly what this rule change would mean to serials catalogers, here are some samples of title-pages with the same words switched around to show how title-page variations would affect title recording. Note that this change does not yet affect entry. All of these examples would still be entered under American Medical Association.

TITLE PAGES	RECORDING OF TITLE
American Medical Association Journal	
	Journal - American Medical Association
Journal American Medical Association	
American Medical Association Journal	American Medical Association journal
Journal of the American Medical Association	Journal of the American Medical Association

Fig. 2-6. Chart of sample of title-pages and title recording under new rule 162B.

All through this discussion the words "generic term" have appeared. A question foremost in the minds of many librarians, especially serials librarians, is "What does this mean?" The question is a good one and is not easily answered. Hopefully, some answer will be reached on an international level, for it will affect many of the international serials projects underway at this time. Something of an answer has appeared already in *Cataloging service bulletin* 112. An attempt at further expansion of that answer appears in the appendices to this book. (See Appendix C.)

The *Cataloging service bulletin* defines "generic terms:"

162

Generic terms. In *Cataloging service bulletin* 110, p. 3, it was announced that the Library of Congress has adopted the following practice in the case of a serial whose title consists solely of a generic term: in recording such a title the generic term is followed by the author statement, the two elements being separated by a space-hyphen-space (-). The following guidelines have been drawn up for determining whether or not a title consists solely of a generic term. It is based on unpublished guidelines of the ISDS, which have been adopted by the national ISDS centers.

1. ISDS definition of a generic term: "one which indicates the kind and/or periodicity of a publication." Every attempt is made to adhere to this definition.

   Examples:

   > Annual conference proceedings
   > Annual report
   > Bulletin
   > Circular
   > Journal
   > Membership directory
   > Occasional newsletter
   > Official report
   > Pamphlet
   > Preliminary report
   > Proceedings of the conference
   > Program
   > Record
   > Research paper
   > Review
   > Special report
   > Transactions

2. Titles which contain (or consist of) terms indicating subject content or coverage *are not to be considered generic.*

   Examples:

   > Anthropological reports
   > Seismological bulletin
   > Astronomy
   > Behavioral science series
   > Chemical bulletin
   > Clinical science
   > Science bulletin
   > Medical series bulletin

3. Titles which include words other than those indicating periodicity or kind of publication *are generally not to be considered generic.*

   Examples:

   > Average monthly weather outlook
   > External trade statistics
   > Employment statistics
   > Nationalities papers
   > Staff papers series
   > Services and organization guide
   > Summary of general legislation

Technical services program
Training & methods series
Tutorial lecture series
State salary survey

4. Titles which contain (or consist of) acronyms or initialisms *are not to be considered generic.*

Examples:

B.E.A. staff paper
B.I.S. report
Research report ADM
Bulletin GT

5. In general, titles consisting of more than five words (exclusive of "empty words"), *are not to be considered generic.*

Examples:

Directory of faculty, professional and administrative staff, and students
Appropriation statements by departments and agencies, all funds
Annual descriptive report of program activities for vocational education
Annual report: National resources and recreation agencies

6. When there is doubt that a term is generic, it will be considered that it is.[29]

This is getting us very deeply into description of the publication itself, and you are probably wondering why we are going on at great length on this subject. The answer is partially to be found in the Ad Hoc Discussion Group's memorandum, in the last paragraph. It has been suggested that rule 6 be dropped completely in favor of title main entry for serials. As the rules are written now, this would mean title as defined in rule 162. Rule 162 has just increased considerably in importance, hasn't it? For more discussion of title main entry, see Chapter 4.

FOOTNOTES

1. Seymour Lubetzky, *Code of cataloging rules, a partial and tentative draft for a new edition of bibliographic cataloging rules prepared for the Catalog Code Revision Committee* (June, 1958), p. ix.

2. *Anglo-American cataloging rules. . .* North American text (Chicago: American Library Association, 1967), p. 2.

3. *Ibid.,* p. 10.

4. *New rules for an old game; proceedings of a workshop on the 1967 Anglo-American Cataloguing Code held by the School of Librarianship, the University of British Columbia, April 13 and 14, 1967* (Vancouver: Publications Centre, University of British Columbia, 1967), p. 64.

5. *Anglo-American cataloging rules*, North American text, p. 10.

6. *Ibid.*, p. 3.

7. International Conference on Cataloguing Principles, Paris, 1961, *Statement of Principles* ...annotated edition with commentary and examples by Eva Verona (London: I.F.L.A. Committee on Cataloguing, 1971), p. 44.

8. Andrew D. Osborn, "International aspects of code revision; the long-standing desire for standardization of cataloging rules," paper XI in Institute on Catalog Code Revision, Stanford University, July 9-12, 1958. *Working papers* (Stanford, Calif., 1958), pp. xi-5, xi-6.

9. *Cataloging service bulletin* 96 (November, 1970):2.

10. Michael Gorman, *A study of the rules for entry and heading in the Anglo-American Cataloguing Rules, 1967 (British text)*, (London: Library Association, 1968), p. 26.

11. Seymour Lubetzky, *Principles of cataloging. Final report phase I: descriptive cataloging.* (Los Angeles: Institute of Library Research, University of California, July, 1969), pp. 41-42.

12. G.E. Hamilton, "Chapter 7: Serials (rules 160-168)" in Seminar on the Anglo-American Cataloguing Rules (1967), Nottingham, Eng., 1968. *Proceedings of the Seminar...*(London: Library Association, 1969), pp. 56-57.

13. *Ibid.*, p. 64.

14. Colloquium on the Anglo-American Cataloging Rules, *The code and the cataloger; proceedings ... held at the School of Library Service, University of Toronto on March 31 and April 1, 1967* (Toronto: University of Toronto Press, 1969), pp. 9-10.

15. *Ibid.*, p. 25-26.

16. *Ibid.*, p. 25.

17. The British text of 6C reads:

> C. Entry under personal author. Enter a serial of which one person is author or principal author, or which is the result of collaboration between two or three persons, according to rules 1-3. Make an added entry or reference under the title of the serial unless this begins with the name of the personal author in the form used as heading for the main entry.

18. *Cataloging service bulletin* 96 (November, 1970):2.

19. *Cataloging service bulletin* 79 (January, 1967):1-2.

20. Announced in *Cataloging service bulletin* 104 (May, 1972):4.

21. Huibert Paul, "Serials: chaos and standardization," *Library resources and technical services* 14 (Winter, 1970):21-22.

22. *Cataloging service bulletin* 112 (Winter, 1975):11-12.

23. *Cataloging service bulletin* 103 (March, 1972):9.

24. Ad Hoc Discussion Group on Serials Data Bases. Working Communications Subcommittee. *Memorandum*, 14 December, 1973.

25. *Cataloging service bulletin* 108 (April, 1974):2.

26. *Cataloging service bulletin* 109 (May, 1974):9-10.

27. *Anglo-American cataloging rules Chapter 6, separately published monographs* (North American text, 1974), p. 67-68.

28. *Cataloging service bulletin* 110 (Summer, 1974):3.

29. *Cataloging service bulletin* 112 (Winter, 1975):10-11.

Chapter III

Title Changes: the Bane of the Serials Cataloger's Existence

The problem of entry for serials is further compounded by the fact that serials are dynamic publications; they are not static. They change their names! This is a lamentable practice, loudly booed by a recently-commissioned facetious organization, LUTFCSUSTC (Librarians United to Fight Costly, Silly, Unnecessary Serial Title Changes), who have a periodical, *Title varies,* to proclaim loudly the vagaries of publishers. Its founder, David Taylor, says:

> The point is that librarians can help stop silly serial title changes if they get angry enough to do something about them... LUTFCSUSTC is now an organization dedicated to channeling that anger.[1]

Serials librarians have leaped onto the bandwagon, writing irate letters to publishers, with copies to *Title varies,* thus making themselves honorary presidents of the organization. Awards are given for Worst Serial Title Change in the hopes that publishers will take note. It is this practice of changing titles that also serves to make serials cataloging interesting and challenging. We have to devise some methodology to meet the challenge, for it would seem that we cannot stop it, as exemplified by the attitudes of serial publishers and the fact that serials are still changing their titles at an often alarming rate. The race for the LUTFCSUSTC award is often a tight one. It also provides for light-heartedness amidst what seems often like drudgery.

There are three basic ways of dealing with title changes: cataloging under earliest title, latest title, or successive titles, with some variations on these three basic themes.

Cutter, in a note to his general rule dealing with periodicals, said:

> When a periodical changes its title, the whole may be cataloged under the original title, with an explanatory note there, and a reference from the new title to the old; or each part may be cataloged under its own title, with references, 'for a continuation, *see* _____'; 'for the previous volumes, *see* _____.[2]

Later he decided to make his second choice his first, and vice versa, but still he felt earliest title to be a viable choice, perhaps due to the prevalence of printed catalogs at the time. The British 1908 rules also made this choice.

The following title would then be cataloged under earliest title thusly:

```
Midwest  journal of political science.
   v.-            May 1957-
   Detroit, Wayne State University Press.
      v.  23cm.  quarterly.

   Title varies, 1973-      American journal of
political science.
   Published by the Midwest Conference of Poli-
tical Scientists, 1957-1966; by the Midwest
Political Science Association, 1967-      .
   Bibliographic footnotes; book reviews.

   1.Political science--Period. I.Midwest Con-
ference of Political Scientists. II.Midwest
Political Science Association. III.Title:
American journal    of political science.
```

Fig. 3-1. Title cataloged under earliest entry.

Evelyn Wimersberger, in her thesis,[3] gave this example from a library actually following this procedure at the time. Note the holdings statement and reference information:

The London forum (incorporating "The Occult review"); a monthly magazine devoted to the investigations of super-normal phenomena and the study of psychological problems.
London.

Set comprises vol. 1, no. 1 (Jan. 1905) and later numbers.
For a record of changes in title, see under its original name: The OCCULT review.

Fig. 3-2. Later title reference card for title cataloged under earliest entry.

There are pros and cons to this, as to all of the choices. For this one, the most obvious problem would be that the main entry would be an archaic one. If all records agreed in entry, which would seem wise, the payment, check-in, and other records would be under an old and perhaps not even recognizable entry. Who would recognize *The Daily universal register* as being *The Times* (London)? It would make procedures such as mail check-in or the claiming of missing issues very difficult. Main access for these functions would always have to be through a cross-reference. It might be wise to give a publication a more lasting entry. Publications foundering at their start may go through a number of changes before settling down. The library may not even have issues under the first title, which the records are under. A solution, of course, would be to catalog under the first title the library has. However, think of all the redoing if the library acquired a backfile prior to that title change which bears the title that the library has chosen for main entry. The whole situation would become very confusing to acquisitions people and library users as well.

However, a definite pro is putting the title in one place, rather than scattered throughout the catalog. There is stability in the entry.

Latest entry cataloging was the order of the day under the ALA red book rules (Rule 5C1), which originally sprang from the American 1908 rules. Our example would look, then, like this:

American journal of political science.
   v.1-   May 1957-
   [Detroit] Wayne State University Press.
     v. illus. 23cm. quarterly.

   Title varies: May 1957-Nov.1972, Midwest
journal of political science.
   Published 1957-1966, by the Midwest Conference
of Political Scientists; 1967-   by the
Midwest Political Science Association.
   Bibliographic footnotes; book reviews.

   1.Political science--Period. I.Midwest Con-
ference of Political Scientists. II.Midwest
Political Science Association. III.Title:
Midwest journal of political science.

Fig. 3-3. Latest entry cataloging.

This provided the library and the patron with a more current entry than earliest practices, but with the integrity of the file intact. This gave those who were interested in the history of a publication the entire file at their fingertips. Bibliographic searchers and other acquisitions people were thus aided. However, with the exception of these library employees, it was hard to determine if people ever really wanted to know about the entire run of something. This procedure, however, hobbled the person looking for title-as-published from a citation in an index or other source. Like with earliest title cataloging, the user was dependent upon references or added entries to lead him back to the proper place and he loses another step, especially if this is where the holdings and other information is. However, proponents of this system feel that the latest title as main entry gives more direct access to current material, which is what most people want. There is the problem here that titles which are dying might grasp wildly at straws to pull themselves out of their death throes. They may go through a number of identity crises and name changes as they go under. The alternative here, of course, is to go to the most common, or longest-lived title, with references. However, uniformity starts to break down then.

The library suffered the most from latest title cataloging, for the costs of recataloging can be very great. Recataloging might be quite frequent, even incessant. Getting the entire history of a new title recently acquired, but with a long history, might be time-consuming and expensive. It's hard to write accurate history statements for broken runs, too. And it's also hard to catalog what you don't have, if you are to keep up with the cataloging, even though you no longer receive the set. However, if you do not keep up, there will be problems with identification of your set with relationship to someone else's, as in a union list situation. Marking costs would jump if shelving is to be under the newest title, or if the book number is changed. And the catalogers would constantly be battling an uphill slowdown to keep current with acquisitions. Arnold Trotier found this to be quite a pressing problem when he wrote:

> I have been particularly concerned over the effect on . . . costs of certain rules of entry affecting serials. I have in mind the rules whereby serials entered under title must always be entered under the latest title and publications entered under a corporate heading must always be entered under the latest form of that corporate heading. No one who has had extensive experience in the cataloging of serials can fail to be impressed with the costs involved in recataloging made necessary by the application of these rules.[4]

It was these rules which made Trotier say, ". . .the chief item of cost in serials processing is the cataloging cost."[5]

Some libraries found it practical to wait until the serial ceased to provide permanent catalog cards for the catalog. This shortchanged everyone and still demanded that typing and other functions keep up with the changes anyway. Not a particularly good solution at best.

The Department of Agriculture Library used to catalog under earliest title in hand, then recatalog the series fully in the light of its history when it ceased. The central serial record, however, was under latest title — an interesting combination of the first two choices.

Problems were encountered when libraries tried to combine rules. Successive entry for monographs under corporate authors and serials under latest made for awkward explanations, to be sure. Too, some libraries, like Denver Public, used latest entry for their classed collection and successive entry for their alphabetically arranged unclassified collection, another curious and confusing mix of choices.

When Miss Iskenderian wrote her thesis, in 1942, she encountered another variation on this method of entry. Two libraries in her study entered the work under the title on the piece when it was cataloged — that is, under latest entry.

References were made under earlier and subsequent title changes. This was not condoned by any of the cataloging rules, but it was simply expedient for the libraries at the time. The problems are obvious in the light of the other methods. Still, it seemed worthy of brief mention as one of the possible alternatives.

Ultimately, it was decided that recataloging of serials was one of the most expensive procedures in a library and it should be avoided. Principle access under references should also be avoided. Even before Lubetzky's proposals, some libraries such as Newark Public and New York Public had already turned to successive entry cataloging as a way out of the problem. Although the 1960 *Code of cataloging rules* gave the choice of all three, except for dead serials, which were to be put under latest title, the pendulum was already swinging back to Seymour Lubetzky's 1958 proposal of successive entry cataloging for serials.

Under successive entry cataloging, each part is cataloged under the title it had at the time of publication and the record of parts is brought together by notes. Our by-now-familiar example would look like this:

```
Midwest journal of political science.
   v.1-16; May 1957-Nov. 1972.
   Detroit, Wayne State University Press.
   16v.  23cm.  quarterly.

   1957-66, publication of the Midwest Conference
of Political Scientists; 1967-72, publication of
the Midwest Political Science Association.
   Continued by the American journal of political
science.
   Bibliographic footnotes; book reviews.

   1.Political science--Period. I.Midwest Con-
ference of Political Scientists. II.Midwest
Political Science Association
```

```
American journal of political science.
    v.17-          Feb. 1973-
  ₍Detroit₎ Wayne State University Press.
    v.  illus. 23cm.  quarterly.

  Continues Midwest journal of political
science.
  Official journal of the Midwest Political
Science Association.
  Bibliographic footnotes: book reviews.

  1.Political science--Period. I.Midwest
Political Science Association.
```

Fig. 3-4. Successive entry cataloging.

This is a more bibliographically accurate process. It is especially helpful to the patron who has a citation to the title-as-published. The entire history of the title is not given, but this can be discovered in one place in bibliographies. (The knowledgeable can even follow it in the catalog, if he so desires, although few probably would.) In fact, Seymour Lubetzky feels that few would even care about the publication's history at all:

> ...in the case of a periodical or serial which appears over a long period of time and is subject to various changes of title, it is not to be expected that a writer citing a given volume will inquire what the original title was, or what the relation of the given title is to any other title, and the purpose of the catalog will therefore better be served if each title is entered separately and provided with notes indicating its relation to any other titles.[6]

It can also be argued that patrons do not generally read notes on catalog cards. If this is so, successive entry is most certainly the best choice as being the most straightforward.

It should be pointed out here that successive entry refers only to those titles which have changed without a change in numbering. If the numbering changes, the entry is not successive. However, since we treat these title changes as separate entities, it should stand to reason that the others, which are successive, should be treated in a like manner. The fact that a title starts with something other than volume 1 should not be a consideration, although it has often been cited as a reason against the use of successive entry. Patrons, however, would not be looking for volume 1 of that title if that title never had a volume 1 and should not be confused! For the curious, the explanatory note should suffice.

The entry is stable, up-to-date and exact. The public and public departments are better served, with shortcuts in cataloging. The average patron can find his material quicker and is more easily helped by reference librarians. The catalog cards are briefer and clearer. Closing out of a title can easily be done by clerical help. (Some libraries ignore this procedure on secondary entries, a practice which is not recommended, as these may be the primary avenue of access for some patrons.) The cataloger, knowing only the one previous title, makes a linking note and catalogs the title just as any new title. Things are much cleaner in the technical processing departments as well.

Isadore Mudge once said:

> Economy in cataloging is economy that actually saves expense in money or time on the library budget as a whole and does not merely save this expense in the catalog department to transfer it to another department or some future time.[7]

Successive entry cataloging does not lay the burden elsewhere and efficiency is much more easily achieved in most areas. It is a true economy in serials cataloging.

Successive entry is the only rational alternative if a collection is not classed. Collocation of volumes with different titles becomes too cumbersome without some kind of symbol or classification scheme to hold continuations of the same run under different titles together. As mentioned in the chapter which covers classification, classification can even be a means for collocation of a serial "set" with successive entry cataloging. This is really the best of all possible worlds, for then you can have main entry access under titles-as-published, but all of the titles can be found together in the shelflist for that kind of an approach, if desired. You can actually have your cake and eat it too in this case. However, successive entries in the shelflist under the same call number need some sort of stamp, note or symbol so that cards will not be thrown out when someone discovers cards already there with the same call number. This is a definitely acute problem for those with automated shelflists. All titles should have cards in the shelflist to show the history of the title and they should be arranged in the appropriate chronological order. If the collection is heavily browsed, however, giving each title its own call number might be the best way to serve the patron. This part of the treatment is best left up to each local library situation.

Successive entry cataloging can be further clarified in serials records if necessary. Cornell stamps its serials catalog holdings cards "See earlier title: [title]" and "See later title: [title]" to fill in the spaces and to call the patron's attention to information on the catalog cards. The central serial record can also have notes such as: "For [v. 1-27] see [former title]" written across the first check-in line to call the user's attention to the fact that another record may be involved. Continuation notes can likewise be penciled across the last check-in line. This can help acquisitions staff immensely.

The problems of acquisitions staff were discussed when the new rules came out and it was pretty strongly felt that acquisitions people would have extra work, since dealers generally put their catalogs under latest entry. This seems to have become less of a problem than originally thought, although you still have to watch for it occasionally. Acquisitions people can be trained to look in all places, and private notes, such as previously mentioned for the check-in records, can help them. The patron cannot have crutches like these, so he must be more directly served. However, if all bases are adequately covered, all can actually be served. Economy and efficiency again!

Seymour Lubetzky feels that successive entry is the most viable alternative for the following reasons:

(a) a serial is, in its course of existence, susceptible to a change of scope and character which makes it in fact a different serial, and the new title may well signify that such a change has taken place, despite the continued numbering of the volumes; (b) a serial does not have the organic unity of a monographic work, it is rather a source of various works, and both the one who cites and the one who looks for a serial is almost always concerned with the part identified by a particular title, not the history of the whole serial; (c) this course is technically more suitable to the changing course of a serial.[8]

He summed it up quite adequately.

The AACR requires successive entry for serials under the provisions of rule 6D:

D. Change of title, author, or name of corporate body

    1. If the title of a serial changes, if the corporate body under which it is entered ceases to be its author,[11] make a separate entry for the issues appearing after the change.[12]

    If the change in title is either of very short duration or of a very minor character, however, it is simply noted on the existing entry (see 167K).

2. If the corporate body accorded an added entry for a serial changes or undergoes a change of name, make an added entry also under the new body or the new name of the body.

(11)Note that the person who is the author of a work issued periodically in revised editions is still considered to be the author even after his connection with the work ceases unless the new editions clearly indicate that the work is no longer his.

(12)The Library of Congress catalogs each serial as a single bibliographic entity, regardless of change of title, issuing body, or name of issuing body. The entry is taken from the latest volume.

AACR/NA.

The British text says much the same thing, in somewhat different wording:

6.D. If the title of a serial, or name of a body used as a heading for a serial, changes, the first issue showing the change is entered in B.N.B. under the new heading, with a note referring to its previous title or heading.

AACR/BT.

Footnote 12 in the North American text came about by request of the Catalog Code Revision Committee. It was felt that too much valuable bibliographic information provided by latest entry cataloging would be lost. This footnote and other like it were stricken from the AACR in April 1971 by *Cataloging service bulletin* 99:

Cataloging of serials

In *Cataloging service, Bulletin* 83, the Library of Congress announced its policy for cataloging serials from the first issue received. In a further effort to expedite the handling and cataloging with changes in title and in name of corporate author. As a result, the Library has decided to abandon its long-standing practice of cataloging all issues of serials under the latest title and name of corporate author and to follow the *Anglo-American Cataloging Rules* as printed. Footnotes number 12 on page 22, number 1 on page 232, and number 4 on page 238 of that volume, describing the Library's present practice, will be canceled. A new card will be printed for issues appearing under a changed title or changed name of corporate author. *New Serial Titles* and the *National Union Catalog* will follow the same policy.

This change will allow the Library of Congress to control its serial receipts faster as well as to provide card subscribers with a quicker and expanded service for serials.[9]

This was followed up by *Cataloging service bulletin* 109, May 1974, which actually brought about the update in the rules. The Library of Congress discovered latest entry cataloging to have all of the costliness mentioned earlier in this chapter and joined the other libraries who had already adopted this section of AACR. LC reports finding it much easier to keep up with current acquisitions now that it no longer has to do costly searching and recataloging.

Cornell University sought further information regarding the rationale behind LC's radical changeover to the AACR as printed and this was the response:

> The basic reason for changing our policy and procedures is that we were losing the serial battle at LC and something had to be done. We have an average of approximately 30,000 titles and it was growing rapidly. Successive entry cataloging allows us to work from the piece in hand and to limit the amount of bibliographic searching done since we no longer need the complete history of a particular title.[10]

Successive entry, although hailed as salvation from eternal drudgery by many, was not welcomed with open arms by all.

Opponents of the successive entry principle, such as F. Bernice Field, felt that "cataloging changes in serial sets as separate entries does not facilitate service either to readers or staff except when a person is checking specific bibliographical citations."[11] However, it would appear that most people are approaching the catalog with specific citations.

Lack of in-depth cataloging and insufficient bibliographic information is often blamed on successive entry. The problems of the order librarian, already mentioned, were brought up again and again in the brouhaha this rule stirred up. However, most of them can find the information needed under successive entry. This does not seem to be the great problem it threatened to be, although one must be careful when searching catalogs still. The Paris Principles even give an "out" by allowing an added entry to be used as a collection point for all entries. This is rarely done in American libraries, however, and does not appear in the AACR.

The proponents felt that there were two acts of cataloging going on — the ceasing of the old entry and the cataloging of the new; and that, although some recataloging is a good thing, too much work would be involved. Actually, such recataloging can be treated pretty much as a routine cataloging problem with the added "trailer" of closing out the old cards, which can be done by a typist and requires only technical kinds of decisions, such as "where to type the information," and "how many cards need to be changed." This can be carried by the normal typing workload, which covers a great many of these kinds of things as "corrections." Training can be pretty minimal and the person involved will build up expertise through practice and experience. This problem hasn't really materialized either in the years libraries have been using the AACR. And it sure beats retyping cards for long history statements!

Another problem cited often by those who do not believe in this system is that of duplication of added entries and subject headings in the catalog.

A serial entry, *one* single entry, can take the place of a group of entries in the Catalog.[12]

This would not seem to be such a great problem in the light of so many advantages. Also, some shortcuts could be taken, if desired, particularly in the subject area. (See Chapter 8.) However, this practice of shortcuts should only be used if there is virtually no room for expansion in the catalog. Most people expect to find information in the card catalog for journals under successive entry — that is, title-as-published. They should find complete access under all entries, which should justify duplicate cards under subjects and added entries. The specialist knows the journals in his field, so libraries providing service only for specialists need not be quite so concerned with this problem. (However, most specialized libraries have different classification and subject schemes, or none at all, which tends to make this a different problem. The catalog may be the check-in record, too, which would shed a different light on the problem.) Those libraries concerned with the ordinary public, or students at the undergraduate level as well as faculty-specialists, should provide all of the access possible. The intellectual processes that generate these extra cards are performed by most catalogers anyway as a matter of course in cataloging a publication, so there is really no extra work involved, except fairly negligible typing and filing. Patrons are shortchanged in the subject and added entry areas when the library uses either earliest or latest entry cataloging, and this should never be tolerated.

The proponents continued on with their arguments. When a title is received all at once, and there are several title changes, there is a lot of time involved in making several entries. When gaps occur in the "run" of a "set," titles are left dangling and the continuity of connecting notes is lost in the catalog. At the Las Vegas ALA convention in 1973, this still was cited as a problem; and it was suggested that cards be put in the catalog indicating that the library did not have one of the titles in a chain. This was loudly shouted down as a silly and unnecessary idea — after all, you don't do that for the monographs you don't have — but it is a solution to the problem. Perhaps a better solution, if the library finds this a problem, would be a note on an internal record such as the central serial record. Linking notes on the other titles could also indicate that the library did not have a given title, although this would cause extra work in the finding and removal of such notes if the library did get the title later on. There may be ways to ride herd on such notes, though, if the library wished to take this approach. Still, catalog records have been made in the past for titles about which little was known, and the sprinkling about of blanks and question marks didn't seem to bother many people then. Besides, none of us really catalogs in a vacuum, especially as more and more union list and automated serial control projects get underway. It may happen sometime in the future that all of those blanks and question marks will be filled in and the links found by some other library with the title in another part of the nation, and maybe even the world.

It was pointed out that indexes and supplements would be hard to handle. This is true to some extent, but procedures can be worked out by references and connecting notes. (See Chapter 7.) A lot of added headings would be needed if a book about a periodical which changed title were written and cataloged too. Back to the same problem of an overabundance of cards, an argument which really shouldn't loom so large in cataloging discussions.

Paul Dunkin, who presented a paper on serials cataloging at the Paris Conference, expressed concern about the loss in consistency as the library world changed systems from latest to successive. He was worried about user irritation, which certainly should be considered. This concerned few of the other librarians at the conference, however. There seems to have been very little complaint, at least audible complaint, so superimposition of this change, as well as all of the others, upon the old scheme of things seems to have been accepted, perhaps as an inevitable in a confusing world, by the long-suffering patron.

Successive entry may also be a problem when cataloging microfilm. Should one cut the microfilm if the change is in the middle of a reel? This may be the only answer now that so many networks and systems are becoming involved, but, up until now, the best alternative was to catalog the individual library's set under latest entry. This was a question which never seems to have been raised at the incendiary discussions about successive entry, perhaps due to the fact that there were fewer sets being filmed then and librarians didn't purchase them in as large quantities as they do now. The problem is the same with reprints, particularly those without distinct title-pages so you cannot tell where the breaks occur, or those with other publishing problems making it impossible to break up the volume. (These latter would probably be treated as "bound-withs.") Libraries not concerned with networking can still use their judgement and would probably opt for latest entry as the wisest way out of a sticky situation.

There can be problems with specific titles cataloged under successive entry, as many catalogers were quick to point out when the topic was first brought up. Here are some lovely ones.[13]

A title first appeared in 1930 as *Textile economist*. It had this title for six months before it became *Textile organon* for four years. It was *Rayon organon* for sixteen years before it reverted to *Textile organon* in 1952.

An Italian philological review first appeared in 1934 cataloged under the name of the society because its name was *Bolletino*. The second volume was still called *Bolletino*, but the society had changed its name. Volume 3 was published under the title, *Rivista inguana e intemelia*. The society changed its name with volume 7, but the serial waited until volume 8 to call itself *Rivista di studi liguri*. "Yuch!" you may well say to yourself. The ISDS would put all of these under separate entries, with different ISSN. This is probably what we will all eventually come to. However, at present we can call at least some of these "titles of short duration," the last sentence reprieve of rule 6D1.

This last section indicates that titles that do not last very long, or are very minor, can be dismissed in a note. They should be given an added entry, too. "Short duration," unfortunately, is not defined anywhere, making it very hard on the neophyte, who is fervently hoping that someone else has already done this so he will have guidance. It is probable, however, that with the automated systems coming along and the need for standardization as a result, this will need to be clarified. It may even have to be written out of the rules since short duration is really only valid in retrospect and would be hard for these automated programs to implement. (It is interesting to note that the British text does not have this provision.)

A perfect example of the use of this rule is the periodical with the following history: January-June, 1933, *Management methods;* July-September, 1933, *System and management methods;* October-December, 1933, *System and business management*. The only answer here is the latest entry, since the problem is solved by the rules for titles of short duration, and these really are very short. Another alternative might be to shoot the publisher, but this would likely be frowned upon outside circles of serials librarians!

Opponents have been quick to point up the problems of serial entry in relation to the goals of the catalog. When one tries to ascertain what is desired from a catalog, one comes up with a dual purpose:

1. To locate a particular publication by its author's name or its title as given in the publication.

2. To bring together entries for all editions and translations of one work and all work of one author[14]

These two objectives seem to be at variance when it comes to serial entries. The first objective would seem to call for successive entry cataloging, while the second would seem to indicate that one entry is desired to preserve literary units. However, if you follow Seymour Lubetzky's rationale that a title change means a change of identification, you are all right.

According to Lubetzky's point of view, a title change usually heralds a complete change of editorial policy. In effect, a completely new periodical has been created.

When a serial changes its title, this may mean that it has changed its identity as measured by a change in its aim or content. Such a change should logically be treated as a new serial.[15]

Such scope changes may be accompanied by a change of class, which cannot be done under the other alternatives.

The concept of successive title cataloging for serials, while not wildly supported by all on the home front, received support at the ICCP. Section 11.5 of the Paris Principles relates specifically to successive entry cataloging:

11.5 When a *serial publication* is issued successively under different titles, a *main entry* should be made under each title for the series of issues bearing that title, with indication of at least the immediately preceding and succeeding titles. For each such series of issues, an added entry may be made under one selected title[12] If, however, the variations in title are only slight, the most frequently used form may be adopted as a uniform heading for all issues.

[12] If it is desired to collect information about the serial as a whole in one place in the catalogue.

Paul Dunkin commented at the ICCP on a questionnaire distributed with his working paper. Preference was overwhelmingly in favor of successive entry and few felt that this decision was inconsistent with the aims of the catalog. Many apologetically felt that economies should be taken into consideration, which might have prompted some to respond as they did. Although it was a new concept for many, 54 out of 60 votes were cast for successive entry at the conference. The concept was written into the AACR, but not all libraries have bowed gracefully to this new wave, still believing the reasons cited in favor of the other possibilities to be valid. They will probably be forced to change through the impact of automated systems.

Just as titles which change are to be cataloged successively, so are corporate authors which change their names. This appears in rule 6D and also in rule 68:

If the name of a corporate body has changed (including change from one language to another), establish a new heading under the new name for cataloging publications under this name...

AACR/NA

When this first came out in the Draft Code, many people objected. The dissenters argued that a person may change his name several times throughout his lifetime and his works get grouped under a standard heading. This should be the same for corporate authors. They were not taking into consideration that a corporate body is subject to various functional and organizational changes which are, in effect, a change of identity. The new entry for the entity becomes its own authority.

The identification of a corporate body rests upon different individuals at different times. It can continue to change and be described in different terms from time to time. In effect, the person still remains the same individual, even though renamed. He has a limited lifetime. The corporate body may continue to exist and publish for an unlimited length of time. The institution may even move to another place. Then how can it be the same? Arnold Trotier summed it up quite well in his paper presented at the Code Revision Institute at McGill University when he said:

> However, any analogy attempted. . . with respect to changed names of persons and corporate bodies will prove imperfect. The identity of a person is immutable; no matter what name or names he uses or is known by, he remains the selfsame individual. The same cannot be said of corporate bodies. These are always subject to various organizational or constitutional changes which may or may not be accompanied by changes in name. But when a significant change in name does occur, it usually reflects a major change in function, organization or constitution and thereby effects a change in identity. If this fact is recognized, the logic of the rule which provides for entry of works under the name of the organization at the time of their publication becomes more apparent. Moreover a rule based on this theory is supported by the following practical results: (1) the entries will conform with the names under which the works of the body are normally cited, (2) the works issued by that body during each period marked by a change in name will be kept segregated in the catalog, and (3) the recataloging necessitated by the rule requiring entries to be made under the latest form of name will be wholly avoided.[16]

Trotier also said:

> Even if you don't like the rationale behind this change, you have to go along with it as one of the most practical and useful changes. . .It is more comfortable and easy to work with.[17]

The choices of treatment of corporate names which have changed are pretty much the same as the ones for titles which have changed, with one addition. The pros and cons are pretty much the same, too, with the one addition. The addition is what Ruth MacDonald describes as "entry under an arbitrary or symbolic form."[18]

Choice of earliest form would be stable and supply the inquirer with complete history. However, it would not serve the patron looking for a current name or a cited reference very well. There is also the problem of using an antiquated form of a name for a recent publication. Costs of adding references, and the bulk of these references, would increase. There would be problems for check-in and claiming of serial titles.

The latest form also provides stability and the complete history, with the extra added attraction of being current. A minimum of catalog cards is needed, although references for earlier headings would be necessary. It's tidier for dealing with corporate changes. It's also easier for bibliographic searching of current publication. You also achieve some form of classification by the clustering of headings. But the use of the current heading might be an artificial modernization. It is time-consuming, and therefore costly, to use this approach. Catalogers would spend all their time recataloging, and cards would be lengthy and expensive to reproduce. There would be a big problem with analyzed monographic series with series added entries. The workload would be cumbersome and the problems persistent. Nor can this practice be reconcilable with the reader's approach to the catalog. The only accurate description of these choices is as follows:

> Neither [a corporate name nor a serial title] can be directly cited except under the name, number, and data it bears at publication. References forward or backward are falsifications.[19]

M. Ruth MacDonald (1958) offers the choice of entry under an arbitrary name. She gives advantages as follows: more general acceptance than other choices; more direct approach from any or all name variations in any language or alphabet; simplicity; the grouping of entries together; the elimination of recataloging; provision of the requirements for cataloging-at-source; the elimination of the amount of republication required in bibliographies and catalogs, and provision of the answer to language barriers and the corporate authorship problem. The only problem is that all approaches would have to be through cross-references. It is a radical departure from cataloging procedures as we know them and has not been considered very widely.

Entry under the form of name used at the time of publication seems to be the best alternative. It means a savings in work and time. It provides direct access from citations. It produces stability, for an entry once established will not change. The cataloger does not need to search out the history of the corporate body, but can catalog from the piece-in-hand. Repeated recataloging is eliminated. The cataloger can concentrate on current work without worrying about ghosts of the past or the future. Continued reprinting of reference tools and bibliographies will be eliminated, except for provisions necessary to tie together past and current names. Cataloging is up-to-date. Uniformity is attained. The disadvantages of this system are relatively minor in the light of these marvelously positive justifications. Successive entry is the "only way to fly," regarding "a change of name of a corporate body at the end of one body and the beginning of another, excepting slight changes of name and changes of short duration."[20]

Of course, the proponents of the old rules came up with reasons for not going along with successive entry cataloging for corporate bodies with name changes, and brought up copious examples to back them up. A perfectly hair-raising example was brought up by Miss Field:

> How far can we go in considering changes of name of this kind as new entries and still have a catalog that is reasonably useful? I should like to consider some specific cases here to bring out the problem more clearly. Take, for example, the Akademie der Wissenschaften in Berlin. This has had twelve different names, according to the Yale catalog, eight of them in German, all of which would file in different parts of the catalog, one in French, and three in Latin. Names often appear in publications in two or three languages, and we make references from the ones not used. But that is not the situation here. Although the society was founded with a German name, its first publication appeared with the name of the organization and the title in Latin. It was succeeded by a publication with title pages entirely in French, the use of French only continued from 1746 to 1804 on this publication; so the French name cannot be omitted from the picture if we follow the rule to use the form of name on the publication. In the latter part of this period (1781-1803), however, the society also issued two publications in German with the name of the organization and the title in that language. Would Miss MacDonald and Mr. Kebabian start with the Latin name, change to the French form and again to the German when it begins to appear, even though the French name also continues? And what would they do with the other nine names? Some, of course, are minor variations that could be cared for by references; but most of them are major changes. Their publications, however, continue with the same titles. It seems to us that a division of the publications of an organization like this, which is really one institution throughout its history, would be an aggravation to the user of the catalog...
>
> The point I am trying to make is that to have in the catalog innumerable entries for what is essentially the same publication makes the catalog unclear, especially when the changes are not distinctive enough to make a clear-cut division in anyone's mind but only enough to affect the filing. Probably Miss MacDonald and Mr. Kebabian would consider some of these changes minor and cover the variations by references, but most of the examples I have mentioned would surely have to have more than one entry in the catalog if the Lubetzky principle is followed. Whether the work is cataloged as one entry or several, the cataloger has to establish the bibliographical history of the publication at the time it passes through his hands; and a clear presentation of this on one catalog entry straightens out the bibliographic pattern of the publication for all who need it and makes it easy to find.[21]

One can always bring up exceptions to a rule. ("Rules are made to be broken."— Popular proverb.) The clarity of the catalog, is, of course, the most important thing, and we must make the best of a bad situation, as Miss Field's example surely is. References, clear history statements, and judicious grouping of like entries is probably the only wise way out of this mess. The rules are flexible enough for this kind of maneuvering; and the cataloger, using the publication-in-hand, bibliographic and reference tools, and his own common sense, must make his decision. It is situations like the one described here that are instrumental in swinging the pendulum toward title main entry, which is one common-sense approach. There will always be uglies like the ones described here, but these are really the exception rather than the rule.

Successive entry is probably the cheapest, most straightforward, and most expedient way of treating serial title and corporate author changes. It is the most helpful for the patron and the most direct for automated projects, such as union lists. It is one of the bases of the International Serials Data System, ISDS (for more information, see Chapter 18), which has many good tips on title changes in its *Guidelines*. It seems to be the best we can do, that is, until the millenium comes and serial publishers stop changing serial titles!

FOOTNOTES

1. David C. Taylor "LUTFCSUSTC," *Michigan librarian* 39 (Winter, 1973):13.

2. Henry A. Sharp *Cataloguing; a textbook for use in libraries*. 4th ed. (London: Grafton and Co., 1944), p. 316 and others.

3. Evelyn G. Wimersberger *Methods of indicating serial holdings in the catalogs of college and university libraries*. M.S. in L.S. thesis, Columbia University, 1939, p. 86.

4. Arnold H. Trotier "Some persistent problems of serials in technical processes," *Serial slants* 1 (January, 1951):8 and elsewhere.

5. *Ibid.*

6. Seymour Lubetzky *Cataloging rules and principles* …(Washington: Processing Department, Library of Congress, 1953, reprinted 1954), p. 47.

7. Isadore G. Mudge "Present day economies in cataloging as seen by the reference librarian of a large university library," *Catalogers' and classifiers' yearbook* 4 (1939) :9.

8. Seymour Lubetzky *Principles of cataloging. Final report, phase I: descriptive cataloging*. (Los Angeles: Institute of Library Research, University of California, July, 1969), p. 43.

9. *Cataloging service bulletin* 99 (April, 1971):1.

10. Judith Proctor Cannan "Serials cataloging: successive entry," *Library resources and technical services* 17 (Winter, 1973):75; and her "Successive entry at C.U.L.," Cornell University. Libraries. *Bulletin* 179 (September, 1972):9.

11. F. Bernice Field, "Comments on papers relating to the application of the Lubetzky principles to serials at the Armed Forces Medical and the New York Public Libraries," *Serial slants* 8 (July, 1956):129.

12. Leo R. Rift , "The girl they left behind … serials and the new catalog code," *MLA quarterly* 18 (September, 1957):85.

13. Elizabeth G. Borden, "Revision of cataloging rules for serial entries proposed in the Lubetzky report," *Serial slants* 5 (April, 1954):95-97.

14. Helen M. Falconer, "Function of the main entry in the alphabetical catalog," working paper no. 1 in Canadian Institute on Cataloguing Principles, St. Andrews, N.B., 1961, *Summary of proceedings and working papers* (Ottawa: Canadian Library Association, 1961), p. 1.

15. Antony Croghan. *A short code of rules for author, title, and descriptive cataloguing; with explanations and examples.* (London: Coburgh Publications, 1971), p. 32.

16. Dorothy Comins, "Catalog code revision for serial publications," *Library resources and technical services* 5 (Summer, 1961):222.

17. Arnold H. Trotier, "The draft code and the problems of corporate authorship," *Library resources and technical services* 6 (Summer, 1962):225.

18. M. Ruth MacDonald, "Entry of corporate bodies under successive names," paper IV in Institute on Cataloging Code Revision, Stanford University. July 9-12, 1958. *Working papers* (Stanford, Calif., 1958), p. IV-3.

19. Marie Louise Prevost, "The Lubetzky report: harbinger of hope," *Journal of cataloging and classification* 10 (April, 1954) :75.

20. Lubetzky *Cataloging rules and principles* , p. 50.

21. Field "Comments," pp. 128-129.

Chapter IV

A Major Controversy: Title Main Entry for Serials

Due to international developments and the appearance on the scene of various standards, proposals have been made to change the existing rules for serial entry. The International Serials Data System and the International Standard Bibliographic Description for Serials (see Chapter 18) do not concern themselves with main entry per se. They are standards for identification and description, using title-as-it-appears-on-the-piece as the basis for the records involved. For the ISBD(S) the initial element is the distinctive title; for the ISDS it is the key title. Rule 162B has been changed, as already mentioned, to go along with the new standards. Now it is proposed that rule 6 be revised to require entry under title for all serials to conform with the ISBD(S) and the ISDS. As a result of all this, the authors of the new AACR are taking a long hard look at rule 6. There are several alternatives, although title main entry seems to have the edge, especially since the Catalog Code Revision Committee of ALA voted in favor of it at the CCRC's July meeting in San Francisco. This is what the current controversy is all about.

There are basically five alternatives to the problem: the status quo; no separate rule for serials; entry under author if there is one; entry under title at all times; and entry under title if distinctive, but under corporate body if generic. Obviously the status quo is no longer viable due to the criticisms it has received so no change in the rule is really not a choice either. This leaves four.

There would be many problems if the choice of entry for serials were to follow the rules for monographs and there were no serial rule. It would be very difficult for catalogers to cope without a separate rule; since one has been in existence for so long, it is expected. It would also presuppose a lot of knowledge on the part of the cataloger. This is one of the faults, if one can call it that, of the present *Rules*: one has to understand the principles behind the rules with a depth and intimacy with which few are adequately equipped. Too, the rules are not, at present, adequately written to cover the changing authorship concept that encompasses serials. This is implied in the rules but is not obvious, except perhaps in the serial rule, where it is masked by other considerations. It wouldn't really be there at all if the rule were to be dropped unless some provisions were made for it. This idea of no separate rules was rejected by the CCRC.

The question of entry under author if there is one, either corporate or personal, goes hand in hand with the above choice. There are many who quarrel with the concept of personal authorship for serials, feeling that the two are incompatible. These people feel very kindly towards title main entry.

In the chapter on entry the problem inherent in the concept of authors for serials was discussed. Many entries which people feel are author entries are, in reality, issuing-body entries. Corporate authorship responsibility for serials is confusing and unclear. Although many would like to see corporate entries for generic title serials, they would not be getting such under strict application of the authorship principle. Cases in which the corporate body denies responsibility for the contents of its journal, as in the case of the *Journal of the American Medical Association,* would not meet the qualifications for authorship entry. According to the rules that would follow from this principle, entry for this title would be under title. This would probably not be desired by those people who want authorship entries. There would be some titles under bodies and similar ones under title due to the intentions of the body with respect to its publications. This would be confusing to the user and very difficult for the cataloger to apply.

The authorship concept is the whole rationale behind rule 6B2, which catalogers have a great deal of trouble interpreting now. Changing to more of the same will not improve things. It was to avoid considerations beyond mere title-page information that drove the makers of the AACR away from the concept of authorship for serials. The same problems still apply.

Another consideration takes us to the projects that brought this all up in the first place: automated projects like CONSER and international considerations like ISDS and ISBD(S). (For a discussion of these, see Chapter 18.) These are based on a title entry concept. This cannot be changed. The problem with the status quo for them is that when a title does not change, but an author does, and the entry is under that author, two bibliographic records are created according to AACR. However, since these projects are based on titles only, there would be only one record for them. This means that there will be only one ISSN, which will be a problem because two cataloging records cannot have one number. These cataloging records may really multiply, as in the case of the

Statistical abstract of the United States. Simple arithmetic trips us up. Authorship is not the way to go in the light of automated projects.

The answer seems to lie in the direction of title main entry for serials. The moment this is mentioned, serials librarians choose up sides. First, before considering the pros and cons of such a radical approach, let us see what the rule might look like. Joe Howard, formerly head of the Serials Record Division at the Library of Congress, came up with an alternative wording for rule 6, calling for the desired-by-some entry for serials under title:

(6) Serials

Preliminary note. This rule for serials (including numbered monographic series) applies also for entries for unnumbered monographic series and to series added entries (cf. 33N) made for monographs in a series (whether numbered or not).

(A) Enter a serial under its title.

If an added entry is required for a serial, and if the title of the serial is identical with that of another serial, add in parentheses the city of publication. If this addition is insufficient, add also the years of publication.

For serials issued by or under the authority of a corporate body, make an added entry for the corporate body.

For serials by a personal author, make an added entry for the personal author.

(B) If the title of a serial changes, make a separate entry for the issues appearing after the change. If, however, the change is of a very minor character, it is simply noted in the existing entry (see 167K).

If the corporate body accorded an added entry for a serial changes or undergoes a change of name, make an added entry also under the new body or the new name of the body.

If the personal author accorded an added entry for a serial change [sic] make an added entry also under the new personal author.[1]

There has always been a fairly large contingent of librarians who have objected to corporate entry for serial publications. Corporate entry is, as Osborn points out, ''the single most troublesome element in reader use of catalog cards for serials.''[2] Yale, he says, cautions its staff by saying:

A cataloger must keep in mind that serials cataloged under corporate entries are difficult for readers to find.[3]

Some libraries have always had title main entry, ignoring the rules for entry, and more seem to be turning to it. Some libraries go against the rules as presently printed for all distinctive titles, even though they should be entered under a corporate body according to the provisions of 6B2 or under a personal author according to 6C. This point of view has really taken hold with the new automated developments in serials cataloging.

Those who advocate title main entry are quick to point out that serials are most definable by title. Most titles are distinctive and the problems only come up with generic titles, a small proportion overall. Too, citations lead patrons to titles, especially in the case of generic titles. Corporate authorship is a concept not easily understood by those who are not librarians and, indeed, not all librarians subscribe to this principle, as already mentioned. Title is more straightforward and direct. The main entry should be the most useful entry and those voting for title feel that this is it.

Not only is title main entry easier on the patron, it is easier on the cataloger. The cataloger can be freed from the cumbersome decision-making processes that correct interpretation of rule 6 entails. Catalogers of serial publications will be able to do their work with ease and accuracy. Standardization will be built into the rule.

There are problems with correct interpretations of the rules now. Some librarians do not follow them, or do not understand them. This tends to give the editors of *NST* and other union lists grey hairs. There is considerable room for interpretation in the rules and different rationalizations and differing knowledge of the publication-in-hand can yield very different results. Joe Howard gives an illustration:

> If a cataloger is working on *External Trade of Liberia: Exports,* issued by the Department of Planning and Economic Affairs of Liberia, he has several decisions to make. If he does not know the frequency of the publication he may decide that it cannot be a yearbook and does not seem to fit the definition of periodical as given in the glossary of AACR. He makes his entry under issuing body. A second cataloger could decide that the publication is, indeed, a periodical; so his entry is under title. A third cataloger, working perhaps from different or additional issues of the same publication, finds information that the frequency is annual. He decides that he has a yearbook in terms of the definition in the *ALA Glossary of Literary Terms,* and his entry, too, is under title. A fourth cataloger, knowing the publication is annual, may feel that he cannot consider the publication a yearbook because as footnote 8 to AACR6 says, "the term 'yearbook' is to be understood to exclude a work the content of which is necessarily the expression of the corporate thought or activity of the body," and so he uses the issuing body as his main entry.[4]

Title main entry for all serials would need little interpretation by the cataloger, the advocates of this position feel, and there would be little variation in the results of cataloging in various situations. A standard would have been reached. It is easier to establish a title main entry than to establish a corporate hierarchy (although, presumably the hierarchy will appear in an added entry).

Another argument is that mail accessioners would not have to learn corporate entry. There would not have to be an intellectual decision made each time a piece of mail was touched. The mail check-in person would not have to decide the entry words (perhaps under a place name or some other artificial structure not on the piece-in-hand — i.e., "Catholic Church. Pope." for *Acta apostolicae sedis*). The piece-of-mail-in-hand would bear the authoritative entry on it and extra work would not have to be performed to write the entry on it or to mark the entry appropriately with slashes, underlinings, or hash marks. Less time would be spent on mail check-in.

It is felt that main entry is no longer really important. This was the attitude A. J. Wells voiced in 1966:

> In many ways it would be easier to plan a catalogue record which began with the title, for this would dispense with the notion of a main entry heading — a notion which has occupied more of our time to little purpose than everything else in librarianship except, perhaps classification and subject indexing. There is little doubt in my mind that we could get international agreement on a standard format for a machine-readable catalogue record if we dispensed with the necessity for a main entry heading.[5]

It is an attitude shared by most people in the field of automation today. Others tend to agree, particularly for serials. Added entries should be made for all possible approaches in the public catalog anyway. Cross-references can be made for a single-access file, such as a check-in file or union list, if desired. The *World list of scientific periodicals* has a title arrangement and seems satisfactory. Indexes for political jurisdictions and corporate bodies would help in accessing the list, as with the *World list*.

Title main entry may be cheaper for bindery lettering. There would not be redundancy and parts could be left off or abbreviated, particularly in the corporate name when added to a generic term.

Title entry would standardize contacts libraries have with publishers and vendors, which would improve communications considerably. The International Standard Serial Number and key title (see Chapter 18) would be the primary identifying factors and main entry under a corporate body would not be necessary to identify a serial title. Vendors would not need elaborate reference structures to get at a title in all the ways needed to serve the vast number of libraries using different approaches. There would be only one approach.

The problem of desuperimposition would be somewhat solved. Since the Library of Congress will drop superimposition in the future, it would be much easier if that were done after corporate authorship were deleted from the Serial

Record. However, there will be a problem with titles cataloged under latest title. Since the proposed rule is so linked to physical appearance of the piece-in-hand, it will be impossible in many cases to reenter the title without going back to the original and essentially recataloging it. For any kind of conformity, most titles will have to be touched, which would be a perfect opportunity to break up sets cataloged under latest title. LC will be able to do a lot of this by machine, but not all of us would be so lucky. We'd be redoing old records until 1984, and beyond! But then, everything would be clean! There are definitely possible advantages to this, if we don't think about the work involved. (Larger libraries will probably just close their catalogs anyway.)

There would be fewer problems with corporate body name changes. Recataloging occasioned by corporate name changes, as with many governmental agencies, would be reduced. When the Bureau of Statistics of Canada changed to Statistics Canada, for example, all serials under the old entry were ceased and new entries cataloged. For the most part, however, the titles had not changed. Most were distinctive titles, such as *Estimates of employees by province and industry,* so that title entry for these would not include the corporate name. Under the proposed rule change, there would be only one entry for these titles with added entries for both of the corporate bodies as authors. (The recent one would be specially tagged in the computer record.) Catalogers wouldn't have to keep up with corporate changes as they do now.

This rationale was stated by Andrew Osborn in the 1955 edition of his *Serial publications:*

> . . .because the cataloger of the corporate entry serial is confronted with two
> elements subject to change (corporate name of the author and title of the work) it
> is only natural to try to reduce them to one: the title.[6]

This above procedure would be in keeping with the ISDS guidelines. The title is the benchmark; and when it changes, the ISSN changes. AACR is out of step because it calls for a new entry when the corporate-author-when-it-is-an-entry changes its name. Thus, there would be times when AACR would call for two entries when the ISDS would not. This is the crux of the problem and one of the basic reasons for the proposed change. Title entry would eliminate the problem.

Authorship is no longer necessary to the ISDS and the ISBD(S) title approach; and, as a matter of fact, it is something of a nuisance, causing duplication of effort and redundancy in the machine files. This is a situation that is not desirable to the computer people. As it is now, there is redundancy in that the corporate author appears twice in the file — in the entry and in the author statement, for example. They want to eliminate this, and this is another basic reason for the proposed change.

Finally, there would be consistency in the treatment of serial records for exchange of machine-readable information and the American library public would be able to accept the international standards being set up. Eva Verona, who has studied corporate authorship with respect to serials, feels that title entry is the only one practical and possible for the international user.

Back when the AACR was first being discussed as a final product ready for employment by the Anglo-American library world, this comment came up:

> A general criticism which could be leveled at AACR is its almost complete avoidance of the needs of computer handling of catalog data.[7]

This criticism was again leveled at the rules in the final report of the National Serials Pilot Project, an investigation into automation of serials records which formed the basis for some of the projects agitating for change now. (For more information, see Chapter 18.) The criticism would still seem to be valid, as evidenced by the desire to change.

Those who do not wish to change argue that, while title main entry may be all right for computer records, which can be accessed in almost any fashion, it is not valid for card catalog files. Most libraries, they feel, will be stuck in the manual mode for a long time to come and even those with machine files may not have the really advanced technology and programing to make these rules work for them. The effectiveness of catalogs would be destroyed by rules designed primarily for computerized files. Ultimately, when machine access is virtually the only possibility, such a machine-oriented approach to cataloging would be acceptable. The doors are being opened now, but the millenia is by no means reached. Such a drastic jump should not be made now when we do not know where it will take us. We need to explore our new frontiers in terms of these automated projects now. We need to build new consortia and add them to the projects. When we move more irrevocably into the Automated Age, maybe then we can think in these terms, but right now the manual card catalog and the patron-off-the-street are the lifeblood of the library. Redundancy in the machine file should be tolerated rather than chaos in the catalog, say those who do not favor title main entry.

One of the first reactions the opponents of the proposal have been vocal on has been filing in a catalog with title entries as set up now. Because of the new rewrite of 162B, there will be titles like:

Journal for the Society of Psychical Research
and
Journal - American Water Works Association

Under this generic title, and a few others like it, there may be other linking words in English, as well as linking words in French. This will create several subalphabetic arrangements under the single generic term. This may tend to confuse patrons, particularly those who do not know what the linking words are, or even if they are there. Patrons coming to the catalog with a citation like *Trans. Am. Phil. Soc.* will have to guess the entry as:

Transactions-American Philosophical Society
Transactions by the American Philosophical Society
Transactions from the American Philosophical Society
Transactions of the American Philosophical Society

and perhaps other permutations of the title. (This one is pretty straightforward; there are others which are considerably less so.) There are at least four possible alphabetic arrangements for this to be in.

This has always been an argument against title entry arrangement. In the past, librarians who wished to make title added entries added linking words like "of the" in brackets to connect the generic work to its author and, thus, make it distinctive. This addition of nontitle words is not allowable any more since it is not accurate transcription of the title-page. The number of titles under "Journal," already great, would swell beyond belief if title main entry were used. Patrons would become lost and confused, particularly in a single-access file, where they would not have added corporate entries.

This has been likened unto the long files that would occur under "University of" or a common surname like "Smith." However, the names of most universities are pretty well fixed in the minds of people, and a patron would have no problem in a long file of Smiths if he were sure of the full name. However, the problem is considerably different if the patron only knows the author's surname. Then even a relatively uncommon surname can present a problem. This is a more realistic analogy. Presumably there would be a title added entry for the patron with the surname problem, but what help is there for the person floundering about in a generic title like "Journal" in a single-access union list?

It is interesting in the light of this new movement to go back to the arguments that came up when the *World list of scientific periodicals* came out (1921): a list arranged under title-as-printed-on-the-title-page. This was hailed as the answer to uniformity in periodical cataloging, even though the rule was, in F. W. Gravell's[8] mind, difficult to apply. Its advocates claimed that this arrangement was simplest for the ordinary reader. However, the arrangement was adapted by seven auxiliary rules and these rules seemed to defy the simplicity and the alphabetical arrangement. Mr. Gravell criticized the arrangement by saying that patrons do not often remember long titles exactly, and, as mentioned before, did not remember the little linking words.

The old *World list* found something of an answer to the filing problem by using a sort of key word approach. This received a great deal of comment back in the Twenties, Thirties and Forties, mostly negative. The same arguments are coming up again in connection with this. It was felt that people remembered key words, but this didn't work out too well and people were only slightly helped. There were other problems, too. This would not really be a viable solution in a card catalog. The person who knows what the title is he is looking for shouldn't be penalized by such an arbitrary system, either.

The rule would be keyed too much to the piece-in-hand. The patron, not knowing the arrangement of the title-page or cover, would look in the wrong place. The cataloger would have to decide which of two pieces to use as an authority, perhaps a problem of fairly great magnitude if they differed very much. There is also the question of how much change constitutes a title change, especially since everything is tied to the physical appearance of the title. This is spelled out in the *Guidelines for ISDS,* but not to everyone's satisfaction. (See Chapter 18.) Many feel that this will only cloud the issues rather than clarify them.

Some feel that because the title approach is so radically different from what has been practiced for so long in libraries, patrons would be confused.

Acquisitions would find it difficult to "psych out" publishers from a "blurb" and it would be hard to set up reliable preliminary entries. It may be ordered under one title and come in under variations which, although previously considered minor, are now problems. Order slips could conceivably not be matched up, since order personnel would most likely not be working from a physical piece, and a snag would be created. Corporate entry could umbrella a lot of little changes that would now stick out like roots ready to trip the unwary. Publishers, unfortunately, find too much enjoyment in rearranging their title-pages and playing around with typography and layouts. Opponents to the proposal are all too aware of what could conceivably occur. Mail routines may not be as easy as the advocates seem to think.

It is generally felt among the opponents that activities such as mail check-in should not determine entry. Cross-references can be used, if needed, as long as there is no spatial problem. Besides, it is much better to train mail checkers in the rudiments of corporate entry rather than spoonfeeding them with simpleminded work. They should be developed into valuable resource people with a deeper understanding of the central serial record. This is an automatic given in an integrated department, and could be developed in other kinds of arrangements as well. Manpower could be better utilized. Payment information could be more easily kept together under corporate entry, under which there would be some gathering of entries. Minor changes could be covered by the corporate umbrella.

Perhaps we should take a good long look at the past and learn from it. LC tried title entry once before in its central Serial Record. This was abandoned. Florida State University used title entry both on the shelves and in the catalog.[9] This procedure was also discontinued for some of the reasons already listed. Why should it work on a greater scale? This is what the opponents would like to know.

The opponents feel that ISDS and ISBD(S) are standards, not codes of cataloging, and to use them in ways for which they were not intended would lead to confusion and anarchy. No longer would catalogers be defining a bibliographic entity; they would simply be describing a physical piece. Changes would be based on title, not bibliographic entity. We would be cataloging "books," not "works." This would be a retrogression in cataloging history back to the very beginnings of title-page transcription, which, to Seymour Lubetzky, is the "ideological deterioration of bibliographic cataloging."[10]

Finally, it is felt that it is wrong to retrogress to the pre-AACR days when rules were based on the type of material to be cataloged. The AACR was built upon sound principles based upon bibliographic conditions. It is proposed that these international principles be overthrown. We do not do our work in a vacuum. Serials must still be integrated into catalogs along with monographs. Both monographs and serials can bear the generic title *Proceedings,* for example. Librarians will find themselves very hard put to explain to patrons why the serial with this title is cataloged under title and the monograph under the heading for the conference or other corporate author. Now the patron can be programmed to look for a generic title serial under corporate body because there is a logical explanation. You can say, "It is more important to you that this is a publication of the American Mathematical Society than that its title is 'Proceedings,' right? Then look under the Society and you'll find it." There will no longer be a logical explanation.

Problems will crop up with other types of materials, the so-called "pseudoserials" and other occupants of the no-man's-land between monographs and serials: looseleaf services, catalogs, books in successive editions, serial supplements to monographic works, etc. When the rules for entry vary so much, people will not know where to look, and trying to explain will be very difficult. It will be harder to recatalog a monograph as a serial. Communications between librarians, catalogers of two progressively more different forms of material, may break down even more. The opponents do not feel the future looks very bright.

C. Sumner Spalding summed it up well:

> What, then, is the impact of the demand for arbitrary entry of all serials under title on the IFLA Paris Principles? First, it proposes a rule of entry that is based on type of publication rather than on bibliographical conditions. This kind of a rule runs counter to the whole history of cataloging rule development in the last half of the 20th century. It runs counter to the fundamental principles laid out by Seymour Lubetzky as the guidelines for this historical development. Second, it introduces an element of irrationality into cataloging with the proposition that if a product of corporate activity is issued in monographic form, the body is to be considered responsible, but if it is issued in serial form, it is, in effect, anonymous. The *Library of Congress List of Subject Headings,* for example, would be entered under the heading for the Library because it is a monographic work but the *Annual Report of the Librarian of Congress* would be entered under title. The corporate

responsibility is the same but the cataloging treatment would be different. The proposal has the effect of completely undermining the theory of corporate responsibility as justification for main entry — not just for serials but for monographs as well.[11]

This is exactly what Paul Dunkin advised against in his working paper at the ICCP. Dunkin closed his presentation with:

> . . .it seems basic that a cataloguing code — and an international agreement on entry — deals with bibliographic facts, not just with the form of a publication. We may not, for instance, enter all serials under title simply because they are serials and retain corporate entry for monographs only because they are monographs. If authorship is the basic bibliographic feature determining entry of a publication, the differentiation in entry must result from the facts of authorship — for example, author entry only for works with authors, title entry for works of changing authors and for works without authors.[12]

There is a chance that all of these arguments against the proposed changes may hold sway, but let us, for a moment, assume that the title main entry concept has won out. What problems, other than those mentioned, might there be, and what solutions might be foreseen?

There are a lot of places where confusion can occur. This will mean uniformity will not be reached unless these problems can be worked out. One problem, explored somewhat further in Chapter 18, is encountered with identical titles. The key title and distinctive title are different here. Which is to be the cataloging title?

There are considerable problems to be worked out with the new system of adding author elements to the title, whether or not this key title is to be used as the main entry or not. For example, the title page reads:

Journal
The Chemical Society

Does this mean the key title is:

Journal – Chemical Society

or

Journal – The Chemical Society?

If the block of type on the page includes the corporate hierarchy and the address, how much should be transcribed as the author? In other words, how full should this be and where do you stop? There are still potential inconsistencies of interpretation. Corporate hierarchy will present more of a problem. The format may not be standard on all pieces of a publication, causing changes in title. One solution is to standardize the order, perhaps by prescribing lowest to highest, or vice versa. Another alternative is to pick one form as standard and to treat deviations as titles of short duration, or variations. This latter is what was done here:

Circular - University of Hawaii Cooperative
   Extension Service. no.1-
   Mar. 1939-
   ₍Honolulu₎ University of Hawaii, Cooperative
Extension Service.
        nos. illus. irreg.

   Supersedes its Agricultural notes.
   Title varies: no.1, Agricultural circular;
no.2-   Agricultural extension circular.
   Some issues have title: Circular - Cooperative Extension Service, University of Hawaii.

(continued ◯ on next card)

2

Circular - University of Hawaii Cooperative
   Extension Service....Mar. 1939-   (card 2)

   Issued also by the Service under an earlier
name: Agricultural Extension Service.

   1.Agriculture--Period. 2.Agriculture--Hawaii.
I.Hawaii. Agricultural Extension Service.
II.Title. III.Title: Agricultural circular.
IV.Title: Agricultural extension circular.
V.Title: Circular - Cooperative Extension
Service, University of Hawaii.

Fig. 4-1. Variant titles under title main entry.

In this case, the most common presentation of the information was used as the standard. LC, however, has indicated that it will probably catalog using the first issue received as an authority, with notes only if the presentation of the title and author information seems to fluctuate. Then notes like the one used here will suffice. However, if there is actually a break that can be established between the information being presented in the form: "University of Hawaii Cooperative Extension Service" and "Cooperative Extension Service, University of Hawaii," this will be treated under successive entry as a title change. This would be a major change because it affects filing.

Another problem is that parts of the corporate author can be left out as exemplified in the new Chapter 6 rules for series. This would seem to be counter to the intent of the ISBD(S), which is supposed to describe the piece-in-hand. It also means applying rules of entry to description, which would seem inconsistent. Supposedly this is explained away by the existence of an entry above and beyond the description, although the description is allegedly to be able to stand alone without the superstructure of an entry. However, one wonders what will happen to this hierarchy if title is made the main entry and the superstructure is gone. Conceivably there could be inconsistent interpretations of what should be included and what left out for complete clarity. So far the entries that LC is assigning cannot stand alone because they are meant to be used with a heading. ISDS would demand qualifiers. What will this do to the cataloging title, catalogers all over the country are asking.

There are still problems with what is considered "grammatically linked" when talking about words in a title. It has been suggested that all words in English should be considered linked if in close proximity so that

American Medical Association
Journal

would be

American Medical Association journal

rather than the inverted form. This would seem reasonable, but it needs to be clarified.

If the suggested rule revision goes through, it will be necessary to inform the patron of possible discrepancies in the catalog — the result of variant rules and practices that may lead to confusion. Following is a suggested explanatory information card. (Another sample may be found in the chapter on Added Entries, Fig. 5-1.)

Such a reference card would preclude the need to recatalog all the titles cataloged under past rules. Some libraries may elect to recatalog anyway, desiring some consistency, but this would be on an individual basis.

The cataloging rules would have to be more specific on what constitutes a

```
PROCEEDINGS...

    Titles which begin with the word Proceedings
may be filed under one of several variant forms,
depending on the arrangement of the title-page.
Example:  the Proceedings of the American Chemical
Society might be filed in any of the following ways:

    American Chemical Society.  Proceedings.

    Proceedings of the American Chemical Society.

    Proceedings  American Chemical Society.

If you have difficulty locating an entry of this type
please ask for help at the Reference Desk.
```

Fig. 4-2. Explanatory reference for variant entry forms for generic titles.

title change. Changes may be simply stylistic, as in the case of typography and layout. Serials can be very mutable. Here is an example of a change which, under the old system would be encompassed by one entry:

```
                    Circular 100




                Cooperative Extension
                Service, University of
                        Hawaii
```

Cooperative Extension Service
University of Hawaii Circular 101

Fig. 4-3. Title change under proposed rules — examples of title pages.

This is a major change under the newly-established system and would demand successive entry cataloging (unless it were a back-and-forth type of thing, with no discernable break). No longer is there a corporate umbrella to envelop all this type of thing. Although the ISDS guidelines do present some good jumping-off points, these need to be codified for the cataloger so that he can interface better with national and international programs. "Titles of short duration" have to be defined better. Mail checkers and others will have to be more aware and call these variations to the attention of the cataloger with more speed and accuracy than in the past, which will be very awkward without really good guidelines.

If the decision on the rules retains any vestiges of author entry, serials catalogers should probably rethink their policies on title added entries. There should be more allowance for title added entries for generic titles, especially if this will be the principal access to a machine file of information on that title.

Another problem with title entry is brought on by the structure of elements in the ISBD(S). The publication entitled *Bulletin signaletique* have been variously cataloged under France. Centre National de la Recherche Scientifique and title. At least they are findable. Who would hope to find one of them easily under such a corrupted entry as that offered as an example in the Standard:

Bulletin signaletique – Centre national de la recherche scientifique. Section 9, Science de l'ingenieur.[13]

You need to know the generic title, corporate author and distinctive subsection title in order to find it. What's more, it's misleading. Unless you know the publication, you would probably assume that Section 9 was part of the Centre instead of the subsection of the title. It is not our job to push titles out of shape so that we present them as something different from what they are.

To put it mildly, not all the bugs are out of the proposed system yet.

The ideological reasons for not changing cannot be played down, for they are valid and of great importance. However, the need to conform to the computer standards is also of importance. It is probable that the AACR authors will weigh the pros and cons very seriously and try to reach some sort of happy medium.

Joe Howard has come up with as close to a happy medium as is likely to occur. His solution calls for entry under title except if the title is a generic term, or a generic term followed by an issuing body:

(6) Serials.

> Preliminary note: This rule for serials (including numbered monographic series) applies also to entries for unnumbered monographic series and to series added entries (cf. 33N) made for monographs in a series (whether numbered or not).

A[sic] Enter a serial under its title.

> If an added entry is required for the serial, and if the title of the serial is identical with that of another serial, add in parentheses the city of publication. If this addition is insufficient, add also the years of publication.

> For serials issued by or under the authority of a corporate body, make an added entry for the corporate body. For serials by personal author, make an added entry for the personal author.

> Exception:

> (1) If the title of the serial as it appears on the piece consists solely of a generic term, enter under issuing body if there is one.

> (2) If the title of a serial as it appears on the piece begins with a generic term followed only by the name of the issuing body[6] (initialisms and acronyms are not to be considered names of bodies), enter under issuing body named in the title.

> (2) If the title of a serial as it appears on the piece begins with a generic term followed only by the name of the issuing body[(6)] (initialisms and acronyms are not to be considered names of bodies), enter under issuing body named in the title.

> If the corporate body accorded an added entry for a serial changes or undergoes a change of name, make an added entry also under the new body or the new name of the body.

If the personal author accorded an added entry for a serial changes, make an added entry also under the new personal author.[14]

(6)[This footnote appears already in the AACR (p. 17) and was not a part of Mr. Howard's proposal. However, it is repeated here for clarification:

Mere sponsorship or commissioning of a work by a corporate body is not to be understood as raising a question of corporate authorship. . .]

This leans more towards the British rules, which call for considerably more title entries. This would be a step toward merging the two editions, a desired thing in the future. It may tend to stretch the authorship principle, as advocated by Lubetzky, out of shape a little, but does not destroy it entirely. It also eliminates some of the problems suggested by those concerned with generic title filing. Distinctive titles, including those issued by governmental agencies, such as *Carload waybill statistics,* and those having initialisms, such as *ALA bulletin,* or the name of the corporate body in the title, like *University of Detroit law journal,* would be granted title main entry. A concession would be made to the automation problems, but card cataloging rationale would not be totally overthrown. There would need to be some redundancy in the machine file, although not as much as the old rules would have warranted. With the addition of the corporate body to generic titles, generic titles would be distinctive, and, as the entry changed, so would the title. Each AACR entry would bear an ISSN and each ISDS change would be reflected by cataloging changes as well (although approached through the key title as an added entry). Most of the desires of both sides would be met.

Thus one sees a tug-of-war between past experiences and traditional rationale and future trends and the automated revolution. Little has excited serials people so much since the dawn of successive entry cataloging. The CCRC has weighed the alternatives and chosen title main entry. There are the other four authors waiting in the wings, however, whose minds are not yet made up. Which path will they choose? This is yet an unknown factor, and we must wait to see what will happen as the votes come in. Hopefully, the answer will weigh all of the pros and cons and not lose the patron, the rationale of cataloging, and other considerations in the speedy rush into the Computer Age.

FOOTNOTES

1. Joseph H. Howard, "Main entry for serials," *Library of Congress information bulletin* 33 (November 22, 1974):A-234.

2. Andrew D. Osborn, *Serial publications; their place and treatment in libraries,* 2d ed. rev. (Chicago: American Library Association, 1973), p. 355.

3. Yale University Library. *Cataloging of serials in the Yale University Library*, 3d ed. (New Haven, Conn., 1969), p. 28. Quoted by Osborn.

4. Howard, "Main entry," p. A-235.

5. The Brasenose Conference on the Automation of Libraries. *Proceedings. . . ,* edited by John Harrison and Peter Laslett, (London, 1966), pp. 24-25. Also in A.J. Tait, *Authors and titles. . .* (London: Clive Bingley, 1969), p. 1-2.

6. Osborn, *Serial publications,* p. 133. Also quoted in Paul S. Dunkin, "Problems in the cataloguing of serial publications," working paper 8 in International Conference on Cataloguing Principles, Paris, 1961. *Report* (London: Organising Committee of the International Conference on Cataloguing Principles, 1963), p. 197.

7. J.A. Tait, "Paper 1; editor's introduction and Chapter 1: Entry (Rules 1-33)" in Seminar on the Anglo-American Cataloguing Rules (1967), Nottingham, Eng., 1968. *Proceedings of the Seminar. . .* (London: Library Association, 1969), p. 10.

8. F. W. Gravell "The cataloguing of periodicals with special reference to the World List of Scientific Periodicals and the Union List of Serials," *State librarian* 2 (May, 1949).

9. Nancy Bird, "Title cataloging of periodicals at Florida State University," *Serial slants* 4 (January, 1953): 19-20.

10. In a speech delivered on May 15, 1975 at the School of Library and Information Science, University of California at Los Angeles.

11. C. Sumner Spalding, "ISBD(S) and title main entry for serials," *International cataloguing* 3 (July-September, 1974): 5. Also in *Library of Congress information bulletin* 33 (November 22, 1974):A-231.

12. Dunkin, "Problems," p. 198.

13. International Federation of Library Associations, Joint Working Group on the International Standard Bibliographic Description for Serials *ISBD(S); International standard bibliographic description for serials* (London: I.F.L.A. Committee on Cataloging, 1974), p. 8.

14. Howard, "Main entry," p. A-234.

Chapter V

Added Entries: Additional Access Points

Added entries supplement the main entry by providing additional direct access to bibliographical items that are represented in the catalog. AACR (North American text, 1967), p. 70, note to rule 33.

Title added entries should always be made for titles which are distinctive, but for which entry has been made under the corporate body. For example: *ALA studies in librarianship, AAUW journal* or *Carload waybill statistics* when the entry should be under American Library Association, American Association of University Women, or United States. Interstate Commerce Commission. Bureau of Economics should have title added entries.

Added entries should also be accorded titles cataloged under personal authors, such as *Poor Richard's Almanack* under Benjamin Franklin. Many libraries, as mentioned before, do not use personal author entries for serials. If this is the case, an added entry should be made for the author.

Added entries should be made for "common titles" like *Anthropological papers* when the choice was to make the main entry a corporate body, such as, in this case, the Anthropology Department of a college or university.

The Library of Congress, as announced in its *Cataloging service bulletin* 96 (November, 1970, p. 24), makes title added entries for the popular names of U.S. government publications when the Serials Division notifies of a needed added entry. A note saying "Commonly known as [name]" will be added to the catalog entry to justify the added entry.

The British rules say title added entries should not be made if the title is a generic one, preceded by the corporate body in the same form as the entry, as *University of London Studies,* entered under "University of London."

However, if you are following superimposition, the entry is "London. University," and the added entry should be made. The American rules are not quite so specific about this stricture, although they also make it in rule 33P. However, for ease of using the catalog, it would probably be a good idea to make such title added entries in most cases. They should definitely be made if the library in question has a split catalog with authors and titles separated.

Title added entries should not normally be made for generic titles like "Journal" or "Bulletin." (For a fuller list see Appendix C.) Exceptions were made in the past for certain of these, such as Russian words. Some libraries wanted to make generic titles distinctive so they added connecting words like "of the" in brackets to make the titles meaningful:

Bulletin [of the] International Association of Concert Managers.

Others did not like this approach because it introduced non-title-page words into the title. However, at one time it was the only way to make a title distinctive and meaningful. Another alternative might have been to add the society or other organization to the title in parentheses, such as:

Bulletin (International Association of Concert Managers).

However, now that ISDS' has chosen to enter under "distinctive generic terms," that is, generic titles with qualifiers, either in the form on the publication or with a space-hyphen-space, it would probably behoove us catalogers to rethink our policies and make added entries under these terms. The title added entry for the title which has been used as an example would rightfully be recorded and traced as follows:

Bulletin – International Association of Concert Managers.

A question comes to mind now. What happens to the patron who is looking for a title like "Bulletin" and suddenly finds that he can find these in the catalog where he couldn't before. He will be confused and think that the library doesn't have some of the titles that he wants because not all of them are there under the generic term. One alternative to combat this is to recatalog all of these titles and give them correct ISDS key titles, which can be traced. But this would not be a very feasible solution if the library is of any size. Offered here is another alternative, a guide card with appropriate information to help the patron find all of the generic titles under both practices the library has followed. (Another such card example can be found in the chapter on title main entry.) Please note that this card can still be used if title main entry is adopted.

Partial title added entries should be made for the distinctive portion of a sub-series title like *Studia iuridica upsaliensia* for the series Uppsala. Universitet. / / *Acta universitatis upsaliensis. Studia iuridica upsaliensia.* This example should also receive a full title added entry since it is entered under the corporate entry form for the University of Uppsala. However, the same would not be true for *Pacific Linguistics. Series A: Occasional Papers. Occasional papers* is a non-

```
BULLETIN


For Bulletins not filed behind this card

see under the name of the issuing organization,


International Association of Concert Managers.
Bulletin.
```

Fig. 5-1. Guide card for generic title.

distinctive generic title that would not normally be cited or sought for by a patron, nor can it be approached in a meaningful way through an ISDS form because *Pacific Linguistics* is not a corporate author. Any manipulation of this title in this way would be misleading and incorrect.

If a title has an "at head of title" note which could be construed as part of the title, this should receive an added entry. For example:

At head of title:	PMLA
Title:	Publications of the Modern Language Association of America

Cataloged as:	Modern Language Association of America.
	Publications of the Modern Language Association of America.

Such abbreviations as "PMLA" are often better known than the real name of the publication and definitely need to be given catalog access. The *Journal of English and Germanic Philology* finally adopted the initialism *JEGP* in 1959. These initials now stand foremost on the title-page; the publisher finally decided to acquiesce to the indexers who have been citing this journal for years by the initials. (This appears as an alternative title and should be accorded an added entry.) *Modern Language Notes* must have given up too, finally, for it changed its name officially to *MLN* with volume 77, 1962.

However, this opens up another problem. What to do with common abbreviations like *JAMS* (*Journal of the American Musicological Society*) which do not appear on the publication? The cataloger simply cannot know that such an access point will be required. Some librarians search for citations in indexes, but this is time-consuming and, therefore, costly. Also, with first-issue cataloging, it is often impossible to know what a publication will be referred to so early in its career. The best thing to do is to treat each one of these on an ad hoc basis as requests are received from the public departments or the patron.

Perhaps a library will choose to make added entries for all index abbreviations, although this is perhaps going overboard a bit. A good alternative is to invest in reference books that give this kind of information, such as *Periodical title abbreviations* by C. Edward Wall (Detroit: Gale Research, 1969). A copy should be kept in the serials area as well as in Reference. Reference and serials staff who work with the public and direct patrons to indexes should call the patron's attention to the explanatory material at the front of each index which gives a key to the abbreviations. This directive should also appear on any flyers on the subject of index use or "how to find a magazine."

This kind of problem is best handled on a local basis, depending on the types of material collected and the types of clientele served. However, any abbreviations or initialisms that appear on the publication itself should be traced, for this will take care of a good percentage of the problem. Notes can justify the added entries by giving such explanations as:

Refers to itself as: [title].

Commonly called: [title].

Indexed as: [title].

Spine, cover or masthead titles should be designated as such, if following the old rules. The ISBD(S) asks only that the following note be used without specification:

Alternative title: [title].

At any rate, all added entries need to be justified by the cataloging.

A good example of both common and variant titles is *Justus Liebigs Annalen der Chemie*. This is clearly the title of the publication, which appears on the title-page. However, most chemists would not be likely to look this up under the actual first word of the title. There should be an added entry for them under *Liebigs*. Because the first two words are a personal name, and also because the title which appears on the signatures is *Annalen der Chemie*, an added entry should be made under this as well. All would seem to be viable approaches from citations.

Added entries should always be made for parallel titles. For example, the following appears on the cover of a journal:

	Soviet	*Union*
Union		Soviétique

The main entry is under *Soviet union.* There should be an added entry for *Union sovietique.*

Always make an added entry for a "title of short duration" which was cataloged under another title. Added entries should be made for titles not used in any case, even under earliest or latest entry cataloging.

Added entries should not be made for superseded or superseding titles since they are not covered by a given set of catalog cards; they are outside the bibliographic entity being recorded. References should not be made for the same reason. Cards also need not be made for titles which the library does not hold under successive entry cataloging, just as the library does not make cards saying it does not hold a given monograph title. Superseding and continuing notes should take care of all necessary linkings.

Additional entries can be made under subtitles if the subtitle added entry would seem to bring an appropriate and useful access to the publication. It is not good practice to make added entries willy-nilly for every subtitle — each situation should be weighed. Often a special subject is usefully emphasized in a subtitle. If this is the case, the added entry should be made.

Added entries should be made for all sponsoring bodies, such as the English department of a university under whose auspices a poetry journal is published or the society which backs a professional journal. If the name of one of these bodies changes, but the journal's name does not, a second added entry should be made for the "new" body in compliance with the provisions of AACR6D2. The *Adelphi papers* is still being published in London. Up until No. 78 it was published by the Institute for Strategic Studies. At that time, 1971, the Institute changed its name to the International Institute for Strategic Studies and published No. 79 of the series. The cataloging for *Adelphi papers* should reflect this with notes and added entries for both organizations.

Added entries should be made for authors in addition to the main entry. An entry should be made under "Addison, Joseph, 1672-1719" for *The Tatler.* A secondary entry should be made for "Steele, Sir Richard, 1672-1729." Of course, this is a distinctive title entered under a personal author so there should be an added entry for the title, too. If the library's policy is not to follow rules for personal authorship for serials, which is indeed true for many libraries, the main entry for this example would be under title with added entries under both Addison and Steele.

Make added entries for important editors. Shortcuts are often taken in editor statements, but this should never be "across the board." Unimportant or constantly changing editors can be ignored with no problem. Others should not be. Editors whose names have been firmly linked with their publications should receive cataloging recognition. Editors who are important literary or political figures, or figures of prominence in their own fields, should be traced. People of local importance such as faculty members of the university or leaders of the community should also get tracings.

Sometimes editors are so well-known that the journal is called by their names. *Silliman's journal* is a perfect example of this. The real title of this journal is *The American journal of science*. It was edited in the late 1900's by two men, father and son, named Silliman. The name has stuck ever since. A note should appear on the cards indicating:

> Commonly called Silliman's journal, or
> Alternative title: Silliman's journal.

An added entry should be made for this title so that patrons will be sure to find what they want. Added entries for the Sillimans might not be sufficient in this case for complete identification from a popular citation. This added entry should not preclude ones for the editors, however. *Annalen der Physik* has been known variously by its editors' names, too.

Make added entries for all series in which a serial appears. If numbered, this series should appear in any serial listing as a numbered monographic series. (For further on this, see Chapter 6.)

Added entries should be used for any access which can be made to a serial publication. (For subject access, see Chapter 8.) They should be made on unit cards so that the patron will not get shortchanged on the information he receives. Cross-references should not be made for these access points unless unit cards cannot be made, such as in the procedures described herein for "uncataloged collections." Cross-references are best confined in serials work to variant forms of the names of personal or corporate authors. (Note, *not* titles!) If our function is to give access to the collection, we must do our best. The added entry on a unit card is the best way to meet this goal and, thus, serve the patron, our *raison d'être*.

Chapter VI

Descriptive Cataloging

As far as the description of serials is concerned, it is most peculiar. Monographs generally are described once and for all. The description can be complete and detailed. Not so for serials. Serials change a great deal, in title, subtitle, numbering, editor, issuing body, place of publication, publisher and frequency *ad nauseam;* and to try to pin them down at the start would be to ask for an inordinate amount of revision in order to keep up with the dynamic nature of the beast involved. There is always a question mark just beyond the present. There can also be a question mark about the past, if the set is not a complete one. For these reasons, the rules for description of serials are a mere skeleton, which the cataloger can flesh out, if desired, upon a serial's demise. Few libraries, however, actually follow all the rules for description that appear in the AACR. Most of them feel that even these few are confining and un-necessary and so they take shortcuts. Some of these will be discussed here as well. It is, however, good to remember that if you are as complete as you can be as you go along, there will be no need to recatalog when the serial dies. There is, of course, also the problem of standardization, which any deviation from the rules puts in jeopardy.

The rules are being revised at this time to reflect the changes demanded by the new International Standard for Bibliographic Description for Serials, ISBD(S) (see Chapter 18). While the rules are still being drafted, some changes have already been reflected in LC's cataloging practices, as announced in *Cataloging service bulletin* 112 (Winter 1975, pp. 12-13), and subsequent bulletins. These changes incorporate some of the practices already in effect as the result of the new chapter 6 of the rules. These changes will also be discussed here.

Chapter 7 of the rules, "Serials," starts off badly in the minds of many serials people, for it seems to indicate that serials are only variant monographs, a feeling that has pervaded librarians' thinking since the beginning of time. Serials people worth their salt feel that serials are significantly unlike monographs and should not be treated according to monographic standards and procedures, which may prove to be both unsuited and expensive. Perhaps it is this feeling that has given rise to the many shortcuts and other deviations.

Nevertheless, let us repeat here the introductory notes for Chapter 7 of the rules as they now stand:

> The general principles for cataloging serials are the same as those for cataloging monographic publications; wherever suitable the rules for the cataloging of monographs are to be applied to serials. Nevertheless, the physical characteristics and the manner of publication of serials necessitate some special rules. The fact that the parts of a serial are published over a period of time gives rise to numerous potential changes in bibliographic details. It is essential to record such information as minor variation in title (see 167K), changes of name of issuing bodies, connection with preceding or succeeding publications, and statement of indexes, to mention only the more important. These items are condensed, tabulated and recorded in a form in which no essential fact is lost, although the exact wording of title-pages is shown less frequently than in the cataloging of monographs. If the serial is still being published or the library has only a part of the set, an "open" entry is prepared according to the rules below; the aim is to prepare an entry that will stand the longest time and will permit the making of necessary changes with the minimum of modification. No attempt beyond the limitations specified in these rules is made to describe parts that are not in hand.
>
> Whether a serial is monographic (i.e., a series) or not does not affect its cataloging, although it may affect its classification, since the separate parts of a series may be classified separately while those of a non-monographic serial must be classified together. For this reason, no special rules for the description of series are necessary, the rules for serials as a whole being applicable. When each volume of a monographic series is cataloged separately, there may be no need for a main entry describing the series as a whole.
>
> Certain types of publications that are not true serials but that are issued frequently in new editions may be cataloged according to the rules of description for serials. These include certain dictionaries, guidebooks, handbooks, etc., even though they may be of personal authorship. [These are, of course, Osborn's "pseudoserials," mentioned already in Chapter 1 of this book.]
>
> AACR/NA.

The British text would seem to be much more to the point when it says in the introduction to Chapter 7 of the rules:

> Periodicals, continuations, and works published frequently or regularly in new
> editions (such as guidebooks, who's whos) of which the library holds several
> parts, either simultaneously or successively, are described as serials according to
> the rules which follow. . .

AACR/BT.

This tends to treat a serial more *sui generis* than the North American text
would allow.

It is only a step away from this point of view to the almost radical viewpoint
which rocked the audience at an institute at the 1975 ALA Convention in San
Francisco. The espouser of this viewpoint, Michael Gorman, British editor of
the current AACR revision, presented his thoughts on cataloging: cataloging
rules should not be constructed for "monographs" and "serials," but for dead
or completed publications and live or incompleted ones. The British text tends
to be more receptive to this interpretation than the North American one, which
seems to deny that serials can have personal authorship, even though rule 6C
provides for this in a "real" serial. It is true that monographic works like
dictionaries coming out in fascicles are much more serial-like than
monographic. Serial procedures for numbered sets on standing order should
have the benefit of orderly serial follow-up procedures — i.e. claiming, which
not all monograph order departments are adequately equipped to handle.
Shadowy areas would be minimized by Gorman's proposal, for many people
automatically assume all open entries to be serials when such is not the case
under present definitions.

There may be problems with the closed serials, however. Many libraries do
treat these as monographs already, since, as Gorman points out, they have
many characteristics of monographs because they are bibliographically complete. However, they were serial-like at one time, and still are in terms of
citations and appearance in serial indexes, bibliographies, and union lists. They
may be partially unbound still, due to lacunae, which would even tend to make
them like current publications. They may be purchased from serial vendors and
so should still remain within the purview of the serials order section. They may
bear relationships to current publications, which would further stress their
serialness, and, even after a hiatus of many years, they may spring full-blown
again. All these factors would seem to render at least part of Gorman's
suggestion impractical, at least in a divided library with division of duties
between Monographs and Serials Departments. It is an interesting thought,
however, and most worthy of consideration.

Mr. Gorman's method of attack is from a practical view on another plane.
The concept of "serial" is basically a librarians' concept, and not one easily
understood by the rest of the world. Perhaps the above reservations can be
worked out to the satisfaction of all.

The introductory notes to the British text would seem to give a better list of aims than the North American one, too. They are:

1) to present an adequate account of the whole published set of each serial,

2) to indicate and describe the library's holdings, and,

3) to construct entries which need the minimum of alteration because of changes during the course of publication of serials.

AACR/BT

This is probably more in keeping with what a lot of American libraries do, too, for the description is for a perfect copy, which the library will probably try to get at some time, if it doesn't already have it. This is more practical in the long run, for filling-in of backfiles will not then generate a lot of recataloging, but only a mechanical chore of adding holdings. The North American text wants the "minimum of modification," but this would seem more in keeping with the perfect copy approach of the British rather than its own of not describing what you don't have. Description from a bibliography should be accepted if it seems reliable to avoid modification later when the issues are acquired. Of course, something which is ambiguous or misleading or not in keeping with what is in-hand should not be considered accurate bibliographic information; but if another librarian's description seems acceptable, it should be accepted. There are several descriptions of the history of *The Churchman*, for example, which are in conflict. It is hard to believe that they came from full sets, and were taken with a grain of salt when this cataloger had to catalog an incomplete set of the title. One must always use one's head when one does not have complete information, but not believing a colleague about a beginning date, for example, when they have it and you don't, seems to be carrying both a cataloging sense and a Missourian attitude of skepticism a little too far.

Chapter 7 of the rules continues:

160. Variations from the cataloging of monographic publications

The rules in this chapter show the application of the general rules to the cataloging of serial publications and provide additional rules as necessary. The chief differences in the form of the cataloging entry for a serial from that for a monograph may be summarized as follows:

A. A serial that changes its title or that is entered under a corporate body that changes its name during the course of publication is normally cataloged with a separate entry for each new title or new name of the corporate body. [There was a footnote[1] here, indicating LC's former practice, which has been deleted, per *Cataloging service bulletins* 99 (April 1971) and 109 (May 1974).] A note relates the new title to the serial it continues.

B. A serial publication in several volumes with varying bibliographical details is described from the latest volume, with the variations from that volume noted, whereas a monographic work in several volumes is cataloged from the first volume, with variations noted.

C. The subtitle is frequently omitted or presented in a supplementary note.

D. The author statement does not appear in the body of the entry; if needed, it is presented in a supplementary note.

E. The editor statement is given as a supplementary note instead of in the body of the entry, because the more prominent position following the title is devoted to the statement of "holdings" and because, when editors change, the adding of that information is more convenient and economical if the editor statement has been given in a note.

F. The catalog entry for a serial publication should show which parts of it are in the library's collection or refer to another catalog such as the shelflist or a special record of serials.

G. An important feature for the characterization of a serial, and occasionally for its identification, is the frequency of its publication.

H. If the statement of holdings does not show the duration of publication, supplementary notes are necessary to show it. This includes the facts of suspension and resumption of publication.

J. The fact that a serial is the organ of a society or other body is stated.

K. Serial publications frequently have special numbers that must be described.

AACR/NA.

Although section F in the listing does make some mention of auxiliary files for serials, the concept of complementary records that plays such a large part in Osborn's philosophy and the workings of so many libraries is lacking from the rules. This is, of course, one of the major differences serials and their treatment have to offer, and one of the least understood by those who work with self-contained monographs.

161. Body of the entry: organization and source of data

A. The body of the entry consists of the following elements, in the order given here: title, subtitle (if required), volume designation and dates of the serial as published (or of volumes held by the library [see chapter in this book on holdings statements]), and imprint. The title and imprint are taken from a single source as far as possible. If the publication has no title page, the title is taken from the cover, caption, masthead, editorial pages, or other place, the order of preference being that of this listing. The source of the data is specified if it is not the title page, cover, caption, or masthead. However, if there is no title page or cover, and the caption or other titles differ, the source of the title used is specified and the other titles are noted.

B. The title page, or title page substitute, chosen as the basis of the catalog entry is that of the latest volume. Exception to this rule may be made in the case of a serial which has ceased publication, if an earlier title has continued for a much longer period of time than the later title. In such a case the title chosen for the body of the entry is the one that persisted the longest.

AACR/NA.

Much of this is straightforward and pretty obvious. Serials should be cataloged using an open entry form, unless the serial is dead. If a serial is dead, the title chosen may be the latest or the longest, depending on the history of the publication, and the choice of the cataloger. This seems to be somewhat in conflict with the rules for entry, perhaps because this section is lifted almost verbatim from the 1949 *RDC*. The British text does not have the provision offered by the last line of the North American text's rule 161B, although it is somewhat implied.

There has always been a considerable amount of confusion and negative reaction brought up by the emphasis on title-pages when discussing serials cataloging, the argument being that, more often than not, serials do not have title-pages. They are usually cataloged from their covers, or perhaps mastheads, and it is felt that the rules perhaps should be reworded to indicate that the source used should be the one with the most complete information, which does not necessarily mean title-page. An old rule, dating at least from Mary Wilson MacNair's time and echoed in the 1941 rules, indicated that a title which was more complete elsewhere than the title-page could be used, if enclosed in brackets, as

The Portrait magazine [containing sketches of prominent persons of the present time]

This rule was fortunately written out of the 1949 rules. The ISBD(S) is moving somewhat more toward the liberal policy most serials catalogers would seem to be wanting.

Rules 162A and B have already been discussed, as they relate rather directly to the question of entry, particularly since entry may be under title at all times, thus according "Recording of the title," the subject of rule 162, a more important place than just description. The latter two sections of rule 162 seem to relate more directly to description and are reproduced here:

[162]

C. If a number appearing as part of the title is considered to be the volume designation it is omitted from the title (without mark of omission); e.g.

> *Report of the first annual meeting* becomes *Report of the annual meeting.*

D. If any other word or phrase preceding the title might be construed and cited as part of the title, an author-title and/or title reference with this form of the title is made on the catalog entry for the serial.

AACR/NA.

The first is covered quite well with the example given. "1st-   " would then be the numbering given.

The second problem can normally be taken care of easily by "At head of title" or "Added title information" notes. Added entries would probably be more appropriate than references.

Rule 163 relates to holdings statements, and section A1 of this rule appears in that section of this book. The other sections are more directly related to description, and appear here.

[163A]

> 2. If the work is still in progress of publication, the statement consists only of the data relating to the first issue.
>
> v.1-   1929-
>
> If the library does not have the first issue, the holdings statement is omitted and a note is added, if the information is available, to provide the date when publication began (see 167D).

AACR/NA.

Many libraries do not follow the second part of this rule to the letter. Because they feel that the opening date may be of importance in the identification of the publication, and because there is the strong possibility of obtaining the back issues not held at some time, necessitating transfer of the data, they put the opening volume and date in this space, whether it is held or not. The library's description is for a perfect copy, which is more in keeping with the British rules than the North American. The British text refers to this section as "Volume Designation and Dating," while the North American calls it "Holdings," which shows the different emphasis. The catalog is not used for holdings in this case and the reader is refered to serials checking records or elsewhere. (See Chapter 12.) The Library of Congress does not observe this rule, however, and, according to Library policy, LC would not go back and recatalog if the first issue is received.

LC may also indicate holdings on its printed cards, as in the second example opposite.

Alabama law review.

[University, Ala.]

   v. 26 cm. 3 no. a year.

Began with fall 1948 issue. Cf. Union list of serials.
Seal of the University of Alabama at head of title.

1. Law—Periodicals—Alabama.   I. Alabama. University.

K1.L3   340'.05   73–647290
ISSN 0002–4279   MARC-S

Library of Congress   74 [2]

Fig. 6-1. LC card showing drop note for opening date.

Musik aus Amerika. Jahrg. 1–5 (Heft 1–58); März 1958–
Dez. 1962. Wien, United States Information Service.

   5 v. ports. 29 cm. monthly.
   L. C. set incomplete: no. 32, 40, 47, 56 wanting.
   1. Music—Period. 2. Music, American—Hist. & crit.   ı. U. S
Information Service, Vienna.
ML1.M9936   67-33225/MN

Fig. 6-2. LC card showing LC holdings.

It is interesting to note that the British text does not give this as an option. The British prefer always to indicate perfect sets. If a title is no longer being received, but is still being published, a note may be added in parentheses, as

vol. 1-   1887-   (still current 1964)

per the provision of rule 163A5. The British would seem to prefer "vol." rather than "v." for volume and also allow for the use of the plus sign + to indicate open entries as well as the dash favored by the Americans.

B. Designation

1. The statement of holdings is limited to volume designation for those publications that do not carry dates by which the parts are identified; volume designation may be a volume number, edition number, or other designation according to the usage of the publisher.

2. The date may consist of the month, day, and year; month or season and year; or year alone, depending upon the frequency of publication and the usage of the publisher. If each issue of a serial bears both a date of publication and an indication of period covered by the contents, the latter is given in the holdings statement. If the statement of date is not in terms of the Christian era, it is followed in brackets by a statement of the corresponding year or years of the Christian era.

C. Abbreviation and numerals

Terms used in volume designations and for months are given in the vernacular, abbreviated if possible. Arabic numerals are normally used (see Appendix III [of the AACR]).

AACR/NA.

Emory law journal. v. 23–
winter 1974–
Atlanta, Emory University School of Law.

v. 26 cm. quarterly.

Continues the Journal of public law.

1. Law—Periodicals—Georgia.   I. Emory University, Atlanta.
School of Law.

K10.Q885   340'.05   74–644258
ISSN 0094–4076   MARC–S

Library of Congress   74 [2]

Directory: planning, building & housing libraries, United States & Canada. 1st-
ed.; 1969–
College Park, Md.

v. 28 cm.

Issued by the Planning, Building & Housing Section, Special Libraries Association.
ISSN 0420-0659

1. Social science libraries—United States—Directories. 2. Social science libraries — Canada — Directories. 3. Regional planning — United States — Directories. I. Special Libraries Association. Planning, Building & Housing Section.

Z675.S6D57   026'.3092'1202573   73-645951
                                                          MARC-S

Library of Congress   75

Television news index and abstracts. Jan. 1972–

Nashville, Tenn., Vanderbilt Television News Archive.

v. 28 cm. monthly.

"A guide to the videotape collection of the network evening news programs."
ISSN 0085-7157

1. Television broadcasting of news — United States — Indexes. 2. Video tapes—Indexes. I. Vanderbilt Television News Archive.

AI 3.T44   011   74-646462
                                                          MARC-S

Library of Congress   75 [2]

Fig. 6-3. Examples of various numbering and dating systems.

Some serials may have more than one numbering system. The one which seems most prominent should be used and others relegated to notes for the sake of clarity, although it is sometimes LC's practice to put both in the "holdings" statement. Usually the most prominent one is the one using the term "volume" or its equivalent, although some do prefer to use continuous numbering. The one chosen should be the most consistent system, if that can be established, so that volumes can be bound by it. Notes for numbering irregularities or variations can be brief if all information is adequately maintained on the central serial record for detailed reference work.

"Number" numbering, rather than volumes-and-numbers, can be ambiguous and may provide a potential pit for the unwary cataloger to fall into. The numbering may be continuous, as in:

> no. 1-12, 1973; no. 13-24, 1974; no. 25-36, 1975; etc.

or it may be repeating, as in:

> no. 1-12, 1973; no. 1-12, 1974; no. 1-12, 1975; etc.

These two cases should be treated differently. The first is appropriately indicated as "no. 1-   1973-   ;" the second is not. There is a no. 1 for every year that it is published, and 1973 may not even be its first year of publication. Let us say that it is, though, for the sake of illustration. In this case, the year is the primary element of the numbering scheme and should receive prominence. The numbers are not necessary, except for the bindery, which should know that, if year 1973 of this title has to be bound in two parts, they should be marked like this:

1973		1973
no. 1-6		no. 7-12
	not	
no. 1-6		no. 7-12
1973		1973

The catalog card should only indicate "1973-   " in a case like this.

D. Punctuation

1. Volume, report, and edition numbers are separated from the dates by a semicolon. If there are two or more series volume numbers, commas are used between volumes and dates, and semicolons between series. Whole numbers, i.e. the numbers of parts which continue from one volume to another, are enclosed in parentheses following the volume numbers.

AACR/NA.

The Millennial harbinger ... v. 1-7, Jan. 4, 1830-Dec. 1836; new ser., v. 1-7, Jan. 1837-Dec. 1843; 3d ser., v. 1-7, Jan. 1844-Dec. 1850; 4th ser., v. 1-7, Jan. 1851-Dec. 1857; 5th ser., v. 1-7, Jan. 1858-Dec. 1864; v. 36-41, Jan. 1865-Dec. 1870. Bethany, Va., The editor ₁etc.₁ 1830-70.

41 v. 21ᶜᵐ. monthly.

Editors: 1830-66, Alexander Campbell (with W. K. Pendleton and others, 1846-66)—1866-70, W. K. Pendleton, C. L. Loos. No more published.

1. Disciples of Christ—Period. ı. Campbell, Alexander, 1788-1866, ed. ıı. Pendleton, William Kimbrough, 1817-1899, ed. ııı. Loos, Charles Louis, 1823-1912, ed.

21—7900

Library of Congress   BX7301.M5

Fig. 6-4. LC copy showing punctuation of several series.

Club Filatélico de Caracas.
Reevista del Club Filatélico de Caracas. año 1–
(no. 1–   ; set./oct. 1961–

₁Caracas₁

v. ill. 23 cm. bimonthly.

1. Postage-stamps—Collectors and collecting—Periodicals.

HE6187.C56a   769'.56'075   74-647835
                                           MARC-S

Library of Congress   75

Fig. 6-5. LC copy showing continuous numbering in parentheses.

Sometimes, to alleviate the clutter, catalogers may prefer to put secondary numbering in a note, as mentioned previously. This is sometimes clearer. The note should be positioned with those listed here for numbering irregularities.

2. A diagnoal line is used in recording the date of a report or other publication that covers either a year that is not a calendar year or a period of more than one year. A dash connects the dates of the first and the final issue.

AACR/NA.

National Monuments Record.
    Report. 1964/65–
    ₁London₁ Royal Commission on Historical Monuments (England)

    v. illus. 25 cm. annual.

    Continues the publication with the same title issued by the body under its earlier name: National Buildings Record.

    1. Architecture—Great Britain.

NA105.N33   354'.42'0086   73–646810
                                                                    MARC–S

Library of Congress   75

○

Fig. 6-6. Use of diagonal line for fiscal years or periods longer than a year.

This reflects a change from the earlier LC rules which, for this example, would have used: "1964-65-   ." The newer version is much less confusing.

The data in the statement of holdings are not enclosed in brackets when assertainable from the issues being cataloged even though they do not appear on the title page or title page substitute which forms the basis of the catalog entry. Brackets are not used to enclose the "v." or comparable designation if it appears in a later volume of the publication.

AACR/NA.

This is a useful rule, considering how wayward serials publishers can be in numbering their publications, which includes the lengths they go, at times, to hide the numbering from the casual observer. Current policy seems to be to put it on the contents page, front cover, title-page, or spine. Things were not so easily findable in the past, and even now there can be problems, as any mail accessioner will readily tell you. Sometimes the numbering can be discovered in the running title, or at the beginning of each signature. In old sets bound without title pages or covers, the latter may be your only salvation for locating numbering. Other cute things have been known to happen, such as stars for the numbering: Volume 1 has "★," volume 5 has "★★". Serials publishers can be very clever! But at least numbering not on the title-page can be presented in a straightforward manner, without brackets, on the catalog cards.

Rule 164 covers the imprint:

A. General rules

1. The imprint in the catalog entry for a serial publication is limited to the place of publication and the name of the publisher if dates are recorded in the statement of holdings following the title. (See also [rules] 138-140.) If dates are not recorded in the statement of holdings, they are given in the imprint, as for monographs (see [rule] 141).

2. If the record of the final volume is not included in the statement of holdings, the imprint begins a new line in the catalog entry.

B. Place of publication. Changes in the place of publication that do not warrant specific description are indicated by the abbreviation "etc." following the place of publication (see 167P). If the name of the place has changed during the course of publication of the work being cataloged, the earlier form of name is added, within parentheses, after the latter form; e.g. Oslo (Christiana).

C. Publisher

1. If the name of the publisher is essentially the same as the title of the publication, as is often the case with periodicals, it is omitted from the imprint.

2. Minor changes in the name of the publisher as it appears on the various volumes, and changes of publisher not warranting specific description, are indicated in the imprint by the use of "etc." after the name of the publisher (see 167P).

AACR/NA.

These are fairly straightforward and do not need much explanation. The following example shows the monographic type of date recording, as called for in rule 164A1 when the date is not given in the statement of holdings after the title.

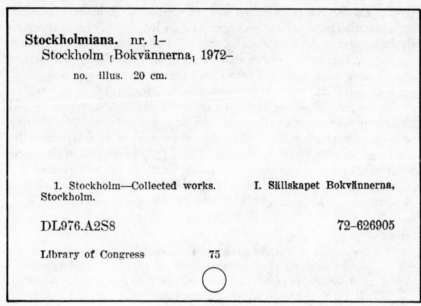

Stockholmiana. nr. 1–
Stockholm ₍Bokvännerna₎ 1972–

    no. illus. 20 cm.

    1. Stockholm—Collected works.   I. Sällskapet Bokvännerna,
Stockholm.   Stockholm.

DL976.A2S8   72–626905

Library of Congress   75

Fig. 6-7. Date in imprint.

This particular set-up is not advisable for serials because it can be confusing if a serial goes into several series or does other odd things serials have been known to do. Beatrice Simon was probably thinking of just such problems when she said:

> There is nothing more confusing, and lending itself more easily to untidiness, than the form of card which tries to imitate the form which was devised for books.[1]

The only time this might be seriously considered is if there are actually two sets of dates, one for the period covered, which should appear at the top, and one for the date published, which might appear here. This publishing phenomenon is true of some almanacs, indexes, and the like, as well as dated publications like conferences.

    The example also shows the use of brackets, not specifically indicated in this part of the rules, but called for elsewhere. Brackets are used to enclose information not found on the title-page. The use of brackets will be considerably less pronounced with the ISBD(S) than it is now.

One of the economic measures taken by libraries, which is not recommended, is the dropping of imprint elements, although some skimping might be allowed for variations, if they aren't important ones, or for dropping repetitions, as in the entry or subtitle, if quoted and includes the organization's name. The point is, however, that place of publication, and sometimes publisher, are vital clues towards identifying publications, especially when it comes to commonly used titles like *The Critic*.

An update in the *Cataloging Service Bulletin* (no. 112), refers the user to revised chapter 6, rules 136 and 137, which are to be used except for prescribed punctuation. These rules are the updated rules already mentioned in the rules in the monographic chapter already cited. This gives the source of the elements and some description of the form they should take. An innovation, not found in the older version of the rules, provides for Latin abbreviations [s.l.] and [s.n.], meaning *sine loco* and *sine nomine* ("without place" and "without name," respectively), indicating that either the place or publisher is unnamed in the publication. If both are unnamed, a printer's statement is used following the abbreviations in brackets.

If there is a choice of place and/or publisher, the first one is generally used as the predominent one, unless information is given to the contrary, perhaps by typeface or position on the publication. If an American imprint place and an American publisher are given in secondary position, these, too, should be included in the description. The place chosen should not be the place which awarded the postal license, for it is only a mailing point. The location of the editorial offices should be used. Phrases like "published by" or additions to the name of the publisher, such as "Co.," "Inc.," "Ltd.," etc., can be eliminated from the publisher statement, as with monographs.

An example of a publisher as discussed in 164C1 is Monthly Review, Inc., which publishes *Monthly review; an independent Socialist magazine*.

165. Collation

A. General rule. The collation statement describes the completed set for serials that have ceased publication. If the library does not have a complete set and if the information is easily ascertained, the total number of volumes is indicated. Illustrative matter is described for the set as a whole. If the serial is still in process of publication, the collation describes the set as it is at the time it is cataloged.

B. Volumes. The statement of the number of volumes is left open until the serial has ceased publication and the total number of volumes or the pagination can be recorded (see 142B).

AACR/NA.

Arkansas law review and Bar Association journal. v. 1–21; winter 1946/47–winter 1968.
Fayetteville, Arkansas Law Review and Bar Association Journal, inc.

21 v. ill. 23 cm. quarterly.

Vols. for 1946/47–1968 published under the auspices of the School of Law of the University of Arkansas; 1946/47–1952 with the Bar Association of Arkansas; 1953–68 with the Arkansas Bar Association.
Title varies slightly.
Continued by Arkansas law review.

1. Law—Periodicals—Arkansas.   I. Arkansas Bar Association. II. Arkansas. University. School of Law. III. Bar Association of Arkansas.

K1.R552   340′.09767   74–648926
                                                         MARC–S

Library of Congress   75

Fig. 6-8. Ceased title showing closed volumes in collation.

One of the shortcuts often taken by libraries is not filling in the number of volumes or numbers when the title ceases, although some do this on the shelflist only. It is a nicety of cataloging to do it, but not necessary for identification. The information can be easily ascertained elsewhere, if desired.

C. Numbers. If the parts of a serial are described as numbers in the publication and there is no comprehensive volume numbering, they are designated as "no." in the collation. If they are bound together, the number of volumes is also given.

25 no. in 3 v.

D. Pagination. The pagination of a serial that is complete in one volume is recorded according to the rules for describing the pagination of separately published monographs (see [rule] 142A).

AACR/NA.

This last rule is usually followed only if the title has used continuous pagination in one physical volume. Many libraries do not follow this rule, however, and simply describe such a serial brought up by section D as "lv.," which they feel is more in keeping with serial treatment. Such a deviation is not an important one.

E. Illustrations. Only those types of illustration that are, or probably are important to the set as a whole are included in the description of a serial publication. A single illustration of a given type (map, plan, port., etc.) is always ignored. (See also 142C).

AACR/NA.

Most serials are adequately described in terms of the general "illus." With the coming of the ISBD, however, this abbreviation has given way to the more universal form "ill.," as shown on the following cards.

Ontario bar news.

₍Toronto₎ Ontario Branch, Canadian Bar Association.

    v. illus. 29 cm.
    Began with June 1972 issue. Cf. New serial titles.

       1. Bar associations—Ontario—Periodicals.   I. Canadian Bar Association. Ontario Branch.

340'.05

74–641060
MARC-S

Library of Congress   74 ₍2₎

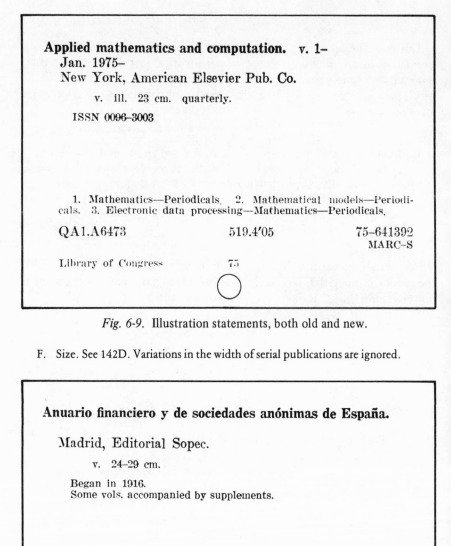

Applied mathematics and computation. v. 1–
Jan. 1975–
New York, American Elsevier Pub. Co.

    v. ill. 23 cm. quarterly.

  ISSN 0096–3003

    1. Mathematics—Periodicals. 2. Mathematical models—Periodicals. 3. Electronic data processing—Mathematics—Periodicals.

QA1.A6473   519.4′05   75–641392
                                                   MARC-S

Library of Congress   75

Fig. 6-9. Illustration statements, both old and new.

F.   Size. See 142D. Variations in the width of serial publications are ignored.

Anuario financiero y de sociedades anónimas de España.

Madrid, Editorial Sopec.

    v. 24–29 cm.

  Began in 1916.
  Some vols. accompanied by supplements.

    1. Corporations—Spain—Finance. 2. Stock companies—Spain—Finance. 3. Securities—Spain.

HG5631.A47   74–642352
                                                  MARC-S

Library of Congress   74 [2]

Fig. 6-10. Size of serial noted; this one varies from volme to volume in the run.

However, as shown by the example above, variations in size throughout the set are considered important. Size is also indicated if the height is less than the length of the publication, as shown in the example below. Serials are measured in centimeters in the same way that monographs are, according to the reference to Chapter 6 of the rules cited in this part of Chapter 7 of the rules.

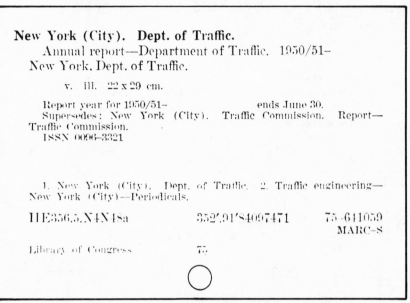

Fig. 6-11. Collation showing serial whose longest side is its depth.

Size is another factor that serials people feel is less than important. The class mark will no doubt show bound holdings that are oversized by "f's," "*'s," or whatever symbol the library uses for folio volumes. In large classes of oversized material, such as general periodicals, the shelves may be extra large or adjusted to fit the bigger volumes. Size is less crucial as a piece of description on the catalog card. Librarians are especially wary about pinning this kind of information down, particularly since it changes so radically (especially in the middle of volumes, much to the chagrin of serial bindery preparation staff). It is not so crucial that this information be included, although it is necessary for complete and first-class description. This is one of the major shortcuts.

Susan Grey Akers recommends that no collation be used for serials because it is so changeable and because it is not necessary for identification purposes. A number of others tend to agree, although some of the information can be considered useful by both librarians and patrons, particularly illustration notes.

There has been some opposition to this section of the rules since it seems to want description of something which the library does not have — namely, the entire run of a serial. This has rarely been a real problem, however, for you can usually get a pretty good idea of the publication from representative issues. Even if you neglect elements, such as illustrations, due to the fact that the issue you looked at didn't have any, it is such a minor error that it can be easily overlooked. Such information may be updated, if desired, but it is not really necessary.

166. Series statement

 A. The series statement for a serial issued as part of a larger serial (i.e. as a subseries) generally does not include volume numbers. If, however, 1) the larger series is numbered, and 2) the subseries has ceased publication, and 3) the numbers are few (generally not more than five), the series statement includes the volume numbers.

AACR / NA.

Tennessee. University.
 Report on research and publications.
 Knoxville.

   v. 25 cm. annual. (The University of Tennessee record)

   1. Tennessee. University—Bibliography. 2. Research—Tennessee.
 Z5055.U5T2512a   016.378768'85   74–644906
 ISSN 0049-3414   MARC-S
 Library of Congress   74 ₍2₎

Fig. 6-12. Series note for a serial located after the collation.

 B. When only some volumes of a serial are issued as a subseries, this information is presented in a note.

AACR / NA.

Great Britain. Dept. of Trade and Industry.
Continental shelf act, 1964; report.

London, H. M. Stationery Off.

  v. 24 cm. annual.

  Issued in the series of Reports and papers of the House of Commons of Parliament.
  Report year ends Mar. 31.

  1. Petroleum industry and trade—Licenses—Great Britain.
  2. Petroleum in submerged lands—Great Britain.

HD9571.2.G73a   354'.42'00824   72–626954

Library of Congress   74 [2]

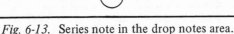

Fig. 6-13. Series note in the drop notes area.

The fact that a serial can be part of another series seems to be very difficult for some people to understand. This problem can be further compounded if the series is to be traced. If the series is to be traced, and it is unnumbered, there is not too much of a problem, for the series would not normally be construed as a serial, since it has no "numerical or chronological designations." It is an unnumbered monographic series, of which some parts just happen to be the numbered issues of a serial. It is being subarranged by author and/or title, depending upon which is appropriate. The problem is usually in the mixing of the terms "monograph" and "serial." A serial can be found within a larger series which is basically monographic. A good example would be the publications of a university, all of which are numbered in some all-encompassing "publications" series which counts for all of the university's publications. Within this series can be found the annual report of the school (a serial), the catalog (a serial), various bulletins (serials), and perhaps even the student newspaper (also a serial). Also within this series might be found the various addresses at graduations (which might be better treated as a series of monographs), scholarly papers by professors (monographs), and other monographic works. The items are diverse and should be treated as individual things; it's just that some of them naturally clump themselves together with the others of their ilk into serial runs. Once this is accepted there is no problem. There is a problem with numbered series, however, for the rules say that the numbers should be ignored when it comes to serials. This is obvious, since the numbers will not be in any sequence and it would be awkward to make a card for each item in the series. Future numbers of the larger series would be random and unknown. Some libraries follow the rules, as does LC, but others find it hard to integrate serials with monographs in the same larger series when the larger series is collected numerically by added entry. They get around this by bending the rule and using the series name, followed by the number of the series borne by the first issue of the serial being cataloged. This number is followed by "[etc.]" to indicate that there are other numbers to follow, not necessarily in sequence. In this way, the serial will fall in the series sequence where the first number of the serial fell in publishing order numerically. Thus, a serial card would not be sent back for the addition of numbers for a series normally listed by number in the catalog. This larger series is cataloged separately and is, therefore, a numbered monographic series which is scattered or cataloged separately. If the serial is the first number of that larger series to be cataloged, and the decision has already been made that the larger series should not be classed together, the series should be set up by the serials cataloger as a "monographic series, traced by number." (See series authority file card in Chapter 9.) It is, of course, possible to catalog the larger series as a serial, with an analytic for a subserial within it, but this should be decided within the guidelines set up for determining whether a monographic series should be scattered or collected, regardless of the fact that the publications which fall within it are serials. It is even possible for all of the subordinate parts of a larger series to be serials. This larger series is still a "monographic series," since all parts are actually cataloged separately by their own authors and titles.

Titles that fall partially within a series, or within several series, pose analogous problems and should be treated in basically the same ways. Series should be represented and traced in almost all cases. Some libraries ignore microform or reprint series, however, preferring to treat the publication as much like the original as possible, with notes indicating format changes.

The next rule, 167, deals with notes. The British text gives the functions of notes in its rule 167A, which does not appear in the North American edition:

In addition to qualifying and amplifying the formal description in the body of the entry. . .notes in serial cataloguing serve specifically to show the relationship between the individual parts of the serial and the whole, and to record the variations from the general picture in the body of the entry that occur in individual volumes or parts.

AACR/BT.

To continue with the North American rules:

167. Notes

A. General rules

1. Many of the supplementary notes necessary to the cataloging of serial publications are presented in a conventional style. Although the circumstances of the case must necessarily govern the phrasing of any note, the following paragraphs indicate what types of information are essential, and suggest but do not prescribe forms. At times unnecessary repetition can be avoided without sacrifice of clarity by combining two or more conventional or other notes.

AACR/NA.

The Library of Congress has updated the last part of this rule with the following, from *Cataloging service bulletin* 112 (Winter 1975, pp. 12-13):

Combining Notes. Since the various types of information in notes must be put into MARC tags, combinations of information are difficult to handle. Therefore, two different types of information should not be combined into one note even though, by doing so, repetition can be avoided.

Examples:
   Combined: Began with vol. for 1963/64, superseding in part the society's Bulletin, and continuing its numbering. *Cf.* New serial titles.

   Separate: Began with vol. for 1963/64. *Cf.* New serial titles.
   Supersedes in part: Society for Testing and Materials. Bulletin.

The second note of the second part of the example also shows something which was covered in the same bulletin:

Notes Which Refer to Another Publication: Notes which refer to another publication which has been cataloged in LC should give the other publication in its *exact* catalog entry form, even if this requires repetition of a heading or title. (See also 167A "Language of Notes.")

Examples:

   This: Continues: Canada. Bureau of Statistics. The printing trades.

   Not this: Continues its Printing trades.

   This: Continues: Wisconsin. University. Land Tenure Center. A research paper.

   Not this: Continues the publication with the same title issued by the center when the university's name was University of Wisconsin.

The reference to the ''Language of Notes'' section also refers to the same *Bulletin*. This section reads:

> *Language of Notes.* All notes are to be in the roman alphabet unless the information is being quoted from the publication and placed in quotation marks.

It may be that some of the examples in this section do not correspond to these notes. That is because they are older LC cards. This is a comparatively new innovation due, as it states, to MARC-S and also to the ISBD(M), which the Library of Congress is trying to adapt for serials cataloging as much as possible, awaiting the ISBD(S).

Back to the old Chapter 7 of the rules:

2. In describing bibliographical changes in a serial publication, reference is generally made to the date of the volume or issue showing the change rather than to its volume designation, unless the date of the volume or issue is not sufficient and volume designation must be used. Dates, and the designation of volumes when used (except in contents notes) are given in English, with appropriate abbreviations, unless the vernacular is essential to clarity. Dates may be described by the month, day and year, by the month or season and year, or by year alone, as the situation may require. If any change described in a note occurs with the first issue in the month, the day is not specified; if it occurs with the first issue in the year, the month or season is not specified.

3. In general, the order of the items given in the rules below is observed in the catalog entry.

AACR/NA.

The order is given by the North American rules as follows:

[A. General rules]
B. Frequency
C. Report year
D. Duration of publication
E. Suspension of publication
F. Numbering
G. Connection with preceding publications
H. Publications absorbed
J. Organ
K. Minor variations in title
L. Issues with special titles
M. Issuing bodies
N. Editors
P. Variations in imprint

Q. Connection with later publications
R. No more published?
S. Contents

This is basically that used in the LC *Rules for descriptive cataloging,* with some modifications due to the change from latest to successive entry cataloging and the need for additional notes. The British text gives the following listing:

1. Frequency
2. Source of title
3. Changes in title
4. Changes in author and author's name
5. Editors
6. Issuing or responsible body
7. Duration and suspension of publication
8. Numbering
9. Imprint
10. Series
11. Bibliographical history and relationships
12. Supplements
13. Holdings
14. Indexes

[The latter three are covered by other rules than the rules for "notes" in the North American text and are covered in this book by Chapters 7 and 12, as well as the paragraphs discussing "holdings" earlier in this chapter.]

It has been stated by some librarians that the British text has more appropriate and logical listing of notes, thus bringing related information together. Be that as it may, the North American text's so-called "haphazard" order will be used here. It should be remembered that these rules are guides rather than mandatory instructions. Depending on the situation, some of these may be more important than others. The order may then need to be rearranged. Not all will apply for all titles either. Each situation has to be evaluated on its own merits and the possibility of notes considered as necessary. Notes should be brief and clear. They should not show bias on the part of the cataloger, but should simply state the known facts.

B. Frequency

1. If the frequency of publication can be described by a single adjective or brief phrase, it is given immediately after the collation, unless it is obvious from the title of the publication, i.e. *Library quarterly.*

AACR/NA.

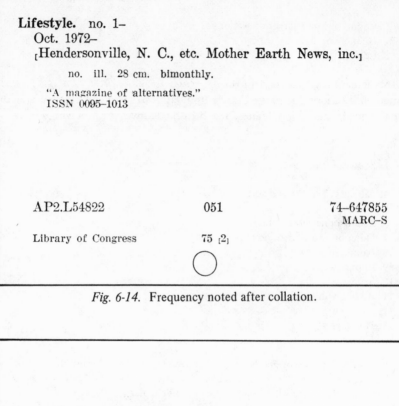

Lifestyle. no. 1–
Oct. 1972–
[Hendersonville, N. C., etc. Mother Earth News, inc.]

  no. ill. 28 cm. bimonthly.

"A magazine of alternatives."
ISSN 0095–1013

AP2.L54822   051   74–647855
                                                     MARC-S

Library of Congress   75 [2]

Fig. 6-14. Frequency noted after collation.

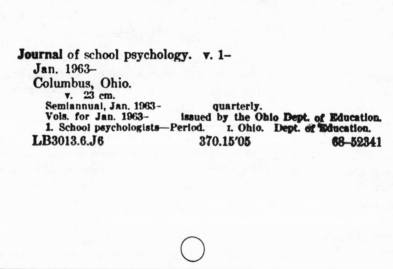

Journal of school psychology. v. 1–
Jan. 1963–
Columbus, Ohio.
  v. 23 cm.
  Semiannual, Jan. 1963–   quarterly.
  Vols. for Jan. 1963–   issued by the Ohio Dept. of Education.
  1. School psychologists—Period.   i. Ohio. Dept. of Education.
  LB3013.6.J6   370.15'05   68–52341

Fig. 6-15. Frequency in a note form.

2. If there are numerous changes in frequency of publication, the information is represented by the general note "Frequency varies."[3]

[3]The Library of Congress uses this note if there are three or more variations.

AACR/NA.

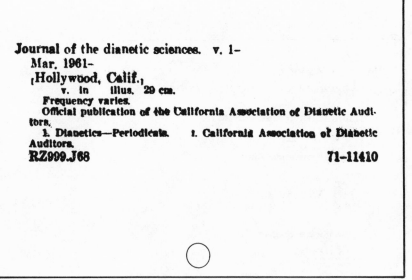

Journal of the dianetic sciences. v. 1-
Mar. 1961-
Hollywood, Calif.,
v. in   illus. 29 cm.
Frequency varies.
Official publication of the California Association of Dianetic Auditors.
1. Dianetics—Periodicals.   i. California Association of Dianetic Auditors.
RZ999.J68   71-11410

Fig. 6-16. "Frequency varies" note.

One of the complaints about this section arises from the fact that there is the potential of three places for a user of the catalog to look when trying to find frequency information. First of all, it can be found in a title like *Urban affairs annual reviews.* If not there, it can be found in the collation. Lastly, it can be found in the notes, either by itself or perhaps as a quoted subtitle or other characterizing note. This can be a burden to the user of the catalog.

Coupled with the above objection is the objection that such information be found in the catalog record at all. Such information is rarely updated on cards and could easily be left off, to be considered an auxiliary and augmentative function of the visible file. A large number of libraries eliminate such information from their cataloging records.

However, the rules do state that frequency is an important feature of a serial and it is sometimes necessary for identification. Its retention is suggested for this reason.

    C. Report year. If the period covered by an annual publication is other than that of the calendar year, the fact is noted.

AACR/NA.

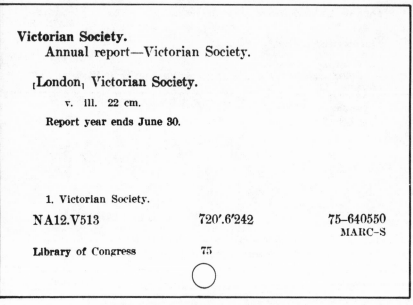

Victorian Society.
    Annual report—Victorian Society.

ₜLondonₗ Victorian Society.
      v. ill. 22 cm.
    Report year ends June 30.

    1. Victorian Society.
NA12.V513   720'.6'242   75–640550
                                          MARC–S
Library of Congress   75

Fig. 6-17. Note for "report year."

    D. Duration of publication. The duration of publication is stated in a note, unless it is shown by the statement of holdings. The authority for this information is generally cited.

AACR/NA.

Anglesey Antiquarian Society.
Transactions—Anglesey Antiquarian Society and Field
Club.

Llangefni, Wales.
v. ill. 22 cm. annual.
Began in 1914. Cf. Union list of serials.

1. Anglesey, Wales—History—Periodicals. 2. Anglesey, Wales—
Antiquities—Periodicals. 3. Anglesey Antiquarian Society.

DA740.A5A66a   942.9′21′005   74–648194
                                              MARC-S

Library of Congress   75

Fig. 6-18. Opening date in a note, with source authority given.

As already mentioned, this is standard LC procedure when the first volume is
not held. Unfortunately, LC catalogers complain that they very rarely seem to
catalog from v. 1, no. 1 — it is usually v. 1, no. 2 — so this note appears often
and is not revised. This information is much better located after the title in the
fashion of "perfect copy," especially since it is valuable for identification purposes.

E. Suspension of publication. If a serial suspends publication with the intention
of resuming at a later date, the entry is left open and a note is used to show
date, or the volume designation, of the last issue published. If publication is
resumed, the note shows the inclusive dates of the period of suspension.

AACR/NA.

Journal of Philippine statistics. v. 1–
July 1941.–
Manila.
    v. tables. 27–33 cm. monthly.
Publication suspended   –Dec. 1948.
Issued July 1941–   by the Bureau of the Census and
Statistics of the Commonwealth of the Philippines;   by
the Bureau of the Census and Statistics of the Republic of the
Philippines.
    1. Philippine Islands—Stat.   i. Philippines (Commonwealth)
Bureau of the Census and Statistics. ii. Philippines (Republic) Bu-
reau of the Census and Statistics.
    HA1821.J68   319.14   44–22992 rev*

Publisistik.
  [Djakarta, Lembaga Publisistik, Universitas Indonesia;
distribusi : P. T. Gramedia]

    v. 21 cm.

  Began with June 1964 issue; suspended 1966–1971.

    1. Mass media—Indonesia—Periodicals.   I. Djakarta. Univer-
sitas Indonesia. Lembaga Publisistik.

P92.I72P8   S A 68–19183

                              PL 480: Indo–S–168
Library of Congress

Fig. 6-19. Suspension notes.
            (Note that the second one is a combined note, now a "no-no.")

This is fairly straightforward, except to note that sometimes you may need to sprinkle some question marks through this section due to uncertainties. Unstable governments, possible insurrection and fickle clientele sometimes mean that even the publisher cannot adequately respond to claims. This is often true with Latin American periodicals, which are notoriously difficult to control adequately. One must do the best one can to "second guess" what is going on and to make notes accordingly.

F. Numbering. Irregularities and peculiarities in the numbering of a serial publication are described, unless they are limited to the numbering of the parts of a given volume. These include double numbering, combined issues or volumes, confusion in the use of series numbering or whole numbers, the publication of preliminary editions not included in the regular series numbering, numbering that does not begin with volume one, etc.

AACR/NA.

Herder correspondence. v. 1–
   Jan. 1964–
   Dublin, New York, Herder.
      v. 26–28 cm. monthly.
      Vol. 1, no. 1 preceded by numbers called v. 0, no. 0
   and v. 1, no. 0
      1. Catholic Church—Period.
   BX801.H38   282'.05   68–5069

Photo merchandising. v. ₁1₁–   May 1956–
  ₁New York, Photographic Trade News₁
      v. in   illus.   29 cm.
      Quarterly (irregular) May 1956–Nov./Dec. 1957; bimonthly, Jan./
  Feb. 1958–
      Issues for May 1956–Nov./Dec. 1957 have no vol. numbering but
  constitute v. 1–2.
      1. Photography—Apparatus and supplies—Period.   I. Photo-
  graphic Trade News, inc., New York.
  HF6201.P55P5   60–41541

Publicity & printing.

  ₁Brisbane₁
      v. in   24 cm.   bimonthly.
  "Established 1924."
  Vol. numbering irregular: v. 26 repeated.
  "The national journal of the printing and allied trades in Aus-
  tralia, New Zealand, and South Africa."
  1. Printing—Period.
  Z119.P985   66–98612

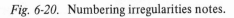

Fig. 6-20. Numbering irregularities notes.

This can be one of the most fun rules to try and follow for this is where the publications we dearly love tend to show their perverse nature, sometimes quite by accident. A publication entitled *Socialist thought and practice* was published for twelve years in Belgrade with no problems at all as numbers 1-59. Then the publisher switched to volumes-and-numbers, with six issues numbered v. 14, no. 1-6/7, published in 1974. In 1975 a strange malady seems to have struck the people involved with this publication, causing them to have problems with counting, and the following chart shows what happened.

v. 15 no. 8
v. 16 no. 9
v. 17 no. 10
v. 18 no. 11
v. 12 no. 12
v. 13 no. 1
v. 15 no. 2

This cataloger gave up and wrapped it all up nicely with a note "Volume numbering irregular" and had the title bound by year subdivided by months. All the appropriate numbers that appear on the issues should be recorded on the Kardex, however, so that the receipt file can be referred to for specific numbering problems or reference questions. The catalog cannot hope to cope with a long and involved statement of irregularities such as this and be clear about it, so it is best to give up and let the serial records do it. This is a case in which Osborn's concept of complementary records is a real help.

Numbering notes may also include double numbering used, including double numbering with another publication, which should be specified. This problem has already been discussed earlier in this chapter when talking about "holdings".

Notes may be needed to explain the numbering used in the body of the entry, too. For example, a congress was not published for the first sixteen years it was held. The numbering statement should show "17th-   ." There is an obvious discrepancy here that needs to be explained and this can be simply done with a note like:

1st-16th congresses not published.

Allow me to call upon Sarah Dickinson of the Crerar Library to tell us some of the numbering idiocyncracies of periodicals she's known and loved.

And I am sure many of you know *System,* which became *Magazine of Business,* and then was replaced by *Business Week;* and then a new *System* started with volume 1, no. 1, so it had to be treated as a new journal; and just after everybody had gotten it cataloged and the cards printed, it jumped from volume 3, no. 6 to volume 52, adopting the numbering of its predecessor which had died, and announced, if you please, that it did so at the request of the librarians!

One more illustration of this sort — this time an English one: *Education Outlook,* of London, started in 1924, but absorbed *Educational Times,* a journal with an honorable record of forty-five volumes. Proud of the marriage, the *Outlook* adopted the volume numbering of the *Times,* and although it was the first year of its own existence, it called itself volume 76.

All went merry as a wedding bell for six years. Then *something* happened. A dignified silence is observed — no explanation vouchsafed. But divorce followed. And in the *Outlook,* volume 81, 1929 was succeeded by volume 7, 1930.

The *Educational Times* soon found another partner, who was proud of the association, and announced itself to the world as *Journal of Education,* with which is incorporated *School World and Educational Times,* And a lot of recataloging and altering of records had to be done.[2]

The only thing one can do is try to explain as best one can what one thinks the publisher is doing. Lest one think this is only a curiosity from the past, here is a modern example. The publication *The Green revolution* changed its numbering to correspond better to its history, the change announced in v. 12, no. 5, summer 1974 as follows:

THE GREEN REVOLUTION is now in its 31st year. Originally published under the title "The Interpreter," its name was changed to "The Way Out," and later — in 1961 — to "The Green Revolution." In 1973 it merged with "The Modern Utopian," and with "Alternatives," formerly published by Richard Fairfield.[3]

The card showing this is reproduced opposite. Note the notes and the numbering statement.

Miss Dickinson also has examples of numbers not published:

The most remarkable example of this kind of thing was the *Altruist* of St. Louis. [We] started out with it bravely in 1903, paid our agent, but though it was a monthly, numbers 1 to 6, and 12 were not published. The next year 4 out of the 12 came; the next, 3 out of the 12; but always numbered as though the others had come out. And when I claimed and claimed, the same answer would come: "I called it no. 10, because it would have been, if numbers 1 to 9 had been issued; I still hope to catch up."

```
AP2    The Green revolution; perspectives on major
G737     problems of living.  v.1-12, no.5, 1961-
         summer 1974; v.32-
         1975-
         ┌Los Angeles┐
              v.  illus.

         "Official journal of the School of Living
         ┌West┐."
           Frequency varies.
           1973-      merged with The Modern Utopian and
         Alternatives.  1975-       called v.32-       in
         continuation of the numbering of The Way out
         and other titles which precede this one.

           I.School of Living - West.
```

Fig. 6-21. Numbering irregularities, history and absorption.

But alas, a record of 14 years showed that out of 204 due, only 89 arrived. But who can blame that publisher? The price was first 10 cents a year, then 25 cents — postage from St. Louis included.

And when in 1917 it expired, with only one issue for that year, we even had our 25 cents refunded! It was well named *Altruist.*[4]

All serials librarians have their favorite horror stories to tell. This is just one area where one learns to cope!

G. Connection with preceding publications. The relationship between a serial and its immediate predecessor or predecessors is indicated. A serial that appears under a different title or different name of corporate author but continues the numbering of its predecessor is considered to "continue" that publication;[4] If the numbering has not been continued, however, it "supersedes" it.

[4] [This footnote was a lengthy description, with examples, of the Library of Congress' practice of using latest entry cataloging. This practice, already discussed in the chapter on title changes, has been dropped in favor of the successive entry practice which the AACR advocates, and this footnote has been deleted per instructions in *Cataloging service bulletin.*]

AACR/NA.

Amerikastudien. American studies. Jahrg. 19–
1974–
Stuttgart, J. B. Metzlersche Verlagsbuchhandlung.

v. ill. 25 cm. 2 no. a year.

Continues Jahrbuch für Amerikastudien.
English or German with summaries in English.
Issued under the auspices of Deutsche Gesellschaft für Amerikastudien.

1. United States—Civilization—Periodicals.   I. Deutsche Gesellschaft für Amerikastudien. II. Title: American studies.

E169.1.J33   973.92′05   74–646602
                                                      MARC–S

Library of Congress   75 ₍2₎

(a)

**United States. Library of Congress. Library of Congress
Office, Karachi.**
Accessions list, Pakistan. Annual supplement: cumulative list of serials.
1973–
₍Karachi₎

v. 28 cm.

Continues a publication with the same title issued by the Office under its earlier name: American Libraries Book Procurement Center, Karachi.
ISSN 0097–7985

1. Pakistan—Imprints.

Z3191.U53 suppl.   015.549′1   74–648198
                                                   MARC–S

Library of Congress   75

(b)

Ubumwe. 1.–
31 mars 1972–
Bujumbura.

    v. illus. 30–44 cm. weekly.

With the Rundi edition of the same title supersedes the bilingual
(French and Rundi) edition.
In French.

AP27.U272   054.1   73–645944
                                              MARC-S

Library of Congress   74 [2]

(c)

Saturday review/world. v. 1–
Sept. 11, 1973–
[New York]

    v. illus. 28 cm. biweekly.

Formed by the union of Saturday review of education, Saturday
review of society, Saturday review of the arts, Saturday review of
the sciences, and World.
Running title   : SR/world.

   I. Title: SR/world.

AP2.S273   051   73–645517
ISSN 0091–620–X   MARC-S

Library of Congress   74 [2]

(d)

Fig. 6-22. Various forms of superseding or continuing notes:
      (a) continuation
      (b) continuation due to a change in corporate author
      (c) superseding
      (d) merger of several titles to form one

The continuation note may include the numbering, particularly if more than one title is involved, indicating which numbering is being continued.

Some libraries append a note after the earlier title when it is not held by the library which says: "(Library does not have.)" The note is lined out if the title is acquired. This can be done for succeeding titles as well. This is a nice help for the patron, but it provides extra work and the information can be easily found by checking the catalog under the title in question. Librarians may wish to consider the practice, however, if they feel it is of help, regardless of the work involved. It is not a practical solution, however.

Many librarians feel that the use of both the terms "Continue" and "Supersede" are unnecessary and will choose one or the other and further qualify as necessary, such as in:

Supersedes _____ and continues its [volume] numbering.

This is often easier for local libraries, but would be hard to justify in a union list setting since all terms would not be equal, causing confusion.

> H. Publications absorbed. If a serial has absorbed another one, the publication absorbed is named and the exact date of absorption is indicated, if possible.

AACR/NA.

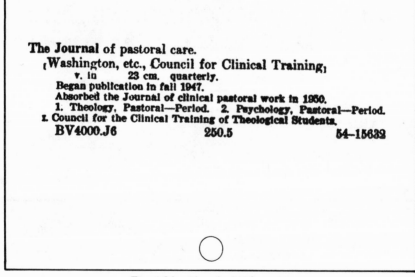

Fig. 6-23. Absorbed title note.

This is also a fairly straightforward situation. It should be noted, however, that this is only done when the continuing title remains the same. If the title is changed to indicate the presence of the new title, the provisions of 167G should be followed and the new title cataloged as a separate entity.

Absorptions can be pretty interesting affairs, however. The example given below is absolutely violent, as reported in a letter to the Editor of *Title varies:*

> While the world shuddered and gasped at the outbreak of World War II, another monster frolicked freely in the Caribbean. And because of the biased media and international cover-up, the event did not come to the attention of the librarians of the world.
>
> Even now many of you are not aware of the savagery which took place in August 1940. Who was to know that *Jamaica* would open its jaws and swallow *West Indian Review? Jamaica* and *West Indian Review* had existed side by side since 1934 and CHOMP! *West Indian Review* was chewed and swallowed. . .but divine grace interfered.
>
> On a foggy, clammy morning in March 1944, what rose out of a nearby print-shop — yes! It was *West Indian Review* resurrected as a Series 2. For five years *Jamaica* sulked and *West Indian Review* grew strong. Understandably, *West Indian Review* had not forgiven the one-time hostility of *Jamaica;* for on May 7, 1949 *West Indian Review* gobbled *Jamaica,* producing *West Indian Review* Series 3.
>
> The revenge may have been sweet, but *West Indian Review* suffered acute indigestion. The publication hiccoughed and introduced Series 4 (1951). For years *West Indian Review* sat placidly as Series 4, but soon its tail began to twitch and its eyes rolled up in the sockets. Oh, the guilty conscience of *West Indian Review!* *Jamaica* was no more, and this ached *West Indian Review's* title page. Was an apology and reconciliation in order?
>
> Apparently so, for in September 1963, a Series 5 entitled *Jamaica and West Indian Review* reached the outside world. And to this day, these two beasts remain friendly and their title constant (we hope)![5]

No one could show such an inventive mind, nor such a love for serials, better than the contributor of this newsworthy item. This example also shows title changes and numbering changes as well. When a serial begins to deviate from the straight-and-narrow, it often does so on all fronts at once. (One of the true challenges of the serials cataloger.)

> J. Organ. The fact that a serial is the organ of a society or other body is noted if it can be presented in the terms, or the English equivalent of the terms, used by the publisher, even if the name of that organization serves as the author entry of the work.
>
> AACR/NA.

International journal of government auditing. v. 1–
Jan. 1974–
[Toronto, International Organization of Supreme Audit
Institutions]

v. 28 cm. quarterly.

"Official organ of INTOSAI."

1. Finance, Public—Accounting—Periodicals. 2. Auditing—Periodicals. I. International Organization of Supreme Audit Institutions.

HJ9701.I 55   350'.7232   74–645051
                                                           MARC-S

Library of Congress   74 [2]

◯

The Law librarian. v. 1–
Apr. 1970–
London.

v. 30 cm. 3 no. a year.

"Bulletin of the British and Irish Association of Law Librarians."

1. Law libraries—Periodicals.   I. British and Irish Association
of Law Librarians.

Z675.L2L38   026'.34'00942   74–236032

Library of Congress   74 [2]

◯

Fig. 6-24. Notes that a serial is the organ of an organization.

Most libraries, in an effort to save time and space, will not make the note if it means repeating the main entry, however. This is in keeping with the old green book rules. They also will not usually repeat the society's name if it is listed as publisher, although some will prefer to leave off the publisher statement and amplify the body's connection with the publication further in the notes, either by a direct quotation, as in the examples, or in a conventional note. Note that the second example may be a subtitle which is being quoted. Often subtitles give important amplication to titles.

K. Minor variations in title. Changes in the title of the several volumes or parts of a serial so slight that they do not affect the location of the title in an alphabetical file, or conceal the identification of the parts, are mentioned in a general statement such as "Title varies slightly" or "Subtitle varies." The varying forms of a title used on different parts of the publication are reworded in the catalog entry if they contribute to the identification of the publication.

If the varying form of the title appears on all volumes of a work that has ceased publication, the inclusive dates are unecessary in the specification.

AACR/NA.

Underground evangelism magazine.

ₗGlendale, Calif., Underground Evangelism, etc.ₗ

   v.   ill.   28 cm.   11 no. a year.

Title varies slightly.
ISSN 0097-6784

   1. Evangelistic work—Communist countries—Periodicals.   2. Communist countries—Religion—Periodicals.

BV3777.C62U53   269'.2'091717   75–642063
                                                          MARC–S

Library of Congress   75

Fig. 6-25. "Title varies" note.

Cataloging service bulletin 112 gives further amplification to the part of this rule relating to titles on different parts of a serial:

Titles on Different Parts of a Serial. Notes regarding titles on different parts of a serial should use only the terms listed below. Any locations which are not specifically listed below (e.g., masthead title, colophon title) should be described as "other title."

> Cover title
> Added title page title
> Caption title
> Running title
> Spine title
> Other title [other title appearing on the piece and not specified above]

In general, title variations appearing on different parts of a serial are not specified unless these variations are important enough to require added entries.

Even though a serial is in two languages and/or the title in two languages has been used in the entry, notes regarding titles on different parts of the serial will record the title in one language only, usually the language of the title recorded first in the entry.[6]

El Dorado. v. 1–
　Aug. 1973–
　[Greeley, Colo., G. E. Fay]

　　　v. 28 cm.

　　　"A newsletter-bulletin on South American anthropology.
　　　Added title, 1973–　: Relaciones antropologicas.
　　　ISSN 0095-165X

　　　1. Indians of South America—Collected works.　I. Title: Relaciones antropologicas.

　F2229.D67　　　　　　　980'.004'98　　　　　　74-643045
　　　　　　　　　　　　　　　　　　　　　　　　　　　MARC-S

　Library of Congress　　　　75 [2]

(a)

Communio. v. 1–
spring 1974–
₁Spokane, Wash.₁´

    v. illus. 25 cm. 4 no. a year.

  At head of title, 1974–   : International Catholic review.

    1. Catholic Church—Periodicals. 2. Theology, Catholic—Periodicals.   I. Title: International Catholic review.

BX801.C63   282′.05   74–644864
ISSN 0094–2065   MARC-S

Library of Congress   74 ₁2₁

(b)

Quebec (Province). Bureau of Statistics. Finance Service.
Finances municipales: Municipalités du Québec.

Québec, Service des finances, Bureau de la statistique du Québec.

    v. ill. 28 cm. annual.

  Cover title   : Municipalités du Québec: Finances municipales.

    1. Municipal finance—Quebec (Province)—Statistics—Periodicals.
I. Title. II. Title: Municipalités du Québec: Finances municipales.

HJ9014.Q39BS7a   352′.1′09714   75–640996
                                            MARC-S

Library of Congress   75

(c)

West Virginia Education Association.
WVEA school journal.

₍Charleston₎

v. illus. 41 cm. bimonthly.

Continues West Virginia school journal.
Running title : WV school journal.

1. West Virginia Education Association—Periodicals. I. Title.
II. Title: WV school journal.

L11.W33 370′.9754 74–642452
ISSN 0094–176–X MARC–S

Library of Congress 74 ₍2₎

○

(d)

Fig 6-26. Other title variants noted.

Sarah Dickinson again, on the subject of variant titles:

Small annoyances are the variations in the title. I remember I cared for the *Army and Navy Journal,* of Washington, for a full year, all records under that name, to be much surprised to have the title page, when it arrived, read *American Army and Navy Journal;* and consistency obliged me to make a number of changes.

Some carry one name on the outside and another on the inside, and still a third hidden discreetly on the editorial page. We don't know yet whether to say *Farm Journal,* or *National Farm Journal.* And the *Creamery and Milk Plant Monthly* hides *Creamery* in the smallest possible type, and shouts the *Milk Plant Monthly* at you. These are puzzles more for the binding and cataloging departments.[7]

Minor changes can be ignored or passed off with a brief note, but the real challenges are those that actually present alternative entry points to the catalog.

These should be traced, particularly if they might be mistaken for the title. Note that LC has traced the alternative titles listed in all of the examples in Fig. 6-26. Real title variants, cataloged under rule 6D, should be noted and traced.

Subtitles are usually not used in the cataloging of serial publications because they tend to vary so much. Such a practice might be termed "preventative cataloging." However, they may be used to further identify publications in notes. Their changes may be briefly characterized as "subtitle varies," if, indeed, they are given prominence on the card.

Subtitles should be quoted in almost all cases if they contain the name of the sponsor or issuing body. Subtitles may also be another place where frequency statements may be found. They may give clues as to the nature and scope of the work. The character of the publication may need to be described if the title is not specific, as in a title like *Omega,* which could mean several things.

Other descriptive phrases may also be used to identify a publication, if desired. Quotations from the publication itself should be enclosed in quotation marks. Here are some examples:

NLR: national library reporter. v. 1–
Oct. 7, 1974–
Columbia, Md.

    v. 28 cm. semimonthly.

    "An independent newsletter covering library and publishing news in the nation's capital."
ISSN 0095–053X

    1. Libraries—United States—Periodicals. 2. Publishers and publishing—United States—Periodicals.   I. Title: National library reporter.

Z731.N2   021'.00973   74–647994
                                          MARC-S

Library of Congress   75 [2]

American Baptist Convention.
Directory—American Baptist Convention.

Valley Forge, Pa., American Baptist Convention.

  v. 25 cm. annual.

"American Baptist Women, American Baptist Women of the Regions/States, Division of World Mission Support, Regional State Convention Executive Secretaries and Directors of Promotion, American Baptist Home Mission Societies, American Baptist Foreign Mission Society of the American Baptist Conventon."
ISSN 0096-3380

  1. American Baptist Convention—Directories.

BX6207.A323   286'.131'025   75-641375
                                                     MARC-S

Library of Congress   75

Fig. 6-27. Additional characterization of a serial publication through subtitles, etc.

L. Issues with special titles. The presence of special titles of individual issues or volumes is mentioned in the catalog entry, the various titles being specified, if the individual volume is likely to be known by the special title. If the serial is in progress, this note should be the last one.

AACR/NA.

Many convention proceedings have special titles for each volume. If the title is cataloged as a serial, special title analytic cards can be made to refer back to the main entry, or added entries may be made for each special title.

M. Issuing bodies. If the statement of issuing or sponsoring body is complex, if the name of another body appears as the publisher, if there are changes in the name of the issuing body of a serial entered under title,[5] or if a serial entered under title has more than one successive issuing body, the necessary information is added in a supplementary note. Minor variations in the form of the name of the issuing body (see 68, footnote 7) are also described.

[5] [The Library of Congress uses this form of note also for serials that are entered under the issuing body.]

AACR/NA.

Consumer electronics product news. v. 1–
Jan. 1975–
[New York, St. Regis Publications]

    v. ill. 29 cm. monthly.

ISSN 0097–8329
Issue for Jan. 1975 called also Inaugural issue.
Running title, Jan. 1975–   : CEPN.

    1. Electronic industries—United States—Periodicals. 2. Electronic apparatus and appliances—Periodicals.   I. Title: CEPN.

HD9696.A3U533   338.4′7′62130973   75–642304
                                                           MARC-S

Library of Congress   75

Consumer behavior. v. [1]–
1954–
New York, New York University Press.
    v. 29 cm.
    Each volume has also a distinctive title: v. 1, The dynamics of consumer reaction.—v. 2, The life cycle and consumer behavior.
    "Sponsored by Consumer Behavior, Incorporated" (called in 1954, Committee for Research on Consumer Attitudes and Behavior)
    Editor: v. 1–   L. H. Clark.
    1. Consumers—Yearbooks.   I. Clark, Lincoln Harold, 1910– ed. II. Consumer Behavior Incorporated.
HF5415.A2C57   **54–11984 rev**

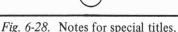

Fig. 6-28. Notes for special titles.

Canadian materials. 1971–
ₜOttawaₗ Canadian Library Association.

    v. 26 cm. annual.

Vols. for 1971–   issued by the Canadian Materials Committee, Canadian School Library Association.

    1. Canada—Juvenile literature—Bibliography—Periodicals.   I. Canadian School Library Association. Canadian Materials Committee.

Z1378.C33   016.9171′03   74–641664
                                                      MARC–S

Library of Congress   74 ₜ2ₗ

Southeastern Europe/l'Europe du Sud-Est. v. 1–
1974–
ₜPittsburghₗ University Center for International Studies, University of Pittsburgh.

    v. 23 cm. 4 no. a year.

Vols. for 1974–   issued jointly with Temple University.

    1. Balkan Peninsula—Collected works.   I. Pittsburgh University. University Center for International Studies. II. Philadelphia. Temple University.

DR2.S65   914.96′03′05   74–644117
ISSN 0094–4467   MARC–S

Library of Congress   74 ₜ2ₗ

Australia. Bureau of Census and Statistics.
Rural land use, improvements. agricultural machinery
and labour. 1971/72–
Canberra.

    v. illus. 30 cm. annual.

Supersedes its Rural land use and crop production.
Vols. for 1971/72–   issued by the Bureau under a
variant form of name: Commonwealth Bureau of Census and Statistics.

    1. Land—Australia—Statistics. 2. Agriculture—Australia—Statis-
tics.   I. Title.

IID1031.A35a   338.1'0994   74–643468
                                           MARC-S

Library of Congress   74 [2]

Dunia maritim.

   [Jakarta, etc.]
      v. ill. 28–31 cm.

    Issues for   published by Jajasan Penerbitan Mari-
tim, Departemen Perhubungan Laut; issues for
published by Direktorat Jenderal Perhubungan Laut (–
July 1972 under an earlier name of the directorate: Direktorat
Djenderal Perhubungan Laut)
    1. Merchant marine—Indonesia—Periodicals. 2. Shipping—In-
donesia—Periodicals.   I. Indonesia. Direktorat Jenderal Perhubungan Laut. II. Indonesia. Direktorat Djenderal Perhubungan
Laut. III. Indonesia. Departemen Perhubungan Laut. Jajasan
Penerbitan Maritim.

HE887.D85   75–640860
                                           MARC-S

Library of Congress   75   S A

Fig. 6-29. Notes for issuing bodies.

It is probable that few make notes like LC did (see the footnote) except for minor changes of corporate name, such as the American Society for Testing Materials, changed to the American Society for Testing and Materials. LC deleted the footnote with *Cataloging service bulletin* 109 (May, 1974), which also added the note to see rule 68, footnote 7. This footnote gives the provision for latest entry cataloging for changes of names of corporate bodies which are very slight.

N. Editors

    1. Unless a serial has ceased publication and has had the same editor or group of editors throughout its life, the editors, compilers, directors or founders who are important to the identification or characterization of the work are named in a conventional note. (Editors for whom added entries are not to be made are not noted.) The following are considered to have such importance:

        a. Persons whose names are likely to be better known in relation to the work than the exact title of the work itself.

        b. Persons who have been associated with a publication (except minor works, such as house organs, student publications, etc.) throughout the lifetime of the serial or for a notably long period.

    2. The conventional note begins with the word "Editor" or "Compiler," or other appropriate designation, and shows the inclusive dates of the contribution of each person named.

    An informal statement is preferred to a conventional note in cataloging a work that has ceased publication and has had the same editor or group of editors throughout, or if an informal statement is more satisfactory for other reasons.

                                          AACR/NA.

Very few libraries make note of editors, except for very prominent people, such as H. L. Mencken, the example given in the "blue book." The argument is that people who really want to evaluate a person's editorship will go to the publication and look for themselves and not rely on notes made by a cataloger. However, prominent editors are another "handle" by which a publication can be grasped in the catalog and should not be eliminated if important or necessary for retrieval purposes. Surely the presence of a prominent person as editor in the history of a publication is too important an item in its description

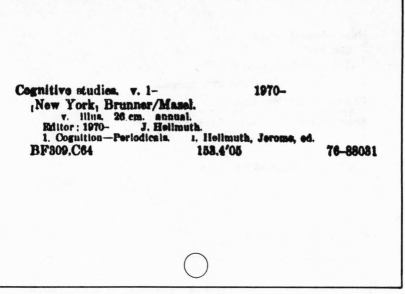

Fig. 6-30. Editor note.

to be ignored. To do so would be a grave neglect of a bibliographic duty. Note that the rules specifically say that not all editors should be so treated though.

P. Variations in imprint. Important variations in the place of publication, changes of publisher, and important variations in the name of the publisher are shown in notes. A change in place of publication is generally considered important if it also involves a change of publisher, if it occurs after a long period in the previous city, or if it transfers the publication to another country or region. A conventional note beginning with the phrase "Imprint varies" is generally used unless there has been but one change of place and publisher. An informal statement is used if the change is that of only the place or of the publisher, or if the change consists of an important variation in the name of the publisher.

AACR/NA.

Experimental review. v. 1–
Apr. 1940–
₁Woodstock, N. Y., etc:, 1940–

   v. in   plates. 22½-30ᵐ. irregular.

Title varies: Apr. 1040, Ritual.
  Nov. 1940–   Experimental review.
Editors: 1940–   Robert Symmes and others.

    1. Symmes, Robert, ed.

                                                      45–23125

The Nation, a weekly journal devoted to politics, literature,
science, drama, music, art, finance. v. 1–
July 6, 1865–
New York, J. H. Richards & co. ₁etc.₁ 1865–19

   v. 30½-3:ᵐ.

Editors: July 1865–1890, E. L. Godkin, W. P. Garrison.—   1899–June
1906, W. P. Garrison.—June 1906–May 1909, Hammond Lamont.—May
1909–Mar. 1914, P. E. More.—Mar. 1914–   H. de W. Fuller.
  Published by J. H. Richards & co., 1865–66; E. L. Godkin & co., 1866–
81; the New York evening post company, 1881–19
  1. Godkin, Edwin Lawrence, 1831–1902, ed. II. Garrison, Wendell
Phillips, 1840–1907, ed. III. Lamont, Hammond, 1864–1909, ed. IV. More,
Paul Elmer, 1864–1937. ed. V. Fuller, Harold de Wolf, 1874–   ed.

                                             4—12681

Fig. 6-31. Variations in imprint.

Compendio statistico della Somalia. Statistical abstract of
Somalia. no.   -5; 19
68. Mogadiscio. Statistical Department.

    no. in   v. 34 cm. annual.

English and Italian.
Continued by Somalia statistical abstract.

1. Somalia—Statistics.   I. Somalia. Statistical Dept.
II. Title: Statistical abstract of Somalia.

HA2167.S6A2   316.7'73   74–644533
                                                 MARC-S

Library of Congress   74 [2]

(a)

Faculty research journal. v. 1–
1974–
Raleigh, N. C.

    v. 26 cm. 2 no. a year.

    Vols. for 1974–   issued by the Research Committee of Saint
Augustine's College and the Research Committee of Voorhees College.
    Supersedes: Saint Augustine's College, Raleigh, N. C. Faculty re-
search journal.

    I. Saint Augustine's College, Raleigh, N. C. Research Committee.
II. Voorhees College. Research Committee.

AS36.S17A27   378.756'55   74–645837
ISSN 0094–758X   MARC-S

Library of Congress   74 [2]

(b)

Canada. Marine Sciences Branch. Pacific Region.
Annual report—Marine Sciences Branch, Pacific Region.
19 –71.
Victoria, B. C.

      v. illus. 28 cm. (Pacific marine science report)

      Continued by the publication with the same title issued by the agency under the later name of the branch: Marine Sciences Directorate.

      1. Oceanography—North Pacific Ocean—Periodicals. 2. Hydrography—North Pacific Ocean—Periodicals. 3. Ocean engineering—Periodicals. I. Series.

GC781.P32   subser   551.4'6'008 s   74–644776
                          354'.71'008232   MARC-S

Library of Congress   74 [2]

(c)

Fig. 6-32. Connections with later publications:
    (a) continuation
    (b) superseding publication
    [Note that (b) uses the correct form according to the update in the *Cataloging Service Bulletin.*]
    (c) continuation due to change in name of corporate body

This rule is self-evident. It is also one that is considered too fine a delineation in serials cataloging, and is often ignored or not updated.

Q. Connection with later publication. If a serial is continued, superseded, or absorbed by, or merged with, another publication, this fact is noted. If the library's holdings are not complete or if the change does not follow immediately after the publication of the last issue, the date of the action is indicated.

AACR/NA.

Much of the mechanics of successive entry have already been taken up in this chapter and elsewhere, so that, by now, there should not be much question about this section of the rules. To make things even clearer, reproduced below are two cards for the "before-and-after" publications of a continuous title.

The National maritime SAR review.

₍Washington, D. C., U. S. Coast Guard₎
    v. illus. 27 cm. quarterly.
    Continued by On scene.

    1. United States. Coast Guard—Search and rescue operations—
Periodicals.   I. United States. Coast Guard.

VK1323.N35   363.3′4   74–641541
ISSN 0047-8946   MARC-S

Library of Congress   74 ₍2₎

On scene. Jan. 1972–
 ₍Washington, D. C., U. S. Coast Guard₎
    v. illus. 24 cm. bimonthly.
    Continues the National maritime SAR review.

    1. United States. Coast Guard—Search and rescue operations—
Periodicals.   I. United States. Coast Guard.

VK1323.N35   363.3′4   74–641542
ISSN 0093-2124   MARC-S

Library of Congress   74 ₍2₎

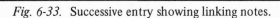

Fig. 6-33. Successive entry showing linking notes.

R. "No more published?" A note reading "No more published?" is added as the last note before the contents, if there is doubt as to whether or not the number designated as the last issue was in fact the final issue.

AACR/NA.

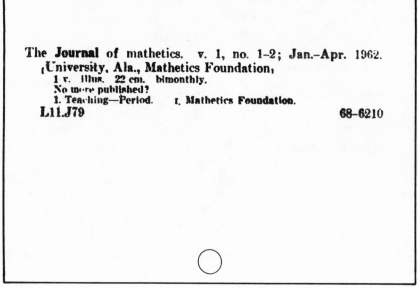

The **Journal** of mathetics. v. 1, no. 1–2; **Jan.–Apr.** 1962.
₁**University, Ala., Mathetics Foundation**₁
   1 v. illus. 22 cm. bimonthly.
   No more published?
   1. Teaching—Period.   ₁. Mathetics Foundation.
L11.J79   68–6210

Fig. 6-34. "No more published" note.

If the cataloger is sure that the publication has ceased, the question mark is unnecessary. This note is not used if the title is followed by some other title. Some libraries use the expression "Ceased publication."

S. Contents

1. Contents are not specified in the catalog entries for serials that consist of a sequence of monographs that are, or may be analyzed or that are relatively unimportant. Analyzed parts are represented by unit cards under the name of the series.

2. Notes concerning the inclusion of other serials in the contents are used to characterize the work as a whole, to indicate parts that are necessary for the completeness of the volumes, and to specify special items that are important enough to warrant added entries.

AACR/NA.

Florida. State Dept. of Education.
Community education: The Florida Community School
Act of 1970, report.
1971/72–
Tallahassee, State Dept. of Education.

v. ill. 28 cm. annual.

Report year ends June 30.
Vols. for 1971/72–1972/73 also contain an Interim progress report
for the succeeding year.
ISSN 0097-7438

1. Community schools—Florida. I. Title. II. Title: The Florida
Community School Act of 1970, report.

LB2820.F67a   379′.152′09759   75–640439
                                                                                        MARC-S

Library of Congress   75

The Journal of Roman studies. v. 1–   1911–
London, Society for the Promotion of Roman Studies.
v. illus., plates, maps, plans. 28 cm. semiannual.
Includes Proceedings of the society, report of the council, lists
of members, etc.
Vols. 13, 15–20, 22–29, 37 include Supplement v. 1–7, 8–16, 21 to the
Subject catalogue of the joint library; vols. 9–13, 15–20, 22–29, 37 in-
clude 6th, 8th–25th, 30th List of accessions to the catalogue of slides.
INDEXES:
Vols. 1–20, 1911–30 (Issued as v. 20, pt. 2)
Vols. 21–40, 1931–50. 1 v.
1. Rome—Antiq.—Period. 2. Inscriptions, Latin. 3. Rome—Hist.—
Period.
DG11.J7   26–2981 rev*

Fig. 6-35. Notes for contents.

The first part of the rule, that which covers analytics, is more fully discussed in Chapter 9 of this text. The old method of adding analytics to contents cards has proved an effective cover-up for a considerably large number of important works in libraries across the country and it is really a monumental step forward to have discontinued it.

Contents notes may be interpreted to cover accompanying materials such as recordings or other audiovisual materials. If such a note is called for, mention should also be made of the location of this material, if it is not to be shelved with the bound volumes. See also Chapter 10 of this book for procedures covering multimedia serials. Supplements will be covered in the next chapter, which will also include such things as serials within serials or special issues like directories.

Contents notes may also contain notes indicating the scope and nature of the work, like:"Minutes of its sessions."

It is always helpful to indicate to readers if the journal being cataloged includes bibliographic references; review material: book reviews, film or performance reviews, reviews of recordings, etc.; or bibliographies, filmographies, discographies, etc. — if this is substantial to the journal or important in the field. The Library of Congress does not usually do this, which is unfortunate, for many libraries, especially academic ones, would find it of value. Often their catalogers will add such notes.

Other notes may be employed, if desired, depending on the situation. The following is a discussion of some of these, although it makes no attempt to be a complete listing. It would depend on the situation being covered, and the policies of the library concerned, where these would come in the outline of notes.

If the library does not use the rule for entry of a serial under personal author, there will need to be a note of this personal author so that he can be traced. Because such a note reflects an alternative form of entry, it would probably be a good idea to make such a note early on in the notes section, perhaps even the first one, depending on the publication.

Although not specified adequately in the rules for serials, LC obviously felt it necessary to indicate the language of the text of the serial shown on the next page.

Summaries in one language for articles in another is often a useful note.

Another note which would be highly desirable would be one indicating that the serial being described is a translation of another serial. *Radiophysics,* for example, might be described as "Translated from the Russian periodical Radiofizika."

Irish folk music studies. Éigse cheol tíre. v. 1–
1972/73–
₍Dublin, Folk Music Society of Ireland₎

    v. 22 cm. annual.

    English or Irish.

    1. Folk music, Irish—Collected works.   I. Folk Music Society of
Ireland. II. Title: Éigse cheol tíre.

ML3654.I 7   781.7′415   74–648187
                                             MARC-S

Library of Congress   75 ₍2₎   MN

Fig. 6-36. Language of serial note.

Bucharest. Universitatea.
Analele Universitaţii Bucureşti: psihologie.

₍Bucureşti₎

    v. 25 cm. annual.

    Romanian with summaries in French and Russian.

    1. Psychology—Periodicals.   I. Title.

BF8.R7B8a   74–644059
                                             MARC-S

Library of Congress   74 ₍2₎

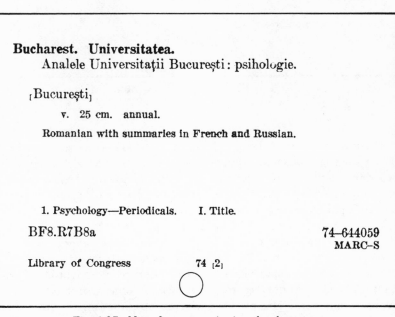

Fig. 6-37. Note for summaries in other languages.

A tracing should be made to make this fact an access point as well. The following is a Library of Congress card. The note is made, but unfortunately the added entry is not. Libraries, particularly libraries with both titles, would find this added entry of use.

Shipbuilding.
Warsaw, Foreign Scientific Publications Dept., National Center for Scientific, Technical and Economic Information.
  v. illus. 24 cm. monthly.
Translation of Budownictwo okrętowe.
  Vols. for   "published for the U. S. National Marine Fisheries Service, National Oceanic and Atmospheric Administration, U. S. Dept. of Commerce, and the National Science Foundation, Washington, D. C."
  Vols. for   available from the National Technical Information Service, Springfield, Va.
  1. Ship-building—Periodicals.   I. United States. National Marine Fisheries Service. II. United States. National Science Foundation. III. National Center for Scientific, Technical and Economic Information. Foreign Scientific Publications Dept.

VM4.S448   73–648133
                                                       MARC-S
Library of Congress   74 ₍2₎

○

Fig. 6-38. Note for a translation.

Note that this is not to be used for another edition of the same serial in a foreign language, which is a different case entirely and usually noted in the main entry, with perhaps notes such as: "Also published in French and German editions." Such translations as discussed here are usually done by special translation publishers, not the original publisher. Note the example.

The title of a publication which is not in the Roman alphabet, and which has a card typed in the appropriate alphabet, should have a note for transliterated or Romanized title, so that the card can be more easily merged with Roman alphabet files. Rule 150 provided for such a note at the lower right-hand corner of the card and many libraries still put it there. In order to facilitate machine processing, however, LC has put the title at the top of the card in curves.

Социалистическая индустрия.

₍Москва₎

    no. illus., ports. 60 cm. daily.

"Газета Центрального комитета КПСС."
Began in 1969.

    1. Russia—Industries—1957-   —Periodicals.   I. Kommunisti-
cheskaȋa partiȋa Sovetskogo Soȋuza. TSentral'nyĭ Komitet.
                Title romanized: Sotsialisticheskaȋa industriȋa.

HC331.S495   73–648573

Library of Congress   71 ₍2₎

(Vyzantina)
Βυζαντινά.
Θεσσαλονίκη.

    v. 25 cm. annual.

    Organ of the Kentron Vyzantinōn Ereunōn of Philosophikēs
Scholēs of Aristoteleiou Panepistēmiou Thessalonikēs.
    English, French, Greek or Spanish.

    1. Byzantine Empire—Civilization—Collected works.   . Thes-
salonike. Panepistēmion. Kentron Vyzantinōn Ereunōn.

DF503.V97   74–644915
                                   (MARC-S)

Library of Congress   75 ₍2₎

Fig. 6-39. Transliterated title notes.

Notes may also be needed to clarify the conditions surrounding a publication's state of being. The next note indicates that the publication is a supplement to another publication. Sometimes history statements have to be written explaining that a publication was issued inside something else, but is now a separate publication. This one, however, has always been separate, although issued together with the *Guide*.

Directory of State, county, and Federal officials. 1973–

Honolulu, Legislative Reference Bureau.

v. 28 cm. annual.

Continues the publication with the same title issued by the bureau when it was a part of the University of Hawaii.
Vols. for 1973–   issued as a supplement to the Guide to government in Hawaii.

1. Hawaii—Registers.   I. Hawaii.   Legislative Reference Bureau.   II. Guide to government in Hawaii.

JK9330.H38a   353.9′969′002   74–644932
ISSN 0440–4947   MARC–S

Library of Congress   74 ₍2₎

Fig. 6-40. Note indicating publication is a supplement to another publication.

For further discussion of supplements, see the following chapter.

It may be that notes are needed to indicate the extent of a publication in terms of volumes or parts, since it is usually assumed that a publication comes out in one piece per volume, unless the contrary is indicated, as shown.

Librarians may wish to characterize a publication further by such physical description as "Mimeographed." This is really an unnecessary and trivial detail, although it was probably useful when pagination was given in terms of leaves, as, perhaps, with analytics. It is an unnecessary piece of description.

Government publications and special technical reports, such as those put out by the Rand Corporation, may be restricted in their circulation. Libraries may wish to make note of this fact so that patrons will understand that some issues may be unavailable to them, or at least unavailable without special clearance. Notes may be like those which follow.

Kuala Lumpur. Pesurohjaya.
   Laporan tahunan—Pesurohjaya Ibu Kota Kuala Lumpur.
19   –69. ₍Kuala Lumpur₎

   v. 27 cm.

   Reports for 19   –69 published in 2 parts.
   Continued by its Lapuran tahunan.

   1. Kuala Lumpur—Politics and government—Periodicals.

JS33.K8K84a   74–645175
                                               MARC-S

Library of Congress   75

Fig. 6-41. Note indicating several parts per volume.

For use by the U.S. armed forces only. Not for sale.
Issues for April 1944 — March 1946 are "secret" or "restricted."

Sometimes a library may have a title with lacks that cannot be filled in except by another edition of the publication. If the desire is to keep these together as one set, rather than as two distinct bibliographic entities, a note should be made to explain the situation. This is quite often the case with reprints, which may have elaborate explanations in the introduction about how difficult it was to get a perfect set, how after much perusal of libraries, this was the best they could do, etc., etc., etc. While not specified as a needed note in the rules, such a note is necessary to describe adequately a given situation.

The Library of Congress may have cataloged a series as a monographic series when it first started as a series on a number of diverse topics. However, the title may have changed character, as discussed in the chapter on monographic series. Rather than recataloging the older issues as a serial so that they will stand with the newer issues, which have become more serial-like, LC will make a note indicating that the older issues were individually treated. Below is an example of such a note. It would be best for smaller libraries to recatalog the older volumes in such a situation.

Bremer archäologische Blätter. 5–
Bremen, in Kommission bei R. Habelt Verlag, 1969–

 no. illus. 27 cm.

Earlier no. classified separately in L. C.

  1. Europe—Antiquities—Periodicals.

D80.B85   913.36′03′05   73–642563
                        MARC-S

Library of Congress   74 ⌊2⌋

Fig. 6-42. LC note for earlier numbers classified separately.

Below are two examples of how the Library of Congress treats reprints.

Ça ira. no 1–20; avril 1920–jan. 1923. Bruxelles, J. Antoine, 1973.

 256, 210 p. ill. 25 cm.

Reprint, with an introduction, of a periodical published in Antwerp.

  1. Arts—Periodicals.

NX2.C22   700′.5   75–641414
                         MARC-S

Library of Congress   75

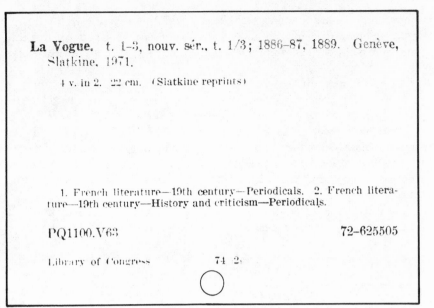

La Vogue. t. 1-3, nouv. sér., t. 1/3; 1886–87, 1889. Genève, Slatkine, 1971.

4 v. in 2. 22 cm. (Slatkine reprints)

1. French literature—19th century—Periodicals. 2. French literature—19th century—History and criticism—Periodicals.

PQ1100.V63   72–625505

Library of Congress   74 2)

Fig. 6-43. LC cards for reprints of serials.

A lot of libraries prefer to catalog reprints as the original, however, including the original imprint in its normal place. A note, "Library has reprint edition," is made. It is felt that the patron would miss the identifying imprint information if it appeared later on on the card and that it is better to sacrifice bibliographic niceties and absolute accuracy according to the rules for usefulness. The patron rarely cares that the publication is a reprint and doesn't normally look for either reprint publishers or reprint series. Libraries following this procedure don't usually include the reprint series and those who do very rarely trace it for serial material. Extra introductory matter or criticism and commentary which appear as footnotes or afterpieces are included in the note for the reprint edition, in a similar manner to that used by LC in the first example.

A serial which has some volumes in reprint editions may need such a note. If the serial is still continuing, or if the backfile is incomplete, there is no need to try to pin down which volumes are reprints, since these may change. If the serial is ceased or complete to date, the volumes in reprint may be specified if desired, although there is very little real need for such notes. "Library has some volumes in reprint editions" should suffice.

Although this is a deviation from LC- and AACR-authorized practice, this author feels that such a procedure is more in keeping with rules for serials, and with the practical workings of serials departments, and recommends it over the more cumbersome and monographlike authorized procedure, which relegates more important serial identification factors to notes. It will be noticed that this procedure is also the basic one for microforms and other formats, discussed later on.

A single reprinted issue of a periodical (if not the only one issued) or of a newspaper should be considered a monograph. This should also be the treatment for reprinted or offprinted articles from journals. Added entries should be made for the journal involved, but in no way should this be considered part of a journal run, since the emphasis is now on the monographic entity of the article itself. A collection of articles extracted from several issues of a journal is not part of the journal run either, even though the specific issues can be identified.

The International Standard Serial Number (ISSN) came out after the 1967 rules, so its use does not appear in the printed rules. The ISBD(S) calls for the area which contains this information to be the last one on the bibliographic record. LC has been using this note on all its recent cards, as shown.

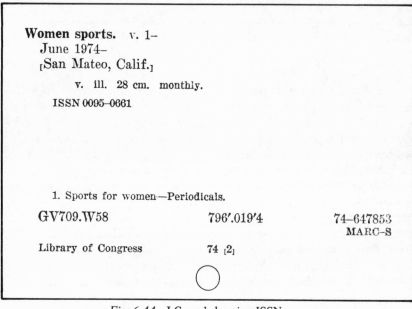

Fig. 6-44. LC card showing ISSN.

Additional notes may be required for supplements, indexes and other matter. These will be covered in the next chapter, since their existence may extend beyond that of mere description.

All the examples that have just appeared have been chosen merely to illustrate the rules a little more fully and to amplify those examples which appear in the text of the "blue book" itself. Cards have been used because most catalogers find these more helpful in order to see the relationships of various elements of bibliographic information. There are many books of illustrations of cards that have come out over the past few years to illustrate the rules, and the reader is encouraged to explore some of these for further illustration by consulting the bibliography to this volume.

For further examples of notes, the reader is directed to the fine compilation by Ruth Schley and Jane B. Davies entitled *Serials Notes compiled from Library of Congress cards issued 1947 - April 1951.* (1952). Although old and published to complement the *RDC,* it still illustrates the serials description found in part II of the AACR. The examples are very comprehensive, rather than selected, as here, and give a good overview to the kinds of notes used, with directives on order, etc. Because of the comprehensiveness, the neophyte is guided tremendously in the conventional wording of such notes.

And to test one's skill in cataloging, one should really tackle the Gordian knots in Johanna Tallman's article on "The Family of 'Electronics World'" in *Title Varies* (v. 1, no. 5, pp. 29, 31-33, September 1974). Truly a challenge for the composition of notes and the connecting of many links! Building up to this task, one should peruse Osborn (1973, Chapter 11) for a half-dozen case studies of descriptive cataloging of serials.

It will be useful to interject a statement about the rules right here, since we are talking about catalog cards. The AACR has been accused of not having enough consideration for automated methods, which would seem to be a valid argument. However, the MARC projects and other automated projects have shown that the AACR has been used in bibliographies, too. It would be foolish to limit a cataloging code to only one medium. Because of this, the editors of the first edition of AACR put the examples in a free format. They did not use catalog cards, although there are some vestiges of this when you see the corner lines in the section on references. This lapse into formatting will be eradicated in the next edition, making the code as universal as possible. The use of catalog cards here is not an attempt to limit the code in any way. It is hoped that catalogers who work with card formats, as so many of us still do, will find this useful. Those who work with computer catalogs or other formats hopefully will be able to abstract the rules from the card format enough to be able to work with the rules and interpretations found here.

One of the major criticisms of Chapter 7 of the rules has been that it is much too detailed for normal library use. As remarked all through this chapter in the discussion of the rules, there are considerable shortcuts that are taken. The librarians who do this argue that from practical aspects it is better to simplify. They feel that this helps their patrons. This is questionable, however, when it comes to a problem of identification.

The advocates of shortcuts also feel that absolute up-to-the-minute cataloging can only be had on the central serial record and that it cannot be adequately recorded in the catalog. To a point this is true, but the catalog entry should give adequate direction for the check-in and processing of current issues, including whether supplementary material should be checked-in or sent elsewhere; tell what to do with variant titles or subtitles or issues without titles, or the like; tell which numbering should be considered predominent for marking or binding, etc. Current specifics and handling directives can be covered by notes in the central serial record, which is also the master list of holdings, and in these ways the record is an extension of the catalog. However, for the major changes that will affect all records, catalog notes should also be made. Later on in this book, methods for doing this will be discussed.

There is also the argument that, since there are serial bibliographies like *ULS, NST, BUCOP,* etc., there is no need to do all of this detailed work, for it will be found there. The problem is, if adequate cataloging is not done, the researcher has no way of knowing if the title he has found is the right one. The problem becomes one of insufficient information for proper identification. This will be alleviated to some degree by the arrival of the ISSN, but it will still be necessary to provide adequate description for identification and retrieval purposes. Besides, if the contributing libraries were to back out of their bibliographic duties, *NST* would not be an adequate reference tool. The rationale upon which this argument is built can easily crumble, for it would become part of a vicious circle that feeds on itself.

There is still a need to standardize, and this is not fulfilled if some libraries try to be complete and others not. Cataloging records for serials should be as complete as possible. This is necessary for proper identification and complete compatability of records. It is needed for proper reference assistance and patron service. It provides for as complete a bibliographic description as possible to give direction to serials workers in one's own shop as well as to others through union lists, cooperative cataloging, and other ventures. It can only be through our own efforts that such tools as *NST* can be proper bibliographic reference works and cooperative projects such as CONSER (see Chapter 18) can survive.

Serials work is becoming more detailed and involved than it ever has before, for libraries are no longer cataloging for themselves alone, but for their neighbors as well; and any serials librarian who does not recognize that fact is indeed living like an ostrich with his head in the sand. At long last, it is being decided that it is foolish to reinvent the wheel all across the country when it comes to each individual serial problem. In the past, there were dreams of centralized cataloging and cooperation, but these dreams never materialized, partially because they were too "pie-in-the-sky," with little in the way of proper mechanics and architecture to support them, and partially because librarians were leery of accepting each others' cataloging, particularly if it didn't come "up to snuff." These attitudes are changing significantly, for even the Library of Congress is willing to accept the serial cataloging of other CONSER participants. The computer offers the mechanical means for making the dreams come true. Now it is up to serials catalogers across the country to do the best they can to provide up-to-snuff cataloging. This should be a matter of course when the new International Standard for Bibliographic Description for Serials, the ISBD(S) (see Chapter 18), is adopted and incorporated in the AACR. The handwriting is already on the wall and this standard is likely to be adopted in the near future for serials after a few modifications are made. The monographic one is, of course, already in effect and is being practiced by libraries across the country. It is interesting to note that much of the detail, so abhorred by critics of the AACR, is still being retained by the ISBD(S). It is obvious that we must continue to use it for the betterment of our bibliographic control of serials.

> The essence of standardized cataloging is widespread availability and generalized acceptance of the data. . .The national structure for communicating standard cataloging data today is mainly printed tools, but tomorrow local library terminals on-line to a shared computer data bank may provide the instantaneous access needed.[8]

Serials cataloging and serials catalogers must be ready for the call which is already sounding. Serials are much too important to be lost in the massive shuffle of data.

FOOTNOTES

1. Beatrice V. Simon, "Cataloguing of periodicals," *Ontario library review* 33 (August, 1949): 241.

2. Sarah S. Dickinson, "Idiocyncrasies of periodicals," *Catalogers' and Classifiers' Yearbook* 2 (1931): 97.

3. *The Green revolution* 12 (Summer, 1974): 3.

4. Dickinson, "Idiocyncrasies", p. 95.

5. *Title varies* 2 (May, 1975): 19.

6. *Cataloging service bulletin* 112 (Winter, 1975): 13.

7. Dickinson, "Idiocyncrasies", p. 95.

8. Stanley D. Truelson "The need to standardize descriptive cataloging," *Bulletin of the Medical Library Association* 57 (January, 1969): 21.

Chapter VII

Supplementary Material

Publishers may send out "extra added attractions" to the serial itself. These must be processed in the Serials Department in an appropriate manner. The cataloger should make the decisions on such matters, or at least be consulted on the best treatment.

First of all, there are supplements. These are covered by rule 168:

168. Supplements.

    A. Serial publications may be accompanied by supplements that are monographic or that are themselves serial publications. The former, if important, are described in the same manner as supplements to monographic publications (See 155). The latter may be described in a similar manner with a "dash" entry, but following the cataloging rules for serial publications. If they are likely to be known as independent works, or if they are to be classified separately, they are cataloged as independent entries.[6]

    B. Irregular and unnumbered as well as unimportant supplements *are noted* informally.

(6)If an independent entry is required for a supplement with a title dependent on that of the main work. . . . the entries would read as follows:

Verein Deutscher Ingenieur.
  Zeitschrift. Beihefte Verfahrenstechnik. . .
Blätter fur Volksbibliotheken und
  Lesehallen. Ergänzungshefte.

[Rule 155 prescribes dash entries in which the supplements may be described in detail. They may also be noted briefly, and even be included in contents listings. These rules are analogous to the ones listed here for serials.]

AACR / NA.

Although still in the rules, it would seem that libraries are moving away from dash entries. Since the MARC format cannot handle such entries, the CCRC has voted to have the provisions for dash entries stricken from the rules. LC uses dash-ons only for issues and photoreproductions. Real supplements are awarded full cataloging entries now.

Important monographic supplements received on serial orders should be sent to a reviewer — whether it be a language or subject specialist, a department head, a reference librarian, a collection development officer, or a committee — for review as a candidate to enter the collection on its own merit. Upon its acceptance, the volume should be cataloged on its own merit as a monographic publication. As a general rule of thumb on these decisions, the following is pretty good advice:

Monograph supplements [,] Festscrift volumes, and other individual items issued as addenda to an issue or a volume, should be completely analyzed and appear in the catalog as separate entries. . . (Simon, August 1949, p. 242).

Notes should be made that the publication is a supplement to a serial work, if this is stated in the book. Serial records should state that the supplement was received and was sent for review as a monograph. The note should not be all-inclusive so that mail checkers will simply follow it blindly. Supplements may vary and each should be judged by itself. The next supplement may well be the start of another serial publication.

Dash entries can be made for serial supplements as well as for monographic ones. Here is an example:

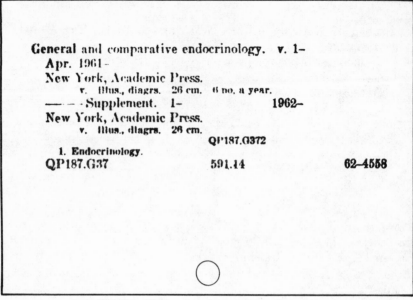

Fig. 7-1. Dash entry for serial supplement.

The trend is to move away from such practices, however, as already mentioned. The rules provide for separate entries if the supplement is to be treated in its own right, which is what most libraries should do. This is the current practice at LC.

Another problem with the use of dash-ons is that serials can be dashed-on to cataloging for monographs and vice versa. This may put the serials department in the bad situation of having to control monographic material. This is not desirable and most serials catalogers have preferred making separate entries. It is a good thing that dash-ons are on their way out.

The serial supplement should be judged on its own merit, just as the monograph was, through the normal library mechanism for serial selection and review. If it is a monographic series, as so many of them are, it should be further judged as to analytical entries, or perhaps catalog-as-separate treatment. If the decision is made to keep the publication as an additional serial, a separate card set should be made for it, as below:

Bureau of National Affairs, Washington, D. C. Tax Management.
 Tax management—primary sources. Supplement.

Washington.

  no. 28 cm. monthly.

  1. Income tax—United States—Law.   I. Title.

KF6365.B872   343′.73′052   74–646258
                                             MARC–S

Library of Congress   74 [2]

Fig. 7-2. Separate cataloging for a serial supplement.

This is the treatment which the Library of Congress accords this kind of material now, as indicated in the following rule interpretation, issued January 1972:

> *AA168. Supplements, etc.* Serials which would normally be dashed on to a serial or a monograph will be given independent entries by the serials descriptive cataloger and an added entry will be made for the work it supplements. If these publications have a dependent title, the independent entry will follow the provisions in footnote 6.

The description which is put on the card is for the supplement, not the parent title. Notes are not usually necessary to tie the supplement to the parent title, because this is pretty generally inherent in the supplement's title: "Supplement," "Beiheft," etc. If this information cannot be gained from the title, however, it should be included as a note. (See *Fig. 6-40*). Notes may be necessary to explain numbering or some other area of description, but this is in keeping with the serial rules anyway.

Sometimes a publication is related to another one because it is issued as its supplement, perhaps only for a short time. If it has been decided to treat this title separately and the title does not show the relationship, notes should be made to describe the relationship, as indicated above. The *American Foundation news* started out as a supplement, and then became a more substantial publication in its own right. The card should bear a note like this:

> Issued June 1949-Sept. 1951 by Raymond Rich Associates as a supplement to American foundations and their fields.

A classic example is the monographic series, *Memoirs of the American Archaeological Society*, which is issued as no. 2 part 2 of every volume of *American antiquity* since volume 7. This is a series which should be analyzed. Rather than making duplicate added entry cards when analyzing for each series, a shortcut can be taken by making a note on the card for the series explaining the relationship of the two series, complete with numbering. The patron can be served without cluttering up the catalog.

> Issued as supplement to American antiquity v. 7– 1941/42–
> Called no. 2 part 2 of each volume.

Unimportant supplements can be briefly described in notes. These would be unnumbered supplements, or they would bear some numbering relevant to the parent title, like ''Supplement to v.4.'' Notes might read something like this:

> Supplements accompany some numbers.
> Vol. 7 accompanied by separately paged supplements.
> Includes supplements.
> Vols. 16-21 include supplement: British empire vegetation abstracts.

The LC cataloger who cataloged the title with the last example as a note did not feel that it was even important enough to give an added entry to the supplement. It would probably be a good idea to make such an added entry, particularly since the supplement is an abstract. In another library, it might be decided to catalog this as a separate entry.

Another variety of accompanying material is the special number, covered by rule 169:

> 169. Special numbers.
>
> > Special numbers of serial publications present, as such, no particular problem of description. They are cataloged as separate works, with the relationship to the regular numbers shown, cataloged with analytical entries, or simply noted informally. If they are to be shelved with the regular numbers and are of minor importance, they may be disregarded.

AACR/NA

Each special number should be reviewed on its own merits, as in previous cases of received-with material, to decide which form of treatment should be given to it. It would probably be best to treat all special numbers of one serial title in the same manner, so as not to confuse the patron unduly, but this would depend on the individual interests and policies of the libraries involved.

The decision to treat both supplements, especially monographic supplements, and special issues, separately might well be tempered by what the index to the publication says. There is a stronger affinity with the serial publication if the supplement or special number is indexed in the serial. In this case, it should generally be decided that the publication in question should be put with the serial. Analytics can be made for these, if desired. Special numbers on a particular topic, but still retaining the running numbering of the set should generally not be extracted from the set, and certainly not without adequate explanations all around if this is done. Similarly, if extra material mentioned in the table of contents or index is extracted, a note should be made on the serial records and in the volume itself.

Another curious problem with serials is the partially dependent title issued inside a parent work. An example is the *School library journal,* which used to appear as a section bound in the *Library journal.* If it were not for an added complexity, this journal could have been extracted from *LJ* and cataloged as a separate entity. This, however, was not possible because the title bore not only its own pagination, but also that of *LJ.* Since the title could not practicably be extracted, one had to settle for a contents note and an added entry even though the title obviously was meant to be a separate publication. Since it has now broken out, as others have done, and is a separate publication in its own right, notes referring to its history as part of *LJ* are necessary.

Special issues may be important enough to require separate entries and notes and added entries linking them to the parent work, even though they actually are a part of that work. Examples might be the MeSH issue of *Index medicus* or the California Library Association Directory issue of the *California librarian.* This problem is discussed as a special aspect of the location chapter and of the analytics chapter. Although not specifically supplementary in nature, it is fitting that the problem be mentioned here as well.

One of the major problem addenda to serial publications is the index. Indexes are covered in AACR by rule 170:

170. Indexes.

> Indexes to single volumes of serial publications are not recorded. Other indexes are cataloged with the set which they index. They are normally recorded in a conventional, tabular form, or in an informal note or by a combination of the two. When more detailed description of an index is required, the provisions of 155A[*] may be applied. The information given

for each index includes some kind or all of the following items, and in this order:

a) Kind of index, i.e. author, subject, chronological, etc.
b) Volumes or numbers of the serial indexed.
c) Dates of the serial indexed.
d) Location of the index in the set, i.e. "in" if it is included in the paging of an issue, "with" if separately paged, or unpaged, and bound with a volume.
e) Statement of number of volumes of the index if not "in" or "with" a volume of the set.
f) Size of the index if it varies from the size of the set.[*]
g) Other miscellaneous bibliographical data, such as the volume and number of the issue of the serial if the index comprises a whole number, or the number to which the index is a supplement. Compilers of indexes are not ordinarily noted.

B. An informal note is used for a single index to a serial that has ceased publication and in other cases if the tabular form is impractical.

[*155A calls for dash entries. Few libraries record size of periodicals.]

AACR/NA.

Indexes can be indicated by dash entries, as provided for in the reference to rule 155.

Journal of nuclear medicine. v. 1–
    Jan. 1960–
    [Chica o. etc., S. N. Turiel]
        v. in   illus., ports. 26 cm.
    Frequency varies.
    Official publication of the Society of Nuclear Medicine.
————KWIC index to the Journal of nuclear medicine. [v.
1/8]–   1960/67–
    Rockville, Md., National Center for Radiological Health.
        v. 26 cm. (Public Health Service Publication)
                            RM845.J7812
    1. Radiology, Medical—Periodicals.   I. Society of Nuclear Medi-
cine. II. U. S. National Center for Radiological Health.   (Series.: U. S. Public Health   ice. Publication)
    RM845.J78   616.07'57'05   64–6090

Fig. 7-3. Card showing dash entry for an index.

However, dash entries are being used less and less today due to economy measures. (It is very expensive for LC and other libraries to recatalog a title each time an index is added.) The fact that automated catalogs cannot cope with dash entries also provides some of the impetus.

Catalogers of serials today tend to lean more toward the note approach for indicating indexes. Here are some examples of index notes, first in tabular form and then as informal notes:

INDEXES:

> vols. 1-9, 1882-90, with v. 9.
> vols. 10-15, 1891-95, in v. 16, no. 1.
> vols. 1-20, 1882-1900, 1v.

INDEXES:

> Author index.
>> vols. 1-6, 1915-21 (suppl. to v. 6) with v. 6.
> Subject index.
>> vols. 1-6, 1915-21 (Its Bulletin, no. 14) 1v.
> General index.
>> vols. 1-10, 1915-24, 1v. 28cm.

Includes index.
No. 158 constitutes index to no. 1-156.
Quinquennial indexes, 1925– .
Annual index in no. 1 of next year's volume.

Cumulative indexes should be noted on the catalog card when they are bound. Each one should be added, even if there is some overlap. It is also suggested that indexes, superseded by indexes for longer periods of time, such as a ten-year index, followed by a twenty-five year index covering that ten years plus more, should not be discarded. Volumes often get lost and the shorter index will at least suffice for some of the volumes. Indexes received at regular intervals do not need to be listed individually on the card. This can be taken care of in notes, like the notes above for the annual and quinquennial examples. Notes should be brief, but also as clear as possible.

Indexes which cover more than is in the volume should be noted on the spine of a volume, unless the issue is a numbered issue of the title. Then, the notes should suffice so as not to clutter the spine with lengthy explanations in order not to be misleading. Thus, index notes are very important.

Successive entry was hailed as a boon for the cataloger, getting him out from under piles of work. It really is an easier way of doing things, in most cases, but it can be the cause of knotty problems when it comes to indexes. Indexes which cover more than one title can cause something of a sticky problem, and this situation is very often caused by successive entry cataloging.

If the index is not too lengthy — say, in the vicinity of fifty pages — it might be xeroxed and bound with both titles it indexes. Or, another copy might be solicited from the publisher. Thus, the sticky problem is avoided.

If, however, the index is beyond the possibility of photoreproduction, notes should be made on the catalog cards and other appropriate records: central serial record, serials holding list or catalog, etc. These notes should be explicit, yet succinct. One title, usually the one indexed the most, is chosen as the main one as far as the index is concerned. The index is shelved with this title. The cards for this title can simply have a straight index note. The other title(s) indexed should have notes like:

> Index for [vols. 1-20] is bound with [vol. 70] of [title index is shelved with, give call number for this title.]

This is advisable over the examples given in the rules:

> Index included with that to v. 5-8 of the journal under its later title.
>
> Index to v. 3-4 included with that to v. 5-6 of the journal under its later title.
>
> Indexed in the index of v. 1-25 of the Mennonite quarterly review.

By the suggested note, the patron is given not only a clue as to why he must look elsewhere, but he is also given the place to look. He does not have to interpret the card, looking for the later or earlier title, and he does not have to search again for the call number for this title. The note is really a whole lot clearer.

Indexes also bring up other problems not in the text of the rules. For example, what should be done with indexes published separately — that is, by a different publisher? This index can be considered *the* index to the publication, particularly if there is no other index. This violates the bibliographic integrity of both publications, making purists cringe, but it is the most practical approach. If, however, the decision has not been made to treat this index as a subsidiary to the publication it indexes, notes can be made to see a certain call number for the index, which has been treated as a separate monograph. For indexes which do not cover all of the material in a serial title but only selected articles, such as the fiction in *The New Yorker*, this is the only answer. The index will either have a main or added entry for the periodical it indexes so the patron will find it in the catalog. However, it would behoove the serials cataloger to review all such indexes after they are cataloged for appropriate notes to assist the patron and to append to the central serial record and other serial records for help in serials reference work. The same treatment would be suggested for all of the *Vestnik* publications of Moscow University which were indexed in a single monograph that could not appropriately stand with any single one of the umpty-odd *Vestniki.*

Some indexes, of course, are serials in their own right. *Palmers' index to the Times* is a separately-published and nonofficial index to the London *Times.* This could be treated as the subsidiary index to the *Times,* except that there is also an official one, which should take precedence. The solution in this case is to treat both separately from the thing they index. This is also reasonable since the "indexee" is a newspaper and probably not cataloged anyway. This is a wise decision, too, because both indexes are reference tools in their own rights, quite apart from being newspaper indexes. All of this entitles them to separate treatment on their own.

The index to the *New York times* is also a serial, and a reference work in its own right. The Library of Congress cataloged it as follows:

The **New York times** index for the published news. The master key to the news. v. 1–
Jan./Feb./Mar. 1913–
New York, New York Times Co. ₍etc.₎

    v. in   26–29 cm.

    Quarterly, 1913–29; monthly with annual cumulations (1930 has also quarterly cumulations) 1930–47; semimonthly with annual cumulations, 1948–
    Title varies slightly.

    1. Newspapers—Indexes.   2. Indexes.

AI 21.N44   13—13458*

Library of Congress   ₍56r52e1₎

                               ◯

Fig. 7-4. Serial index to newspaper.

"Bound-withs" happen very rarely in serials. Let it suffice here simply to quote rule 171 regarding this phenomenon. The reader is referred to pages 245-246 of the AACR for appropriate examples, if needed.

171. "Bound withs"

A. If a second serial or a monograph is bound with a serial and cataloged separately, it is mentioned in the catalog entry for the serial in a "bound with" note. The form of this note varies from the form of note used in cataloging two monographs bound together, because of the necessity for showing exactly where the second publication is located, and, if the second publication is a serial, the issues of it that are included. For the same reasons the corresponding note in the entry for the monograph or the second serial varies from the form used in cataloging a work bound with a monographic publication.

B. The "bound with" notes consist of the name of the author of the serial (if any) in catalog entry form, brief title, size if it varies two or more centimeters from the size of the other work, and the specific issues contained in the work. If the serial cited in the note is entered under title, the dates covered by the volumes are also included in the note.

AACR/NA.

Once in awhile reprints will appear on the scene of several serials together, such as the reprint of the two avant-garde periodicals *Work* and *Wh'ere,* but usually this problem is confined to older publications, not often encountered.

One of the real problems of the past was that serials used to contain other serials within their covers. Fortunately, this is no longer such a big problem. Sarah Dickinson describes the hair-raising experience of such added attractions:

I wonder how many of you who care for periodicals, have the complications I have always had, due to the various paginations. So many of the foreign journals delight in wheels within wheels; — periodical after periodical, all inside of the one which bears on its cover a simple name like *British Journal of Photography, Chemiker-Zeitung, Elektrotechnischie* [sic] *Anzeiger, Deutsche landwirtschaftliche Presse, Journal of Botany, Revista de Archivos, Bibliotecas y museos*—and dozens of others. This method of publishing half a dozen journals together, under one cover, and books within periodicals, is one of the heaviest taxes on our time, patience and accuracy. For at the Crerar, it must all start right from the periodical room, all the sections be separated, and sent in the right direction. The English *Journal of Botany,* for instance, has since 1902, issued twenty-two different booklets, as separate paginations in the *Journal* — a few pages at a time, a single book sometimes running for several years. You can easily comprehend the care needed to avoid mistakes.

Der Praktische Maschinen Konstrukteur of Leipzig had at one time five regular separate journals in its insides, — all cataloged with different call numbers. And as for the Spanish library journal *Revista de Archivos* — words fail me. I have already puzzled over twenty-seven different supplements, some of which have been running for sixteen years, and have neither beginning nor ending. Of course they did all *start* sometime, though owing to an unfortunate gap in our files, I can't tell *when;* and apparently some of them are never going to end.

So far as I know, it is only the technical journals that do this particular thing; but I can't tell how many of that sort are on our list. (Dickinson, 1931, pp. 95-96).

In this case, the journals should be extracted and a note probably should be put on the checking card indicating that all such journals are cataloged separately. Proper guidance needs to be given to the check-in staff, and this is one of the ways the serials cataloger can help out in the Serials Department.

The cataloger is cautioned that this chapter concerned itself primarily with publications issued with, or subsidiary to, other publications. Publications received with a subscription or a membership do not necessarily fall into any one of the aforementioned categories. Each publication received in this manner, as, indeed, every serial publication received in the library, should be reviewed for cataloging purposes on its own merit. The guidelines given here are only sketchy for it is here that the cataloger must trust to the policies and procedures of his individual library and to a lot of good old common sense!

Chapter VIII

Classification and Subject Cataloging

Nonmonographic serials, it has been said, are approached only through indexes. Thus, it is a waste of time to classify them or give them broad and meaningless subject headings. This is indeed an unfortunate attitude. Not all serials are indexed, for one thing, and not everyone looks for the indexes, or even knows that they exist, for another. You would be eliminating access even to these indexes by eliminating your basic subject approaches, for most indexes are serials. These two subject approaches are basic to the accessibility of the collection and must not be eliminated, thus rendering a large number of serial publications unfindable to a large number of people. It is our duty to enhance the accessibility of the collection, not wipe it out. Serials are too important for that.

First of all, the patron looking for a subject tends to look in the card catalog first. He should find periodicals listed under his subject, even in a general way, or he might not even think of serial materials at all. He will get some idea of the titles available that might help him.

If he approaches an index, he will get citations to some of the journals he already found listed. Those he can scratch off his original list.

What is left on his list might yield great possibilities, but he might have missed them if he'd only used the index approach. Perhaps another index will help him or perhaps the only hope is to go through a self-index to the periodical in question or maybe only an issue-to-issue search will yield anything. But at least he has not stopped short without an approach to all possibilities. All material in the library should be as approachable from as many angles as possible. In these days of the unit card, there should be full unit cards for all serials under all appropriate subject headings, no matter how broad.

174

An argument for the successive entry type of cataloging should be reiterated here when dealing with subject headings, for it is here that the patron is especially short-changed by the other systems. He may only remember a title vaguely, but he knows what it is about. Taking a subject approach, he will miss his title if it is only a note on a card under another heading. Patrons probably use the subject approach more than we realize.

Classification does not always provide the same function that subject headings do. It may be possible to classify broadly with narrow subject headings, or vice versa. Classification of periodicals integrates the journal materials with the monographic materials on the same general subject matter on the shelves, and subject headings integrate the same materials in the catalog, in various levels depending on the schemes used. Just as the browsers in the subject catalog can be served by headings for serials, so can the browsers in the stacks be served by call numbers. A scholar can find a new journal in his field with ease as he looks among his old favorites. The new one may become a favorite, too. The two browsing facilities may work hand-in-hand, or they may work independently of one another. One may be more appropriate for one area of study and the other in another. Both should be available, and both should be tried by the patron. They may be both supplementary and complementary.

Sometimes the crossing of subject boundaries by a journal can be educational to a patron who has always sampled things in a narrow area, either in call number or subject heading. The classification should be given to the primary scope of a periodical but subject headings can scatter this scope. Finding a catalog reference outside his normal field of vision could open up new vistas. As subjects become interconnected and interwined, one needs to take a broader view, but this is not always the case. Libraries should help their patrons to open their minds to the new renaissance.

Since form headings are not used in American libraries, it is useful to have form subdivisions like "PERIODICALS" to give patrons some of the form information they might not otherwise receive. The Library of Congress uses the following form subdivisions for serial publications: "COLLECTED WORKS," "CONGRESSES," "DIRECTORIES," "INDEXES," "PERIODICALS," "SOCIETIES, ETC.," "SOCIETIES, PERIODICALS, ETC.," and "YEAR-BOOKS."

LC uses the term "COLLECTED WORKS" as a form subdivision for comprehensive anthologies of works by separate authors in an irregularly published serial. This would also be the subdivision for a monographic series cataloged as a serial — that is, classed together.

"CONGRESSES" is used subordinate to the heading for the subject covered by the congress. It may relate to proceedings, programs, lists of members present, or anything else emanating from a congress. Periodical publications should not be further subdivided by the word "PERIODICALS." Most congress publications are not cataloged by the Library of Congress as serials anymore; but for those outside who would like to do so still, these guidelines may be followed for subject cataloging.

"DIRECTORIES" is used under headings for kinds of newspapers or periodicals, such as "AMERICAN NEWSPAPERS—DIRECTORIES." It can also be used for directories of persons or organizations. It should not be subdivided further.

"INDEXES" should be used under topic headings for works providing a comprehensive approach to printed subject material. For periodical indexes, the heading would be "PERIODICALS—INDEXES." This subheading can also be used after names of periodicals or newspapers to indicate index materials. This might be applied to a monograph or to a serial such as the printed index to the *New York Times*.

"PERIODICALS" should generally be used after a topic or geographic heading for publications which are more frequent than annual or are irregular.

"SOCIETIES, ETC." is to be used after a subject heading for publications that discuss the activities of several organizations active in a given field. This is not to be used for society publications. It should not be used under phrase headings such as "MEDICAL SOCIETIES." It is very rarely used for serials anymore by the Library of Congress.

"SOCIETIES, PERIODICALS, ETC." is to be used for serial or society publications about a person or about the serials and societies specializing in the study of that person.

"YEARBOOKS" is for annual publications that summarize the activities or events of the year in a subject area. For those annuals that do not summarize, the subdivision "PERIODICALS" should be used according to the Library of Congress. Catalogers often make the mistake of putting this subject subdivision on any annual publication.

Some obsolete form subdivisions may crop up on LC cards for serials of bygone years. The subdivision "COLLECTIONS" was dropped in 1973 to be completely superseded by "COLLECTED WORKS." There formerly was a distinction, primarily based upon the potential confusion of having a collection of objects versus that of works on a subject. "SOCIETIES" was dropped in 1971. It was used as a form subdivision for society publications in a field. For example, the *Journal of the American Medical Association* would formerly have gotten the subject heading, with subdivision, thusly: "MEDICINE—SOCIETIES," because it was a society publication. Now it would simply get the heading: "MEDICINE—PERIODICALS." It does not fit the criteria for "SOCIETIES, ETC." "SOCIETY PUBLICATIONS" has also been dropped. It was created in an attempt to be unambiguous, like "COLLECTED WORKS" was. There was the problem of publications about societies versus those about societies of beings, as "INSECTS—SOCIETY PUBLICATIONS." Publications that cover the affairs of a particular organization are not given any subject heading because either the main or added entries will supposedly take care of that aspect. "ABSTRACTS" is no longer applied to serials per se. A heading that normally would have been "MEDICINE—ABSTRACTS" now must be further qualified by the term "PERIODICALS" to indicate periodicity.

Some subject and geographic headings were not allowed to have form subdivisions in the past, which caused confusion and a burgeoning of subject headings. Osborn[1] uses the example *Journal of experimental medicine,* with double headings under "MEDICINE, EXPERIMENTAL" and "MEDICINE —PERIODICALS." Fortunately this practice has ceased, as the journal now has only one heading: "MEDICINE, EXPERIMENTAL —PERIODICALS." The old practice still shows itself in old LC cards so catalogers of today must take heed and watch for such problems, as well as updating the terminology used like "SPANISH AMERICA."

An interesting problem is pointed out by Osborn[2] regarding law periodicals. These are not treated strictly as periodicals, but are subdivided by place, as in "LAW—PERIODICALS—ARGENTINE REPUBLIC." Even though periodicity is shown, Osborn points out, this may be superseded by another of the form headings listed as possibilities. Osborn (1973), gives excellent examples in his Chapter 13 on "Subject cataloging" and the reader is directed there for more details. He points up some interesting inconsistencies. LC is revising a lot of its thinking about subject headings right at this time, however, and welcomes input from librarians on the subject. The new eighth edition of the *Library of Congress subject headings* (LCSH) has provided some impetus for this, as well as pressures due to problems in the structure of the subject headings in general. Some of these problems and discrepancies may be resolved.

There are problems in that some serial publications do not get subdivisions (or even subject headings) and their serial nature is not obvious. This is unfortunate, but it is not suggested that one invent headings, for it is not good to tamper with the system. However, it is up to individual libraries to service their patrons, and they must make these decisions.

Some libraries, in addition to the regular subject headings, give the form heading "PERIODICALS" to all serial publications to form a sort of mini serials catalog within the framework of the larger public catalog. LC once tried to do this, but it has since been abandoned. Others have chosen similar alternatives. Individual libraries would have to decide if this practice fits their needs. It would probably be unnecessary if the library has a serials list, especially an automated one in which data could be manipulated easily.

Many libraries are turning more toward KWIC indexing for serials to give better subject approach than the traditional methods allow. There is also considerable manipulation of subject headings, particularly to get at geographical names. Unfortunately, in the LCSH, geographic names can appear in many places in the heading, as adjectives, in inverted positions, and indirect as well as direct entry. This poses considerable problems to area specialists. This is one of the problems being looked at in LC's reevaluation of its subject headings. Periodicals and serials can be looked at at the same time as part of the greater problem of subject approach.

There seems to be a great fear of "bloating" the catalog with a plethora of subject heading cards when serials change their titles and are cataloged under successive entries. This would seem to be a very minor problem in the light of all the advantages gained from direct approach to title-as-published and should not deter libraries from the adoption of this rule. However, it would still seem to be a live issue in the minds of some serials librarians, expressed at conferences whenever the problem of serials cataloging comes up.

If space is really a problem in the catalog, with no likelihood of relief, perhaps a solution like the following could be adopted. Put guide cards in the catalog under subject headings that are getting crowded with notes like the following:

ITALIAN LITERATURE--PERIODICALS

   For periodicals on this subject consult the
stacks under the following call number(s):

   PC4001

   For additional titles see cards filed behind.

Fig. 8-1. Subject guide card/reference.

The shelflist might be referred to if the library has a public one. (It is not wise to refer to a record if the public cannot get to it at all times the library is open.) Then all cards for titles having the primary call number(s) listed could be pulled from the catalog and destroyed. Cards having that call number that are to be filed after the guide card was put in could be "bumped" by the guide card. Cards for titles receiving other class numbers would continue to be filed behind the guide card, as it directs. Large files could be whittled down considerably if space is really a problem. Of course, this system will only work with a classed collection. It should be noted that this is only a suggestion and should only be used if the problem is acute. It is considerably better than closing that part of the catalog and ceasing to make subject cards for journals, or throwing out old cards and putting in only new ones, which are the only other solutions this author has heard. Subject headings for serials are important and should never be compromised unless the library is in really dire straits.

There is the argument that subject headings for serials do not describe adequately the content of each individual serial. This is true. The real subject access to serials is through indexes. But until *everything* is indexed, there needs to be some sort of subject access to serial publications, no matter how broad. Subject headings is one of the answers. Another is classification. KWIC and KWOC indexing provide a third, although a set of predetermined descriptive words is needed, like with subject headings. PRECIS (Preserved Context Indexing System) is an example of a more sophisticated approach, with more potential for permutations than either LCSH or its counterpart for smaller libraries, Sears. All of these give different kinds of access and all have their own importance. The third is still off in the future for many libraries, though, and the first two must continue to suffice. But in order to have complete subject access to serials, even in a gross way, both of these methods should be used.

Libraries have always felt a little unclear about what to do with periodical publications. Should they be classified or not? Some classify them and shelve the bound and unbound issues together in call number order. Some classify all but those in the *Readers' guide* and maybe a few other indexes. Some classify none of their serials; some class "continuations" only. Some don't classify publications that appear more frequently than once a year (periodicals), but do classify serials appearing once a year or less frequently—classifying or declassifying as the publication changes frequency. Some cover only subscriptions and gifts and some only defunct titles and short runs. Some do not classify ephemeral materials. The whole concept seems to be on fairly shaky ground.

Classifying periodicals does have a number of advantages. The principal one of these is that subject matter can be kept together. It can be argued that subject areas for periodicals are very broad and that classification is less relevant. Certainly this attitude comes through in the following quotation:

According to the Fussler (Library quarterly 19:19-35, Jan. 1949, 19:119-43, April, 1949) articles, only 30.5 percent of the serial titles used by the chemists were classified in chemistry and only 20.2 percent of the serial titles used by physicists were classified in physics. The importance of the figures is emphasized by the added information that almost 3/4 of the titles and over 9/10 of the references used by chemists were serials. More than 2/3 of the titles and over 9/10 of the references used by physicists were serials. . .[3]

This trend, however, seems to be changing as more and more fields are springing up and are being developed into whole disciplines. The character of the classification schedules is changing as knowledge expands, and this is reflected in periodical classifications. The *Journal of algebra* can be included in the number for algebra and need not be lost under the general mathematics number—that is, unless it is desired that *all* math journals be together, in which case QA1 or its Dewey equivalent can be used for all journals on algebra, calculus, etc., as well as general mathematics. An individual library can tailor its classification guidelines to fit its usage. The point is, serial publications should be classed. And it is not always true that the classification areas are so broad as to be meaningless. Newer serials are being published on comparatively narrow subjects.

Additional subject headings would have helped the chemists and physicists in the above example, too. Also, they might have discovered new journals to explore. There will always be broad areas, such as "SCIENCE—PERIODICALS," which are very general, but for which there are other approaches, such as indexes.

For titles accessed through indexes, the call number becomes an arbitrary shelving device, but some titles may have no access through indexes. Even a general classification can be a hint as to the contents of the publication. Finding it among the journals and monographs on similar topics will guarantee chance use of it. Professors and students may browse the call number area of their choice and find a title they'd never heard of, but one they would like to explore again. A collection that is not classed cannot easily be browsed. It is most easily approached by those looking for a specific title. A title not indexed will be overlooked and, no matter how good it is, it should be abandoned by the library as unused and unnecessary and as an incumbrance upon the budget. Even a broad classification number would ensure its being found. Although some titles do not fit cleanly with a subject field, classification numbers can help in guiding browsers.

Newcomers to the library can learn about the "system" through looking for periodicals among books on the same subject. Those not well-acquainted with a subject area will find the majority of the materials necessary for an in-depth study all together. They can learn about the literature of the subject and may be encouraged to sample journals that are not indexed. Subject headings and cross-indexing may lead them to related areas under other class numbers with useful materials. Very often students look for "What you have on education." Ideas for term papers may burst upon them as they browse through the tables of contents of a few journals in the area. Those entrenched in the "old stand-bys" might happen to glance down the shelf and see a new title in their field that they had hitherto missed. This title, too, may prove indispensible, now that it has become known.

When polled in 1959, 5 out of 16 reporting libraries indicated that they had serials shelflists. Most were arranged in call number order.[4] Hopefully the number has gone up since, for this can prove a valuable aid in serials reference work. Patrons often indicate that they would like to read in a foreign language by asking, "Where are your periodicals in German?" Usually this means "general periodicals." A quick consultation of the schedules in an LC library would indicate AP30 as the appropriate basic number. This is a lot easier than telling a patron to look in the reading room for a German title. The shelflist can be consulted and several specific titles can be given to the patron for consideration as desired reading. Other areas may be subdivided by language as well. Perhaps the request is really for German history or literature. This request, too, can be answered by a quick trip through the schedules, followed by an excursion through the shelflist. Requests may be even more specific than that, such as materials on the Republican Campaign of 1860. Some retrieval can be done through the subject headings, but sometimes these two subject approaches complement each other rather than give duplicate information. Having a serials shelflist to consult in the serials department while the patron is asking the question also gives the library a better image to the outside world than shuttling the patron off to the public catalog on the first floor or elsewhere. The person answering the question can give immediate title access, call number access, and suggested subject heading access from the tracings on the shelflist card for the person to find specific serial publications, and, if desired, other entry points in the catalog and the collection for additional serials and monographic publications. The patron can be further directed to Reference, Government Publications or elsewhere, if necessary. However, his initial question has been adequately answered and he may need only what has been given. Being shuttled all over the library becomes his choice and he is not a pawn of the system.

A lot of material can be manipulated via computer if the information is there to input. Printouts can be generated on various subject areas by sorting on the class numbers. Such printouts can be distributed to academic departments or individuals. They can be placed in strategic locations around the library, far from the catalog or the shelflist. For example, a list of sociology journals might be put on a table adjacent to the stacks where these journals are primarily shelved. The list would become a miniature catalog of the collection. It might also give additional places to look if the browser didn't find what he was looking for on his first try. Many library users do not use the catalog, but simply go directly to the shelves. In this case, a wrong first guess does not necessarily mean an extra trip to the catalog and back to the stacks in another place.

Call number sorts by computer or manually in the shelflist can provide data useful in periodical selection, just as call number arrangements by Dewey numbers in the subject-arranged *NST* can. In fact, these can be coordinated somewhat, particularly in a Dewey-arranged library. A library can analyze its collection in a subject field by such a mechanical means. This is rough analysis, to be sure, but faster and more convenient than any other method and seemingly highly regarded in the library world as an accurate sampling procedure. A field can be analyzed for periodical support in a way that would be awkward without a convenient means such as this.

A by-product of the current economic situation — rampant inflation and tight budgets — is the need to "deselect" titles no longer centrally relevant to the library's needs, or titles the library cannot support. A method of going about this weeding process might be a list, preferably computer-produced, like the ones just mentioned, sorted by the discipline supported. Then, the selection officers in each area can pare away at their own disciplinary interests. Profiles of various subjects could be coded by class numbers and matched with each other to show overlaps. This can be a great time-saver at budget time or when the serials come up for renewal. Many automated procedures would be facilitated by call numbers.

Serials do not become less accessible in the collection because they are not monographs. They are not given less than first-class coverage. Furthermore, all serials should be classed so as to avoid confusion and extra work in classifying and declassifying.

Micro and other forms should also be classified. The tendency is to treat these as lesser citizens in the library world, even lesser than serials, and this is unfortunate. They should be included in call number sorts and deselection lists, too. They should be accessible by subject approach in the shelflist just like hardcopy material. As will be mentioned in the chapter on other formats, the text is just as important and librarians should not be swayed by form. What is true for "books" should be true for "magazines," "little boxes," and "cards," too. Other numbering systems are a confusion and a disservice.

Classification is useful, too, because it makes reshelving easier. A page does not have to guess a probable entry or know specialized filing rules. Shelving becomes mechanical. There is no longer the problem of what to do with similar titles. Titles are put into unambiguous pigeonholes that call numbers give them and there is no problem with identical titles being interfiled and volumes potentially lost. There is no confusion on the part of the patron looking for a title, for it is in its little cubbyhole. There may still be confusion, but there is less confusion between numbers than between spellings of similar titles with words like "Biblioteca," "Bibliotheca," "Bibliothèque," "Bibliothek," etc., or various not-very-different titles beginning with the phrase "Journal of . . ." Patrons looking for volumes under their generic title - corporate author, which are shelved under main entry, might be confused if the titles are shelved by entry. They would be especially confused if the issues didn't say on them quite the entry they were shelved under. (This could be fixed by marking or labeling, but then there really is very little reason why the whole process isn't completed, with call numbers as well.) Classification allows for the shelving together of minor title changes that would cause different runs if shelved by title. Even long runs can be shelved together despite title changes. The pigeonhole effect is most useful here.

Titles that have changed can be shelved together, even with successive entry cataloging. When LC adopted successive entry cataloging, the Subject Cataloging Division began assigning new class numbers and more specific subject headings to the new title, without regard for what had been done to the old title. This proved unacceptable and the Division revamped its thinking. The original class number and subject headings are now used for title changes unless they are unsatisfactory and the Library does not have too many bound volumes, making it unfeasible to update the title. Recataloging will be done if the original cataloging is proved to be incorrect in some way.

The arguments made in support of latest entry cataloging can be restated here with regard to the desire for having all issues of a bibliographic entity together. There is considerable strong feeling that this should be done for all titles that change, so that the complete history of the publication in its many guises is available. This can be done if the same call number is retained for all issues, no matter what the title. Complete bibliographic history is available in the shelflist under the collecting point of the call number. All of the issues are together on the shelves for easier bibliographic checking for lacunae, too. Many librarians find this a viable alternative to latest entry cataloging. It also serves all of the people who would be served by title-as-published information. There are a few little traps that one has to watch out for, however, if one decides to take this procedure. Shelflist cards need to be marked, perhaps with a stamp saying "Successive entry," so that the cards will not be discarded as duplicates or cause other problems because there are several cardsets with the same call number. Libraries using this system and thinking of automating their shelflists should also be aware that special provisions need to be built into the system to take care of the problem, or the computer will reject all cards for a successive entry serial but the first. Some provisions for numbering the cards need to be made so that the various titles will file in the proper chronological sequence. Libraries considering this kind of collocation should seriously consider classifying their serials, if this is not the case now, for it is much easier to shelve together in this manner than with systems based on entry or dummies under successive titles. For many this is the happy meeting ground between successive and latest entry cataloging.

However, before a library jumps in and does the above, it should seriously consider the browsing aspect of its service. A patron may often bypass the aids to stack material such as the card catalog or serials list because he feels that he knows where to find things. He may look under the entry he is looking for in the alphabetical arrangement of things under the broad class number and not find it because it is under a Cutter number for an older title. Too, a mixture of titles under the same call number in the shelflist, especially if public, and on the shelf, could be confusing. This is an extension of the theory of title-as-published argument for successive entry that the library should take into consideration when trying to determine its practice.

It is up to each individual library to choose its way of doing things. The second method is easier because it is more straightforward and fits in with the theory behind successive entry cataloging. You also have the potential problems of what to be done if a title had been acquired with a history that you didn't know; would you Cutter it from that title? What would you do when you uncovered others in the chain? Would you recatalog all? It would seem to be confusing to mix the two systems, and others trying to Cutter in the shelflist would be very confused by titles and Cutter numbers that bore no obvious relationship one to the other. Browsers might be helped by dummies in the stacks under the alphabetical sequence, giving the call number where all were collocated. This might not be very useful, through, because such dummies might get lost easily and might prove more of a burden than a boon. (A "dummy" is a piece of cardboard or wood holding a specific place on the shelf and referring the user elsewhere.) For those libraries which really do care about the history, the answer seems easy, but browsers should not be forgotten either. Each library needs to consider the pros and cons of both sides, as in everything, and make a choice.

Titles that change scope should generally change call number. The Armed Forces Medical Library (now NLM), got out of this situation by "classifying" its serials very broadly to type: medical serials in W1, document serials in W2, and congress publications in W3. These classifications do not change. Any expansion or contraction of subject matter is lost in the broad areas upon which the library is based. However, the effect of pigeonholing, mentioned earlier as an admirable aspect of classification, is retained. Special libraries, however, have already a fairly narrow scope of collecting and do not have the same problems that general libraries have. Such a scheme as this "weasels" out of the sticky problem that will now be described.

Patrons often ask why *Vogue* is classed in the T's rather than in the AP's with the rest of the general periodicals. After all, it is indexed in the *Readers' guide to periodical literature*, isn't it? It used to be a dressmakers' magazine, which, through the vagaries of the LC classification scheme, puts it in T, along with car driving, electronics and other technical things. Since then, it has lost a little of its former thrust, although the classification is still appropriate.

An even better example is "Silliman's journal," the *American journal of science*. This journal started out covering various phases of science and LC classed it in the general Q's. Somewhere along the way the journal dropped all the other sciences and decided to concentrate on one, geology. This is such a major shift that it probably should be reclassified, although perhaps only a specific subject heading would suffice to bring out the different thrust of the publication, depending upon the interests of the library.

This can become a problem. There are alot of journals that could be put either here or there, and it is the duty of the cataloger to put them in the best place. There are numbers for world politics in D and J. One title goes in D and one in J, perhaps by different catalogers or through the influence of LC copy. They are both acceptable numbers, but you get reaction from patrons who would expect to find the two side by side. Should you change one of the titles? Which one? This can be a problem in serials cataloging.

A general rule-of-thumb would probably be to change the class number if a sufficient number of volumes warrants it, as in the case of the *American journal of science*, particularly in a primarily physical science-oriented library, but not to change the number if it is an adequate and appropriate one still. At any rate, such changes should be made sparingly and only when the situation warrants it.

There are quite a number of librarians who feel that classification is a waste of time for serials. This is not true, as already described. The benefits are numerous, so the time is more than offset. Also, the cataloger must "read" the publication to catalog it and to get ideas for subject headings. Looking up a class number and fitting the title into the shelflist will not add appreciable amounts of time or costs. If LC or other copy is used, a call number will be given. The cost of labeling the spine would be minimal, too. Nothing that helps the patron or gives order and some measure of usability to the collection should be considered a waste of time.

There are other anticlassificationists who feel that it is a disservice to make patrons look up call numbers before they look for their desired periodical. This argument can be countered with the following: a patron will look for a title in the card catalog or the serials list, particularly if he is being led to it by an index, for he will want to know if the library he is standing in has the title he wants. He should also find a call number in the list or catalog he is looking in. Very few patrons would not write that number down. Patrons have also been trained in a library that the approach for monographs is very rarely, if ever, direct. Hopefully this has trained them in good library habits. Hopefully there will also be sources of information that will give some idea of where unbound issues are, if not shelved with the bound issues: either in the list or catalog (for possible stamped messages, see Appendix D.), on a sign, or at the Reference Desk. There might also be further elaboration in a handbook or flyer on library use. This should lead the patron sufficiently so that he will not become confused. If the issues are all unbound, there are several alternatives, such as temporary cards without call numbers or plastic jackets that mask the call numbers until they are bound. However, if there is a serials list or catalog supplementing the main card catalog, this kind of information should be the duty of this record. At any rate, none of these solutions should be a valid argument for nonclassification, although definitely should be taken into consideration when the library devises its methods of giving holdings and location information. (See subsequent chapters.) Just because serials spend some time in an unbound state should not be a criterion for whether or not they get classified.

There are also arguments that periodicals are scattered among books, which can be inconvenient if the patron only wants periodicals, and that the checking of holdings would be cumbersome. Neither of these arguments seem to be very important or very valid. Most periodicals fall to the front of classes and stand somewhat by themselves anyway. They should be findable as periodicals through the catalog or the shelflist or the serial records. Checking holdings can be done through serials records, too, and be considerably more up-to-date than the shelves would be, unless you are searching for missing volumes. You would have the call number in front of you if something caused you to want to look at the stacks, and you would probably remove the Kardex and take it with you to double check. It doesn't need to be a cumbersome procedure if you don't make it so.

Basically, the arguments for classification seem to have won out, for the majority of libraries classify their serial publications, with the exception of small college and public libraries and special libraries. These situations are less crucial than in the larger academic and research libraries and large public libraries for, on the one hand, in the small public and college libraries, there are relatively few serials on really specific subjects and generally even fewer that aren't indexed; and, on the other, in the special library, all the serials are on specific subjects in a pretty limited area of interest, where classification would be of little use since most of the publications would fall in the same numbers. Indeed, in special libraries, the periodicals may tend to become the featured part of the collection, as is true of the Linda Hall Library of Kansas City. The visible file could even take the place of the card catalog, the titles shelved in alphabetical order. In both cases, the collections are not scattered all over the realm of knowledge, which makes classification necessary, and the clientele is probably looking for specific titles-as-published, rather than runs of historical backsets, which tends to make classification pigeonholing useful. In other than these special cases, the shakiness of the past seems to be dwindling away in the light of the many advantages to adequate subject approach. Librarians are perhaps realizing that the more diverse the library collection and the higher the level of library use, particularly for scholarly pursuits, the greater the need to class all serial publications.

Classifying serial publications is not really very difficult. Most schedules give slots for publications of this type. However, there is the question of what to do if there is not a specific-enough serial number for the publication in hand. Some libraries use the specific number, with a double Cutter using ''A1'' as the first part of the book number to indicate that it is a periodical and so it will stand at the head of the class. LC cautions against this practice, except where it is specifically called for in the schedules themselves, yet seems to have done it sometimes itself without apparent cause. LC has special Cutter tables it has finally agreed to let the masses on the outside see. Some of these special directives appeared in *Cataloging service bulletins* 110 (Summer, 1974) and 112 (Winter, 1975). These directives will be explored soon.

More and more specific serial numbers seem to be being built into the scheme as it expands. Individual library practice, as mentioned before, might determine how best to handle such situations: whether all journals should go at the head of the general class, such as mathematics, or whether the specificity of certain numbers might better serve the goals of the individual library. This would probably have to be tailor-made, at least somewhat, but following the lead of the Library of Congress is almost always a wise choice in case of doubt.

LC's special Cutter tables were just mentioned a moment ago. Let us see what secrets LC is letting us in on.

Cataloging service bulletin 110 informs us that the procedures listed below are used for monographs and serials under corporate headings and have been in effect since May of 1973.

Upon receipt of a publication cataloged under a corporate heading already represented in the particular class to which the publication has been assigned, LC disregards all previously assigned author Cutter numbers for that heading and formulates a new number for the heading that will shelve immediately after all existing ones used for the body.

1. *Cutter numbers.* All publications cataloged under a corporate heading and classified under the same number are assigned the same Cutter number. In formulating a Cutter number for a corporate heading, all subheadings are disregarded. . .

However, any word or phrase at the end of a corporate heading which distinguishes between two bodies having the same or similar name is regarded. . .

When the entire class number is for the official documents of a specific country, the Cutter numbers are based on the name of the particular agency. If the name of the country appears at the beginning of the entry it is disregarded. As stated in the preceding paragraph, subheadings that appear in the heading are disregarded. . .

3. *Serials.* To formulate a distinctive call number for serials (e.g., periodicals and collected series) cataloged under a corporate heading, successive work letters, beginning with "a" for the first serial, are added to the Cutter number for the heading in the order of receipt of the publications. . .

xxxx	United States. Army. General Staff.
.U3	[Monographic title] 1958.
1958	

xxxx	United States. Army.
.U3	[Multivolume monographic title] 1963-1964.
1963	

xxxx	United States. Army. Far East Command.
.U3	[Monographic title] 1963.
1963a	

xxxx	United States. Army. Corps of Engineers.
.U3a	[Open entry serial title] 1957-

xxxx	United States. Army. General Staff.
.U3b	[Closed serial title] 1956-1963.[5]

Cuttering of serials under conference headings is covered in *Catalog service bulletin* 112:

5. Serial publications cataloged under the heading for a series of conferences, or under title with an added entry for the conference series, are cuttered alphabetically by the name of the conference series before all publications of individual conferences in the series. Call numbers for different serials of the conference series are formulated by assigning consecutive Cutter numbers.

xxx	Conference on serials.
.C63	[Serial title] 1964-

xxx	Conference on serials, 1st, 1964.
.C64	[Monographic title] 1965.[6]
1964a	

Perhaps future bulletins will further explain the peculiarities of LC's Cuttering which appear nowhere in the schedules, but manifest themselves on LC card copy to the confusion of serials librarians everywhere. We eagerly await these explanations.

Perhaps worthy of brief mention are the document collections abounding in university, particularly state university, libraries that are full or partial state and/or federal document depositories. These are usually housed separately and not integrated into the collection by location, classification, or even representation in the library's major bibliographic tool, the card catalog. These collections are generally ignored by the average student, unaware of the wealth housed there. This is substandard treatment, unworthy of a great research library. Imposing the Superintendent of Documents Classification on people is even worse than accession numbers for microforms: the numbers are awkward and long and hard to remember or understand, and many problems can result, such as confusion when publications change issuing agency. There is no subject access through the classification scheme, for it is built upon issuing agency. The patron has to digest another numbering system, or even more than one, since some libraries use several numbering systems for documents. It is no wonder that patrons are loathe to walk into this bewildering mass, even though reassured that this is where the answer to the question already raised lies. More should be done to integrate government publications into the regular collection, especially those documents which are popular and less "governmental-looking," like *Arizona highways.* Even the *Monthly labor bulletin* is indexed in the *Readers' guide* and should be out for public use rather than tucked away in a corner of a documents department. Much more should be done to bring document serials to the people and to make them usable from all access points, particularly the subject point of view, which seems to be virtually ignored in most cases.

The whole point of using classification and subject headings is to draw attention to the purpose and contents of all serials publications and to bring them together with monographs on the same subject so that the entire library collection can be used comparatively, effectively and in depth.

FOOTNOTES

1. Andrew D. Osborn, *Serial publications; their place and treatment in libraries,* 2d ed., rev. (Chicago: American Library Association, 1973), p. 253.

2. *Ibid.,* p. 257.

3. Edgar G. Simpkins, *A study of serials processing,* M.S. in L.S. thesis, Western Reserve University, 1951, abstracted in *Serial slants* 2 (January, 1952):16.

4. Gloria Whetstone, "Serial practices in selected college and university libraries," *Library resources and technical services* 5 (Fall, 1961):287.

5. *Cataloging service bulletin* 110 (Summer, 1974):6-8.

6. *Cataloging service bulletin* 112 (Winter, 1975):16.

Chapter IX

Monographic Series and Other Analytical Problems

One of the distinctly grey areas in serials cataloging in college and research libraries is numbered monographic series. Ideally, it would be nice to have the Serials Department in charge of *all* serials, the definition of which usually includes monographic series that have numerical or chronological designation; however, this is not generally practical, particularly from the cataloging standpoint. The volume is just too great. In the interest of practicality, some kind of compromise needs to be made: the Serials Department will take care of those serials cataloged as serials and let the monographs people handle the rest. How deceptively easy! But how is this to be done?

Harry Dewey suggests that the following list of considerations should be looked at with the question of whether to catalog separately ("scatter") or as a set ("assemble"). Those series that are scattered then become the interest of the monographs catalogers while the Serials Department concerns itself with the assembled series. Mr. Dewey's list:

1. Regularity of receipt. . . .Regardless of regularity, if there are to be any future acquisitions, by accident or design, the catalog department will be committed to devote "cataloging time," as opposed to "adding time" (taken to add them to the serial record or shelflist), to them.

2. Series that are "out of scope." Long-established series, the contents of which are known to include only rarely titles within the scope of the library's acquisition policy, may be scattered without a particularly large commitment on future time.

3. Binding. If a series is paperbound, to scatter it is to invoke a commitment to bind separately all future volumes. Even pamphlet binders are expensive. If the series is not to be scattered, several volumes may be bound together. On the other hand, if the volumes are published in cloth bindings, or are too thick as to require separate binding, this factor need not be considered in making the decision to scatter or not.

4. Variety of subject matter. If the series consists of titles on closely related subjects, e.g., the *Census Monographs* of the Bureau of the Census, and would shelve near each other even if scattered, nothing is gained by scattering. On the other hand, such series as the *Reference Shelf* would be more readily located if scattered, by readers browsing in an open-stack library. Libraries with stacks divided on the subject-divisional plan might more logically pursue a liberal scattering policy than libraries with central-core stacks, although such libraries cannot hope to disperse all subject materials appropriately, without resorting to scattering the articles that appear in the general periodicals, or the chapters in books that deal with overlapping subjects, etc.

5. Availability of LC cards. If LC cards are not obtainable for each spearate monograph in the series, then the encumbrance on catalog department time resulting from a decision to scatter the set is indeed heavy, whether or not LC series cards are available. On the other hand, if LC analytic cards are available, but a series card is not, it may be cheaper to prepare the series card locally and avoid the not inconsequential expenses incident to separate classification and cataloging with LC cards. The analytic cards may be used anyhow, if the set is not scattered, at considerably less cost than is entailed in their use as an adjunct to separate classification (see below.)

6. Numbering. If the monographs in the series are not numbered according to a system whereby each title can be identified exclusively by series title and volume number (or date), it becomes impossible or inadvisable not to scatter them. The cataloger must otherwise supply arbitrary numbers to the volumes, and keep up-to-date on the catalog card, a key to these volume numbers; location of the volumes is otherwise impossible. If the series title and numbering are placed on the volumes in a very obscure position, the cost savings must be weighed carefully against the fact that bibliographic citations are apt to omit mention of such series notes, even in such bibliographically reliable publications as the H. W. Wilson Company and LC indexes and catalogs. This is likely to be true of series with complex systems of numbering or cryptic series titles such as the "ARC" series published by the American Red Cross, etc., since these series may go unrecognized as such, or be dismissed as unimportant, by bibliographers, as indeed they often are.

7. Publisher. It is not advisable to classify together monographs in series issued by "trade" publishers, even though numbered for the simple, if technically illogical, reason that libraries (let alone patrons) do not expect to have to look under series titles to find such series, and for the technically valid reason that

bibliographers and researchers almost universally omit mention of such series titles in their catalogs, indexes and bibliographies. This latter factor would render well-nigh impossible the identification and location of such monographs if they were classified as sets.[1]

Some of these criteria may be more important to a single library than others. In most libraries, number 4 is of primary interest because it affects the patron most. The library is supposed to be helping the patron and closely classifying each volume, or keeping sets together because people think of them that way, is an important help, or hindrance, to the patron's use of the library's collections. Numbering that is arbitrarily supplied or is confusing should be avoided. Most libraries, as Dewey points out, do not include publisher's series as serials. His rationale is valid. However, if the series is on a narrowly-defined subject, for example, it might be wise to consider it for serial treatment. *North-Holland mathematics studies* would appear to be a publisher's series on first look, because North-Holland is a publisher and this is often a clue to a publisher's series: the publisher's name is in the title. But the series is presented quite predominantly as such, and the Library of Congress and other libraries have chosen to make it a classed-together series. This would be up to an individual library and is hard to codify. Number 2 is also important from the patron's point of view. If a library has purchased only a few volumes of a series, the interest is primarily in those volumes and not in the secondary fact that they are in a series; a virtually irrelevant piece of information in this case.

Dewey's numbers 1, 3, and 5 are primarily of interest to a library trying to cut costs. This should always be a secondary consideration to patron's needs, except when not cutting corners means that patrons lose out completely by not getting the materials they need due to backlogs, slowdowns, and the like. The patron should always be the library's first concern.

The basic argument for individualized monographic treatment emphasizes that items in a series are monographs with a clear identity and are fundamentally viewed as such. Their individual monographic importance clearly outweighs the significance of a series title, which is not enough to give serial character to the publications.

If this viewpoint is strictly adhered to, there would never be the grey area already alluded to, which would be nice. However, just as it would be virtually impossible to treat every series as a serial, it would be virtually impossible to give every one, and every part of every one, the detailed individual treatment a monograph deserves. Cost of cataloging would skyrocket and backlogs would soon overwhelm the catalog department. The all-or-nothing monographic viewpoint has to be tempered considerably to reach the happy medium.

Andrew Osborn speaks in favor of scattering a series, as follows:

When a library does not intend or need to acquire a complete set, the individual volumes on hand should almost invariably be scattered by subject. When a complete set is on hand or on order, the presumption may be in favor of scattering the volumes by subject in the following circumstances:

1. General series, like *Everyman's Library,* which cover many subjects.

2. In institutions which are connected with storage libraries, those series which have items that should go directly to storage instead of to the classed shelves.

3. In library systems, notably university library systems, those series that contain volumes that ought to be located in the main as well as branch or departmental libraries whenever the acquisition of duplicate copies cannot be justified. Conversely, a branch or departmental library should always scatter the volumes of a series unless all of them are in its subject field.

4. Items whose name or title is apt to change, the evidence being taken from the prior history of the organization which publishes the series or from the set itself when it has been acquired after there has been at least one change of name.

5. Loosely connected series on a diversity of subjects, e.g., the *Publications of the University of Manchester.*

6. Publications which include items on poor paper, since such items will sooner or later cause gaps to occur in a set unless they are preserved under special conditions.

7. Publisher's series, e.g., the *College Outline Series.*

8. Series that clearly should be scattered by subject, e.g., the *University of Minnesota Pamphlets on American Writers.*

9. Sets whose component parts look like ordinary monographs and are generally regarded as such, e.g., the *Rivers of America* series.

10. Special library holdings, except when the institution is a historical research library or when the total set falls within its subject field; also the holdings of school and small public libraries, but this does not apply to complete sets of works such as the *Farmers' bulletin* and the *Pageant of America.*

11. Titles which include reference books in the narrow sense of the term, e.g., *Carnegie Institution Publications,* of which volume 353 is Talock and Kennedy's *Concordance to the Complete Works of Geoffrey Chaucer and to the Romaunt of the Rose.*

12. Unnumbered series to which facetious numbering is not to be supplied.[2]

A basic guideline would be: that which is more homogenous in subject matter is best kept together, for there is not the loss of subject approach through the classification. If you lose this subject approach by not closely classifying, you are violating the objective of letting the patron find material on a certain subject together. This, of course, is an amplification of Dewey's number 4, already listed, as well as a corollary to several of Osborn's points just listed. If a series is very diversified, it would be best scattered throughout the collection where items would be more easily findable. Volumes could be extracted for shelving in special locations or libraries with ease, too. Series issued by universities or societies with a large scope of interest, such as the American Philosophical Society in Philadelphia, would probably be best scattered. The "AS" class in LC (for publications of scholarly institutions) is not really very enlightening to patrons and perhaps should be kept for publications that cannot be broken down into their constituent parts, such as straight periodicals or single monographs of scholarly endeavour.

Of course, the best route is the one taken by LC and a few others: two sets, one classed together and one scattered. But most of us are not as wealthy and cannot take such exorbitant measures for patron convenience, even though we should like to. We must make our choice. Public libraries get very little of this material, but universities and research libraries get quite a bit and must find a solution. Unless cost is an absolutely overwhelming factor, the most rational way out is the subject approach. Treatment may vary from library to library, but this seems to be a useful variation, as long as other approaches to the material are possible, such as adequate catalog representation of the series and its parts.

The best guideline to this subject approach is to consider whether the series title would cover subjects in a narrow area or a broad one. If the coverage were all of one classification, such as a title *Studies in European history* would be, or perhaps many classes, such as *Social science research papers*, the treatment would be best as a monograph. If the subject were narrow, such as *Studies in dance*, it could be done better as a serial. Perhaps serial treatment would be better for a subject fairly scattered in scope, but which the library would like to emphasize. This might be the rationale for serial treatment of something entitled *Environment studies*. This series could conceivably jump from one subject to another, from air pollution to diseases of plants to the economic aspects of new automobile engines to city planning to soil science. This would cover a number of classes, but the thread of "environmental studies" would still be there and would give direction to both the library and the patron, encouraged to explore more widely and to find related things he might not have thought of at first.

Monographic series should be recorded in the central serial record, but, as mentioned before, this may not be feasible. If the library has a serial listing of any kind, numbered monographic series should be listed in it, since these titles may be treated as serials elsewhere, or the patron may choose to take that kind of approach to finding his material. Series received on standing orders, but scattered, should be reported to *NST* and other union lists. Series added entries should always appear in the library's catalog for each title cataloged in that series. Separate added entry unit cards are to be preferred over those that list two or three volumes on the same card. Additional listing on such cards can be too easily missed.

Some libraries may desire to have a main series card for a scattered series, stating the series name and referring to following cards for contents and call numbers. This card is good for the recording of title changes, cross-references, and other information referring to the series. This card might also indicate if the library has a standing order for the series or not. It would be analogous to the serial "cover card" for a numbered monographic series classed together and might, if possible, come under the purview of the serials cataloger. In this way, the serials cataloger could monitor the establishment of the series entries. This card, as shown below, is just like a serial card, except that it does not give a specific call number for the series. Each added entry card behind it gives a call number on an individual basis. This card could be the basis for recording and authority work for the series.

```
Wisconsin commerce studies.  Madison, Bureau of
    Business Research and Service, University of
    Wisconsin.

    For volumes in library, see cards following.




    1. Wisconsin--Commerce.  2. Wisconsin--Econ.
condit.  I.  Wisconsin.  University.  Business
Research and Service Bureau.
```

Fig. 9-1. Cover card for a monographic series cataloged as separates[3].

The following quotation shows that it might be preferable to catalog monographic series as serials however.

> The alternative (to classing together as serials) is to classify serially issued monographs independently on the ground that they are books rather than papers or articles. This treatment fails to take account of the fact that such monographs are intended to appear in an indefinitely continued series. Such monographs, moreover, differ from papers and articles only in having greater length and wider scope; appearing in serial form they are likely to be indexed as serials and to be located by volume and number.[4]

In this point of view, the series is considered the main work. This is a useful viewpoint, especially when reinforced by certain publication practices indicating that W. S. Merrill is right. Sage Publications issues a number of series of professional papers. Each paper is separate, but the publication pattern indicates that four of them go together, as if in a volume, only each has its own set of covers. Although each is separately paged, they really are only long journal articles. *The Racial policies of American industry reports* are published separately. They are also collectively published in hard cover as another series. Such examples only serve to strengthen the arguments for cataloging as serials.

LC tends to follow the general guidelines given in this chapter for the grouping or scattering of series. LC is aware, however, that probably not everyone would feel the same way about series treatment that it does. In order to give other libraries this option, LC made the following announcement:

> Some libraries that use LC catalog cards may prefer to classify parts of certain monographic series separately which the Library of Congress shelves as collected sets. Therefore, the Subject Cataloging Division has started assigning alternative class numbers for all analyzed monographs in collected sets. Thus, in addition to the call number for the collected set, a bracketed monographic class number will be supplied, based on the contents of the monograph represented by the analytic card.[5]

This should be helpful to those acquiring a few selected volumes that are to be cataloged as separates. This policy has been expanded to those items which receive Dewey numbers as well, per *Cataloging service bulletin* 105 (November, 1972), p. 16. Other libraries may then treat as separates what LC classes together under the criteria to follow.

Some series are more effective as collections, such as *Lecture notes in mathematics,* which covers an interrelated and therefore narrow class: math. Close classification would tend to put all volumes very close together on the shelf, so why not dispense with that extra work and treat as a serial? Some series are thought of as series of collected papers, such as some society publications or series issued by a university department. These are much better kept together. Publications of congresses or symposia are probably best classed together too, although this is much more a local library decision, since LC is moving away from this idea.

Andrew Osborn gives the following list of circumstances as criteria for keeping a complete set together in serial fashion:

1. Government documents such as the congressional set or geological society publications.

2. Items whose parts are not regular bibliographical units, e.g., the *Cambridge History of the British Empire*.

3. Near-print, e.g., technical reports.

4. Pamphlet series which obviously do not need to be scattered and whose parts might otherwise end up in pamphlet volumes. Many German series belong in this category.

5. Publications with continuous paging.

6. Sets on a narrowly defined topic, e.g., Byzantine art.

7. Sets whose parts might prove difficult to classify, especially when the monographs are written in Latin or any of the less common languages.

8. Unanalyzed series, even when the analyzing is merely postponed.

9. Well-known sets which are likely to be asked for as such, e.g., *The Harvard Classics*.

10. Works for which a cumulative index is issued. e.g., the *Skrifter* of the Norsk Folkeminnelag, which has an index covering v. 1-49.[6]

Although some of his examples are multivolume monographs, like *The Harvard Classics,* Osborn's arguments for serial treatment are quite valid.

Classing together as a serial can be a considerable savings in time and money. Separate classification would not be necessary for each volume. The costs of adding to serial records would probably be significantly less than the costs of special handling for each volume. Volumes classed together can be bound together, if unbound, saving money and perhaps keeping a space or two open for other materials if the library has a bookbinding quota. The individual items in a series might not even need to be cataloged individually. This latter practice would tend to be considered overmuch, however, if the library felt it should get away with such minimal, yet "adequate" cataloging for a large part of its collection. Future volumes would just be added, as in a regular serial, and that would be all of the handling necessary. As Kathryn Luther Henderson indicates, this is not a good idea:

Many libraries continue to give only inventory control to monographic series. This is certainly one type of serial where a careful review of local policy needs to be made. Too often the availability of Library of Congress cards for the analytical parts of such series is probably the deciding factor here. Many potentially useful materials can remain hidden away on the shelves because of the lack of indexing of the individual item. Some of these series do not even have the rudimentary internal control which contents notes afford. Even if the series is eventually analyzed in some printed bibliography, the bibliographies are often late in appearing and the book may not be available until such time as its immediate use has long since passed.[7]

Let's see what Mr. Dewey has to say about the analysis of serials:

1. Availability of LC cards. If LC analytic cards are not available, the work of analysis will be overly time-consuming and costly. The list of series for which analytics are prepared locally will be scrutinized by the economy-minded cataloging administrator.

2. Availability of printed indexes. Printed indexes available to the public and to the reference librarians may be substituted for costly catalog analysis. Such indexes as Firkin's *Index to short stories* and the *LC Subject catalog* are expensive, they do not earn their purchase price if their contents are duplicated in the card catalog. This is not to say that series analyzed in the LC printed catalogs should not be analyzed in the library's card catalog; however, the titles chosen for analysis should be chosen with cards and with expectation that the cards will be frequently used.

3. Library holdings. If the library has a limited amount of material in the subject area of a particular series of monographs, more serious consideration should be given to analytics.

4. Demand. Institutional and reader interest in the subject area, or lack thereof, may dictate the decision.

5. Local interest. If the series contains monographs by leading local citizens, members of the faculty, or about local persons, places, organizations, etc., analytic cards may be made for these.[8]

For the most part, these suggestions are good, but they should be used only if something is questioned or is of minor significance. All major series should be analyzed without question since they form the backbone of a good collection in many areas.

It has already been mentioned that large numbers of serials need not be purchased if they are not to be classed because they are not indexed and would not get any use, except maybe by accident. Further savings can be made if monographic series to be treated as Mrs. Henderson just described were not purchased as well. The collection would, of course suffer enormously as a result. This is not good.

Of course, such monographic materials have another treatment as well, as monographs. The fact that so many are given such rudimentary treatment as serials gives rise to the extremist viewpoint presented at the beginning of this chapter demanding total treatment as monographs. After all, if a series is scattered, it is automatically analyzed. If it is kept together, it may not be. Savings can still be made by classing together, without the hidden costs of bibliography searches and patron frustration.

Bibliographies are often used as substitutes for analytical entries. This may be fine in some areas, such as for those titles listed in *Titles in series*. This is somewhat useful for a closed title or series of a title. The catalog card can say:

For contents see Titles in series [call. no. for Titles in series], or

For contents of old series, see Titles in series [call no.].

You should always give the call number of another title being referred to in the catalog so that the patron does not have to make a second search in the catalog. Some libraries have stopped making analytics for series they had formerly analyzed when it was discovered that the title was indexed in a bibliography. Notes like the following could be put into the catalogs:

Beginning with no.[ ] separate cards will not be made for each number. The set is indexed in [Titles in series, call no.]

Form cards could even be made with such a legend to be filed after the last analytic card.

Other bibliographies can also be used, but it is unfortunately true that a lot of bibliographies leave a great deal to be desired. They may leave important information out, which makes them somewhat less than satisfactory as substitutes for analytics. For example, they may not indicate that a series is covered. The analytic entry may leave out a series statement; and such information, if it is included, is frequently wrong according to several complainants. There may not be a series approach. Also, the patron may have to search a lot because he doesn't know what it is exactly that he is looking for. The cataloger would probably have to search very carefully for an adequate substitute for his cataloging. Some of this problem may vanish with the new LC catalog on *Monographic series,* but this has yet to be tested, since the first volume only came out at the end of 1974. The whole procedure is very questionable in the light of service to the patron, and only very minor series should probably be treated in this way. It is most advisable that all material in the library be exhibited as fully as possible in the library's catalog.

Bibliographies have traditionally been the accepted mode of approach to government publications, and, even though the indexing is quite good, the patron tends to ignore it and, hence, misses out on some of the library's most worthwhile sources. This approach is not really adequate and should only be used if there is not another choice. As Mrs. Henderson indicated, this is not really a desirable alternative, although it's better than nothing. The indexes will get their share of use, from patrons approaching from that direction, who may not have thought of approaching the catalog until after receiving the additional information that the index gave. Mr. Dewey does not have to worry that the indexes will sit idle.

The best answer is to catalog monographic series as serials when the series fits the criteria mentioned earlier for assembled series. Then analyze each volume for fuller coverage in the catalog. The Library of Congress gives considerable help in this area, especially in recent years. According to *Cataloging service bulletin* 104:

> Since the middle of June [1971] the Library of Congress has analyzed all analyzable monographic series currently being acquired and cataloged by the Library except for those that are documents, technical reports, reprints from journals, and those requiring page analysis. This extends and completes the coverage in the provision of analytics which is now being given to monographic series from NPAC shared cataloging countries.[9]

However, even if the Library of Congress has not made analytical entries for numbers in a series, they should be made for material that has been, or is likely to be, cited as a separate work. Savings are still made, yet the patron's needs are also met.

The title would be classed together under a single call number, which would be a considerable savings in cataloging time. The main, or cover card, would be for the series and would contain all bibliographic information for the series as a whole, including subject headings and added entries. A stamp or typed note should be appended, as in the case of all serials, indicating that holdings are to be found in the central serial record (see Chapter 12). If analyzed, as it should be, a note, preferably in red, should also state that

> For contents of this series see following cards

or some similar wording. Then, analytics cards, filed by series added entry overtyped on unit cards, should follow.

```
QA3   Lecture notes in mathematics.
L4      no.1-            1964-
         Berlin, New York; Springer-Verlag.
         no.

         English, German, or French.
         For contents of this series see cards filed
         behind.



            1. Mathematics--Collected works.
         anals.
```

Fig. 9-2. Cover card for a monographic series cataloged as a serial with analytics.

The old practice of listing contents should definitely be discontinued if it is substituted for analytics for monographic series. This is a practice of very questionable worth since it is usually overlooked by the patron whom it is attempting to serve and it makes much more work for the cataloger than adding a series entry to the foot of a unit card ready for photoduplication. The boon to the patron in this case would be a great one.

Those who fear for space in their catalogs might opt for gathering the individual cards for the series together under the call number in the shelflist, without the series added entry in the public catalog. This is an alternative, to be sure, but it is not particularly useful for the patron and should only be used if the library is in dire straits and if the shelflist is open to patrons. Libraries that only have this information in their shelflists, which are locked away in a backroom of their catacombs, are frustrating their patrons who try the series approach. Too many patrons try this access point to allow them to be short-changed. All access points should be available to them. Of course there is no problem if the shelflist is a public one.

The series should never be an access point that is unavailable to the patron, whether the series is assembled or scattered. Added entries should always be made, except for publisher's series, and even some of these may be desirable at times. Patrons should not have to depend on the fact that a title is classed together on the shelves for series approach either. Some libraries do this to their patrons, which is an unfortunate shortcut. A few access points can be eliminated as excess verbiage, however. A series issued by a society should have the society's name traced on the series card. LC will make added entries for such a society on all of the analytics. Some time and space can be saved if this were not done locally, if such shortcuts are desired for savings, as long as the name appears in the catalog in connection with the series. Shortcuts can sometimes be made in descriptive cataloging for analytics as well, although this is generally not advisable.

A shortcut can be taken in the analysis of minor series that are fairly homogeneous and closely classed as serials. For example, take a series such as *Notes and essays on education for adults* issued by the Center for the Study of Liberal Education for Adults. The class number is LC6251. The subject heading for the series is: ADULT EDUCATION — COLLECTED WORKS. Each volume is on a special aspect of adult education; and, while the volumes differ in approach or specific subject matter, the library has collected them basically because of the general subject matter: adult education. This series can be more briefly analyzed by being given author and title analytics. There is complete bibliographic description, and author and title added entries are made for each monograph, as well as main entry and series approaches. Individual subject headings are not given because the heading given for the serial can take care of all the parts adequately. In this example, the savings isn't great because the subject headings are not difficult or numerous. There are other possible titles that might be treated in this manner and where the savings due to volume or the somewhat esoteric aspects of hard-to-find subjects might be more. This can help if the library is afraid to bloat its catalog with lots of cards on the same subject. Such an approach might be taken for lecture series where the authors, and not the subjects, are of interest. Such a shortcut should not be employed for a major series.

Other than some of the shortcuts already mentioned, the cataloging of each individual analytic should follow monographic cataloging rules for entry, including added ones, and description. Series statements should be made in the normal place, including the numbering. Numbering should also appear in the call number. This should be the numbering for the individual volume or volumes being described, not the collective volume they might be bound in, for this information will be contained elsewhere. It is best not to consider serial analytics as bound-withs, for this can lead to confusion. Added entries should be made for the series. Editors for the series do not have to be considered for each volume, for they should be considered for the series as a whole, if at all; serial cataloging usually ignores editors unless they are important ones. Additional series should be traced, but they should be considered as either subseries of the main serial, if they are subserviant to that series, or larger series if such is the case. Subseries need to be mentioned in the cataloging for the series as a serial. The larger series should be mentioned if it is constantly part of the series, such as *Fieldiana* appearing in the Museum's *Publications* series. If it appears once or twice only, such mention is not necessary. Added series should be traced. They should be treated as numbered monographic series cataloged separately. Here is a sample of an analytic card:

Mundell, Robert A

The dollar and the policy mix: 1971 ₍by₎ Robert A. Mundell. Princeton, N. J., International Finance Section, Princeton University, 1971.

34 p. (p. 29–34 advertisement) 23 cm. (Essays in international finance, no. 85)

1. Monetary policy—U. S. 2. Balance of payments—U. S. I. Title. II. Series: Princeton University. International Finance Section. Essays in international finance, no. 85.

HG136.P7 no. 85   332 s   70–165467

[HG588]   MARC

Fig. 9-3. Analytic card.

Sometimes analytics may continue for a number of volumes within the series. The analytics may even be serials themselves.

Because the public catalog is not to be a place for holdings statements for serials (see Chapter 12), additional cards for numbers out of sequence are not necessary. For example, there need not be a separate card in the series listing for additional numbers of *Lecture notes in mathematics* following no.39, as below:

```
QA3        Séminaire de probabilités, Université de
L4            Strasbourg.  1-          1967-
no.39,       Berlin, New York, Springer-Verlag.
51,88,         v. (Lecture notes in mathematics, no.39,
124,191,  51, 88, 124, 191, 258, etc.)
258,etc.
             "Exposés faits, pendant l'année universi-
           taire, au Séminaire de probabilités de l'
           Université de Strasbourg."

             1. Probabilities--Addresses, essays,
           lectures.  I. Strasbourg. Université.
           Institut de Mathématique.  II.  Series.
```

Fig. 9-4. Analytic card for continuing monograph in series.

There should be one in the shelflist, however, as a space holder.

```
QA3   Séminaire de probabilités...1967...
L4

no.51      See no. 39 of this series.
```

Fig. 9-5. Space holder card in shelflist for additional volumes.

Additional cards can be made, if desired, following the pattern set up below.

```
          Lecture notes in mathematics, no. 51.
QA3       Séminaire de probabilités, Université de
L4             Strasbourg. 1-        1967-
no.39,           v. (Lecture notes in mathematics, no. 39,
51,88      51, 88, 124, 191, 258)
124,191,
258        "Exposés faits, pendant l'année universi-
           taire, au Séminaire de probabilités de l'
           Université de Strasbourg."

              1.Probabilities--Addresses, essays, lec-
           tures. I.Strasbourg. Université. Institut
           de Mathématique. II.Series.

                           ◯
```

Fig. 9-6. Additional number added to series added entry making a new card.

In this second case, it might not be advisable to use "[etc.]" in the call number, unless space on the card is really a problem.

Temporary catalog cards would not be needed for the series added entry while the cards are being typed for each monograph due to the serials stamp on the cover card. This needs to be pointed out to staff and patrons alike. This can be especially helpful and timesaving if there is a backlog in cataloging or if serial analytics are sent on for monographic treatment by a monographic cataloger, who traditionally and notoriously puts serials work off in a large number of libraries. There should be temporary cards under the separate main entries for each monograph in the series, in the catalog as well as in the shelflist, while cards are being made.

There is a problem inherent in the decision to scatter or not to scatter a monographic series: you generally have to decide from the first issue received. Sometimes you can tell by the title. *Studies in history* could cover at least four major classification sections of the LC classification. Even *Studies in English history* would be broad, covering the entire DA area. *Social science monographs* would be even broader, covering H, a huge schedule by itself, and possibly J, also large, K, and L, with the possibility of touching upon B for psychology, R for medicine, and maybe T if discussing a technological subject, like air pollution. *Studies in librarianship,* however, would be more narrow in scope and a prime candidate for classing together as a serial. The title itself can sometimes be a big clue. If you are lucky, there will be a list of volumes already published or projected in the series, hopefully in the volume in-hand, or perhaps in a publisher's "blurb." If the series is an already-established one, the LC catalogs would give a clue as to what has already appeared. LC tends to use the same criteria for treatment of series that are listed here, so their choice of classification might be a good guideline for a library, although local preferences might take precedence since the people involved have to work at the local level.

> In theory, each monographic serial should be tested in order to determine whether it is to be analyzed or not, using as a touchstone the usefulness of that series in a given library. More specifically, a book which would be given "normal" cataloging if it did not belong to a series should definitely be analyzed if it is published in a series.[10]

Reference people, subject specialists, serials acquisitons and cataloging staffs should somehow be involved in these decisions, depending on the situations and, possibly, the organization of the library. Economies in cataloging are not economies if they result in more work for patrons or public service staff.

> The decision to scatter or not to scatter is, in the aggregate, one of the most important made in college and research libraries.[11]

There are problems sometimes with series that should have analytics. They may start out as perfectly respectable periodical publications, as *Revue des lettres modernes* did, and then split into series and subseries, some volumes analyzable and some not. *Fennia* spent many years being a collection of articles before, all of a sudden, its publishing pattern changed and each one of the articles was numbered separately and it suddenly became an analyzable series of single monographs. Some university or society publications may have monographs for a long time and then a totally unanalyzable volume of a periodical nature, with many articles by many people and with not even a collective title, comes along. Tulane University has been guilty of publishing several such series.

The only hope for such a situation is a note on the cover card for the series which says something like: "For contents of this series under individual authors see cards filed behind." This wording could be reworked if the analytics are not generally under author, such as literature series under uniform headings or some variation such as "authors and titles" if the series has a lot of title entries. The idea is still there, and the holdings note still covers the series for those looking for a volume the library may have, but cannot analyze at all.

Another alternative, definitely second-rate, is to refer to the shelflist for partial analyzed series. This provides a hardship for the patron, which, as mentioned before, is unfair.

It is also possible for the change to occur in the other direction as well. *Figure 6-42* shows a title LC chose to scatter early in its career; then the title changed character and LC cataloged it as a serial without changing the older issues. In smaller libraries it would be advisable to recatalog the older issues with the later set, still analyzed if desired, for ease of use, particularly since the older monographic issues were so few in number.

Notes can be made if special issues get analytics, too. Sometimes a straight serial may have special monographic issues. If these bear serial numbering, they should be analyzed within the set. If they bear separate monographic series numbering rather than that of the parent publication, they should be treated as a separate title, with the same criteria holding about cataloging separately or as a serial with analytics. If they bear no numbering at all, they should be considered separate monographs.

An advantage of the integrated Serial Department is that, with the cataloger there, the rest of the serials personnel are more aware of cataloging problems. Thus, they will question issues they feel should be analyzed. They will be able to see, as they check-in mail, that a serial has changed character, and can bring this to the attention of the catalogers. Notes that a series has analytics should appear on the check-in record and checkers should be taught, as part of their job, that such discrepancies should be questioned.

Partial analysis might be made for a series whose volumes are of unequal importance. A contents note could be made on the main entry and those numbers that received full unit cards could be starred or otherwise marked. Then, volumes that have important authors, titles or subjects could be analyzed. Insignificant volumes could be virtually ignored. This has been suggested as a timesaver, but it defeats the purpose of the catalog, which should be as full as possible, and may create problems later on. Going back and redoing is always harder than doing it right in the first place, and it is strongly suggested that all volumes should be analyzed when looking toward the future. There may be considerable patron confusion resulting from a partially-done job, too.

It may be that special volumes, such as bibliographies, may have to be extracted from the series to be classified separately to suit reference librarians. This should be done only if the book is out of print or the library cannot afford a second copy. Notes should be made on the catalog cards, shelflist, serials check-in record, and automated serials list, if the library has one, adequately explaining what has been done. The cataloging for the extracted volume should also include a series added entry. If a second volume has been purchased and closely classed, notes should also be made on serials records, and on the series authority file, so that serials catalogers and others looking in the catalog will not think the duplicate cards are a mistake and pull them. If the volume has not been reclassed, but simply taken from the stacks and shelved elsewhere, the different location should be stated in all records. If a series is to be scattered in many libraries or different locations of the same building, however, it is best treated monographically.

A series authority file should be maintained so that catalogers all over the library will know what the authorized treatment of a series is. The following is a very simple authority card. It can be used for either monographic or serial treatment, with or without analytics. The authorized form of the series name, as it should be traced, should be entered at the top of the card. Any references needed should be put in the space next to the "X" and cross-reference cards should be typed. Stray volumes of serials that land in monographic catalogers' hands can be routed through the serial record. Orders for individual volumes can be sent from monographic acquisitions people to serials acquisitions people when the proper treatment of a series is discerned from the file. Authority file cards for serials treated with, or without, analytics should be typed and filed when the title is first cataloged so that further volumes might not bypass the serial record and be treated improperly. The call number for the serial should be indicated under the word "Series."

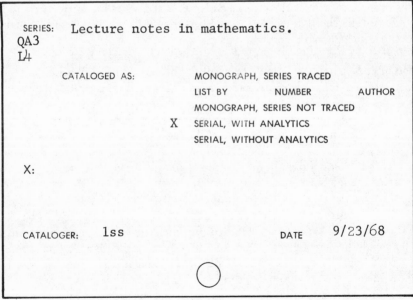

Fig. 9-7. Series authority file card.

Periodicals need not be included in the authority file and need not be indicated as "serials without analytics." This category should be used for those series which could be analyzed but are not (Kathryn Luther Henderson's bone of contention) for some reason.

Whenever there is a discussion of monographic treatment of serial publications, there is automatically a question that raises its ugly head: who should do the work? The monographs people or the serials people?

The monographic argument is that monographs people can catalog monographic material better, which is probably true in many cases. You also have a network of subject specialists, most likely, who would be interested in the materials received in their subject areas, particularly if they also do bibliographic and selection work. The second problem usually can be worked out in some way. The people who are knowledgeable in a subject area will always be called upon for help in that area, if their advice is needed. The first argument is, of course, argumentative. However, most serials catalogers have been through the library school, or technician training route if nonprofessional, which emphasizes monographic cataloging.

When considering a monographic series cataloged as a serial, it must be remembered that the serial nature of the publication has been considered the most important. This is usually overlooked by monographic catalogers and played down, even to the extent of virtually ignoring it. Volumes in a series may be distributed to a number of different people. This means the treatment will probably be inconsistent, even with the authority work soundly built as a basis. At least with a small number of catalogers, as in the Serials Department, the procedures can be more standardized and in keeping with the coverage expected of the Department when it placed the material on order. It is not good to have two departments responsible for the bibliographic control of the same material, as many serials catalogers will testify. It can be done, but communication would have to be considerably better than it usually is in most libraries.

Monographic departments are usually not set up for routines based on frequency, such as the monthly receipt of *Adelphi papers* or a fistful of *Exchange bibliographies* put out by the Council of Planning Librarians. Monographs people tend to procrastinate when it comes to serial publications and the material will sit and wait. The CPL *Exchange bibliographies* are timely and should not wait. Professors will start to send in orders for publications in the *Janua linguarum* series (of which there are five) without indications of series as they order from current catalogs that do not mention series. These separate orders will probably go through for purchase while the books sit nearby with no indication of their receipt except for anonymous check marks in the serial record. Analytics need to be processed, searched, and cataloged rapidly to avoid duplicate orders. Generally this can be more efficiently done in the Serials

Department, where the records are. Too, the workflow is smaller and perhaps more easily managed. Titles newly cataloged as serials may be analyzed at the same time, necessitating only one scrutiny and intellectual decision rather than two. The serial cataloging can depend and build upon the monographic cataloging and vice versa, all at the same time. Problems with titles that receive partial analytics can be resolved within the Serials Department. Numbering and other variations can be caught and records changed almost immediately. Small variations can be caught by those who are trained to catch serial irregularities and cope with them. Such inconsistencies would probably confuse the mind primarily concerned with orderly monographs.

It is strongly suggested that monographic series be analyzed within the Serials Department framework. Article analysis, to be discussed next, is even more involved in the daily processing of the Serials Department and should also be located there, although this function is most often done in public libraries by the reference librarians.

Whatever the decision as to who will catalog, communication on treatment of series should be as clear as possible. This is best done by the series authority file card already shown.

Analytical entries can also be made for articles, as well as for monographs, in serial publications. Here the reliance should be more on indexing and abstracting services than with monographs, which are generally not so well covered by indexing media. However, if the serial is not covered by an index, or if the library finds need for analyticals in a certain field, such as local history, a library may choose to analyze articles in its journals. Special libraries find often that they need to analyze articles that may for many years be the only thing published on a special aspect of their confined sphere of interest. In most of these cases, actual cataloging rules have been kept to a minimum and may even be nonexistent. This is lamentable. Even though a library may make decisions to catalog above and beyond the rules, these rules should still be used as general guidelines insofar as they apply. It is perfectly possible to catalog an article of a few pages within the framework of a monographic catalog card, and this would be the suggested practice as it would reinforce the patron's concept of the catalog rather than throw something new at him.

Rule 142 defines the series area in the description of a separately published monograph (rule 143 in the old edition of the rules), showing how the series should be represented. In the presentation of rule 6, it is stated that added entries for series should follow rule 6, too; 33N indicates added entries should be made

> . . .under the series for each separately cataloged work (adding after the title the numerical designation of the work as part of the series if it is numbered) if it can

be reasonably assumed that the work might be cited as part of the series or if the series might be reasonably cataloged as a collected set.

AACR/NA.

Old rule 151, superseded in part by new rule 151, covers tracings of secondary series as well. Rule 156, referred to in rule 172, covers "analytical entries," which are defined therein as

> . . .an entry for a part of a work or series of works for which another, comprehensive, entry is made.

AACR/NA.

The rules wave off individual volumes in rule 156 with this sentence:

> If the part analyzed is an independent work, it is cataloged according to the rules for separately published monographs, with a series note indicating its relationship to the more comprehensive work.

AACR/NA.

This, of course, brings us back to the rules for series recording and added entries, already quoted and discussed. The rules for analytics continue, but only to describe analytics that are not independent, which are called "page" analyticals or "in" analyticals. Even the Library of Congress does not use this format very much any more. Most libraries have chosen to use the same format for analytics that is used for monographic cataloging.

The AACR does not give any kind of guidance as far as guidelines for cataloging choice are concerned. Only such outside sources as Osborn or LC give this kind of guidance, and individual libraries must make their own choices on individual matters.

The volume or number or part would appear in the call number of a normal monographic series analytic. This could be amplified to include page numbers for articles, if necessary. The format and rules would still be basically the same. Subject headings may need to be expanded because of the need for finer delineation, especially in special libraries. The format for page analyticals is still in the rules and pretty much calls for what is outlined here.

```
Z881     Paltsits, Victor Hugo, ed.
N4          Family correspondence of Herman Melville,
v.33     1830-1904, in  t he Gansevoort-Lansing Collec-
no.7     tion. New York, July, 1929.
p.507-     ₍68₎p. illus. (New York₍City₎Public Library.
525,     Bulletin, v.33, no.7, p.507-525, v.33, no.8,
v.33,    p.575-625)
no.8,
p.575-   Includes explanatory footnotes.
625

            1.Melville, Herman, 1819-1891--Correspon-
         dence. 2.New York₍City₎Public Library. Ganse-
         voort-Lansing          Collection. I.Title.
         II.Series.
```

Fig. 9-8. Suggested format for analyzed article.

It is probable that, as time goes on, less and less of this type of analysis will have to be done. Computers have already shown their worth in information retrieval, primarily in the science areas. Medicine, chemistry and agriculture are all very well covered by data bases and the methods to retrieve information from them. So far there have been some advances in the social science areas with *Social science citation index* and *Psychological abstracts.* Someday there may be no need to index serials article-by-article and page-by-page, for everything will be retrievable through the computer. However, until this millenium arrives, we may be stuck with little "3 x 5" cards for serial articles.

Even in general libraries, particularly university libraries, there may be a call, from time to time, to analyze an article or a volume of a serial not usually analyzed. The same procedures should be followed in the cataloging of these as of anything else. Control cards should be kept as a record of what has been requested and perhaps, sometime in the future, an entire series might be picked up and analyzed as the result of requests for so many of its volumes or parts. Nowadays, this very often comes as the result of publishing practices. Many issues of serials are now being reprinted as monographs, and libraries discovering this are tending to analyze their serial copies rather than spending a few pennies of their evershrinking budget on another copy.

When a collection of miscellaneous periodicals on a specialized subject are received in the library, a subject analytical may be made as follows:

```
NX600 DADAISM--PERIODICALS
D3A1
        Single and scattered numbers of periodicals
    and other serials, containing material on this
    subject, and not otherwise recorded, will be
    found on the shelves under the above call number
```

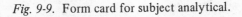

Fig. 9-9. Form card for subject analytical.

Pamphlet collections and minor monographic material may also be treated in a like manner. The subject analytical for the serial should have the holdings statement stamp or legend, as all serial cards should. The central serial record can record holdings, including titles, or these can be treated as an uncataloged collection, to be discussed in Chapter 11.

A point should be made here about materials abstracted from a journal or other serial publication. Photo-offprints of articles published originally in a serial issue should be considered monographs, if the library decides to keep them at all. Added entries should be accorded the serial, but this single article should not be equated with the serial publication. In this case, the monographic nature of the work is more important, even if it is only a few pages long. Clippings from newspapers and journals should likewise be treated with an emphasis on the monographic aspects — that is, individual authors, titles and subject matter. If fully cataloged, rather than being assigned to a pamphlet collection, these entries should suffice for the serials aspects of these publications. They should not be entered on the serial record.

The *Anglo-American cataloging rules* virtually ignore the problem of analyzing series, except for the problem of serials that appear within serials. This area is covered in rule 172:

172. Analytical entries

    A. Serials that are parts of other serials can generally be described by means of an informal note in the catalog entry for the main work. An added entry for the title, or the author and title, of the part serves as an analytical entry.

    Beginning with 1920, includes Oudheidkundige mededeelingen uit het Rijksmuseum van Oudheden.

    Vols. 1- include Proceedings of the 27th- annual meeting of the Pacific Coast Branch of the American Historical Association.

    B. Titles which are sufficiently important to require separate analytical entries, or for which special secondary entries need to be made, are cataloged according to the rules for cataloging other serial publications, with an analytical note taking the place of collation, or imprint and collation, as in other analytical entries (see 156). This note follows the form of other "in" analytical notes, the reference to the main work containing the same data as the "bound with" notes for serials (see 171).

    American Historical Association.
    Proceedings. 1st- 1884-
    (In its Papers, 1884-1888. New York. 25cm; and in its Annual report. 1889-91, 1893-1917, 1919-32, 1935- Washington. 25cm.)

                                             AACR/NA.

FOOTNOTES

    1. Harry Dewey, "Handling monographs in series," *College and research libraries* 15 (July, 1954):272-273. Also in Harry Dewey, *Specialized cataloging and classification theory and technique* (Madison: College Typing and Printing Co., 1963), pp. 36-37.

    2. Andrew D. Osborn, *Serial publications; their place and treatment in libraries,* 2d ed. rev. (Chicago: American Library Association, 1973), pp. 276-277.

    3. Dewey, *Specialized cataloging,* pp. 36-37.

    4. W. S. Merrill, *Code for classifiers; principles governing the consistent placing of books in a system of classification,* 2d ed (Chicago: American Library Association, 1939), p. 14. Quoted in Edgar G. Simpkins, *A study of serials processing.* M.S. in L.S. thesis, Western Reserve University, 1951, p. 56.

    5. *Cataloging service bulletin* 104 (May, 1972):6.

    6. Osborn, *Serial publications,* 2d ed., rev., p. 275.

    7. Kathryn Luther Henderson, "Serial cataloging revisited — a long search for a little theory and a lot of cooperation" in *Serial publications in large libraries,* ed. by Walter C. Allen. (London: Clive Bingley, 1971, c. 1970), pp. 56-57.

8. Dewey, "Handling monographs," p. 275; Dewey, *Specialized cataloging,* pp. 36-37.

9. *Cataloging service bulletin* 104 (May, 1972):6.

10. Marian Harmon, "Policies for analyzing monographic series, part II: University libraries," *Serial slants* 4 (July, 1973):130.

11. Dewey, "Handling monographs," p. 271.

12. Esther Anne Smith, "Form cards," *Catalogers' and classifiers' yearbook* 5 (1936):59.

Chapter X

Micro and Other Forms

Serials have managed to make themselves interesting for many years in the conventional manner: by never remaining too much the same. They have the possibilities of interminable change, even within the conventions of the printed book form, the codex. However, with the increasing technology, they are branching out into all sorts of further possibilities to trap the serials cataloger.

Microforms are bailing a lot of libraries out of ''hot water'' in this era of the ''budget crunch.'' Microforms are cheaper. There isn't the cost of binding or of keeping up with replacements for lost, stolen or mutilated issues. Expensive stack space can be reserved for other materials. It is cheaper than buying expensive backsets. There isn't the need for a second subscription to insure good binding copies. Newspaper and newsprint materials are more accessible and better preserved. And, of course, many things are within the range of the average library in terms of microtexts which, in hard copy, would be rare and unobtainable items. Hopefully, however, if the library has a choice, the choice of microeditions has been made wisely in terms of the publication's suitability on microtext (i.e.: illustrations, reference value, length of articles, issuing pattern of the publication and indexing). Assuming that all these preliminary matters have been taken into consideration upon order, there is still the problem for the cataloger: ''What to do with the blasted things?''

The first hurdle to jump is that of accepting the fact that they are serials too, and not second-class serials either. In fact, as time goes on, more and more material may be published originally in a microform. They deserve full treatment in the same way as hardcopy. The format may be different, but the information is essentially the same and needs to be indexed for the collection.

The content of microform materials does not differ from bookform publications, and hence it ought to be considered an integral part of the library's collection, i.e., each microform entry should be fully classified and cataloged, with author, title, subject, and added entries filed in the public catalogs. . . . Incomplete cataloging of microforms seriously limits access to the material, while an un-classified microform collection is indeed de facto separated from the total library collection.[1]

For all of these reasons, it is not wise to take shortcuts in the bibliographic control of microform serials. They should be fully cataloged and, if the library classifies its serials, these should also be classed. If the publication would warrant full treatment in its hardbound form, it should also in its microform. The need for full bibliographic description should be determined by the con-tents, not the physical format. If a library catalogs hardcopy material, but does not its microform collection, it is almost saying to the patron that a murder mystery by Agatha Christie in eye-legible print is more important than the Dead Sea Scrolls in microform. Not particularly good logic. The patron should be able to find in the catalog adequate representation of the things the library has to offer.

A minor shortcut can be made in the description of the microform as such. The title can be cataloged as if it were the original hardcopy, with a note over the call number: "Microfilm" [etc.], just like a location symbol, and in the descriptive notes, an abbreviated note like "Library has microfilm edition" can appear. This is a lot easier than a full description of a microform set and LC or other catalog copy is easily adapted. But the essential bibliographic history and description of the hardcopy title should not be compromised, however.

Osborn suggests that

Because there are mixed situations, it is wiser to catalog microcopies as though they were originals and to indicate the parts that are microreproductions.[2]

This can easily be extended to include all micro-published serials, even if the library has no hardcopy issues at all. The philosophy is still the same. Micro-forms should not be considered second-class in any way.

Although some have accepted the idea of cataloging microtexts, the idea of classing them has not fared so well.

. . .It may be well to note that a majority of the writers on the cataloging and classification of films have reached the general conclusion that while the cataloging of films is both desirable and necessary, the classification of films is neither. The assumption is made that films may not be consulted on the shelves.[3]

This is simply not so! It is advisable to class microform serials for the same reasons that it is a good idea to class the hardcopy. For example: subject searches can be made in the shelflist for material in esoteric areas or for inventory of a subject collection. If computer listings are made of serials by call number, these would be left out if not classed. Also, classifying a microserial can provide continuity for the patron who is used to finding *Life* under AP2.L4 in the bound stacks and comes looking for the microfilm armed with the same call number. Boxes of film could even be shelved with the bound volumes, although it is probable that there are only a few libraries where doing this would be wise. Although there cannot be complete browsing of microforms, being able to retrieve them by call number from a drawer of similarly-classed titles can provide some of the advantages anyway.

Call numbers do provide the patron with a location symbol he is used to and, if he is a sophisticated user, may be of great meaning to him. To make him learn a whole new set of contrived accession numbers, as so many libraries do when in the realm of microtexts, may be very awkward and confusing to him. Another shelflist for microforms tends to divorce these publications even more from the general collection so that consultation will be overlooked. Large libraries will also find it awkward and unwieldy to maintain a set of accession numbers.

Providing a location symbol for these materials over the call number such as is already done for things not in the general collection such as reference, documents, or special collections has already guided and conditioned the patron. Providing the same treatment for microforms would simplify and amplify the already-working system. For this reason, class numbers with accession numbers as Cutters is not a good idea, either. It does not relate to the normal scheme of things, although it does a much better job of it than a straight accession number arrangement. The general argument for accession-type arrangements relates to an unwillingness to do a lot of shifting. This is, of course, a recognizable problem, but it can be solved. If microfilm is kept on shelves, spaces can be kept open for ever-growing sets. If it is kept in drawers, it would be a little harder, but could be done. Card forms would not cause so much of a problem for the space would not be so great. Still, arrangements could be made for adequate storage. Such questions as this should not affect cataloging and classification of the materials.

For serials there is another problem. Perhaps a run of a title is not completely on a microform. This was touched upon earlier by Osborn as a justification for full cataloging treatment of microreproductions of serials. What note should be in the public catalog? Osborn feels that complicated descriptions of micro and hardcopy holdings should not appear in the card catalog, and, of course, he is right.[4] Such information should appear in the official serial records and holdings lists, however. If the issues are scattered, an easy solution is a note like: "Library has some issues on [microfilm]." This is best if the department is unsure of its policies, if it is filling in scattered volumes, or there are problems otherwise. It does not cause problems nor does it need to be updated. The shelflist or central serial record can record individual blocks of holdings of a microfilm. If a defined number of volumes were purchased in the past, a note more specific like "Vols. 1-100 on microfiche" could be used. If the library has a current subscription for a micro title, continuing a bound backfile, a note like "v.24- 1972- on microfilm" could be used. However, this would not be advisable in the case of a microfilm edition coming at the end of a year and superseding unbound hardcopy, for it would be misleading (indicating that there is no hardcopy at all after a certain point in time). Then it would be advisable to use the note first suggested: "Library has some issues on microfilm." This function should be reserved for a central serial record, which should also answer the same questions for microform holdings as it does for hardcopy. Such holdings should also be included in the serials list, if such a list exists for that particular library. If the library maintains a shelflist of bound holdings, these holdings should be included there as well. To distinguish from hardcopy, some designation should be used. Since a serial may appear in more than one microformat, designations should be specific, especially if the locations may vary. The following are suggested short abbreviations for microformats:

mc	microcard (opaque cards, usually 3x5)
mf	microfiche (transparent cards, 3x5 or 4x6)
mfm	microfilm (film)
mp	microprint (opaque cards, 6x9)

Microtext volumes could be indicated by these abbreviations and shelflisted along with the hardcopy volumes to insure continuity of holdings statements in the shelflist. Other abbreviations could be devised as necessary.

A second copy might be acquired in one of these forms. Notes would be worded as appropriate: "Second copy on microprint."

If the library has more than one copy on a microform, notes might read like this: "Library has copies on microfiche and microcard."

Because situations like this can occur, it is better to use call number designations than to classify each set separately in different schemes for different forms. It is advisable to keep copies separate even though they complement each other, for they might be filled in eventually. Let the serial record clarify with appropriate notes.

If the library has a copy, even a microcopy, of a title, and then acquires another copy of the same title in a big series, such as the *Americal periodical series* or *English literary periodicals,* the single title should be considered copy one, with notes indicating call number and reel number(s) for the second copy. Each title in one of these sets should be analyzed as a complete title, with added entries or cross-references for variant titles, etc. Many of the big series do have catalog cards available.

The Anti-jacobin; or, weekly examiner. 4th edition, revised
and corrected. London, Printed for J. Wright, 1799.

2 v.

Originally published in 36 no., Nov. 20, 1797-July 7, 1798.
Edited by William Gifford.
Microfilm. Ann Arbor, Mich., Xerox University Microfilms, 1972.
1 reel. 35 mm. (Early British Periodicals, reel 230)

I. Gifford, William, 1756-1826, ed. (Series)

AP4.A65

Fig. 10-1. Catalog card for *Early British Periodicals* series.

Each should also have other appropriate records, such as serials list listings and
representation on the central serial record. Not analyzing the contents of large
series of microform serials tends to result in expensive duplication and
frustrated patrons. Analysis of such series is very important.

Sometimes having microforms tends to make things interesting for the
cataloger. When *Harvest years* changed to *Retirement living,* it did it in the
middle of a volume. This was indeed unkind of them and the people of LUTF-
CSUSTC (Librarians United to Fight Costly, Silly, Unnecessary Serial Title
Changes) probably sneered. The problem was easily solved by successive entry
cataloging for the hardcopy. But the microfilm came in all together! What to
do? It seemed silly to cut the film, so the title was recataloged under latest entry. It seemed the easiest way out of a sticky problem. This particular problem
was furthered by something of a confusion in the title on the piece, resulting in
some overlapping. The new title was treated as a subtitle until the break was
finalized and the situation was covered by notes. Things may not be so easy in
the future, however, due to international developments, but we still have to see
about that. Right now on the home front one can be sneaky.

Another problem came up with *Senior scholastic's Teachers' edition* and
Scholastic teacher, a supplement to it. Usually these are different titles, but
they were microfilmed together. The sneaky solution here was to mark the box

for one title (in this case *Senior scholastic* was picked as the more important title) and make notes on the cards as follows:

On *Senior scholastic. Teachers' edition:*
Some issues on microfilm. Microfilm, Sept. 1972-May 1973 also contains Scholastic teacher [Junior/senior high teachers' edition].

On *Scholastic teacher:*
Sept. 1972-May 1973 included in microfilm for Senior scholastic. Teachers' edition. (AP2.S46)

An added entry was made for the secondary title on the primary title cards so that attention would be drawn to it in the catalog. This could not be considered a merger since the library still receives the two titles in unbound current issues. The integrity of the two entries was maintained and the problem was fixed with explanatory notes, which also appeared in the other pertinent serial records in the hopes of turning any inquirer in the right direction. Note that the note for the secondary title gives the call number for the primary title so that the patron does not have to look up the other title in the catalog.

Absolute bibliographic description would not seem necessary for microform serials. There can be too many changes, such as from 3x5 to 4x6 inch microfiche. This kind of description would be best kept on the check-in record, which would also serve as a complete location file. Notes can be made saying: "For v. 16- see 4x6 file." Another location device for such a split record would be a dummy in the drawer bearing the same note. Some libraries put dummies in the general stacks for volumes extracted from the general collection for special locations, and this is just an extension of their practice. Notes whether microfilm is positive or negative are of little real use to the patron who just wants to find the words necessary for his research. Sure, it is true that one is easier to read on the machine and one is better for printing, but they are both legible for the use of the general patron. Such information may be added to the boxes, if not already there, as Nitecki suggests,[5] or it may be included on the central serial record. However, putting it on the catalog card makes it awkward to add further notes to a card, particularly if a hardcopy edition is purchased later. In such cases, it would seem more appropriate to make the paper edition the first copy, since this would strike the patrons' attention first and would probably be the one he would prefer reading.

Tauber has a long list of items that need to be included in the cataloging of microforms:

Place and date of microfilming and printing, used as imprint

Number of reels

Type of container

Collation of original

Note that it is a film reproduction

Name of the photographing agency

Location of originals

Owner of originals

Contents of the reels

Nature of the film (positive, negative)

Date microfilm made (as separate note)

Reduction ratio of film

Placement of film (position)

Title on microcopy

Kind of film (e.g., Eastman microfile)

Accession number of film item

Entry in printed bibliography

Amount of material (e.g., 44 boxes)

Number of frames to reel

Pages per frame

Form headings

Manufactured title (for newspapers)[6]

He then goes on to state that the number of reels is needed, as well as other bits of information. This is really not necessary. Even this much description is too much for serials in the minds of many serial librarians, and the 1967 rules improved on this immensely by trying to describe the original as much as possible. Negatives are indicated and the kind of microreproduction is specified, along with a brief physical description. The publisher is included. Fortunately, the rest of Tauber's list is not deemed needed. The only thing you really need to tell the reader is that he will be using some kind of a microform, which he can find in a certain place, along with machines for his use, and that he should be prepared to take notes or pay for a copy rather than take the material home with him. All of this can be wrapped up in a simple description of the material as "microfilm," "microfiche," or whatever. Very few would care for all of this type of information and Osborn feels that such refinements are not necessary, except perhaps at the Library of Contress.[7] This takes us right back to the suggested method at the beginning of this chapter, the shortcut of adding notes to copy for the original. The cards would look like this:

microfilm
AP2   **Time; a monthly magazine …**
T5   London, Kelly & co. ₍etc.₎ 1879–

        v.   illus., plates, ports.   22–22½ᶜᵐ.

Title varies: 1879–84, Time: a monthly miscellany of interesting and
    amusing literature … (Cover-title: Time, a monthly magazine)
    1885–88, Time: a monthly magazine of current topics, literature & art.
    1889–90, Time: a monthly magazine.
    1890–   Time.
Editors: 1879–81, Edmund Yates.—1885–86, E. M. Abdy-Williams.—1888–
    89, Walter Sichel.—1890–   E. B. Bax.
    Library has microfilm edition.
    I. Yates, Edmund Hodgson, 1831–1894, ed.   II. Whishaw, Mrs. Ellen
Mary (Abdy-Williams) ed.   III. Sichel, Walter Sydney, 1855–   ed.
IV. Bax, Ernest Belfort, 1854–1926, ed.

Fig. 10-2. Suggested cataloging format for a microform.

One of the major uses of microfilm has been in the reproduction of newspaper files. Newspapers are bulky to store, expensive to bind, and awkward to use. Even patrons have readily accepted microfilm for newspapers where they might not have otherwise; patrons basically don't like microforms. For the cataloging of newspapers, see Chapter 11.

While we are on the subject of microformats, let us discuss other noncodextype formats. The first that pop into mind are recordings. Since many books are issued with recordings, libraries tend to be more accepting of recordings than other audiovisual materials, which, particularly in a university situation, are relegated to the status of classroom aids in the various academic departments.

Serials in recording formats should be treated just like microeditions. If the serial is an original in that format, one can bend the description slightly to fit the format without going into the lengthy Library-of-Congress-type of description.

```
Recording/CA
PS324     BLACK box.    ⌜no.⌝ 1-
A1B58     1972-
          ⌜Washington, D.C., The New Classroom⌝
          nⴰ. bimonthly.


          A periodical of poetry and music in
          cassette form.



          1. American poetry--Period.  2. Music,
          American--Period.

                                        CU-Riv/1ss

                        ◯
```

Fig. 10-3. Catalog card for a cassette serial.

As can be seen in the example, the collation still indicates that the periodical is issued in numbers, which it is. The only description necessary is the note, and the location symbol over the call number. This symbol indicates that the publication is on a cassette. The following chart shows other suggested symbols:

Recording	—	Phonodisc
Recording/CR	—	Cartridge
Recording/RT	—	Reel tape

The use of such symbols makes the collection a portable one. It might conceivably be housed at first in Special Collections or some other guarded place, and then, as it becomes a larger and more substantial collection, it is given its own room with appropriate housing and machinery. With the advent of *Black box,* it is highly possible that serials will start to be published in such a genre as this.

The serial published in another format, just like the microedition of a serial, should be completely cataloged and classified, and for the same reasons. After spending time and money acquiring the title, and time and money to house it properly, there should be complete access to it so that it will not be buried in the collection. Serials in further formats have not made themselves known yet, but perhaps they will in the near future.

Serials have, however, made themselves obnoxious by publishing themselves in a variety of formats, differing from issue to issue. *McLuhan dew-line* and *Aspen* are two of these. *Aspen* is subtitled "the magazine in a box," which is an apt description. It has had issues composed of booklets, poetry and pictures on separate card-sized sheets of paper, records, photographs, a portfolio of Oriental art, posters, film, and a black paper put-together box kit! *McLuhan dew-line* was deceptively orthodox, being a newsletter or a booklet for most of its issues. However, it was not the same sized booklet or newsletter through all of its career. It also manifested itself from time to time as a booklet with recording, a booklet with slides, a deck of cards, and six posters. Probably the best way to deal with these is to house them in a special area of the library, such as Special Collections. They should be checked in on the central serial record, with a succinct description of the item received, such as "v.2, no. 3; 6 posters." If the library maintains a shelflist of bound holdings, this could be the place for a more detailed description, if desired. Or the shelflist could refer to the central serial record for description. The second choice would probably be a better one since there would be less handling of problem material before it was sent on to its final resting place. There would also be less duplication of effort in the recording of the issues. Public catalog description would be kept to a minimum with catch-all phrases such as: "In various formats; see central serial record for description," or the like. The material could be housed in boxes or large manila envelopes adequately labeled in the special holding area.

A serial may decide to try another format for an issue or so, such as the 12th issue of *Dryad,* which appeared on reel-to-reel tape. In such a case, the cataloger might elect to describe the one issue on the cardset and give it a special location, as might be done with an oversized volume of a bound serial run. However, the cataloger should guard against having to give complex descriptions of many varieties of oddments which a serial might choose to be from time to time.

The same basic approach could be taken with material issued with standard serial issues, such as recordings. The issue may be pamphlet bound and shelved separately with the record or tape in an area where the recording might be played. Location would have to be given and a justification for this issue being extracted from the set. Another alternative would be just to shelve the odd piece separately, with a note in the issue saying where the additional material might be found. This, however, is not a good idea, since the patron might miss the note and take the issue home only to find that it was only half there. Some additional material comes out with some serials on a regular basis, such as the maps in *National geographic* and some geography titles. These can be bound with the issues in pockets, but there should be some mention of them in the description of the serial as well. For the unbound issues, there should be some kind of holding place where these will be kept and not lost; perhaps the Bindery Preparation Section's file of title-pages and indexes.

The new technology has opened the doors to a veritable Pandora's box of evil possibilities for serials. So far only a few radicals have dabbled their toes in the avante-garde waters, but give them time! The future may produce serials on videotape as well as audio tape; film, discs, mobius strips, a series of concrete objects, and perhaps even media not yet dreamed of. We must not lose sight of the fact that, even though the media be a totally different one, the essence of the serial should not be lost. If the library feels such material should be acquired and housed, it should be cataloged and classed in the same manner (or as closely as possible) as all of the other serials. Serial catalogers have never balked at publishers' peculiarities before, so why start now? A serial in any other form is still a serial.

FOOTNOTES

1. Joseph Z. Nitecki, "Simplified classification and cataloging of microforms," *Library resources and technical services* 13 (Winter, 1969):79.

2. Andrew D. Osborn, *Serial publications; their place and treatment in libraries*, 2d ed., rev. (Chicago: American Library Association, 1973), p. 344.

3. Maurice F. Tauber, "Cataloging and classifying microfilm," *Journal of documentary reproduction* 3 (March, 1940):13.

4. Andrew D. Osborn, *Serial publications; their place and treatment in libraries.* (Chicago: American Library Association, 1955), p. 254.

5. Nitecki, "Simplified classification," p. 82.

6. Tauber, "Cataloging," p. 16.

7. Osborn, *Serial publications* [1st. ed.], p. 344.

Chapter XI

Uncataloged Collections: the Use of Form Cards

There may be materials which the library does not feel should be completely cataloged and which, therefore, would form "uncataloged" collections.

It is obviously ridiculous to make elaborate records for serial materials which is of ephemeral value only or which, because of space limitations, must be discarded.[1]

. . .Since serial cataloging at best is expensive, economical methods of processing less significant serials are highly desirable.[2]

These should be kept to a minimum and should have some listing in the card catalog, for the main catalog should list everything in the library in some form. The term "uncataloged" is, therefore, not technically correct, for some cataloging is done: an entry is maintained, although without description, and holdings are maintained as well, in the central serial record. Perhaps Osborn's term "self-cataloged collection" is more appropriate; however, due to the very minimum of cataloging performed, the term "uncataloged collection" will be used here.

Such uncataloged collections might include corporate annual reports, telephone books, city directories, university, college, and school catalogs, art exhibition and auction catalogs, bookseller's catalogs, and the like. These can be kept together in collections of a specialized nature, with a specialized acquisition and weeding policy. For the catalogs and the telephone books, the latest ones would be kept in most instances. Annual reports might be retained for the last, say, five or ten years.

All such materials should have public access, preferably through the card catalog. Entries can be typed on form cards with the collection name as "call number." As has been mentioned earlier, patrons think of the call number as a location symbol and any hints as to where to find such a collection should be located in the call number area, that is, the upper left-hand corner of the card. Calling the collection by a name, such as the "Annual Reports Collection" will facilitate its maneuverability. A note can be appended to the stack guide indicating where such material can be found and, if it is moved, the notes need only be changed. The entire catalog need not be turned upside down.

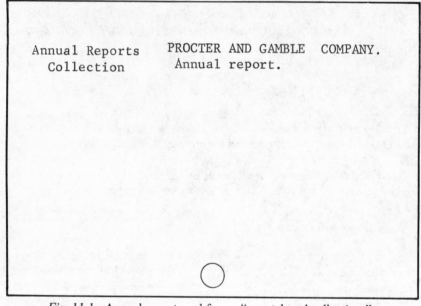

Fig. 11-1. Annual report card for an "uncataloged collection."

Notes indicating that holdings records are in the Serials Department, or elsewhere should be appended to the card, either as a stamp or as a legend on the form card itself.

In situations like this, it is probably preferable to use latest entry cataloging, especially if the earlier editions are discarded. Using such very short forms makes it impossible to have adequate history statements except on the central serial record, where all of these materials should also appear. Cross-references for variant name forms can be traced on the flip side of these cards and reference cards made.

An alternative for university publications could be a form card like the following for all publications of a school:

```
College     UNIVERSITY OF REDLANDS, Redlands, Calif.
Catalog
Collection     Of the administrative publications of
            this college, only the latest issue of
            each title (Catalog, Report; etc.) is kept.
            None more than five years old is preserved.




                            ◯
```

Fig. 11-2. Form card for university publications[3].

A similar sort of note could be made in the central serial record to ride herd on individual titles, if this is the way the library has chosen to go. Such form cards are an easy alternative to original cataloging. LC cataloging would not be obtainable for most of these publications for LC stopped cataloging university and college catalogs, mentioned in *Cataloging service bulletin* 27, due to "frequent irregularities, such as changes in titles, etc."[4] Certainly these irregularities would be downplayed by such form card treatment. LC employs such a method. Often, too, the patron does not know the specific title he is looking for when desiring a publication of this type. He is probably better served by this method. He is most interested in the school in question, rather than specific titles, anyway.

A suggested form card for public school publications, with the same kind of check-in record, is as follows:

```
Education
  Ref      PHILADELPHIA. PUBLIC SCHOOLS.



           Catalogs, courses of study, reports and
           similar publications of the public schools of
           the city, not separately listed, will be found
           in the Education Reference Department.




                              ◯
```

Fig. 11-3. Form card for school district publications[5].

Note that this gives a subject approach rather than a main entry approach.

A form card like the following can be used for the minor publications of societies, institutions and government agencies. It can be adopted for pamphlet collections and collections of minor periodicals on a topic or by a group, depending on the wording used. The following card is for an organization, but other variations can be made. Librarians should not be afraid to use form cards if they feel it will help in their work, and yet not hinder the patron in his library quests.

Telephone books are a unique type of serial with unique problems. Entering them adequately in the catalog might prove to be a bit sticky. As an alternative, there should be adequate signs indicating where telephone books may be found, probably in a special niche of the general Reference Department. A subject card might also be placed in the catalog, indicating the place where phone books were housed.

The books themselves should be arranged in alphabetical order in a geographic arrangement by state or country indexed, subdivided by principal city indexed. (An alternative might be to give them accession numbers, but this could become awkward and everyone would have to check the index first.) Separate yellow pages can be shelved after the regular white pages of the same city or area. They should be adequately indexed with references for the towns

```
Z673      AMERICAN LIBRARY ASSOCIATION.
A5
              Reports and publications not separately
          listed will be found on the shelves under
          the above call number.
```

Fig. 11-4. Form card for minor publications of an organization[6].

that appear in a book, but may not be named in the book's title. These cards should be arranged state-by-state, country-by-country, in the same manner as the books. The card file should be close to the books and also close to the staff who may have to use it on a regular basis.

Check-in records should be kept for telephone books so that new ones can be acquired and old ones weeded on a regular basis. A similar procedure can be instituted for city directories.

Another category of material that should be discussed here is the newsletter-type of ephemera. Some newsletters may be of current value, but the library may consider keeping such current-interest publications for years past their usefulness a waste of time and money. If this is the case, the question will probably come up: why bother to have them in your library at all? The answer is simple. Newsletters of organizations tell of meetings coming up and give current awareness. Newletters of museums give announcements of lectures or special exhibits. People who read these will go to the meeting or see the exhibit if they are interested. But knowing that there was a lecture in 1967 at such-and-such-a-museum on so-and-so-an-artist is not going to be helpful. If the lecture was very good, it will probably be published somewhere, but only finding out that it happened after going through many issues of an unindexed newsletter is not going to be worth much. Such materials can be kept for a short length of

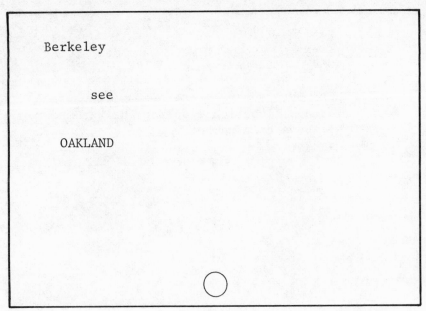

Fig. 11-5. Telephone book cross-reference.

time in the library and then discarded. They can be listed in the card catalog and mentioned in the automated serials list, if the library has one, with notes to see the central serial record and a note of the retention period. People will be able to find a publication under the entry in the card catalog, and will have some idea before going to the shelves of how much the library probably will have of the title. If the periodical shelves are arranged by entry, finding the material will not be difficult. Giving it a general area to shelve in a loosely classed arrangement will also serve the subject approach somewhat, probably insuring more use of the item. Of course, such an uncataloged procedure cannot be done in a library that shelves its unbound issues in call number order (unless the title is classed, and if this is true, it might as well be cataloged completely, although you can still have a short period of retention). Cards for newsletter materials cataloged by this method would look like *Figure 11-6*.

A cross-reference for the title would be traced on the flip side and a reference card made for the catalog under the title. Fully accurate entries should be used for union listings and ease for patrons going from bibliographies such as *NST* to the shelves.

It should be noted here that this is not an all-inclusive suggestion for the treatment of newsletter publications. Some newsletters are more "meaty" than others and deserve full treatment and retention; as, for example, the museum newsletter that bore the text of the lecture on so-and-so-the-artist, mentioned a

AMERICAN THEATRE ASSOCIATION.
ATA   theatre news.

Library keeps current year only.

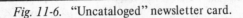

Fig. 11-6. "Uncataloged" newsletter card.

little bit ago. This suggestion is provided only for ephemeral materials and is to be used by those who want to cut a few corners. It should be used sparingly, for it shortchanges the patron.

Such a system can be used to give access to titles the library is "trying out." Perhaps the library has decided to stop throwing away a title that came in unsolicited in the "junk mail" and try it out on the clientele. Or, perhaps, a title has been received with another title and the library is not sure what to do with it. Perhaps a title that was ordered didn't turn out to be quite what was expected. Minimum access to it can be given while the experiment goes on. If the decision is made to discard the whole thing, the cataloger won't be too unhappy to undo the work, for all it was was an entry and maybe a couple of cross-references. If the decision is made to retain the title, the cataloging can be completed. The serial record entry should have been correct from the outset so all that needs to be done is to add the call number and a few notes. Such a system would be helpful to the cataloger, who would thus be armed with more than one issue of a title and also with some receipt history — and perhaps other information that would make the title a little easier to catalog. Looking at the procedure from this angle, it is simply a very long and drawn-out variation on temporary or, as LC called it, "form cataloging," long a burden of serials catalogers, particularly in the days of recataloging problem stacked upon recataloging problem.

This kind of shortcutting should be avoided for regular periodical publications on identifiable subjects (as opposed to annual reports or catalogs or telephone directories, which are really specialized materials), if time can be devoted to full cataloging. It is best to go for full cataloging for these serials, so that the patron gets a full subject approach and all the added entries. Notes can be typed across the face of LC or original cards stating "Library keeps two years only," or some such explanation depending on the retention policy of the library.

Newspapers provide another sort of problem. Newspapers covering a specific subject, like the *Commercial and financial chronicle* or *Variety* can be cataloged and classified as if they were periodicals (in fact, most definitions of newspapers do not include these special publications). But what does one do with the millions of straightforward newspapers that report the news of the world and the locale in which they are published? They cannot be classed with a subject; and LC's AN class is not fully developed, nor is it very useful, unless, perhaps, the library has bound holdings to shelve. What, then, is the answer?

Newspapers form, like other varieties of materials discussed earlier, a specialized kind of collection. They are usually treated separately from other materials. They can be adequately covered with checklists; or form cards can be provided for this collection, too, with the call number "Newspaper." Here is an example:

Newspaper

      The Sun-Telegram (San Bernardino, Calif.)

        X **Keep until microfilm received**
           Microfilm only
           Keep indefinitely
           Discarded after_____

                  (over)

Fig. 11-7. Newspaper form card.

Because a library may have different kinds of formats for a newspaper, or different retention periods from paper to paper, the choices for retention and format have been printed on the cards and one of them can be "X'd," as shown in *Fig. 11-7*. Holdings records should be kept in the central serial record and the stamp appearing on the serial cards can be affixed to these as well.

It is probably advisable to use latest entry cataloging for newspapers. The run is therefore kept together. Sometimes people are not too clear about the title of a newspaper; they just know it is the paper from the city that interests them. Keeping the run together means generally that only one title from the named place need be found. Latest entry cataloging also makes it a lot easier if the backfiles are on microfilm and there is a change-of-title in the middle of a reel.

There are also problems of continuity, such as when the morning paper from San Bernardino, California, formerly called *The Sun,* merged permanently with the evening paper to form *The Sun-Telegram.* This could have been considered a title change except for the fact that for many years the two papers had always joined on weekends for a combined edition called *The Sun-Telegram.* This note appeared on the front page of the February 4, 1974 issue, explaining what happened and what the reader could expect:

> Beginning today, your paper is called *The Sun-Telegram* seven days a week — morning and afternoon editions.

> With this change, *The Sun-Telegram* becomes an "all day" newspaper. As separate names *The Sun* and *The Evening Telegram* no longer will be published.[7]

Friday the first was the last issue of *The Sun.* This was followed by the weekend and then the change on Monday. The only answer was to catalog under the latest title. A lot of pesky brief and confusing variations can be clarified this way.

Cross-references should be made on the verso of the card as in *Fig. 11-8.*

References should be made for all variant name forms, including those of weekend editions (such as *Sun-Telegram* when the paper was still called *The Sun*). References should be made for titles including the name of the city if that does not appear on the masthead. For example, for *The Sun* there should be a cross-reference from *The San Bernardino Sun.* Very often this is the way people will refer to the paper, indicating specifically which one they want, but not necessarily being clear about the actual name of the paper. Newspapers should also be traced with the city of publication as "author." Because so many patrons approach newspapers from the point of view of their location, this can be very helpful. This is not particularly innovative, for Cutter suggested it in his *Rules for a dictionary catalog.*

The newspapers should be shelved in order by masthead title in a separate area distinguished by a sign saying "Newspapers," just as the call num-

```
         ◯

X The Sun (San Bernardino, Calif.)
  The San Bernardino Sun (San Bernardino, Calif.)
  The San Bernardino Sun-Telegram
  (San Bernardino, Calif.)
  San Bernardino, Calif.//The Sun
  San Bernardino, Calif.//The Sun-Telegram
  San Bernardino, Calif.//The San Bernardino

  Sun
  San Bernardino, Calif.//The San Bernardino
  Sun-Telegram
```

Fig. 11-8. Verso of 11-7 showing references.

ber/location symbol on the cards would indicate. This, too, can be a portable collection for the same reasons stated earlier in this chapter and elsewhere.

All the foregoing is, of course, a shortcut in cataloging. It is best not to do this, particularly for important publications. Unfortunately, this is what is primarily done with government publications, which generally receive short shrift all around. Document collections can be self-cataloging to a point. Many of the series are too numerous, bulky and complicated to catalog or analyze, and even LC doesn't try. But one should guard against obscuring material that might be in demand by the library's users. The self-cataloging concept should not be misused. Patrons often miss out on important materials because they are lost in document collections. This is especially true of popular governmental series that people don't think of as documents.

The general rule should be not to have an uncataloged collection unless you have to. Always adequately cover public access by main entry, appropriate cross-references, and some subject or form approach (subject arrangement in the current periodicals reading room, special lists or special shelving, for example). All notes on form cards should be as clear and explicit as possible. There is no reason to have material in the library unless it is made available but, after all, sometimes these special approaches are the *best way* to do so.

FOOTNOTES

1. Beatrice V. Simon, "Cataloguing of periodicals," *Ontario library review* 33 (August, 1949):237.

2. Andrew D. Osborn, *Serial publications; their place and treatment in libraries,* 2d. ed., rev. (Chicago: American Library Association, 1973), p. 212.

3. Esther Anne Smith, "Form cards," *Catalogers' and classifiers' yearbook* 5 (1936):58.

4. *Cataloging service bulletin* 27 (August, 1952):2.

5. Smith, "Form cards," p. 57.

6. *Ibid.*

7. *The Sun-Telegram* (February 4, 1974), p. 1.

Chapter XII

Holding Statements

Just indicating that a library has a certain title is not sufficient where serials are concerned. Very few libraries, except the very oldest and best-endowed, have every issue of every title to which they have ever subscribed. Serials cataloging needs to be augmented with records of holdings — "holdings" being defined as "volumes or parts of the serial in posession of the library."[1] Many librarians feel that because people approach serials through indexes, the library's primary function is the recording of holdings. Although this may not be strictly the most important function of serials cataloging, for identifying a serial correctly would be more important, certainly a list of holdings is an essential of serials work and it is necessary to tell the patron what you have in some way.

The *Anglo-American cataloging rules* indicate that holdings should be listed in the public catalog records.

163. Holdings

    A. General rules

        1. The statement of the volumes "held" by the library is given immediately after the title or subtitle in the catalog entry. If the work has ceased publication, this statement consists of the designation of the first and last volumes or parts, followed by the dates of the first and last volumes or parts.

        v. 1-14; 1929-42.

        If the library does not have all of the volumes that have been published, the extent of the complete set is recorded, provided the

238

information is available,[2] the volumes that are lacking are specified in a supplementary note. If essential data are not available, the statement of holdings consists only of the data relating to the first issue. If information about the first issue is not available, no record of holdings is given.

[2]The chief sources of this information are *New Serial Titles*, the *Union List of Serials*, and the *British Union Catalogue of Periodicals*. The extent of the complete set need not be recorded if the library's holdings are very fragmentary. [Rule continued in descriptive cataloging chapter.]

AACR/NA

This follows the philosophy that

In order to make [the] catalog the most useful to the public, the statement of holdings on the catalog card should show the actual volumes and years possessed by the library[2]

This is further substantiated by Simpkins when he said:

. . .A catalog is of little value to the reader if it does not carry a record of the holdings of the library.[3]

This is an old rule, a remnant of the past, and is rarely followed anymore. However, in the past, holdings were given on the main entry. Instead of added entries, cross-references were employed at other access points in the catalog indicating that on the main entry the list of holdings was to be found. Even when unit cards, a result of new technology in card production, became the going thing, the main entry for a serial was important because it was the only place where holdings were given. (See Appendix D for a representative list of reference notes for holdings.) It came to be that:

The use of stamps on all secondary cards, referring the enquirer to the entry is quite generally established.[4]

Even early on it had been decided that it was too time-consuming to put holdings on added entries, although it was Wimersberger's opinion that a complete statement of holdings on secondary cards gave quicker and better service if one didn't have to look elsewhere. Her second choice was to refer to main entry for holdings if the Library found the procedure too expensive on secondary entries. However, libraries had to be careful in wording their notes so as not to confuse patrons by using terminology unfamiliar to them like "main entry." (There is always that famous library story of the patron prowling around the front door because he was told that he would find his answer at the "main entry!")

There were several ways in which libraries could indicate holdings in the catalog. Notes on catalog cards might say: "Library has June, 1932- date," and/or "v.2, no. 5- date," but these are not very clear to the patron. What does "- date" mean? Patrons might not be very sure, although it seems crystal clear to librarians. The record might even be inaccurate, since v. 3 may be incomplete. It might be bound with stubs, or it might be in some holding place or closed backfile in unbound state. The patron looking on the shelf might be misled by the bound volume or confused by the unbound piece being missing. At any rate, such brief notes can be considerably less than helpful.

The library could catalog only its local set, as specified by the rule, rather than the complete or "perfect" set. There is a problem in this method in that patrons might miss the notes for incompleteness. In an attempt not to mislead the patron, you might confuse him.

Some libraries put penciled notes on the main entry cards themselves. Many complained because the Library of Congress printed cards did not leave sufficient room for adequate holdings records. Some found a solution by filing holdings cards behind the main entry, with reference notes to see the following card(s).

Another objection to holdings in the catalog was that cards had to be constantly removed. Some libraries devised replacer cards for main entries to be refiled in the catalog indicating the cards were "temporarily removed." Another very specialized method was used by large libraries, particularly those which maintained official catalogs: the "traveling card," also called a "return-duplicate card."

> A traveling card is recommended for use in large libraries in which it is not practicable for penciled additions to be made at the catalog or for main entry cards to be removed.[5]

The procedure is described as follows:

> In the traveling card system, an extra card is used. Holdings are added to the official record and to the extra card, and the extra card is then inserted in the public record in place of the entry to which the latest information on holdings has not been added. The card removed from the public catalog then becomes the traveling card to be retained by the serials assistant until holdings have to be changed to record another volume added, at which time the process described in outline here is repeated. To maintain an extra entry card for each serial title adds to the expense of serial processing operations, but the savings in time for changing public records of holdings is presumed to offset this added cost.[6]

If changes in imprint, editions, bibliographical notes, and the like, or additions (other than the latest volume) are made to the cards, the master card is 'flagged' with a tiny red signal. The next time a volume is added this flag acts as a signal to the cataloger that the traveling card which is filed behind the master card lacks certain information, either in the body of the card or in the early holdings, and must be made to agree with the master card. When the title ceases publication, and the library has a complete set, "Library has" cards and traveling cards are no longer needed. All cards are then withdrawn and a complete set of closed entry unit cards is prepared.[7]

Add-to cards work is done in pencil and, when the publication is finally completed, the original cards are completely retyped.[8]

It is exhausting for modern serials catalogers to even conceive of this plan, which is assuredly why it is no longer followed in most libraries. The costs are obviously not offset by savings in time; and, fortunately, automated lists and the central serial record pulled catalogers and their assistants out of this incredible morass of cards.

Now, few libraries maintain public holdings records as they did in the past. Most have given them up as being too time-consuming and sometimes misleading, for only bound volumes are listed. UCLA, for example, has indicated that it would like to cease recording of bound volumes in the public catalog (they do it on holdings cards filed behind the main entry), but has been unable to seek another alternative due to manpower, dependent procedures and the pressure of other priorities. There is definitely the problem there that, as the library grows beyond several hundred thousand volumes, it becomes increasingly difficult to maintain complete records in the public catalog, even under main entry only. Records should be considered from a long-range standpoint; and, all too often, libraries discover this too late.

The following observation would also seem to indicate that public holdings records are not sufficiently understood and utilized by the patron to make the expensive procedures worthwhile.

> My experience is that the public does not use the information [holdings listed on catalog cards]. It is the staff who find it helpful, and as long as the people who answer the questions have easy access to the record that is all that matters. It is an expensive and time-consuming routine to keep the public up-to-date.[9]

Perhaps, too, holdings are not a function of the catalog. The card catalog is at its best as a finding list, not as an elaborate statement of holdings. Public catalog listings that are awkward and confusing do not fit into Kathryn Luther Henderson's summary of the goal of bibliographic work in a library at all. She defines this goal as:

Getting it *if* you want it without labor, without difficulty, and without confusion.[10]

Because public catalog holdings only obscure the goal, they should no longer be a part of serials card cataloging. But this does not mean that you can forget about holdings. Serials processing is best served by a number of records. The same holds for serials cataloging, which is part of this overall processing. The holdings have to be somewhere. Where can this be if not the catalog itself?

One of the aspects of serials cataloging that, according to the AACR, makes it different from cataloging of monographs, is given in rule 160F:

> The catalog entry for a serial publication should show which parts of it are in the library's collection or refer to another catalog such as the shelflist or a special record of serials.
>
> AACR/NA

This last phrase is the "out" that serials catalogers needed.

Nowadays, most public card catalog records for serials direct the patron, by means of stamps or typed messages, to other records. (For examples, see Appendix D.) There, depending on the record, more or less complete holdings are given. A library may have a public shelflist, which has holdings cards for bound material. A stamp on the card may say, "For holdings see shelflist." But this is adhering to an antiquated and basically monographic viewpoint that only bound volumes have actually been added to the collection. This does not answer the questions of the patron wanting the most recent issues, or, at least, unbound ones.

Libraries looking for a solution to this problem may list only bound holdings in the catalog, with notes to see serial records for unbound and current issues. The problem with this is that the patron has two places to look; although it does realize the problem of unbound holdings, usually ignored by most methods. Other variations on this method indicate that holdings of unbound journals, or those not listed in the catalog, can be found in a current periodicals reading room. Although a specific record is not referred to, it is assumed that there is either one there that can be consulted, or that there will be no problem once the patron gets to this room.

Many libraries have found that a separate serials catalog answers some of the problems and questions caused by a need to amplify the public catalog record.

> Most libraries find it necessary to provide added aids in the form of separate serials catalogs, visifiles, etc. to supplement the card catalog.[11]

The catalog may be a 3x5 type of catalog with a serial catalog card, followed by holdings cards giving bound holdings, volume by volume. Directional cards in the public card catalog may lead the patron to this special catalog, or the public card catalog may give full cataloging, with references to the serial catalog for holdings, such with such notes as: "In progress. For numbers in library see periodical catalogue." The latter practice is followed with success at Cornell. (See Appendix D for other examples of notes.)

The serial catalog may be a listing of holdings. In the early years of this century, some libraries tried to make sheaf catalogs of one type or another giving lists of holdings on sheets of paper bound into books or loose-leaf binders. Most abandoned these projects for they were too costly to maintain and very difficult to keep up. Now, in the age of the computer, this type of listing has returned to libraries. One of the first projects a library experimenting with automation looks into is a list of serial holdings. Some are very sophisticated. Others are rudimentary, bearing only the essential information necessary to supplement the public catalog records. Some libraries, like the University of Colorado at Boulder, have almost completely supplanted their card cataloging for serials with a computerized book catalog, giving holdings and catalog information. The problem attendant upon such a situation is that there may be little publicizing of the fact that serials are not listed in the card catalog; and patrons, not finding what they are looking for, may assume (heaven forbid!) that the library does not collect serials. Adequate references must be made to the serials book catalog in such a case as this. A patron should be encouraged to ask questions so that he will be led to the right place if he does not realize that what he is looking for is a serial publication.

Such an automated catalog has the advantage of being updated with relative ease (no more penciled notes!) and being distributed to a number of locations for better reference service. Many by-products can result from further sophistication of such lists.

However, there is only one truly accurate listing of serial holdings, and this is the central serial record, whether it be on computer, as at the University of California at San Diego, or a manual record, such as the most of the rest of us have, on Kardex, Acme, or other visible records, or card files.

George Hartje said:

> One reason for establishing a separate serials unit and the resulting central serials record center is the fact that the holdings of a library can be expressed in this records center, thus saving the tremendous labor of adding information to catalog cards.[12]

In some libraries the visible file serial record may serve as the serials department catalog. This was at one time true at the Linda Hall Library in Kansas City. It gives holdings as well as bibliographic information, call number, what is at the bindery, on claim, on order, etc. It is the official record of the library's serial holdings. Patrons can be referred from the public card catalog to the central serial record where he can find all that the library has, either by himself or through a member of the library staff. This second alternative is preferable in most cases, since the patron might not understand the esoteric records, and he might tend to provide a hazard to the record's integrity, by refiling cards or by extracting cards or notes to take away with him, as some patrons are wont to do.

A survey was made by the Serials Section of RTSD in the mid-1960's.[13] It was found that a majority (77 percent) of the research libraries polled on the subject of holdings information used a combination of public records plus staff consultation. There was some variation of location for this service, but most libraries put it in a Serials or Periodicals Section rather than in General Reference and most said it was available whenever public services were scheduled. The majority also indicated that most of the people who gave service to the patron in this regard were also the people who were in charge of checking-in the publications. This is very good, for it shows more development in the right direction, that of developing a qualified staff of serials experts. (For more, see Chapter 15, "Serials Department.") When no public record is available, serials holdings are more generally found in the Serials Department. However, this is sometimes not a complete record but only, for example, the current issues records. Hopefully this augments the public record adequately. The movement, however, seems to be to the use of the central serial record for this type of information and augmentation of records.

Generally the objections to using the serial record for holdings stem from the fact that, in most cases, this is not a public record, available for patron consultation. Most serials departments feel that such records cannot remain the specialized administrative tools they should be if they are to be made open for the public to consult. This is true. It is probably also true that patrons would become confused by the specialized notations used and they might get more misinformation than information if they used the records themselves. The best solution is to have a trained person (or persons) meet the public, field the questions and interpret the record. In this way the user would get the best service possible — accurate, complete, and up-to-date. The library's money would be much better spent in hiring such a public service employee — or better yet, sharing this work among several staff members as an additional assignment — than in employing someone to carry on the impractical system of updating the public catalog record, which the patron may need help with anyway. (For more on the central serial record, see Chapter 14.)

While discussing public holdings, it would be apropos to mention another holdings record. Traditionally, bound volumes have been listed on some variety of check cards, as shown below, in the shelflist. This is a holdover from monographic practices, but can prove valuable in a serials setting, depending on

Library has volumes checked below:

1950	1960	1970	1980	1990
1951	1961	1971	1981	1991
1952	1962	1972	1982	1992
1953	1963	1973	1983	1993
1954	1964	1974	1984	1994
1955	1965	1975	1985	1995
1956	1966	1976	1986	1996
1957	1967	1977	1987	1997
1958	1968	1978	1988	1998
1959	1969	1979	1989	1999

Library has volumes   indicated above.
  For more information   see Serials Dept.

Fig. 12-1. Holdings card for volumes bound by years.

Vol.	Year	Vol.	Year	Vol.	Year	Vol.	Year
1		11		21		31	
2		12		22		32	
3		13		23		33	
4		14		24		34	
5		15		25		35	
6		16		26		36	
7		17		27		37	
8		18		28		38	
9		19		29		39	
10		20		30		40	

LIBRARY HAS VOLUMES   INDICATED ABOVE.

Fig. 12-2. Holdings card for title bound by volumes and years.

that setting. If the shelflist records volumes in a manner useful for inventory purposes, it should be maintained. Bibliographic volumes bound together in one physical volume should be recorded somewhere so that those doing inventory work can know whether that which is missing is one volume or many. The same is true of one numbered volume broken up into several parts for easier handling. Missing volumes can be recorded on the shelflist while the central serial record continues the process with the record of replacements ordered.

If the shelflist records volumes returned from the bindery before these are listed elsewhere, the shelflist has value for public service. However, if the central serial record has either of these two types of information, the shelflist record is less necessary and could be discontinued. Likewise, if such holdings information is adequately given in a separate serials catalog, or in the public catalog (which is nearby), the shelflist is unnecessary. However, if the public or serials catalog is far distant from the serials technical processing staff, such a bound record is important. A manual shelflist could also be used as backup to an automated serials holdings list in case there are unexpected breakdowns in the system.

The shelflist may also be viable for other reasons. For example, a record of disposition of bound volumes may be kept there for use of the cataloging staff. The shelflist can provide many services relating to holdings. Duplication is inevitable in some areas of serial records. All attempts to stamp it out should be given a long hard look first to see what important scrap of information, what valuable approach to a serial and its bibliographic control, would be irrevocably lost by such thoughtless cutting-back.

Holdings are important to the overall concept of complementary serials records, of which serials cataloging is most definitely a part. However, the most important holdings record of all is the central serial record, and all too often it is divorced from the serials cataloger. This should not be allowed to happen, as we shall soon see.

FOOTNOTES

1. Margaret Mann, *Introduction to cataloging and the classification of books* (Chicago: American Library Association, 1930), p. 267.

2. Evelyn G. Wimersberger, thesis, abstracted in *Catalogers' and classifiers' yearbook* 8 (1939), p. 133.

3. Edgar G. Simpkins, *A study of serials processing.* M.S. in L.S. thesis, Western Reserve Univeristy, 1951.

4. Arnold H. Trotier, "Economies in the cataloging of continuations," *Catalogers' and classifiers' yearbook* 4 (1934):32.

5. Wimersberger, *Yearbook* 8, p. 134.

6. Maurice F. Tauber and Associates, *Technical services in libraries; acquisitions, cataloging, classification, binding, photographic reproduction, and circulation operations* (New York: Columbia University Press, 1954), pp. 444-445.

7. Matilda F. Hanson, "Use of the 'traveling card' in cataloging serials," *District of Columbia libraries* 11 (January, 1940):24.

8. Andrew D. Osborn, *Descriptive cataloging,* Prelim. ed. (Pittsburgh: University of Pittsburgh, Graduate Library School, 1964), p. 109.

9. Beatrice V. Simon, "Cataloguing of periodicals," *Ontario library review* 33 (August, 1949):241.

10. Kathryn Luther Henderson, "Serials cataloging revisited — a long search for a little theory and a lot of cooperation," in *Serial publications in large libraries,* ed. by Walter C. Allen (London: Clive Bingley, 1971, c. 1970), p. 50.

11. Hortensia Tyler Gemmell, *A study of the methods used in the cataloging of serial publications of societies and institutions in small college libraries,* M.S. in L.S. thesis, Columbia University, 1940.

12. George N. Hartje, *Serial practices in public libraries* (Urbana: University of Illinois Library School, 1956), p. 2.

13. Rosamund H. Danielson, "Serials holdings information service in research libraries," *Library resources and technical services* 10 (Summer, 1966):261-283.

Chapter XIII

Location Indicators

As far as catalogues and checklists are concerned, it is necessary to represent exact locations clearly in all entries for runs of periodicals.[1]

Shelf location can be easily shown in general by the class mark. Bound issues of serials should shelve in normal order in the stacks with monographs on the same subject matter.

Unbound issues present an additional problem, however. One solution, followed by some libraries, is putting jackets that block out the call number over cards representing unbound runs. This, however, creates extra work for cataloging personnel, who have to remove the jackets when issues are bound. There is still the problem created by serials still "in progress" that have both bound backfiles and unbound current issues. This problem can be solved by shelving unbound issues in the stacks until there is sufficient bulk to bind. However, it is probable that this binding would never happen, for issues can be easily "ripped off" — secreted in one's notebook, purse, or clothing, and carried off without benefit of sanctioned borrowing privileges.

To reduce theft, libraries usually have a closely monitored periodicals reading room where patrons may look at unbound issues before they are sent to the bindery. Current issues may be available on open shelves; the entire run may be open for browsing; or backfiles, perhaps also with the current issue as well, may be closed to patrons and accessed only by pages armed with call slips. Open stacks may be arranged in a number of ways: alphabetical by title or entry, call number, classed (other than in call number order), or perhaps a combination of systems. This arrangement is important for the patron to know. Patrons may be

248

directed to this room by legends on the cards in the library's public catalog or serials catalog. (See Appendix D for sample legends. See also the preceding chapter on holdings statements.) Patrons can also be directed to the unbound issues by methods that supplement the catalog. This is by far the better way, for it leaves the catalog uncluttered for the addition of other information. Such general directions can be given in a number of ways: a brochure on the use of the library, fliers or handouts specifically on serial publications in the particular library, signs in the Reference Department or next to the catalog or serials catalog, the serials holding list or printout, library tours, stack guides, and your friendly reference librarian, information person, or catalog attendant.

However, specialized information should be given in the catalog for individual titles that receive special handling outside of the ordinary run-of-the-mill serial. This would include reference tools, bibliographies and other library tools scattered throughout the library in technical processing or specialized reference areas or branch libraries, titles on reserve for class reading assignments, special collection materials, etc. In short, it should include everything not in the general stack area or the current reading room.

The best way to indicate a special area for all of a title is to put a symbol over the call number. "R" or "Ref" or "Reference" is commonly stamped or typed over the call number of reference tools in most libraries. Curiously enough, the practice is not kept up with respect to other collections, even within the same library. It is felt that the call number should not be cluttered. However, the patron thinks of the call number as a location symbol and an unadorned call number will send him or her to the stacks. "Spec. Coll.," "Catalog Dept." and other symbols should be used for locations of serial runs. They should be as specific as possible.

A library may have several subscriptions for a reference or working tool, with locations in several parts of the library — such as *Books in print, PTLA,* the *National union catalog,* or various almanacs, directories, etc. The cataloger can do one of two things: either make separate cardsets for each location, with the appropriate legend typed or stamped over the call number, or make a single cardset with detailed notes: "Copy 1 in Reference, copy 2 in Govt. Pub. Reference." The second method is adequate, but the patron might miss the drop note. The first alternative is probably more public service-oriented and should be used unless space is at a premium. The second is all right if backed up by a serials holding list that has locations spelled out specifically, however. This can reinforce the catalog notes. Such information should always appear in the central serial record. In case it is missed elsewhere, proper reference service will be accorded the patron at the serials reference desk.

Library systems having branch libraries may elect to have a location check-off card in the public catalog of the main library, as U.C.L.A. does.

ADDITIONAL COPIES ARE IN LOCATIONS CHECKED BELOW:

Arch./Urb. Plan.
___ Lib.   ___ Educ./Psych. Lib.   ___ Physics Lib.*
___ Art Lib.   ___ Eng. & Math. Sci.*   ___ Pub. Aff. Serv.
___ Biomed. Lib.*   ___ Geology Lib.*   ___ Reference Dept.
___ Bus. Ad. Lib.   ___ Law Lib.*   ___ Special Coll. Dept.
___ Chem. Lib.*   ___ Map Lib.   ___ Tech. Services Dept.
___ Clark Lib.*   ___ Music Lib.   ___ Theater Arts Lib.
___ College Lib.   ___ Oriental Lib.*   ___ University Archives

___   ___   ___

                                                         ___

*Consult Catalog at this
location for call number.

Fig. 13-1. Location check-off card.

The main catalog then becomes a union list of locations, as well as titles, but in a more frugal manner than having a card for each location. (UCLA tends to use this card more for monographs, but there is no reason why its function couldn't be expanded.)

Some titles may not always be shelved in a special location. The latest issue only may be shelved in Reference, or elsewhere, because it has reference value only until superseded by the next one. A stamp can be affixed to the cards saying: "Latest edition in Reference," or some similar directive. Such a stamp should be large enough to catch the user's eye without cluttering the card. It could be put in the space under the call number to relate both location devices better and also to call attention to itself in a space not usually utilized on catalog cards.

Columbia University indicates that only the latest volume of a serial is retained in the Reference Department by a blue diagonally-cut guide card which files in front of the card being referred to. The legend on the card reads: "The latest volume of the work represented by the next card is in the Reference Room."

If a title is not retained, except for the latest issue, the stamp is not necessary. The location mark should be "R" (or whatever) and there should be a note, perhaps in red so that it will stand out, indicating that only the latest edition is retained.

Sometimes serials are acquired in several copies, shelved in different sections, moved around as they grow older, and finally discarded. Such directives can be typed on extension cards in the shelflist or serials catalog for the information of processing staff. A sample might be:

c. 1: Latest in Reference. Second latest in Monographs Acquisitions. Others discarded.

c. 2: Latest in Serials Biblio. Others in stacks.

The patron need not have blow-by-blow account of what is done with each volume, but he should get enough information that he knows where he can find the title if he needs it. He can be told only about the reference copy, which would be primarily for his use, or he can know about all copies. This would depend upon library policy, but should be consistent in all cases. Notes should always be clear enough for him to understand and locations like "Serials Biblio" need to be defined for him.

It is not general practice in some libraries to catalog their working tools and behind-the-scenes publications. This is a lamentable practice if it deprives the patron of knowledge about the only copy the library has. This procedure is acceptable if it is one of several copies, and there is a public copy; but if there is only one copy in the building, the patron should be allowed to know about it, even if it is squirreled away in a backroom and only trotted out for a patron's use once in a blue moon. As mentioned many times before, all of a library's stock should be represented in its catalog in some way.

Oversized serials should be integrated into the collection as much as possible by the adjustment of shelving in the appropriate sections. Serials keep on going, and using the library's probably fairly small oversized volume section for serials would squeeze out the monographs for which these sections should primarily be. A large percentage of general serials are oversized; think of the impact the run of *Life* magazine would have! However, if the set is too big for the regular shelves and is put into the folio stacks, such note should be made in the call number as established by the library. Some use "*'s," some use "f's," etc. (It is to be hoped that libraries indicate this in the call number rather than elsewhere because it is easier for the patron. He will copy it down with the call number. The patron should not be expected to look in the collation for location information, for example.)

If there are only a few oversized books in a set, they should be shelved separately, unless the shelving can be adjusted. Dummies can be placed on the shelves or notes can be made on all serials records including catalog cards and bound holdings card, indicating location. If the majority of a set is oversized, or if the set is very small — such as, perhaps, up to ten volumes — the whole set should be shelved together to facilitate its use. Notes are made on catalog cards as appropriate. Notes are probably better than dummies because dummies can get lost. They can also take up too much room, although they actually make the shelving more flexible than notes would.

Serial volumes on reserve for class readings in a university library, or only in a location temporarily, can be represented in a location file as "charged out" briefly to that location. Serials with analytics can have their analytic cards jacketed for a special location, but jacketing a serial card when only one volume has been extracted for temporary shelving elsewhere is misleading to the patron. In this case the location file would be a better solution. The location file is more realistic in terms of continued workload as well. But it is not fair to the patron to make him use a location file for something that will *always* be in a given place; this is much more in keeping with the function of the catalog. A location file like this should always be public.

Another problem that comes up with serials fairly often is the special reference value of one item in a set. For example, the *CLA directory* used to be published in the *California librarian,* usually as the fourth issue of each volume. This issue was extracted from the run each year and shelved in many reference departments until the next one came in and the old one could be bound with its volume. Analytics are a possible solution to this problem, or special notes can be made for the reference title and location on the catalog cards, which is in keeping with the "contents notes" section of AACR.

Location should be indicated in as straightforward a manner as possible. The patron should be able to understand what is meant. Any explanations should be put on the central serial record, which should also record any variant locations. Locations should also appear on other complementary records, such as a holdings list or serials catalog. Separate cards or entries should be made for each location so that inventory can be done easier. As in all serials cataloging work, the needs of the patron should be kept in mind and every care should be made to prevent the library from laying traps for the unwary patron by hiding something.

FOOTNOTE

1. John Horner, *Special cataloguing, with particular reference to music, films, maps, serials and the multi-media computerised catalogue* (London: Clive Bingley, 1973), p. 2 & 5.

Chapter XIV

The Central Serial Record and the Serials Cataloger

With an integrated Serials Department, Osborn's principle of complementary records is easily attained. He stated that:

> No approach to serial cataloging is satisfactory that does not make due allowance for the role played by the visible index [i.e., the central serial record], the *Union List of Serials* [include here *New serial titles,* too], and other serial records.[1]

Such a concept is fairly new, however. It was discovered during the scramble for input into the *ULS* in the Twenties, Thirties and early Forties, that entirely too many files were being kept and too much information was being duplicated. The answer seemed to lie in the setting up of a comprehensive serials record. Even by 1950, when George N. Hartje wrote his thesis,[2] few university libraries had centralized serial records, although many farsighted librarians were discussing the concept. Hartje studied equipment and formats for recordkeeping as well as many individual procedures and practices. This was still a time of holdings listed in the public catalog, but there is also a reflection of change in Hartje's paper and the harbinger of the central serial record as the sole record of holdings. As time moved on, more and more central serial records were established and the literature describes some of the trials and tribulations. A case in point is Ohio State University. James E. Skipper[3] says that a centralized serials record was organized from three files: the current periodical titles, public document files, and gifts and exchange. Four records were abolished: the shelflist, sheet shelflist, accession book and traveling catalog. Five records were consolidated into the incipient central serial record: the holdings in the public periodicals catalog, the bookkeeping record, checking files, unclassified material, and continuations. The files maintained were the public dictionary catalog, order card record, and binding dummies. There is no longer a public holdings record, but presumably this information is available through a staff member, and certainly more speedily than checking the previously established six files: public periodical catalog for bound volumes, current periodical file for unbound classified titles, unclassified file, unclassified state and local documents (two files), and a miscellaneous file for gifts and exchanges. Skipper goes into the details of the whys, the wherefores and the hows. One can only admire that they cut twelve files down to five, and the efficiency has undoubtedly increased tremendously.

About that same time Arnold H. Trotier[4] found that establishing a central serial record cut down expenses a great deal at the University of Illinois, where "persistent problems" existed in the six sections responsible for serials: Periodicals and Continuations Division in Acquisitions, for periodical or serial checking records; Serials Cataloging Division and Binding Section in the Catalog Department, one for cataloging, the other for added volumes; the Bindery Preparation Division, and Book Repair and Pamphlet Binding Division in the Binding Department. Centralization of serials records seems to have been the answer for a great many of the problems dealing with serials. Staffs and the proliferation of records they maintained were cut down. Procedures became streamlined and cheaper to run. Serials processing became more efficient as the result of a multipurpose central serial record.

A good point to stress here is the multipurposeness of the central serial record. It should contain quick answers to questions that can be answered easily, like "What are holdings?" "How do we acquire issues?" "What is bound?" It should be a complete checking record of holdings. It can also provide the shelflist bound volume function, if desired, which would certainly make added volume routines easier. "Cat seps" — that is, monographic series that are scattered — can be included, if desired, thus making it easier to report to union lists. Treatment of analytics can be noted. Duplication of effort, such as public catalog holdings, can be avoided. Irregularities in the history of titles should be included. Cross-references can be incorporated, although this would differ depending upon the use of the file — by the public or only by serials staffers. Claim procedures can be based on the file. Second copies can be listed, as well as treatment of loose-leaf, cumulating issues, and other problem material. Locations can be given, with call numbers and other data. Binding specifications and collation records can be included, along with information on indexes, title-pages and other received-with matter. Closed entries can be provided for (many libraries do this in a separate file adjacent to the active one). Sources and methods of acquisition can be included. Without any problem, payment record cards can be mounted above such visible file records, for example, to further centralize procedures. No longer will libraries learn that they have been paying for years without having received any issues!

The central serial record becomes the principle location of check-in, routing and other information; and other records complement it. Claiming becomes a primary offshoot, as does replacement ordering. The correspondence records that back up these functions become important extensions of the checking record. Bindery records can be cut down considerably if integrated into the central serial record. Many files can be eliminated, as Mr. Skipper and Mr. Trotier and many others have found, and costly duplication can be eliminated. And, in an integrated Department, all these records can become important tools and resources for the serials cataloger. (See also the following chapter.)

The serials cataloger should make the decision about the entry of the publication. This person should be the authority on title changes, variations, references, etc. All these functions can only be done adequately in a total Department where there is complete exchange of information. Then, the cataloger can call upon the expertise of those around for advice, assistance and background information. Then, all records can adequately reflect all these decisions. This will eliminate the problems of the cataloger at odds with the rest of the people who work with the same materials. Often, it seems, communication is not particularly good, and some records may never adequately reflect bibliographic decisions made. For example, the checking records may be closed for a publication that ceases, but the catalog records may never show this. With all hands rallying around the central serial record, with the cataloger at the head of them, such lack of coordination can easily be licked.

To start off with, all records should be under the same entry, the catalog entry. This trains public service personnel in the problems of the patron using the card catalog, so that the patron can be better served. Order and cataloging functions are better coordinated. Initial search for order ends up with a good basis for precataloging search. Multiple order slips can be typed in a packet for bursting and dispersal to the publisher or vendor with return slips if necessary. One slip can be put in the central serial record, which can also act as an on-order file, and others can go to other internal control files. Without extra typing, copies of this slip can be used as an on-order slip or temporary catalog card in the public card catalog and shelflist. With adequate bibliographic training and advice from a cataloger when necessary, entries can be created for the check-in record at order time so that everything does not come to a screeching halt at cataloging time. The entry can be reviewed when the title is cataloged, but usually there isn't too much of a discrepancy.

Having the check-in records (and others) under the catalog entry from the very first tends to make the records conform better to one another. Thus, all records are coordinated into one continuous chain of information about a given title. There are no variants to worry about and there is not an overabundance of cross-references to everyone's idea of entry. Not only within the Serials Department is this true, but Serials Department records are brought into line with the rest of the library and all library records — say, under a given corporate author—are complementary. There is no problem as one goes from the catalog to the central serial record or visible file to the monographs standing order file to the series authority file on the trail of the publications of, say, a museum.

As mentioned earlier, there is quite an argument in favor of title main entry for serial publications. This would be a great boon to mail checkers who must constantly work with the check-in records and may get lost among the tricky problems hidden in the murky waters of corporate entry. However, as also mentioned, this should not be considered a criterion for changing the rules; such a clerical task should not be a determining factor to choice and decision about entry. However, they are deeply interrelated.

You can put your check-in records under anything you like, with cross-references as many and as various as you would care to make them. However, this could be very, very costly, and it might not net you much.

The Library of Congress tried a simplified form of entry in its check-in record during 1951 but it discovered that there was too much time lost in making cross-references and trying to follow them to make the project, designed for efficiency, an effective one. Savings were very slight in arranging and accessioning. There were no savings in cataloging time, and in reference work there was considerable confusion. The Library changed back to its normal procedure of full LC entry on check-in records.

It didn't work for LC, and apparently other libraries do not want to try it since many have indicated a distaste for the proposed changes. Too, there should not be two cataloging procedures, one for the check-in record and one for the public catalog.

It was this latter problem that really turned out to be a messy one for LC. (See Chapter 17.) LC actually had two distinct cataloging functions that were duplicating each other, and one was canceling the other one out. *NST* and *NUC* entries were at sixes and sevens, and there was a backlog steadily increasing as the two cataloging sections pulled against each other. The problem basically was that serials cataloging is too deeply interrelated with the central serial record; and, while this viewpoint was recognized by having a staff to catalog for the incipient Record, there was a reluctance to break away from standard cataloging practices as already established by the Library. Finally, this was resolved in favor of the serials catalogers resident in the Serial Record Division to oversee the Serials Record, and to do the final cataloging as well. This was a wise decision, and other libraries should benefit from LC's experience.

The real answer for the check-in problem is to train staff to look under corporate authors. There would probably be less confusion, even under corporate hierarchies. The checkers would become much more resourceful and creative. Thinking beings, rather than automatons, are a much more positive adjunct to the Department and less mistakes would be made in mail check-in by people who used their heads. In a really integrated department, almost everyone could conceivably be involved in accessioning routines. It would be a break from their normal routines and so would create a needed diversity. They would not check-in mail all of the time, which would become monotonous and boring. They would enrich their own serials experience by coming into contact with the most basic and most important record in the Department; and they would give to the record their experience gained in another guise as cataloging assistant, public servant, invoice clerk, claimer, etc. Searching and cataloging people would know the intricacies of corporate authorship. Others should learn the basics. Cataloging personnel, housed in the Department, can advise and lend linguistic expertise to the whole operation. Such use of staff will tend to keep the record up-to-date and accurate because staff members who use the record constantly wearing their "other hats" will try harder when checking-in because they will know how it will affect *them*. Such an outlook would ensure a more bibliographically intact record as more high-powered and well-trained people scrutinize the publications that pass through their hands and discover slight variations that could become problems. On such a personal basis things tend to be done a lot better, and this philosophy of organizational administration should prevail in all but the largest departments.

Catalogers of serials play their biggest scenes backstage in the Serials Department as they try to reconcile the problems that daily come to them from other members of the staff as well as from cataloging assistants. Their greatest role is that of bibliographic authority for the Department. The cataloger is asked to interpret a cryptic note from a publisher, which he or she translates into appropriate bibliographic jargon to be added to the central serial record, catalog cards, and other appropriate records, by means of the change memo mechanism (see Chapter 16). The cataloger's advice will be asked on numbering problems, perhaps as an offshoot of bindery preparation, or as a corollary to mail check-in. This explanation should be put on all records, too. Eagle-eyed checkers continually cause grey hairs to rise on the heads of serials catalogers as they show them variations to the nth degree. Decisions must be made, perhaps in consultation with others, and appropriate notes dispersed to the records. Almost all bibliographic, fiscal and physical changes must be recorded accurately. Serials work is definitely a challenge, as the literature indicates. The challenge has to be answered speedily because the record is waiting and future issues loom just over the horizon waiting to cause more problems. Serials record work demands both speed and accuracy. Things cannot sit and wait.

A public-oriented Serials Department learns to check its material in on the central serial record accurately, efficiently and speedily, for it knows what will happen if the issues aren't on the shelves when the patrons come clamouring to the desk. A policy should be set to indicate all varieties of numbering, whenever possible, on the record. The cataloger will have picked one numbering for the publication out of a possible two, three or more. This will be the authority for binding. However, citations come in all kinds of ways and perhaps one author has chosen to footnote using whole numbers rather than volumes-and-numbers. The patron is liable to become very confused, even frightened, by the prospect of having to dig in large piles for what he wants.

The check-in card should be the key by providing the information that what was wanted was vol. 37, no. 45. Fishing it out of the stack and handing the single issue to the patron just saved this patron's sanity! Is he ever grateful as he carries his prize away! This is the kind of decision a cataloger can make regarding information other than entry on the central serial record. The serial record can help to explain the very brief note that the cataloger has probably written about this on the catalog cards, too.

Public service may even be the most important goal of the central serial record if it is decided that this record be the serial catalog for the library. Small libraries may choose to go this route. The Linda Hall Library began this way, but it eventually discovered that the central serial record could not be both the catalog for serials, serving the patron and interlibrary loan and reference functions, and still be the administrative instrument of the Serials Department. Complete and adequate cataloging was then supplied.

Very few libraries are really small enough to substitute the visible file for complete card cataloging. Such libraries are apt to be small special libraries, many of which are composed almost completely of periodical publications, as Linda Hall was. When monographs make up a large part of the collection, or when more than straight magazine publications, easily displayed or made noticeable in special areas, are involved, it is better to take the card catalog route. If serial publications are not listed in the general collection, they can be easily overlooked. The record can be referred to for holdings or other information, even to the extent that all that is in the catalog is a reference to another file. At least, in this way, the material is not overlooked. Visible file records used as public tools need to be clear, concise and easy to use. They also need considerably more cross-references than ones closed to the public.

Some of the original records can be withdrawn from the direct use of the patron. This can be substituted for by adequate communication through a public service assistant trained to interpret the file correctly. The patron will be helped, and probably more adequately than if he'd blundered about trying to do it himself in a highly specialized file, and time would be saved. The integrity of the file would also be saved. Considering the destructiveness of some of the fingers that have walked through card catalogs and excised cards or perhaps only corners of the cards with call numbers on them, this might be a considerably eloquent argument in favor of this sort of system as well. With an integrated Serials Department, the central serial record will not need to be consulted so repeatedly by outside departments. They, too, can be assisted by a person trained in reading the record; and this training should be extended to everyone in the Serials Department, so that help on any problem can be efficiently handled and passed along. (This should not preclude monographs acquisitions people, for example, from using the central serial record themselves, but experience seems to dictate that few do.)

The central serial record may be the only record for holdings information; or it may be coupled with a serials shelflist (much preferred), or a binder's record indicating bound holdings. If a complete record is needed for inventory purposes, a shelflist would probably be preferable. However, this function could be performed by the check-in records, which do this service for unbound issues anyway. If this is the case, the records must be much more specific than they usually are. Such is the case in the Library of Congress.

Because of the presence of the central serial record, serials cataloging has changed a great deal over the recent years. It may be partially responsible for the philosophy of entry under successive titles, for it is a single-access catalog, and perhaps the most important one in any library. Its presence may sway the decision to go to title main entry. Certainly its presence has marked the demise of public catalog holdings statements, as remarked upon and discussed in one of the previous chapters. It provides for interim description while a live title is still in process, allowing for very skeletal description on catalog cards. Because of the eternal change serials go through, serials cataloging records can never be totally accurate. This is why serials cataloging is usually very sketchy — the more you pin down, the more you have to change later. However, the really up-to-the-minute information is essential for accurate bill-paying, reference work, etc., and the central serial record has this. A serials cataloger who works in close cooperation with a serials recordkeeping section will be more on top of changes than one who does not, but even such a person cannot hope to keep up completely. The visible file will always have the most information, for this is really the place for it; and patrons can be directed here from the cataloging for even more information than just the the usual holdings, if desired. The central serial record can fill in the loopholes in the card cataloging, even to the extent that card cataloging doesn't even have to be completely revised when the publication dies, except that the dates of publication and numbering should really be closed. The checking record demands fairly current handling of problems so that backlogs of problem mail do not stack up. (Although notes can be put on check-in cards so that people know the cataloger is holding a problem, most material is probably hurried through pretty rapidly, except where large arrearages or staff shortages do exist.) First-issue cataloging came about as a result of the central serials record's demands, too. Serials cataloging then becomes extremely involved with recordkeeping because the record-keeping is really an extension of what the cataloger does. This is a concept foreign to monographic catalogers, but absolutely essential to good serials handling.

The central serial record is the port of entry of serials into the system. It is an important tool for the cataloger and the rest of the serials staff. It should be accorded a dominant position as the administrative instrument of any serials department. The primary role of the cataloger is bibliographic control of serials, which is what the record is "all about." In order to reach the goal of complete control over serials, the serials cataloger and the central serial record must work together, and this is best accomplished within the framework of a self-contained and integrated Serials Department.

FOOTNOTES

1. Andrew D. Osborn, *Serial publications; their place and treatment in libraries.* (Chicago: American Library Association, 1955), pp. 121-122.

2. George N. Hartje, *Centralized serial records in university libraries,* M.S. in L.S. thesis, University of Illinois, 1950.

3. James E. Skipper, "Organizing serial records at the Ohio State University Libraries," *College and research libraries* 14 (January, 1953):39-45.

4. Arnold H. Trotier, "Some persistent problems of serials in technical processes," *Serial slants* 1 (January, 1951):5-13.

Chapter XV

The Serials Department and the Serials Cataloger

Serials Departments have tended to evolve and grow like Topsy, depending upon the situations encountered by the libraries and the farsightedness of the library director and members of his staff. Generally they have evolved as custodians of serials reading rooms of current issues or as acquirers of problem titles that kept coming and coming and needed to be checked-in and ridden-herd-on. Each situation in each library was different. Different files were kept, different locations were maintained for different things, and different library floorplans called for different treatment of materials and their housing. Files multiplied. Each area kept its own file so that others on another floor would not need to be consulted. There were acquisitions files in the acquisitions department, cataloging files in the catalog department, holdings records in several places, all of which were totally or partially duplicated elsewhere. Serials work, usually considered second-rate by essentially book-oriented departments, backlogged enormously. This state of affairs was well hidden by the compartmentalization of the various activities.

However, libraries were asked to contribute bibliographic information and holdings to the *Union list of serials*. As more libraries delved into their closets and backrooms, more librarians became horrified as the piles of periodicals, plethora of records and the duplication of effort became known. The records seemed to have multiplied at an alarming rate, like rabbits, and nowhere could you get the "whole story." It also was beginning to become plain that "something needed to be done" due to burgeoning collections. The periodical was finally being recognized as an important medium for the communication of ideas. As the periodical came into its own, so did the concept of a special department to cater to its needs.

The answer, of course, was the central serial record, discussed in the last chapter. This would contain all information pertinent to serial functions and those who worked with them. It would contain the current checking records, useful for acquisitions and public service. Bindery information for serials might also be included so that everyone would know what was at the bindery and those who prepared the bindery would have assistance in tracking down issues. Claiming, so ultimately tied to the checking records, would be in the midst of, and not divorced from, acquisitions functions. The knowledge of the claimers would be of paramount aid to the reference person answering a patron's inquiry about an issue not received. Issues would be checked-in and files kept up-to-date by those who knew what would happen if there was any delay. It all seems to blend so nicely. The Serials Department as we know it today evolved and revolved around the central serial record. The trend started in the late Thirties and early Forties and still is underway, although most libraries of any size have centralized pretty much.

Even now, although many Serials Departments have centralized along these lines, with everyone working together and complementing each other in serials work, the serials cataloger is still left out in the cold. Usually this person is a member of the catalog department. Sometimes "he" is not one person, or even a small knot of people, but all the catalogers working in various subject or language areas. This is another example of trying to press serials into an essentially monographic mold. These catalogers do not do enough serials to become fully conversant in serial problems and peculiarities. They retain their monographic *Weltanschauung* and this usually proves detrimental to good smooth serials processing.

This workflow is usually justified for two reasons, either because the subject specialist feels to be in more control over the subject matter that way or because only people in the catalog department can catalog. Certainly there are other solutions to the first problem — such as review of new issues, the reading of reviewing media, the printing of subject lists for those with special bibliographic interests, or other selection and reviewing techniques. As for the second problem, whereas good working relations are essential between the serials cataloger(s) and the monographs people, such judgement upon catalogers need not be true. Many serials catalogers do reside in the catalog department, where their relationships with other catalogers are excellent, but they may be divorced from the serials technical processing personnel with whom they should communicate intimately, but may not. This would be detrimental to the good handling of serials. Also, while serials cataloging is a like task to monographic cataloging, in that a bibliographic entity is still being described, and that description must eventually mesh enough to interfile with monographic works in the same catalog, it is pivotal to the work of the Serials Department and it is much more advisable to put the serials cataloger(s) in the Serials Department, with outside liaisons to other cataloging sections. Then, book cataloging influences will not deter the serials cataloger in the performance of his tasks, and more thorough and efficient work in a serial mode will result.

The production of catalogs and the concepts underlying this function affect all other types of control — that is, the functions of identifying and describing a serial. Thus, the serials cataloger should be central to the Serials Department in its role of bibliographic controller of serials, and should not be shut off in some room elsewhere. Serials cataloging work is much more closely allied to the recordkeeping functions of the Serials Department than it is to the activities of the catalog department, even if the two functions are both called "cataloging."

The serials catalogers should function as the bibliographic authority for the Serials Department. This means that all authority for entry and change of entry should emanate from the informed knowledge of the cataloger. All authorization for change of other bibliographic information, other than price, address, and other acquisitions-oriented information, should be centralized with the cataloger. All the rest of the Department works with the same problems the catalogers do and can give excellent advice and background to the solving of a problem. It's funny, but the mention of a single serial problem to a number of staff members from a single Serials Department will set off a chorus of groans. Similarly, a chorus of groaning can be heard across the country as familiar titles are mentioned to a number of serials people. Then, the groaners will come up with solutions to the problems. There is a basic need for national work on the solving of serial problems, something currently being worked on in various aspects connected with cooperative cataloging and union-listing ventures across the nation. But it first needs to be settled in the single library's Serials Department mentioned earlier. People are getting together and working together and working on common problems involving the titles they are familiar with. The serials cataloger must be involved in this, for this is generally where the trained knowledge is to provide the best solutions for all concerned. Otherwise, things will be as confused as they were in the past, with each record reflecting different things. Somehow in the past, cataloging records were notoriously overlooked and ended up as the ones that were out of line and didn't agree with anyone else's. All Serials Department staff need to work together, and this means the cataloger too.

> For the best results, the serials department should be organized as a whole in which case many minor details, difficult problems if tackled separately, will actually work themselves out, and the result will be an efficient homogenous group of functions. . . .
>
> . . .the serials department is as important as other library departments. . .with the intense specialization required of serials workers and the complex nature of the material handled, it is no longer possible to leave this work to the tender

mercies of the circulation or reference department without the service suffering as a result. . .[1]

Periodicals need not assume any greater importance than at present to warrant the division to books and serials functions. The uniting of all serials activities under one department would result in a measure of economy for the library. In the first place, the work may be handled more easily and efficiently where the records are kept, which, in addition, the work will be done more expeditiously by trained serials workers.[2]

Serials catalogers should be among these "trained serials workers" so that serials will be appropriately handled.

Staff are made much more aware of each other's operations, functions and needs with centralization. There are more opportunities for consultation between areas and more opportunities for cross-training in related procedures. This enriches and broadens the staff and adds depth to the degree of public service given.

Serials Departments that have public service and reference functions always seem to come out best when it comes to working together. This is especially true if there is a sharing of staff, which can be so easily done with an integrated Department. Reference service is certainly enriched by the presence of technical "backroom" staff and their familiarity with the vagaries and idiosyncrasies of periodicals.

The fact remains that all too often providing the reader with needed material requires a thorough knowledge of the serials collection. Such a knowledge can be acquired in a fair-sized library only by those who handle the material frequently and constantly. A member of the staff who prepares or sees the original order for material, who is closely associated with cataloging and classification, and with the binding process, must of necessity be more familiar with the material than an assistant who does not see it until it is ready for the shelves.[3]

In the first edition of *Serial publications,* Osborn tells a story that the head of Reference at Harvard insisted that his new staff members become completely conversant in serials cataloging in order to give adequate help to the patrons.[4] Those who work with the publications on a daily basis not only understand the publications, but also their attendant records. And who should understand these records better than the serials cataloger, who must authorize the information that goes onto these records? Serials catalogers are better able to cope with the corporate author problem, too.

The people working public service desks in addition to other assignments can go back to their "regular" jobs with a sense of priorities instilled in them by patron requests. Each also has renewed vision of his or her job as something worthwhile in the light of the library's primary mission. Each becomes more than a "gnome in the catacombs." For the cataloger, this means a sense of priorities on what to catalog first because the patrons need it or because a certain course is being taught this year and the students will need one title more urgently than another. If elections are coming up and one title on your desk has a lead article about one of the candidates, do it first. Catalogers very rarely get experience first-hand with the patron who is looking at the records the cataloger has created. The cataloger can tailor the cataloging, particularly in subject areas, to the use that the material will get in a particular library. In a Serials Department with such an outward-looking policy, the cataloger, as well as everyone else, does not suffer from the typical "tunnel vision" that technical processing librarians are so often accused of having. This can improve cataloging service immensely, and it can also improve the public relations the library may be trying to establish.

A cataloger may remember well enough what went over his or her desk last week to suggest to the patron a title that had an article on just what is wanted. It's not indexed yet and the patron thinks you're marvelous because you found it. This gives you a sense of accomplishment and pride as the patron walks smilingly away, and with a whole lot better opinion of the library, too. It's amazing what you can remember if you try to develop such a skill in the light of public service work.

The cataloger has a better grasp of the classification schedules than other personnel and can help patrons find specialized titles like "periodicals in French" or "women's magazines" or "publications on Dada art." Because catalogers tend to think in logical blocks of publications, along with related publications in other call numbers, the serials cataloger can give invaluable service at the reference desk. In response to a request for material on a certain topic, the serials cataloger will unwittingly spew out call numbers, possible titles, subject headings, indexes and other useful aids. A brief consultation with the schedules, LCSH, and other tools can assist him if memory fails. A lot of knowledge about the collection seeps into his or her head, unbeknownst to the cataloger, as work crosses and perhaps recrosses his or her desk. There is no substitute for this kind of knowledge, nor can it be learned except through the blood, sweat and tears of actual labor. This kind of experience is too important to be relegated to the backroom as it so often is.

The serials cataloger is probably the most knowledgeable in the library about corporate entry, except perhaps the person who does government publications (often the same person). This expertise should be called upon to unravel the convolutions and intricacies of corporate authorship for patrons and staff members.

The language expertise of a library is usually found in the cataloging staff. The serials cataloger is often one of the best qualified linguistically (even if it is only "title-page" knowledge) because of the need to touch all languages in some depth in a research library of any consequence. This is often useful in serials reference work, particularly if the patron has an enigmatic and cryptic abbreviation of a serial title to decipher. The combined language and serial knowledge of the cataloger is the key needed to unlock the problem.

In his discussion of reference work with serials, Osborn points out the problems brought up by abbreviated serial titles. Often a Serials Department staff member will be called upon to interpret the meaning of such cryptic alphabet soup. There are guides to help one, but often these are not complete and thorough enough for the needs of this particular patron. The patron may be sent away without help, but only after the librarian has exhausted all possibilities. First of all, the librarian should try to rationalize the data at hand to see what kind of clues they offer. Osborn used two examples, *"ZDMG"* and *"BSOS."* It was assumed that the first title was German and the *"Z"* stood for *"Zeitschrift."* Assuming this to be correct, *"D"* probably represented an inflected form of the word *"Deutsch."* The *ULS* was consulted for a "Deutsche m. . .Gesellschaft" and Deutsche morgenlandische Gesellschaft was the obvious candidate since the article which had these curious footnotes was about Asian studies. The second one progressed from the knowledge found with the first, so *"O"* probably meant *"Oriental."* The *"B"* most likely stood for *"Bulletin."* It was probably an English title since the word order was wrong for French, which would have put *"Oriental"* last. *'BSOS"* stood for, it turned out, *Bulletin of the School of Oriental Studies.* This serial, however, is cataloged under *"London. University."* This kind of ferreting-out of publications can only be done by someone with a lot of language knowledge and expertise. This can be found very often in a serials cataloger. Such a specialized librarian can also reconstruct titles from knowledge gained over the years of looking at publication after publication. Osborn also brings up the problem of titles such as *Annales Academiae Scientiarum Fennicae,* entered under Suomalainen Tiedeakatemia. *Toimituksia.* The Finnish title does appear on the publication, but most non-Finnish speakers tend to prefer the Latin alternative. Appropriate references or added entries should have been made for this, it is true, but since this did not happen in this particular case, someone had to do the bibliographical digging. The serials cataloger would be an excellent choice, particularly since, at the end of it all, the appropriate references would surely be made for posterity! Further sleuthing might be necessary, by going back to the original citation, especially if the citation has come secondhand, or by going forward and trying to find better citations or a different approach through serials reference tools: indexes, abstracts, union lists, catalogs, bibliographies and the like.[5] Only after all of this has been properly searched, can one with any kind of certainty send the patron unhappily away. Few will probably suffer such a fate, however, knowing how most serial people operate. And the foremost of these should always be the cataloger, seeing the shortcomings of the system, particularly in the realm of corporate authorship, which is difficult for most patrons to grasp, and plugging up the holes so that the next unwary patron will not fall into the same trap; and giving of an expertise and knowledge derived from an intimate contact with serials in all of their vagaries, peculiarities and many guises. Catalogers are probably the most valuable reference and resource people a library has, but it is rare that they come up from their catacombs to see the light of day. It is absolutely necessary that they do so, for the services rendered back and forth can be of great benefit to the library and to the departments they represent. For a serials cataloger, performing serials reference service is, or should be, an important aspect of the job.

The Serials Department will always be called upon to do reference service for those patrons in need, even if the department doesn't have a full-fledged reference staff. The Serials Department person should be able to give an answer, or find someone who can, without shuttling the person all over the library.

> . . .This service can be greatly extended if librarians with a knowledge of serial publications and an interest in them are employed as serials department reference assistants.[6]

And who can be more knowledgeable and interested in serial publications than the serials cataloger?

When talking about serial publications, one must speak of both bound and unbound issues. Bound issues should be integrated into the library's collection by means of call numbers, and should no longer be the concern of the Serials Department staff, except in terms of replacements for lost or mutilated volumes or pages, rebinding, recataloging, withdrawal and the like. Circulation, inventory, searching, etc., would be within the purview of the circulation department. But what about the unbound issues, what is to be done with them?

There are several alternatives. One might be to shelve the unbound issues with the bound ones in the stacks. This would probably help the patrons, but would be a hardship for the library. Issues could be easily lost, mutilated or mysteriously spirited away. Replacement costs would skyrocket and future patrons would suffer from the library's lacunae. Both bound and unbound issues could be put together some place under a guardian. This would ensure that the unbound issues would be left for posterity, but would defeat the purpose of trying to integrate the collection. The real answer, which would probably benefit both patron and the library most, would be the separate current serials reading room. This could be more easily guarded, with special procedures instigated, peculiar to the singular nature of unbound periodical issues. Some or all issues might be paged from closed stacks. Reading rooms can be set up for current periodical reading, often a leisure function and different from the research aspect of consultation of the bound volumes. Some issues might be displayed to catch the readers' eyes. There are many variations.

This is the basis upon which the Serials Department being discussed here is built. But how does this affect the cataloger? The cataloger should bring his or her expertise to the discussion regarding the arrangement of the reading room. If a large part of the collection is to be displayed — perhaps, the latest issues of every unbound title — how should it be done? There are basically three alternatives: alphabetical, under title or main entry; by call number; or by the use of a classified arrangement not necessarily based on call numbers, but perhaps more on descriptive words or general designators. Perhaps main entry would be too difficult, if the main entry is convoluted and not well-displayed on the piece-in-hand, as in Catholic Church. Pope. // *Acta sanctae sedis.* Title might be a problem, unless the library used straight title cataloging. The alphabetical approach would defeat the idea of a classed and, therefore, browsable, library. If the library feels that this browsing feature is important, it might choose one of the classed alternatives. Yet, people may not think of unbound pieces with call numbers on them, so call numbers might be confusing. (It would also be *very* time-consuming to do.) There might also be confusion due to the vagaries of the classification system being used, especially in the light of the fact that only periodicals are involved, with considerable gaps of knowledge between titles, which then would seem to have no relevance one to another, as happens in the H's, G's, T's and other LC classes. The last arrangement is some sort of classed arrangement, but not using call numbers. What about the first letter of the LC classes for each section? This might be an idea, but H is unwieldy and G is too diverse, having geography, anthropology, and physical education in it. With the cataloger's knowledge and experience, the areas can be refined to the desired needs of the library and the collection. Such an arrangement might instruct the patron subtly in library procedures while it eases the shock of moving from an unbound to a bound situation. The browsing the patron has learned in the reading room can be transferred to the stacks with only a little modification.

Talking about the arrangement of serials reading rooms may seem inappropriate in a book about serials cataloging, but such is not the case. The serials cataloger should have a vested interest in serials all along the way. In an integrated Department the department head would surely ask for input from knowledgeable parties on matters affecting the Department. This particular issue is a matter of some concern to the cataloger and is only another way in which he or she can perform in relationship to public service. At the same time, acquisitions staff may be arguing that marking all the mail which is checked-in and destined for the reading room is too time-consuming. Expert minds can get together and discuss and solve problems like this of mutual concern. Each and every worker in an integrated Department becomes an expert not in a job, but in serials as a whole.

Public service duties affect a cataloger's cataloging duties substantially, for an entirely different outlook is created. The cataloger will think of additional helps for the patron while cataloging. Added entries will be made that will help the particular clientele of a given library find something more easily. Subjects that are of especial interest will receive emphasis. The kinds of cross-references that would be the most effective would be utilized. The cataloger would know whether to class broadly or narrowly, depending upon the use of the material. He or she would participate in discussions on filing or other aspects of cataloging work with a different kind of viewpoint than a lot of the others. Awareness of the signs and other cataloging aids that might be necessary or useful will be heightened, as would the awareness of useful or confusing directives or location symbols. The list could go on and on; but, the point is, the public will always be in the mind of the cataloger, and

> Cataloging policy which never loses sight of the public who will use the catalogue will always be more successful than that based solely on the book in hand.[7]

Those who scream that cataloging should all be done in one place do not comprehend the essence of serials cataloging. While it is still cataloging, the cataloging of serials is much more integrated with the recordkeeping of the Serials Department. A few of the basic tools of cataloging are utilized, such as the *National union catalogs*. However, the serials cataloger also relies heavily on serials tools like *ULS, NST,* and, most important of all, the acquisition and check-in record of the Department itself, the central serial record. This is most central to the serials cataloger, as already described, and there should be fewer steps to this than anything else in the library. Essential tools need not be transferred, although it should be top priority to duplicate some of these essential ones if funding permits. It will increase the whole effectiveness of the Serials Department and can only be better for the patron, the library's ultimate *raison d'être*.

Cataloging and acquisitions functions are not, and should not be, divorced one from the other. Cataloging can benefit from the information generated by an order, such as the results of bibliographic searching or instructions on housing, as might be precipitated by a reference order, or the like. Acquisitions expects fast cataloging so that subsequent issues to the one sent to be cataloged can be gotten out to the shelves before the acquisitions staff is smothered with them!

Sufficient identification is desired so that duplicates will not be ordered. Acquisitions expects guidelines for difficult titles, such as those with numbering problems for check-in. Adequate cross-references are also needed. Acquisitions may ask for the assistance of the cataloger in the establishing of provisional entries for new titles to be ordered. This is particularly crucial when corporate serials are involved. Advice may be needed on the treatment of provisional or pseudoserials or on titles being extracted from the monographic collection to be recataloged as serials. Publications with supplements, pocket parts, or other attendant matter may need decisions. Title changes need decisions and fast action. All of this demands adequate communication between acquisition staff and cataloging staff for a smooth workflow.

Some notes from dealers are duplicated on catalog cards. Catalogers should be granted access to correspondence files, particularly in cases where only the publisher's explanation can light the way out of a sticky problem. Claim records, too, give priceless information on cessations, changes of title and so on. Sometimes a publisher will publish a monograph as one or two issues, or even a whole volume, of a serial title. The book says nothing about this anywhere on it, so it is sent away. Finally, the Department, wondering where its anticipated issues are, writes a letter. The reply comes back that this unaccounted-for monograph was, in fact, the missing issues. The letter should be circulated and all records annotated. It also gives everyone a good chance to grumble at the publisher for committing a "no-no."

Catalogers also find information of interest and usefulness in cataloging from publishers' blurbs. A few years ago Bowker announced a title as *French books in print*. When it came in, it was probably cataloged by most libraries under the French title that it bore on its cover. Then the French bibliographer, wondering what ever happened to the title ordered some time ago, inquired about *French books in print*. After some scurrying around, it was discovered through the order files that this was the advertised title for *Répertoire des livres de langue française disponibles*. A note should have been made on the catalog cards and other records saying this title was advertised as the English title in order to shortcircuit future runnings-around. An added entry or cross-reference should also have been made. A possibly complex problem was made simple by use of one of the order section files by the serials cataloger.

Announcements also give other useful information. Perhaps a title will plan to be semiannual for the first two years of its existence, and then plans to be quarterly. The blurb may say so, giving the cataloger some inside information. Other statements of intent, not given in the publication, might be given in advertisements. Ads for backfiles may give helpful hints for the cataloging of old sets or reprints, giving names of important editors, illustrators and the like for added entries, or important history statements. Scope may be spelled out better in advertising materials than the cataloger can find out from a cursory look at a few issues, possibly in a language in which he or she is not fully conversant. Sometimes the cataloger can even con an acquisitions person, who is more oriented toward letter-writing than he, into corresponding with a publisher on something to do with a publication that will affect the cataloging of it — say, a possible title change that is wishy-washing back and forth, or a problem in numbering. The cataloger can delegate, procrastinate and come up with a better cataloging result all at the same time—a neat trick! The serials cataloger will find files of order information and correspondence a very useful tool and the people responsible for them very powerful allies.

Binding staff need to have someone to come to with bibliographic questions. Sometimes they have questions about entry or spelling, but usually their questions are about numbering, indexes or supplementary material. These can usually be resolved in short order by the cataloger who can explain these things in appropriate bibliographic jargon, have them added to the records with a "magic pencil," and see that such notes are passed on to everyone else involved.

Catalogers may need to consult the bindery preparation staff because of their own work, too. Ofttimes analytics will come in in two parts: a portfolio of artwork and the commentary on it, text and attendant maps, and the like. The cataloger needs to find out whether the bindery will make this two volumes or one or whether the maps will go in a pocket, so that the item can be correctly described in the collation on the catalog card. Perhaps, too, some decision needs to be made regarding the appropriate spine markings.

Added volumes being returned from the bindery may pass through the serials cataloging assistant's hands for shelflisting. There may be revision work necessary due to errors caught by the cataloging staff. In former times this was also the time when preliminary cataloging was completely revised and updated by the catalogers. Fortunately, few libraries burden their serials catalogers with such time-consuming double handling anymore.

If a library has decided to use abbreviations as binding titles, the cataloger should be involved in this decision. Catalogers, particularly those with public service functions, need to be involved in the discussions of binding priorities, particularly of analytics, which would be affected when the items are cataloged.

Collation has often been a cataloging function because it has bibliographic importance. However, this need not be done by the cataloger if it can be done by a trained bindery or acquisitions assistant. Then, the cataloger can perform more professional duties, such as advising and supervising of this collating function. The collator can make appropriate notes to assist the cataloger in the cataloging of the title and the cataloger can give directions on the checking-in and binding, or possible rebinding, and marking of the issues. Judgements on the completeness and decisions on what to do with supplements and other problem materials can be made without the cataloging librarian's actually having done the clerical work. Of course, there is no way out of this in some next-to-hopeless cases. However, with everyone together under the great Serials

Department umbrella, without the problems of crossing over departmental lines and the jealousies this can create, acquisitions, cataloging, and bindery personnel can all don aprons and share the arduous task together or on some other departmental "share the agony" basis.

Many libraries have incorporated their bindery preparation functions with the catalog department because of the logical interrelation of the two functions, one growing out of the other. This is true for serials, too, and perhaps even more so, since serials departments work more with multivolume sets than with single pieces — with considerably more potential for problems. Sometimes serials sets need to be recataloged. This may also mean remarking, since the entry, Cutter number, or even whole call number may have to be changed. The set might be desired by the reference department, which just got some more stack space; or, perhaps the title ceased and the reference department feels that it would no longer have any value in its collection and asks for it to be removed to the stacks; or perhaps the space in reference is at a premium and they can only afford to have the latest volume of a title rather than all the volumes shelved there. With serials, things like this are always happening. The reference symbols go on or come off both the cards and the books, and this should be done almost simultaneously. They should be done by the same department so that attendant problems can be taken care of at the same time and all the records annotated. Marking is really a subfunction of cataloging and can be given to that section, or it can be given to bindery preparation as an extension of that function. In either instance, the cataloger had better have a say in what goes on for best results. Set departmental standards can be maintained, as they often cannot be if material is handled by someone else.

The self-contained Serials Department is the only solution when there are automated functions, since centralized coordination is essential for automation. Because most automated projects deal with bibliographic control, there is a natural relationship with cataloging, demanding open channels of communication. (See Chapter 18).

Hopefully the serials catalogers bring with them from the catalog department, if it is on another floor or area of the library, a serials shelflist or catalog that has bound holdings, if these are still shelflisted. Such a catalog is most useful as a tool for everyone else in the Department. It can provide an inventory record, including stubs and missing volumes. It provides a list of "haves" and "lacks," in addition to, or as an extension of, the central serial record. It gives a mirror image of the public catalog record the patron has already seen, so that problems and questions about that can be solved. It provides a more complete bibliographic record than the central serial record in some areas and can be used as an extension of it. It is a reference tool for the serial collection in the same way that the public catalog is for the whole collection, and, if it is in shelflist order, it is also a classed catalog. It can also perform as an official catalog for the serials collection, with corrections for cardsets emanating from it as a master file. Such a tool may become a secondary pivot point in the Department, but is logical only if the catalogers are there, too.

Cataloging policy is related to, and follows from, acquisitions and preservation policies. For the best and most efficient flow of information and materials, all sections that handle the material should be united. Communication is better, for departmental lines do not have to be crossed. Duplication of records is eliminated. There are fewer problems. Time is better utilized and people are used more effectively. The same people use the records so there is less chance of error. The materials are better controlled — bibliographically, physically and intellectually. Most integrated Serials Departments have proved they can do the job with a smaller staff, yet more efficiently. There is economy in administration and less over-departmentalization. Knowledge, skill and enthusiasm are built up. People are better trained and they take pride in their work. They become specialists. An *esprit de corps* develops. A sound serials collection is built. There is improved service to the reader.

> The greatest gains are possible when catalogers give recognition to the contributions of other serial librarians, notably those who are working with the current checking records and in the periodical reading room.[8]

The advantages of such a departmental arrangement — with the give-and-take, economy, efficiency and good service — cannot be beaten by any other arrangement!

Beatrice Simon described the problems and the solution very well when she said:

> Now, serials are a complicated and difficult form of material to deal with. They can only be put to their best use when administered by a staff thoroughly familiar with all their vagaries. A book is a relatively simple matter, except in the rare books area, and that does not concern more than a handful of people throughout the country. Once you have catalogued a book, you can forget about it. The most useful feature about it is the subject, and the most complicated thing that can happen is a new edition, completely revised by someone else.

> But a periodical is never static. It changes title. It changes its frequency. It merges into and out of other publications. It starts out as a simple bulletin of some society or other and ends up as a very learned journal on some new subject, or, it ceases altogether for a time, and then breaks out again in an entirely new guise, usually just when you have altered all your records.

> And every time this happens, it affects the Order Department, the Binding Department, and the Catalogue Department, to say nothing about the long-

suffering Reference Department for whose benefit all the other departments toil so dilligently.

The amount of time wasted on cross-consultation; the number of costly mistakes made because each assistant knows only part of the tale at any one time, is fantastic. Time costs money and money buys more periodicals, or hires more staff, so I am very jealous of time. That is the reason why I believe so wholeheartedly in the separate serials division. If you can delegate all operations concerning serials to one person, or one group of persons, and you have the courage to set up a separate serial divisions[sic], where periodicals are received, processed and serviced as a continuous operation, you will find that great economies will ensue and you will have, in addition, an unusually competent group of people ready to give reference service of a very high quality.[9]

In short:

Complete centralization of functions relating to serials offers the best solution of vexing problems.[10]

FOOTNOTES

1. J. Harris Gable, "The new serials department," *Library journal* 60 (November 15, 1935):869.

2. J. Harris Gable, *Manual of serials work* (Chicago: American Library Association, 1937), p. 38.

3. Fred B. Rothman and Sidney Ditzion, "Prevailing practices in handling serials," *College and research libraries* 1 (March, 1940):168.

4. Andrew D. Osborn, *Serial publications; their place and treatment in libraries* (Chicago: American Library Association, 1955), p. 216.

5. Gable, "The new serials department," p. 870.

6. Andrew D. Osborn, *Serial publications; their place and treatment in libraries* 2d ed. rev. (Chicago: American Library Association, 1973), pp. 357-360.

7. Beatrice V. Simon (August, 1949), "Cataloguing of periodicals," *Ontario library review* 33:245.

8. Osborn, *Serial publications,* 2d ed., rev., p. 229.

9. Simon, "Cataloguing," p. 239.

10. Rothman and Ditzion, "Prevailing practices," p. 169.

Chapter XVI

Cataloging Routines

This chapter will deal with a proposed cataloging routine, based upon the integrated Serials Department just described, which is, in turn, built upon the central serials record concept of the previous chapter. Although this is not meant to be a treatise on "how we do it good" at one particular institution, many of the procedures used in that Serials Department are described here — on the grounds that they are sound, intelligently worked out, efficient and the ones this author knows best. They are also representative of procedures used in similar situations and are adaptable to still other situations. Basically, they are good. They work! (For specifics on this Serial Department, see Appendix E.)

The question of when to catalog a serial has always been a sticky one. According to C. Sumner Spalding,[1] serial record people will opt for doing it whenever the title is recognized as a new one. They need a check-in record before the next piece comes in to require additional costly special handling. Reference librarians will want first-issue cataloging, too, for they wish to direct the patron to the issues with a minimum of muss and fuss.

Catalogers are a conservative lot, and, for the most part, Spalding feels they would want to wait until the first volume is bound. More issues will provide a sounder base for classification. The title might have decided on its name, frequency or other variable data by the time the first volume is complete; and recataloging and costly additions and revisions would be avoided. A title so shaky it drops by the wayside need never bother the cataloger, for it may be decided to discard the whole thing before the cataloger ever sees it. One opinion is that all sorts of problems can be avoided if one waits. Also, it is considered best by some to wait for a title-page, which may come at the end of the first volume or with an index. This is the most formal presentation of the title, traditionalist catalogers argue. But you may be waiting forever, considering the frequency with which some of these arrive!

In the poll taken in 1959 and chronicled in Gloria Whetstone's article,[29] out of 16 libraries cataloged from the first bound volume and 6 from first issue. Some that cataloged from first bound volume had temporary cards in the catalog with the entry on them. Sometimes location symbols and the beginning of the run were indicated. This was only the beginning of a nationwide trend, however.

You can compromise by temporarily cataloging a title and then firmly establishing everything when the first volume returns complete from the bindery and the cataloging can be finalized. This is a very costly procedure. Everything must be handled twice and, in essence, cataloged twice. Double handling does not prove to be either efficient or effective. Very little needs to be changed, usually, from the first time around. The few changes that need to be made do not justify the lengthy procedures taken just on their account. The risks should be taken, especially since the incidence for need of a change is so low. We owe it to our patrons to inform them of our wares. They deserve to be kept up-to-date. Our service to them will improve tremendously if we keep on top of our current cataloging work load and keep the people "out there" advised of our acquisitions in their fields of interest.

It is much better, then, to catalog from first issue. The entry established can serve both the serial record and the catalog. Immediacy of cataloging is essential to this plan because accumulation of backlogs will cause problems in recording operations. Currency can be maintained by cutting out the duplication.

In September 1968, the Library of Congress issued its *Cataloging bulletin* 83, stating the following:

Cataloging of Serials in the Library of Congress

The failure of the Library's long-standing practices to provide satisfactory cataloging control of serials has led to the decision to make some major changes which, in the course of time should do much to remedy the situation. These changes will in some cases provide card subscribers with a better service than they have had heretofore; in other cases services that used to be provided will be discontinued.

Many English language periodical-type serials are now being cataloged from the first issue received instead of from the first bound volume. This practice will be extended to all English language serials and eventually to all serials of this type as rapidly as possible. This should mean that catalog cards for periodicals will gradually become available in many cases years before they would have been available in the past.

Recataloging and reprinting of cards to reflect changes in serials, however, will be discontinued, except insofar as the Library is able to recatalog titles that have ceased publication. These bibliographical changes will continue to be announced in the "Changes in Serials" section of *New Serial Titles,* as they have been in the past. The Library will make interim entries for these changed serials in its own catalogs. These entries will not be printed because they will often not include the bibliographical detail called for under the cataloging rules and hence would not meet the Library's standards for publication.[3]

Most libraries have found LC's service improved with regards to serials. This service was further improved when LC changed to accept the AACR as printed. Advances in technology have meant that LC's cataloging of serials has been speeded up in its travels to the user libraries. Still, there is need for faster service in some areas and libraries still need to catalog titles originally for themselves. Most of these libraries have turned to first-issue cataloging, as LC did, thus increasing the timeliness and usefulness of their catalogs and ensuring bibliographic control from the very beginning.

NST often had delays in reporting because libraries did not report from first issue. This problem does not seem to be great anymore, particularly now that LC has reorganized. Prior to reorganization, most *NST* entries were prepared in the Serial Record Division prior to being cataloged for printed cards. LC's official entries were prepared in the Descriptive Cataloging Division after the necessary bibliographic research was done. Searchers in local libraries looking for *NST* entries in LC volumes often did not find them because of these discrepancies. The procedures have been cleaned up and streamlined considerably now.

Classification from only one issue will probably present problems in only a few cases, most notably monographic series. Serials cover very broad subject areas, broader than monographs, and it is not so easy to make an error if one keeps to the broad areas. Titles like *Journal of African languages* or *American anthropologist* pretty well clarify their subject matter, even with the first issue. Monographic series can also be fairly specific, like *Lecture notes in mathematics,* but this is not always true. Sometimes you are fortunate enough to have a publication list of upcoming titles or titles already published that can help to serve as a basis for classification. Sometimes the publisher's announcement, which the order person in the Department probably still has, will give a prospectus. But very often you have only a single monograph in-hand from which to classify an entire series. In such cases where classification is not possible, temporary catalog entries can be made or the permanent cataloging can be reviewed upon binding or upon receipt of subsequent issues. Cataloging may be slightly delayed by shifting of the current cataloging backlog so that other issues, if their arrival is imminent, can be used for assistance. This, of course, depends on the set-up and communication lines each serials cataloger has with the rest of the Serials Department.

There has been some objection to putting catalog cards for unbound issues in the catalog with call numbers on them. This is a problem innate with serials. There will always be some unbound issues not on the shelf under the call number for the bound volumes (unless the library is one of those that shelves its bound and unbound issues together). The new serial just cataloged fits directly into an already established pattern. The answer is in the stamp on the catalog cards referring to the serial records (see Chapter 12). Even old issues cataloged or acquired through a backfile purchase or gift can go into an unbound backfile and be retrievable by and for the patron in the same manner as the current issues of other titles.

Another solution could be plastic jackets put over the main entry cards blocking out the call number and having this note: "FOR UNBOUND ISSUES SEE SERIALS DEPARTMENT DESK" on them. However, this is a lot of work and the same ground can be covered adequately in other ways. Well-informed reference personnel, descriptive passages in library handbooks, a prominently placed serials list with directions for its use, and signs explaining library procedures can do a lot to ease this problem, as well as brief and to-the-point directives in the catalog itself, referring to all issues of a title, best done by telling patrons to consult the serial record. This is not a problem relating only to first-issue cataloging, although it is usually brought up in this context.

In short, the really most effective way to catalog serials is to do them as soon as they come in. The cards can be typed and filed, the visible file or other receipt record can be typed with an official entry, and the information on the title can be dispersed to all of the individuals who need to know about it, such as bindery preparation people.

It used to be a procedure in some libraries to send materials directly from acquisitions to bindery so that they would be "preserved." It also meant that an additional end-processing function had to be performed to put call numbers on the spine, a task that could have been done at the bindery. Unnecessary corrections would often be avoided by cataloging first to set up a base record. Decisions on peculiarities and additional materials that might or might not be bound in are best made before binding rather than after. Catalogers should make this kind of decision, too, rather than bindery preparation assistants.

However, the procedure for establishing the title for the library comes long before the recently-arrived piece gets to the cataloger's hands. It must first be ordered. Preorder searching must be efficiently done, at least as efficiently as the newness of the title will allow. Perhaps the one establishing the preliminary entry has only a publisher's flyer; well, this must serve. Here it is useful to have the cataloger on hand in the Department to advise on setting up entries. However, if the title is not brand new, sufficient searching should be done in

ORDER NO	ENTRY, FREQUENCY, ADDRESS.
RC870037	EVERY MAN'S MAGAZINE....Item no. 271, Catalogue 129.
DATE OF ORDER	
4-28-75	Peter Murray Hill (Rare Books) Ltd.
DEALER	73 Sloane Avenue, Chelsea, London S.W. 3
Murray Hill	ENGLAND *Shelve in Special Collection*
FUND	TO BE ORDERED: Please send complete
OPP/FK/G	series, Every Man's Magazine, Item no. 271, Catalogue 129, ONLY.
REQUESTED BY	
Gleckner/ Lang	Per your letter of confirmation rec'd.
AUTHORIZED BY	April 24, 1975.
HW/RL	
RECEIVED	CATA. NO: (LIST)/EST. COST
	ITEM NO: $121.00 for complete series
LC. NO. or CALL NO.	
	SERIALS, LIBRARY, UNIV. OF CALIF., RIVERSIDE

(a)

RECEIVED	CHECKED BY *TV*	DATE 4-28-75
O KARDEX	ULRICH	✓✓ UIS *p 1501*
TRANSFER FILE	AN. &IRREG.	NST
O PRINT OUT	UCLA	LC/NUC
PROBLEM FILE	UCB	OTHER *R.F. Lang / Gleckner*
O SER. AUTH. FILE	BRIT. MUS.	*recommendation*
O PUBLIC CAT.	PTLA	

Catalogue 129 of Old and Rare Books, Spr. 1975 Peter Murray Hill. p 63 ✓✓✓

SUGG. CALL. NO.

7/72

(b)

Fig. 16-1. Preorder searching on front (a) and back (b) of order card.

the standard bibliographic sources to establish the entry. This searching information, perhaps on the back of the order card, should be passed on to the catalogers so that it need not be duplicated, but enhanced as necessary. Then the order is typed.

A most efficient type of order is the 3" x 5" multiple-part order form interleaved with carbon paper. This can be printed in as many plies as necessary for dispersal to different files. The first ply should be heaviest, about a 24-pound weight stock. (Don't let the printer tell you you can't do it because you can!) This ply has the clearest typing on it and should be filed as soon as possible in the public card catalog to show that the title is on order. The second ply goes to the publisher or dealer as the official order. The third goes into the central serial record as an on-order form, which can also serve as a temporary

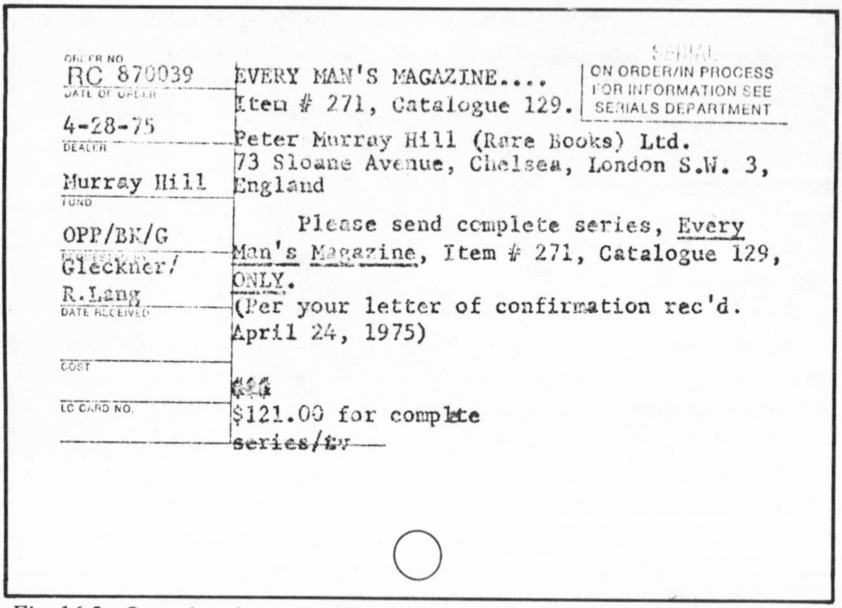

ORDER NO
RC 870039
DATE OF ORDER
4-28-75
DEALER
Murray Hill
FUND
OPP/BK/G
REQUESTED BY
Gleckner/
R. Lang
DATE RECEIVED
COST
LC CARD NO.

EVERY MAN'S MAGAZINE....
Item # 271, Catalogue 129.

SERIAL
ON ORDER/IN PROCESS
FOR INFORMATION SEE
SERIALS DEPARTMENT

Peter Murray Hill (Rare Books) Ltd.
73 Sloane Avenue, Chelsea, London S.W. 3,
England

Please send complete series, Every Man's Magazine, Item # 271, Catalogue 129, ONLY.
(Per your letter of confirmation rec'd. April 24, 1975)

$121.00 for complete series/

Fig. 16-2. On-order slip in public catalog – front ply of multiple order form.

check-in record until the permanent one is made from the finalized cataloging entry. Later plies are for internal records, including one for the serials cataloger to use as a shelflist temporary card. Those after the first can be a lighter-weight paper, like 12 or 10 pounds, depending upon the use of the file. Each ply can have special printing on it, if desired. For example, the part sent to the dealer or publisher can have the library's address on it. Time is saved in typing duplicate records and efficiency is gained. Already the records begin to complement each other.

Filing on-order slips in the public catalog can assist monographic searchers who may be loathe to search serials records but who search the catalog as a matter of course. Expensive duplicates can be avoided. In this way, too, the public is kept informed of serial orders. The serials public service staff are also aware of what is on order by looking at the central serial record, and they can keep patrons informed when issues come in. The title can be rush cataloged for a requester, if necessary. The public is also aware that the title exists before the permanent catalog cards are filed. Any gaps in holdings that delay binding or cause slowdowns in workflow, as those brought up earlier in the discussion of first-issue cataloging, can be conveniently bridged by this slip. Card typing is usually fast enough that putting the call number on the order slips is not necessary. An additional task is avoided and the procedure streamlined even more.

Titles newly-received and not yet cataloged should be checked-in on the temporary record and funneled to the cataloger through a technical processing assistant. The technical processing assistant should keep records of what has been sent to cataloging for retrieval purposes. Anything that needs to be rushed should be so flagged.

The cataloging section should get the piece, the shelflist temps, which are part of the order packet, the preorder searching and any other pertinent information. The searching is completed for cataloging copy, building on the preorder searching base.

The cataloger then catalogs the title from the piece-in-hand, gleaning all the information possible from that piece and using the copy found by the precataloging searcher. If copy or variant copy is found, it can be passed on to a nonprofessional cataloger. The cataloging librarian should catalog all materials with no copy, gathering facts necessary for cataloging according to AACR. Catalogers should always follow the guidelines and rules for the cataloging of serial publications given earlier in this book.

The cataloger must determine the choice and form of entry. The cataloger must read the issues-in-hand very carefully, deciding what the "norm" is and what constitutes variations therefrom. For example, the cataloger must make a note of what the publication refers to itself as, for this may be a useful access point, albeit buried in a preface, introduction or statement of editorial policy. Introductions should always be read, for they give the scope and intent of the serial. They may also give historical information, frequency and sometimes numbering. Numbering may jump out at you, and then again it may be hidden on the spine, back cover, signatures or elsewhere. A neophyte serials cataloger cannot be expected to know all of the places to look, but must build up expertise by being aware and reading completely and technically every issue that goes across his desk. Searching from bibliographies may assist in this, but basically a cataloger's observations are the most important part of the cataloging operation. Even if copy has been obtained, the publication may have undergone considerable changes since the LC card was printed. Care should be taken to make notes clear and concise. Numbering that is the most consistent should be chosen and this should be made clear for bindery personnel. The cataloger should take care to give proper directives for checking-in, binding and other technical processes, if these are not routine. The cataloger should determine the location, if not already indicated on a memo from acquisitions, in consultation with the proper people. Since the subject cataloging of serials is usually comparatively simple, it is customary to have the serials catalogers classify and subject-head their own material, except in a large operation like LC. As the cataloger did the entry and descriptive part of the cataloging, the subject coverage should have been noted too, through the use of tables of contents, indexes, bibliographies, the title, subtitle, introductory matter, name of sponsoring bodies, etc. When in doubt, read an article or two.

The acquisitions area should be so arranged that the cataloger can go back and find other issues received since the one in-hand, in case these would assist in the description of the title. Having more than one issue helps in knowing the publishing pattern of the item, if this is not so indicated on the items themselves. Discrepancies and changes from issue to issue can be easily seen. Having more issues also gives a better idea of subject content for classification and subject headings.

It used to be that catalogers routinely collated runs of old magazines for discrepancies. In this day and age there is little time for the catalogers to do this themselves, and it is also very expensive for the library. It would be better if a clerk did this work, perhaps in acquisitions or bindery. With the serials cataloger so nearby for advice, time and money are better used, and the bibliographic output can be just as good.

Cataloging copy, workcards or worksheets produced by the catalogers then go for card typing. When the new cards for a title are filed, they should bump the on-order slip that has been on file in the public catalog. (Any changes of entry from the on-order slip should have caused the extraction of the slip from the catalog upon cataloging and temporary cards should have been correctly filed as a result of the cataloging process. These would now be bumped out.) Permanent shelflist cards would bump the temporary ones, too.

When the title is cataloged, classed and shelflisted, it is returned to the technical processing assistant with a copy of the cataloging. The permanent check-in records are then prepared. (The assumption here is that the check-in records are manual, since very few libraries have a sophisticated automated check-in system. It would still stand to reason that automated check-in records should be made at this point too, so the theory is still fairly sound. If the library has other automated records, like holding lists, the input for these should be made at this point also, if this has not already been done by the cataloger.)

The method of communication from the cataloger may vary from library to library, depending upon the kinds of records that depend upon this information and the ultimate fate of the communication device. Worksheets that are finally discarded may circulate to touch those files relevant to that title. If the fate of the device is to be filed as part of a record, it may be a card. Below is a "bindery card" record that includes the entry, bibliographic description of the title, the call number and other notes pertinent to that title. The LC card number is recorded if the cataloging was done from copy. If a title is to be analyzed, this is noted. Directives for location or disposition are written on the card and initialed as authorization. Colors of previously bound or publisher-bound sets are recorded so that the bindery preparation staff can match newer volumes and rebinds as best they can. The library feels that such a wealth of information about the title is important, for it has had to recatalog titles for which cards have been lost, and having this file is a boon. Some of the information is transferred to the library's central serial record and the cards are sent to the bindery section where the staff files the cards to use later as a bindery authority, together with the Kardexes, when the title is bound. Subsequent additions and changes for this title are made on this card as well as on other records.

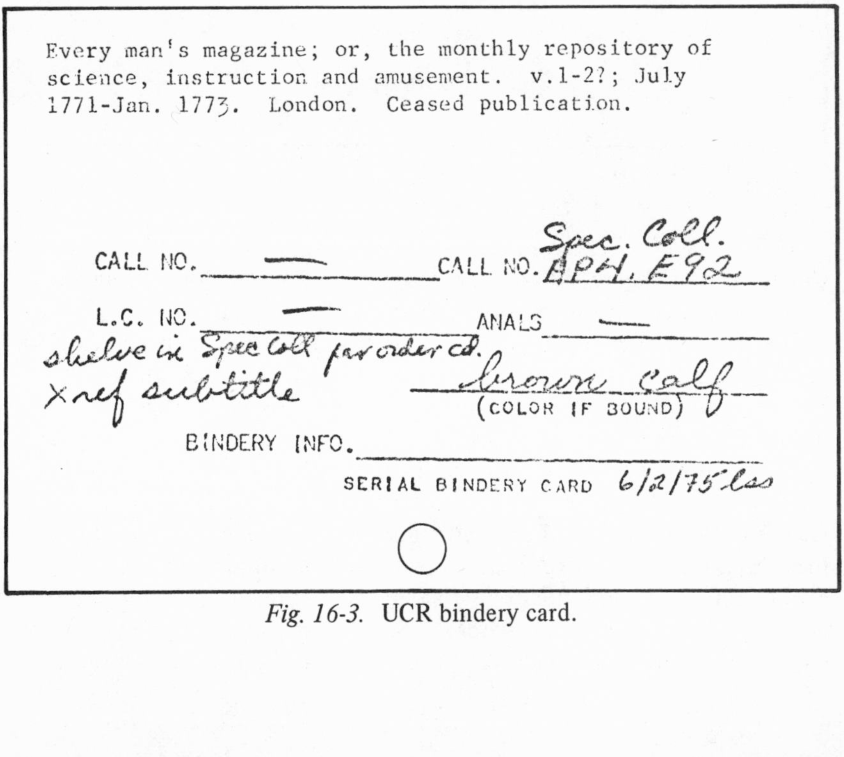

Every man's magazine; or, the monthly repository of science, instruction and amusement. v.1-2?; July 1771-Jan. 1773. London. Ceased publication.

CALL NO. —— CALL NO. Spec. Coll. APH. E92

L.C. NO. —— ANALS ——

shelve in Spec Coll per order cd.

xref subtitle brown calf (COLOR IF BOUND)

BINDERY INFO.

SERIAL BINDERY CARD 6/2/75 cas

Fig. 16-3. UCR bindery card.

This format works best for UCR, which uses the procedure outlined here. Other libraries, like LC, use a worksheet. The University of California at Irvine uses a combination worksheet and computer input sheet. The University of Colorado and the University of California at Santa Cruz use input sheets for their book catalogs. Cornell uses a very brief card form, but it fits the needs of their recordkeeping. Such a reporting device is clearly a necessity for adequate communication.

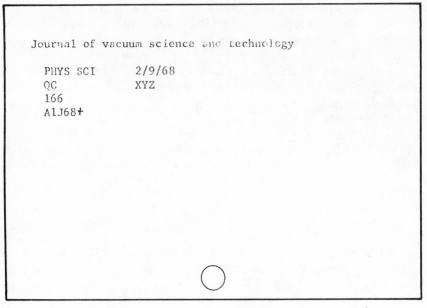

Fig. 16-4. Cornell's central serial record report slip[4].

At the time of serial record typing, an *NST* report slip should also be typed to inform *NST* that the library currently receives a given title. Opposite is an example of a report slip appropriately filled out.

The title is all set for its length of stay in the Serials Department. What happens if there is a change in it? If the title or author entry remains the same, but something else happens to it, like it ceases, suspends, changes its numbering or does something else equally in keeping with its mutable serial nature, all the records need to be notified of the change. This often does not happen. Somebody usually gets left out and notoriously it is the cataloging records that are out-of-step with the others, particularly if the catalogers are not located in the Department. An adequate mode of communication needs to be established. A suggestion is the serial change memo. An example is given in Fig. 16-6. The records listed are for the Serials Department, General Library of the University of California at Riverside, but can be readily adapted to any

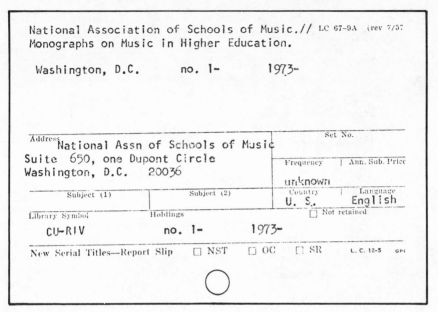

National Association of Schools of Music.// LC 67-9A (rev 7/57

Monographs on Music in Higher Education.

Washington, D.C.   no. 1-   1973-

Address National Assn of Schools of Music
Suite 650, one Dupont Circle
Washington, D.C.   20036

Set No.

Frequency | Ann. Sub. Price

unknown

Subject (1) | Subject (2) | Country | Language

U. S.   English

Library Symbol | Holdings | ☐ Not retained

CU-RIV   no. 1-   1973-

New Serial Titles—Report Slip   ☐ NST   ☐ OC   ☐ SR   L. C. 12-5   GPO

Fig. 16-5. NST report slip.

records for any library. (For the most part, the records are straightforward, but if explanations are needed, they are given in Appendix E). As the memo states, records to be affected are circled and crossed out when the change is made. The memos are funneled through a centralized point where they are read for comprehension and comprehensiveness and then are batched and dispersed and generally "ridden-herd-on." The cataloger should receive all change memos first, unless they were initiated by the cataloging section, which has already been crossed off. This should be done for authorization and perhaps revision into proper bibliographic language. Then it should be routed to the person in charge of each record indicated for changes before it is retired. It is suggested that these memos be retained for a year or two in case questions or problems arise.

The change memo has proved a very effective solution to the communication problem. It can be used when a serial does something requiring a change and it can also be used for changes in records, such as cancellation of a title or change to a different vendor. If the decision is reversed on nonanalysis of a monographic series, this decision can be noted on a change memo and routed for record changes. The memo is a brief outline manual of the Department and its functions, which tends to keep everyone informed and on their toes. It also makes sure that everything gets done: for example, if a title were withdrawn, but someone forgot to remove the bound volumes from the stacks, or the label from the current periodicals reading room when the issues "went away," these errors would cause an undesirable confusion and hardship for the patron.

TITLE _Issues: documents in current_
American government and policies

CALL NO. _J K1 . J86_

LOCATION
DIRECTIVE _____

✓ ADD/CORRECT INFORMATION

_____ TRANSFER OF TITLE
(ATTACH ALL RECORDS)

_____ TITLE WITHDRAWN

_____ CANCELLATION

_____ CROSS REFERENCE NEEDED

_____ CEASED PUBLICATION

_____ ADDED VOLUMES

_____ REPLACEMENT OF BD. VOL.

_____ DECLARE MISSING, REORDER

SOURCE OF INFORMATION _____ _letter_

_____ INITIATOR _cdt_ DATE _8/26/74_

WRITTEN EXPLANATION ___ _Suspended publication_
indefinitely with 1971-72 edition

_____

_____

CIRCLE RECORDS AFFECTED, CROSS OUT WHEN COMPLETE

(SERIALS CATALOGING)

PULLED ____ BD. VOLS.

NOTHING BOUND

PUBLIC CATALOG ONLY

SHELVING AREAS

_____ RR LABEL/ISSUES

_____ BACKFILE LABELS/ISSUES

_____ OUTSIDE SERIALS DEPT.

PROCESSING

(KARDEX)

PROBLEM BOX

STATISTICS FORM

ON ORDER/IN PROCESS FILE

(PRINTOUT)

(TRIP)

NEWSPAPER LIST

BINDERY PRIORITY

(BINDERY) FILE OF INDEXES

PULL ISSUES FOR BINDERY

NOTIFY REFERENCE

NOTIFY MUSIC

CLAIMING-ORDER-PAYMENT

(PAYMENT RECORD CARD)

CONTROL FILE

FUND SLIP

(CLAIM RECORD)

REPLACEMENT FILE

CANCELLATION LETTER SENT

PUBLIC CATALOG

DESELECTION LIST

EXCHANGE FILE

REORDER WITH _____

SERIALS DEPARTMENT CHANGE MEMO 1/15/75

Fig. 16-6. Change memo.

Such errors should not happen, but sometimes they do. The change memo eliminates errors. The change memo also allows the work to be parceled out piecewise to those who maintain the records involved. The responsible people are thus informed of the changes, but their records retain the integrity of having one person responsible for them.

The change memo is effective because it can be initiated anywhere in the Department and for any reason. Claimers are often the first to know about ceasing of titles. They can clip the letter giving this information to the change memo and send it on its way. Catalogers discover an added volume of a monographic series that has slipped by and been cataloged as a monograph. The cataloger brings the volume back into the fold, sending the change memo on with the appropriate place checked off. The "bypass" volume would be added to other serials holding records. Bindery discovers a missed index or a variation in numbering. Public service has a complaint about a necessary cross-reference. Mail checkers discover a new series. All these are written on the change memos and passed along. The cataloger should receive these memos first. This will also ensure that the public records will be changed first. The central serial record should be next in line, unless the change has already affected it, such as in mail check-in or claiming routines. This is the most important record in the Department, and changes should not be made in it without cataloging authority. The central serial record should be touched first, however, in the case of a withdrawal or transfer of title so that mail routines, invoicing, etc., will be nipped in the bud and proper "snag" file ("problem box," on the change memo) directives can be made for proper routing of materials. This is a change that does not require bibliographic authority work. Cataloging should be second in this case so that public records will not be misleading. Cancellation and other invoicing routines do not affect cataloging or authority work, so cataloging personnel need not be involved with those memos. This whole procedure keeps the entire staff alert and constantly working together for better and more efficient service.

Change memos are generally the method whereby the cataloger maintains communication with the other members of the Department. Memos can come as the result of conferences with other people about a particular title, or they can initiate conferences, if a decision seems faulty, unnecessary or vague. Such discussions are useful, for everyone is not off in his own corner of the Department reinventing the wheel when the problem arrives. This is where the cataloger's all-important and time-consuming trouble-shooting function usually shows itself. This is often, too, where the cataloger draws upon the expertise of the rest of the Department.

The procedure for a title change can be handled in somewhat the same way, on a different form (see Fig. 16-7). This can be routed to touch the appropriate records for ceasing the old title after those involved are through with it. Those immediately involved are:

TO __*Iss*__

FROM __*D*__

SOURCE OF INFORMATION __*issues*__

CALL NO.   TITLE

PS 536   *Berkeley*
B46   *Samisdat*
                  review

✓ CEASED PUBLICATION WITH

V __*3*__ NO. __*3*__ PT _____

DATE _____ YEAR __*1974*__

✓ SUPERSEDED BY __*Samisdat review*__

_____

_____

V __*4*__ NO. __*1*__ PT _____

DATE _____ YEAR __*1974*__

_____ SUPERSEDED BY _____

_____

_____

_____

V _____ NO. _____ PT _____

DATE _____ YEAR _____

ADDITIONAL INFORMATION _____

Fig. 16-7. Title change memo.

1. the person who discovered the title changes,
2. the technical processing assistant responsible for title changes, and
3. the serials cataloger.

For them, the procedure is as follows: The person who discovers the title change informs the technical processing assistant of the fact. Hopefully, this discovery was made during checking-in procedures to nip it in the bud, but sometimes the change is so minor it is not discovered until later, perhaps by the bindery section. The assistant should then search the new title or write about it. (This is another nice thing about having an integrated Department; matters like writing letters to publishers asking them what they are doing can fall upon the shoulders of acquisitions people, who are in the habit of letter-writing, and yet catalogers can benefit from the answers.) Then the technical processing assistant should send the cataloger a title change memo, appropriately filled out. Other pertinent information, like letters, should accompany the memo. The assistant should also send the immediate issues before and after the title change. This is useful for noting numbering irregularities, vague and overlapping changes, such as the subtitle becoming a title or wandering back and forth from one title to another for a time, or changes in subject content. The cataloger then catalogs the new title and puts the appropriate notes on the cards for the old title and sends the volumes, bindery card, letter and memo back to the assistant who finishes the process as outlined previously for new titles. The title change memo can be routed to close the old title records before it is retired. The new title, of course, creates its own records as it goes through the new title procedures.

Corrections and additions to cards that come as a result of title change or other changes to serial records should be done by the cataloging typist(s). Complete cardsets should be pulled and corrected if the library can spare the time, for cards with varying information tend to be confusing. Catalog cards should never be removed from the shelflist without leaving some sort of replacer to mark the call number so that it will not be used again. Following is a suggested removal slip. Similar ones can be used for the public catalog if desired. More information is given than that usually on a "Card temporarily removed" card.

Issues destined for "uncataloged collections" should be left in a special place for the cataloger to study them. Entries can be set up and cards can be typed from notes left with the volumes, or a clerk can make up entries for the cataloger to pass judgement on. Usually this type of material does not have order slips, but just comes, often by accident. Routines need to be set up for communication, but these do not have to be elaborate, as long as the people involved understand what they are to do. Change memos might indicate arrival of a new newspaper title, for instance. The cataloger could pass the memo to an assistant to type the newspaper cards.

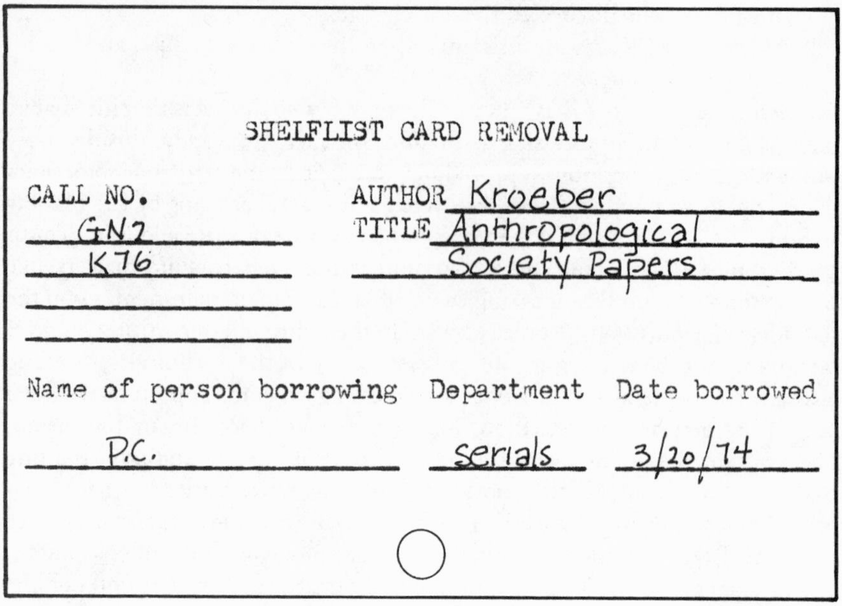

```
            SHELFLIST CARD REMOVAL

CALL NO.             AUTHOR  Kroeber
   GN2               TITLE  Anthropological
   K76                      Society Papers


Name of person borrowing  Department  Date borrowed

       P.C.                serials    3/20/74


                      ◯
```

Fig. 16-8. Shelflist removal slip.

If the cataloging section in the Serials Department also catalogs analytics for its series, procedures should be set up for these as well. Serials to be analyzed should be so noted on the bindery card at time of cataloging and a series authority file card like the one in the chapter on analytics should be filed in the appropriate place. This decision will be noted on the central serial record to notify mail checkers that special handling is required. It would probably be a better idea to let one person be in charge of materials requiring special handling rather than all of the mail checkers, for more expertise in working with highly irregular publications with special requirements would be built up in this one processing assistant. This would provide for better and smoother working relations between the cataloging section and the receipt section.

It cannot be stressed too strongly here that cataloging of monographic series analytics should be done in the Serials Department if at all possible. Uniformity is maintained and the serial nature of the material is not lost. Monographs catalogers may tend to treat the material unevenly, particularly if the materials in one series go to several catalogers, and series treatment may be ignored or incorrect. Procrastination is often the rule of the day, unfortunately, when it comes to analyzing material. For the integrity of records, smoother flow of work and a more efficient operation all around, it is advised to keep all serial material in the Serials Department until it is shelved for use.

Too, monographic cataloging of analytics in a series may be helpful in cataloging the serial that surrounds it, and vice versa. Copy may be found for the analytic, which can help in establishing an entry for the series. Two cataloging operations may be done at once. Subsequent analytics cataloging may also point up changes in the serial, which is then integrated with the serials recordkeeping operations of the Department.

Exposure to monographic cataloging is often useful for serials catalogers. It makes them more rounded people, and they are generally pretty well rounded already from work with so many different kinds of materials and subjects. Their scope is not limited just to serials. They can be ambidextrous, as it were, and versatile. They can take aspects of monographic and serial cataloging and apply them back and forth. They really can become better library people in this way, which is all to the good. They are also doing what is best for the library and the Department.

Part of the searching section should be set aside for continued receipt of volumes to be analyzed from the acquisitions routines. Like the serials, these analytics volumes must be searched for cataloging copy. Unlike the serials, they have not been searched before. There is also the greater possibility of variant copy and copy for other editions. The searcher has to be well aware of monographs searching procedures as well as those for serials. A searcher searching a new serial title for the first time and realizing that it may be analyzed should also search for analytic copy to help the cataloger with the series. Then the analytic can be cataloged too and the process is speeded up considerably.

Libraries maintaining depository catalogs and libraries with standing series orders for Library of Congress analytics cards have devised elaborate systems whereby cards are bumped as they are put into the files or whereby the books are checked when cards are received. These kinds of systems are very cumbersome and can be very expensive. The best method is to search each volume upon its receipt through the *LC catalogs,* on a microfiche retrieval system if the library has such a service, or through an automated cataloging system such as OCLC, if the library belongs to such a system. If the library maintains a proofslip file filed either by title or main entry, this can be searched for serial analytics. Even the depository file can be accessed by something other than these special procedures.

The volume should then be cataloged as a monograph, with complete monographic description and tracings, according to the AACR. The cataloger should be careful, particularly if copy is being used, that the series is correctly represented and traced on the card in the same form that the local library uses. The call number for the series should be typed on the card, augmented by the series, volume and / or number designating the specific monographic title in the series. Dates may be added if desired, but are not optional if they are the only designator given.

Volumes not bound should be sent to the bindery in the same way as unbound monographs, which are already cataloged. A question may be raised about whether it is appropriate to catalog analytics before binding. The answer is a most emphatic "yes." This will cut down on double ordering. It will hopefully discourage wasted time typing orders for titles not indicated in order catalogs as being in series — professors ordering items will find them already in the catalog, thus saving time for their secretaries. Requests through reference librarians for new books just out might be diminished by speedy appearance of cards in the catalog. Temporary cards should be typed for analytics unless the typing is so up-to-date that this is unnecessary, i.e., a week turn-around time in card typing. Analytics volumes received bound should be analyzed immediately as well. They should then follow normal bound volume routines.

Volumes received bound should be immediately shelflisted. If a bound volume has been received as the result of an order and comes to the cataloger for new title cataloging, a written statement of bound volumes needs to be sent back to the processing assistant with the bindery card. The volume should be shelflisted on a holdings card. The call number, including volumes, numbers and dates covered by the physical bound volume in-hand would be penciled on the verso of the title page or wherever the library notes such information. The volume should be sent for end processing. Volumes coming as added volumes that are publisher-bound should already have the call number marked on the inside by a technical processing assistant when they were checked-in. They should be shelflisted, or analyzed and shelflisted, and sent on for marking. Bindery shipments should be checked by catalogers for discrepancies as they are shelflisted. Issues to be pamphlet bound should be routed for shelflisting (and perhaps analysis) before being put in pamphlet covers. (Of course, this all presupposes that the library keeps a shelflist record of bound volumes. If this is not done, as at LC, this step need not be performed by the cataloging section.)

Marking or end processing is really an important adjunct to serials cataloging; and having a staff member or student help devoted to this function within the Serials Department, and preferably within the cataloging section itself, is most beneficial. Material from the bindery shipments can be shelflisted and checked and given due-date slips almost all at once. The material is contained in the Department until it is shelved and under the jurisdiction of the circulation department. This ensures better control and ease of paging in case a patron needs something that is in-process. Having this function is most useful when reclassifications, recatalogings, transfers or withdrawals are at hand. The whole operation can be done in a complementary manner, with cards and books pulled almost simultaneously and fixed under the cataloger's watchful eye. There are no loose ends for later on. Book cards, if the library has these, are part of a marking function to be coordinated with the cataloging process. The clerical help performing these functions might also be responsible for pamphlet binding of small volumes.

The same arguments for a marking section can be used to justify a typist. Corrections and the volume of typing generated by serials and their changes dictate that there should be a serials cataloging typist, specialized in the typing of serials, as opposed to monographs, catalog cards. In the interest of efficiency and accuracy, serial cards should not go through a central typing "pool." The close proximity of the work cards waiting to be typed can often eliminate an extra step in typing or cataloging time if the cards can be found easily and changed. (Serials may be changing even as the cards sit awaiting typing!) Questions about cards and the information on them can be raised immediately and settled. There are fewer send-backs and other delays. Cataloging for serials and card typing for same are much more integrated functions than card typing for monographs is with monographic cataloging because of subsequent and continual changes that need to be made to cataloging records as the result of the dynamic nature of serials. The typist is also caught up in the same public-oriented immediacy that pervades the rest of the Department. Things will tend to be done more efficiently and speedily. Analytics cards would go through the serials card typist for monographic materials cataloged by the catalogers for the same reasons already mentioned. The typist would have to be versatile enough to be able to type both monographic and serial card formats in that case. A typist is an integral and indispensible part of the serials cataloging team.

The counting of statistics seems to be infinitely important to catalog departments. This is unfortunate, for one hash mark on a statistics sheet very rarely, if ever, indicates sufficiently what the catalogers and their assistants do with their time. However, if this is recognized and the cataloging statistics are only used as a guideline for management information purposes, statistics can be useful. The following statistics should be kept for serials cataloging:

New titles cataloged: Number of new titles cataloged permanently, including microform and/or other format titles. The statistics can be kept as a lump sum, or they can be subdivided, perhaps by class number to show activity in various subject areas. This total can be subdivided into:

LC titles: All titles cataloged from LC entries (LC cards, proofslips, entries copied from *LC* or *NUC catalogs,* MARC, MCRS, etc.)

Original cataloging: Titles receiving original cataloging locally. (If changes are made in LC copy, other than adding classification and Cutter numbers or correcting obvious misprints, it becomes original cataloging. Some libraries may further limit this to a certain number of changes or a certain number of elements changed.) This may further be divided into "Variant copy," if desired. Shared copy, such as that obtained from a system like OCLC or

BALLOTS might be considered part of this category, or another statistics category might be set up.

Microform titles cataloged: Each microtext form is counted separately. This is useful since microtexts require additional and special handling. Can be extended to other forms as necessary.

Titles recataloged: Titles requiring significant changes in the cataloging (entry changes, changes in added entries, etc.).

Transfers: Titles that are recataloged and added to serials records. May include transfers involving call number changes, or these and other reclassifications can be a separate category. May also include monographs recataloged as serials, or this may be considered another category.

Withdrawals: All titles that are deleted from serials records should be counted here.

Analytics cataloged: All monograph titles cataloged as individual pieces of serial runs should be counted here. Can be subdivided like "New titles cataloged." (Only kept if serials catalogers do the work.)

Searching: Searching for card copy or cataloging aids in *LC, NUC, NST* and elsewhere should be counted here. This total can be divided into:

Serials titles: All serials titles searched.

Analytics titles: All analytics titles searched.

Accessioned volumes: All bound volumes accessioned, including volumes for new cataloging, added volumes received publisher-bound, volumes returned from the bindery, volumes to be pamphlet bound, added volumes for titles added to the collection through transfers, and microform units. (These latter can form a separate category, if desired.)

Cards filed: All cards filed should be counted. May be further subdivided into "Public catalog," "Shelflist," etc., if desired.

Corrections: All cards corrected as a result of cessation of title, numbering changes, additions of index, suspensions, or other reflections of serial irregularities and peculiarities should be counted here, as well as normal catalog maintenance operations such as correction of typographical errors, updating of subject headings and changes in location.

Individual libraries may vary in the depth and specificity of the statistics required. These are probably the basic ones for a standard serials cataloging operation as outlined here. Marking statistics could be added if a serials cataloging section had end processing chores, but these would vary considerably depending on the variety and complexity of these duties. It would be best for individual libraries to decide what they want to do in this area.

There is no way you can divorce serials cataloging functions from the other workings of the Serials Department; they are too much intertwined. For an efficient process with quality output, the communication and workflow patterns described in this and the previous two chapters are absolutely essential, although not necessarily with all the specifics herein described. A cataloger, especially one working with serials, cannot do his work in a vacuum. He is too involved with other serials processing functions to be separated from them. Communication among all who work with serials is the key, and quality work must follow.

FOOTNOTES

1. C. Sumner Spalding, "Keeping serials cataloging costs in check," *Library resources and technical services* 1 (Winter, 1957):14.

2. Gloria Whetstone, "Serial practices in selected college and university libraries," *Library resources and technical services* 5 (Fall, 1961):287. [The remaining library did not catalog its serials.]

3. *Cataloging service bulletin* 83 (September, 1968):3.

4. Cornell University. Libraries. Manual of cataloging procedures, 2d ed. (Ithaca, New York: Cornell University Libraries, 1969), p. E5.

Chapter XVII

Serials at LC

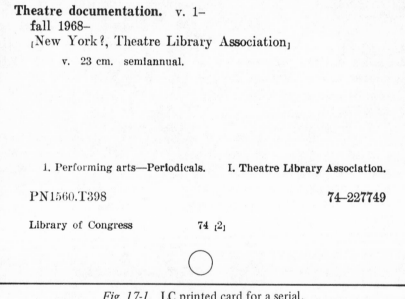

Theatre documentation.   v. 1–
   fall 1968–
   [New York?], Theatre Library Association[
      v.   23 cm.   semiannual.

      1. Performing arts—Periodicals.   I. Theatre Library Association.

PN1560.T398   74–227749

Library of Congress   74 [2]

Fig. 17-1. LC printed card for a serial.

The Library of Congress is one of the leaders of the world in cataloging. Its book catalogs are among the world's finest. It has been involved in all of the cataloging decisions and revisions of cataloging codes that catalogers all over the nation follow. It began producing catalog cards like the one above for sale in the early years of this century and has since come to be the cataloging standard for all of us.

Serials have steadily increased in importance at the Library of Congress. In the early years one could barely find mention of such publications in the *Annual reports of the Librarian of Congress;* but this has changed considerably in recent years, with increased emphasis being placed upon these publications. How has all of this come about?

In the beginning, serials were housed in the Division of Periodicals, later the Periodicals Division, and finally the Serials Division, which is still the custodial section for most unbound issues. There were serials scattered in other areas as well. Each area was autonomous unto itself, with its own acquisitions, cataloging, recording, servicing, and binding personnel and functions. Such a state of affairs continued at LC, as it did at other libraries, far into this century. Serials were virtually ignored as specialized publications of any real importance. There was no unified control.

Like other libraries, LC found it difficult to contribute adequately to the *ULS*. Thirty-two different catalogs had to be consulted for holdings, and the accuracy of what was reported was seriously in question. Another union list endeavour, undertaken around World War I, to compile a *List of serial sets,* was abandoned due to lack of manpower to pursue all of the necessary threads. The Library had no idea of what it had, or even if it could pay a bill submitted to it. Clearly something needed to be done, particularly since such chaos was beginning to affect the public's ease of use of the collections. An advisory committee to the Librarian, composed of Carleton B. Joeckel, chairman, Andrew D. Osborn, and Paul North Rice proposed that a central serial record be established.

Much discussion and furor was stirred up by this proposal. Public areas wanted the record near them, and acquisitions and cataloging staffs made strong arguments for it being near them. A study was made, and it was suggested that two records be set up: one in the Serials Section of the Subject Cataloging Division, which would be the serials catalog of the Library, and the other in the Accession Division for check-in.

The Central Serial Record was set up in August, 1941. It was manned by four people. The first step was to convert index card records to a visible file record.

Steps were taken to standardize processing of serials. Some shortcuts were introduced. Bound holdings were no longer entered on the serials shelflist, which was closed down in mid-1942. The Central Serial Record became the official shelflist of bound serial holdings. Updating holdings in the Official and Public Catalogs was discontinued due to the new Central Serial Record. Form card cataloging was set up.

General Order 1188 created the Acquisitions Department on June 30, 1943. Various adjustments were made in staffing and workflow to accommodate the new addition. In July, 1943, the Central Serial Record was moved to the Annex from the Main Building where it had been set up, and it was given divisional status under the new Acquisitions Department. Centralized acquisitions was begun and some of the chaos and disorder of the preceding years was made orderly and organized.

At the same time, there was reorganization of the Reference Department. The Serial Division was set up as a subdivision of this department by consolidating the old Periodicals Division, Government Publications Reading Room, Pamphlets Collection and War Agencies Collection into one. Issues were sent, as they are now, to this area for custody and bindery preparation. As time went on, procedures were created and hammered into shape for smooth communications between the Serial Record and the Serial Division.

The Serial Record was expanded upon and built up during its first decade by consolidation of other records. In 1942, the Serial Record in the Subject Cataloging Division was abolished. Procedures were streamlined to meet the demands of an increased workload. Accessioning was no longer done by type of publication, but alphabetically, which led to more flexibility. The Serial Record Division became a section of the Order Division in April, 1949, which further increased efficiency by allowing some sharing of staff.

In 1951, to further increase efficiency, simplified checking entries were used in the Serial Record based on the title on the piece-in-hand rather than *ALA cataloging rules*-based headings. Rather significantly, however, this procedure was abandoned in 1952. It had not produced the economies predicted and had resulted in confusion and wasted time.

In 1952, a task of editing the Record was begun, extracting dead serials from the current record for the 3" x 5" dead file, which is located atop the visible file. Entries were searched and revised and all traces of the abortive simplified entry project were erased. Decisions on missing issues and partial runs were obtained. Errors were corrected and serial records were created for publications actually of serial nature but which had been treated as monographs. Each record was made complete unto itself. There was some reorganization of staff activities, and centralization began to show increased economy and efficiency.

In the 1960's there was consolidation of other records into the Central Serial Record. The Serial Record took on information on the treatment of series, conferences and symposia by incorporating the Monograph Record, formerly in the Subject Cataloging Division. Information on retention, routing and processing was added from other files, which were destroyed as the amalgamation of data from these other sources went to build one composite record in the Central Serial Record. There have been other editing projects.

The Serial Record in the Library of Congress records all serials in the Roman, Greek, Hebrew and Cyrillic alphabets. The following genera of publications are not included: newspapers, trade catalogs, telephone books and a few categories of ephemera (such as comic books, which are received in large numbers through copyright deposit). "Serial" is rather broadly interpreted by the Library to include periodicals, documents, annuals, numbered monographic series (including publishers' series), and certain other publications without either a stated or a logical ending.

The Record includes some bibliographic information sufficient to identify the title, such as city of publication and beginning date. For numbered

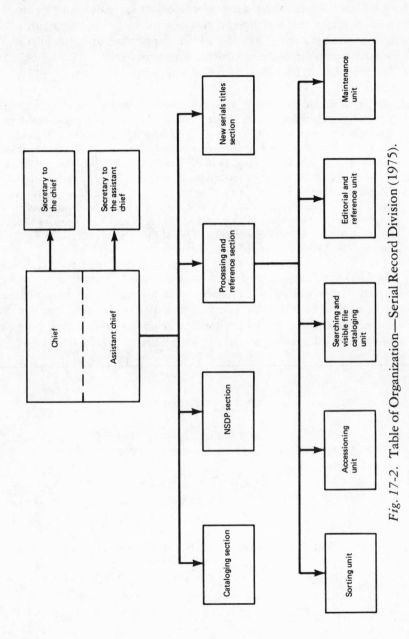

Fig. 17-2. Table of Organization—Serial Record Division (1975).

monographic series, cataloging and classification treatment also appears on the record. Other selection and acquisition decisions are part of the permanent portion of the record, too. Interim checking sheets are the other part of the record, including receipt, location and binding information. From time to time this record is consolidated with the permanent record.

The Serial Record Division is described, at present, as follows:

> The Serial Record Division is responsible for maintaining the record of the Library's serial buildings in the Roman, Greek, Hebraic, and Cyrillic alphabets (exclusive of newspapers). It receives about 6,000 serials each working day which are searched, recorded, and distributed to the public reference divisions or to the classified collections or circulated to more than 100 units in the Library. Out of about 20,000 serials which are identified as new to the Library each year, about 10,000 are selected for retention and so are fully cataloged. All new titles are listed in *New Serial Titles,* which is a union list. It provides reference service in response to questions from Library staff and other government agencies which can be answered from its files.[1] (Fig. 17-2 shows the organization of the present (1975) Serial Record Division.)

The Library of Congress used to do what was called "form card cataloging" for serials. This was a kind of temporary first-issue cataloging done immediately upon receipt for current titles. Check-in files were made using form card entries. Periodicals and collected sets were cataloged for printed cards from first bound volume. This is what a form card looked like:

```
Journal of airport management.

        Published in Wilmington, Del. by American
Association of Airport Executives.


    Until bound and cataloged, issues of the above
will be found in the Periodical Reading Room.

    I.   American Association of Airport Executives.

djg  11June64                          Oct. 1961

LC 64-10    (3/54)
                                              GPO
```

Fig. 17-3. Form card.

Recataloging would be done if the original first-issue cataloging did not correspond with the entry desired when permanent cataloging took place. For this reason, entries in *NST*, provided from form card cataloging, might not agree with final printed cards as they appeared in *NUC*.

Recataloging might also result from changes within the serial itself. Revised cards would be printed for title or corporate heading changes, using latest entry cataloging principles. All bound volumes would be pulled and reexamined. Subject cataloging and classification would be reviewed. Cutter numbers might also be changed for a new alphabetic arrangement in the shelflist. This would involve marking work. New cards would be filed when printed. Old cards would have to be removed. Basically the same procedure was followed for titles which ceased. A lot of time-consuming work was done.

Catalog cards were also printed for updating, such as for changes in numbering or addition of a cumulative index. Notes were made on the Central Serial Record. Usually there was no change in other cataloging data for a change of this kind so the new cards could "buck" the old ones when they were filed.

C. Sumner Spalding estimated a ratio of one recataloging operation to every two-and-one-half cataloging operations.[2] A very high percentage indeed!

Cataloging was done in two places. The Descriptive Cataloging Division handled serials cataloging for the card and book catalogs and for printed cards for sale. A cataloging section in the Serial Record Division concerned itself with bibliographic authority work for the Serial Record entries and *NST*. The coordination between these two was not very good, nor could it really be improved due to the need for speed on the part of the receipt section and the fact that not everything in the Serial Record would be cataloged for printed cards. There was considerable duplication of effort in establishing an entry and describing the physical issues. Considerable effort would be given by each cataloger to added entries, references and other redundancies. This was clearly a waste, particularly if recataloging were necessary, which would also involve changing the Serial Record.

The duplicative procedures were felt necessary because adequate cataloging could not be done from first issue. Form card cataloging would fill in the gap for check-in purposes until the permanent bound volume was cataloged. It would also keep things up-to-date, which the cumbersome final cataloging procedure could not hope to do.

It was C. Sumner Spalding's opinion back in 1956[3] that all of this duplication was unnecessary. He felt that, except for certain problems that could be temporarily handled by form card cataloging until the problems were more satisfactorily resolved, form cataloging should be eliminated. He felt that it should be continued for materials that could not be satisfactorily subject cataloged from first issue. He also felt that form cataloging would be appropriate for titles that were not to be retained. This is similar to the "uncataloged collection" procedures suggested in this book for such titles. He also advocated that titles the library has only a scattered run of be made exceptions to his proposed rule of first-issue cataloging. This should be postponed until the Library either acquired more or discarded the whole lot. If the title were discarded, a great deal of decataloging would not be necessary.

Spalding also advocated notes on the cards indicating that unbound issues were not on the shelves and that the complete holdings records of bound volumes were only in the Central Serial Record. As already noted, the Library of Congress does not shelflist bound volumes anymore.

Another time-consuming practice Spalding hoped to cut out occurred in the Shelflisting Section. The serial would travel from Descriptive Cataloging, where it was entered and described, to Subject Cataloging, where it was subject cataloged and classed. (Unless there was not enough information to do so, whereupon it would be sent back to await more issues, being form cataloged in the meantime.) Finally it wound up in Shelflisting. The shelflister had to copy the information onto a preliminary catalog card to be sent back to the Serial Record Division for completion of its records before the original copy could be sent on to card production. Spalding desired that both the piece(s) and the cataloging information be routed to Serial Record for the staff there to do the work rather than placing the burden upon the shelflisters. Checking records could be made from the card copy, which would also provide input for *NST*. Then the copy would go to the Card Division.

Streamlining the procedures in this way would make bindery preparation much easier. The necessary information would be available before binding, rather than after the first volume was bound, so that there would be considerably less "shooting in the dark." It would be easier for the custodial divisions to ride herd on the issues and make provisions for claiming or replacements, too. Spalding also suggested that the original book numbers be retained rather than re-Cuttering for title changes. This would mean considerable savings in bookmarking time and costs. Spalding's proposals would increase the efficiency in bibliographic control of serials at LC, streamline procedures, save in manpower used and time consumed, and reduce the backlogs significantly.

In May, 1968, serials cataloging activities were consolidated. The Serials Section of the Descriptive Cataloging Division was transfered to the Serials Record Division and merged with its Cataloging Section. Some rearrangements of staff were made.

In order to begin to simplify the cataloging of serials, LC adopted the policy of cataloging from first issue received, rather than first bound volume. This was one of Spalding's main points in his study. This decision was announced in *Cataloging service bulletin* 83 (September, 1968). This effectively canceled form card cataloging and the costly duplications of effort that had disturbed Spalding.

In 1971 a severe crisis regarding serials processing was making itself felt at LC. Only about a third of the new titles pouring into LC were being cataloged by a very small staff. The Library of Congress had followed the suggestions of the Catalog Code Revision Committee and the nation's research libraries, which had convinced it to follow the old ALA rules for entry, — that is, using the policy of latest entry. This gave libraries which desired it the benefit of LC's fairly comprehensive bibliographic research. Such practice was reflected on page 22, footnote 12, page 232, footnote 1, and page 238, footnote 4 of the new printed rules.

However, the backlog was growing by leaps and bounds while catalogers spent hours doing research and recataloging. LC was being literally buried in new serial titles. Finally it was decided that LC would accept the *Anglo-American cataloging rules* as printed and this was announced in April, 1971, in *Cataloging service bulletin* 99. Changes of title or corporate heading would cause new records to be generated as soon as the change was identified. Footnotes describing the Library's practices in AACR were canceled. More serials catalogers were added and catalogers were relieved of marginal duties. Serials cataloging at LC is at present quite up-to-date. Catalogers are even dipping into the arrearages as time permits.

Fiscal year 1971/72 saw an increase of 169 percent in the number of new serial titles cataloged over the preceding year.[4] A loud and clear testimony for the advantages of successive entry cataloging, to be sure!

LC issued *Processing Department memorandum* 111 (May 31, 1971), which also announced that LC would follow the AACR as printed, using successive entry cataloging. The following general practices were outlined:

1. New entries for serials that have undergone changes of corporate author or title will cover only the issues published under the changed name of author or title and will be cataloged from the first issue received that reflects the change. Serial Record entries will be prepared from the new cataloging entries and will likewise be used only for issues received under the changed name of author or title. Earlier holdings will continue to be covered by existing entries in the catalog and the Serial Record.

2. Printed cards will be produced for:
   a. New titles.
   b. Significant changes of title.
   c. Significant changes in a corporate body's name when the serial is entered under that body.

3. Cards will be printed for:
   a. Corrections of errors in the heading and/or title.
   b. Addition of "dashed on" supplements or indexes. Those that are monographic will be handled by the monographic descriptive cataloger and those that are serial will be handled by the serials descriptive cataloger. These are to be reprinted without verification of the original

information on the printed card. [LC no longer uses "dash on" entries, however.]

   c. Other reasons at the discretion of the cataloging section head.

4. Indexes to be listed in tabular form will be added to the main entry in the Official Catalog and sent to Catalog Management Division with a slash card for adding of the information to the Public Catalog.[5]

The procedures outlined in the memorandum are pretty much those that are followed today, although there may be special handling for some materials.

Cataloging is done from first issue. Titles discerned to be new titles are sent for review by a selection officer. This person makes decisions on the retention policy of the particular title. If the title is to be routed to one of the other two national libraries, retained briefly, reviewed later or discarded, the issues and decisions are returned to the searcher who sent them in. This searcher will put a note on the decision into the Serial Record and dispose of the issue as directed. Titles to be cataloged for the collection are given a priority. The title will be sent to a descriptive cataloger along with appropriate slips to be filled in along the way. Catalogers will already have gotten issues with title or author changes, which arrived with the old visible file entry from the searcher.

The cataloger will catalog the issue-in-hand. Searches are generally only to be made in the Official Catalog and the *NST* files, except if a conflict arises. Searches for headings can be done elsewhere. Other titles are not usually examined. Notes are sent to the Catalog Maintenance Division regarding titles superseded or continued by other titles so that this information may be added to the catalog cards. The cataloger also provides *NST* with the necessary data by filling in a slip. The previous entry is photocopied to be forwarded with the current cataloging data and issues to the Subject Cataloging Division.

There are about thirty serials catalogers at LC. They handle material in all languages, but tend to shift around a little because English gets top priority. No one sees every serial cataloged at LC; but a team of eight does see all of the cataloging, so there is some attempt at consistency.

After the descriptive cataloger has performed his work, the cataloging manuscript (See Fig. 17-4 following, and Appendix H for instructions) goes to a typist to have the Serial Record entry typed, including linking notes to and from other titles, other bibliographic notes, and "see references." The typist also types preliminary cards and slips for the Order Division. The typist also checks in the issue or issues-in-hand.

The Duplicating Unit duplicates the information, sending one copy to the Process Information File and the others, with the piece(s), to the Subject Cataloging Division.

The Subject Cataloging Division is divided into two humanities sections (due to the bulk of materials cataloged), and sections for Far Eastern materials, law, social sciences, life sciences, physical sciences and children's literature.

SERIALS

Classified as a collection Call no.:	Classified separately		LAN ☐

ME

FFD

UTI

ENC LVL

1.

TIL Petersen's complete book of Plymouth, Dodge, Chrysler.

2. Conf

3. Type Ser

8. Status

EDN

9. Freq

DAT 1973- ( )

10. Regularity

11. Type Material

IMP ₍Los Angeles, Petersen Pub. Co.₎

12. Nature Contents

COL⧺ (1)v. illus. 28 cm.   FRQ

LANG ENG

15. Date 1

SE

21. Date 2

22. Country of Pub

OAN

23. Repro Form

Spine title, 1973-( ): Plymouth, Dodge, Chrysler book.

25.

PHYS MEDIUM

I SSN 0092 - 4512

26. Mod Rec

1. Chrysler automobile
2. Dodge automobile
3 Plymouth automobile

28.

31. Priority

32. Maj/mn.

33. Internal

I. Title: Complete book of Plymouth, Dodge, Chrysler.
II. Title: Plymouth, Dodge, Chrysler book.

GOVT P

34.

GAC

N-US

CAL	Class *TL 215*	Date	Cutter *C55P47*	Other

COP		DDC⧺b *629.22/22*	CRD 73-83693

Library of Congress   MARC-S

Cds.		Series			Initials	Date
Cataloger's Notes:			Descriptive Cataloger		EB	11Dec73
		Serials File	Reviser		*GBW*	*19 Dec 73*
		Serial Record	Master Typed		*Spr*	*3 Jan 74*
			Subject Cataloger		JK/sc	Jan 21,1974
			Reviser		REM/sc	Jan 21,1974
			Shelflister		JMR/sl	Jan 22,1974
			Reviewer		MRS/sl	Jan 22,1974
			Decimal Classifier		WEM	23Jan74
			Reviewer			
			Editorial Section, SCD			
			To NSDP		Jan 25 1974	
			To MARC-S Project			
			To Card Division			
			To Catalog Mngmt.			

Class x-ref.:

Uniform Title x-ref.:

Cont. of p. 1:

KEY   *Petersen's complete book of Plymouth, Dodge, Chrysler*   ABB

Local Info.:

Tag	Custody		Tag	Custody
901‡c	‡ *Bind / label*		911‡c	‡
901‡c/2	‡		911‡c/2	‡
901‡c/3	‡		911‡c/3	‡
901‡c/4	‡		911‡c/4	‡

ADD   8490 Sunset Blvd.   90069

PRI $2.00

unb

Fig. 17-4. Cataloging manuscript sheet.

If the numbering is continued, and there is no major change in subject matter, a title that has been cataloged for a title change will receive the same call number that the earlier title had. If there has been a major change in subject content, or the numbering has not been retained, a new class number will be assigned. Subject headings will be reviewed on entry-change publications and new ones assigned as necessary. Classification and subject headings will be assigned to new titles. New titles, or titles with new class numbers, will be shelflisted. Temporary cards are put in the shelflist until bucked by permanent cards. These cards give locations and sources of Cuttering (LC is only now starting to publicize its special Cutter tables). Those desiring D.C numbers will go to the Dewey Classification Division.

Titles needing new subject headings or aspects of headings must await authorization of that subject heading. Journal literature must be searched for appropriate terminology. Sometimes this takes considerable time to search. Then this must be approved, which could take up to a month; meaning the semicataloged material sits, making its final appearance in *NUC* or MARC tapes later than usual. It may take several months for the heading to appear in the published subject heading list. Classification proposals also have to await approval, further delaying things.

The cataloging information will be routed, with other information, to other departments as applicable. The custodial division will get a preliminary card (and the piece). Serial Record gets one to update the checking entry with the call number. Other departments will get their necessary slips. Eventually the manuscript sheet will go for card production. New titles receive similar processing.

The National Serial Data Program transferred to the Serial Record Division on January 3, 1975. It receives the cataloging data after the complete cataloging process is through. This data is received in the form of a xeroxed copy of the cataloging worksheet already illustrated and a copy of the cover/title-page/masthead of the piece cataloged, providing documentation for NSDP's work as an ISDS center. ISSN and key titles are assigned. At the present time, ISSN are entered on the Serial Record, but key titles are not. This data is also added to the worksheet, which goes to *NST*.

NST will receive the cataloging from NSDP. The staff will assign a Dewey number, if the title does not already have one, and files the record for further processing and input into *NST*. It routes a copy of the worksheet, with additions such as bibliographic information from outside sources, to the MARC-S people.

Editing is done in the MARC (MAchine Readable Cataloging) Office for content designators and editorial details. Then the information is keyed on a magnetic tape selectric typewriter using the standard 175-character ALA character set. The typewriter cassette is converted to machine-readable computer tape and processed to create the bibliographic record and a diagnostic listing used to verify the record against the worksheet. Twice a week tapes are sent to the Cataloging Distribution Service Division or CDS Division (the Card Division's new name as of 1975), which prepares the MARC-S records for distribution. Generally, MARC-S tapes and proofslips for printed cards will be available about the same time.

Fig. 17-5, following, shows a simplified flow chart of serials processing at LC. The following figures (Fig. 17-6 and Fig. 17-7) show more detailed charts for normal procedures.

Cataloging service bulletin 100 (June, 1971) described "Cataloging priorities at the Library of Congress." The Library further clarified to the library world the priorities it had set up in January, 1969, and had subsequently refined. Eight levels had been established, according to the memo, numbered 1a, 1b, and 2-7. Number 1a denotes rush for governmental requests and number 1b, for Cataloging in publication. Priority 2, enlarged in the revision, covers current American imprints, including:

Current U.S. serials, including government publications selected for research value or for general interest to libraries.

"Other current serials" are included in priority 4.[6]

The memo promises faster cataloging of serials in general. It should be noted, however, that this priority list refers to the order of things being processed each time. The Chinese section might be working on priority 7's, because there were relatively few of each, while the English language sections are still in 1a's and 1b's. The material goes to Subject Cataloging, and must wait in order again. The priority 7's just done by Chinese are still priority 7's and will wait their turn after all of the others which are higher priority already in the Law Section, let's say. Titles needing new subject headings or class authorization must sit around, too. Because of the waiting around, pre-ISBD(S) and ISDS cataloging is still being turned out on MARC tapes and current proofslips, even though LC changed over to the new formatting, punctuation and title recording policy in mid-1974.

LC has just launched a new limited program of cataloging newspapers (announced in *Cataloging service bulletin* 114).[7] Newspapers will not receive any subject cataloging, but will receive normal descriptive cataloging and added entries, including an additional bracketed geographic added entry like:

United States — California — San Francisco

or

Austria — Salzburg

The new newspapers will be added to the normal workflow in the Serial Record Division. Papers already housed in the Serial Division will be cataloged there.

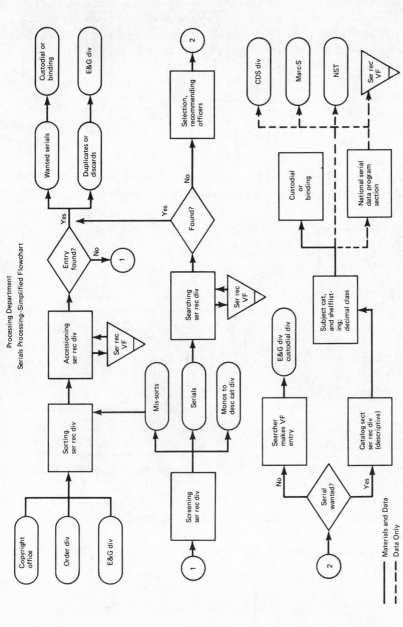

Fig. 17-5. Simplified flow chart of serials processing at the Library of Congress.

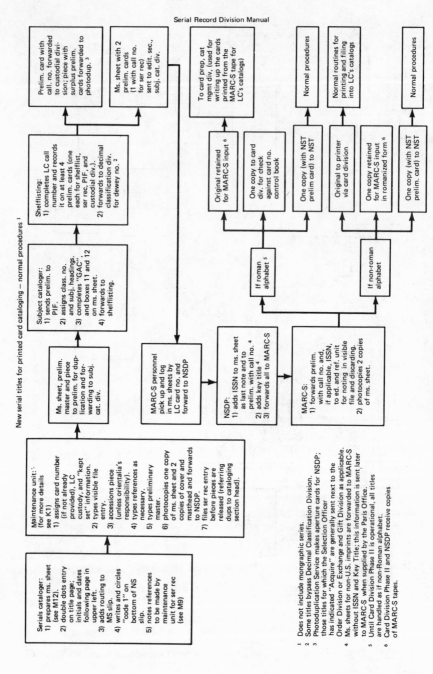

Serial Record Division Manual

New serial titles for printed card cataloging — normal procedures [1]

Serials cataloger:
1) prepares ms. sheet (see M12).
2) double dots entry on title page; initials and dates following page in upper left.
3) adds routing to MS slip.
4) writes and circles "code 1" on bottom of NS slip.
5) notes references to be made by maintenance unit for ser rec (see M9)

Maintenance unit: (for more details see K1)
1) assigns card number (if not already provided), LC custody, and "kept set" information.
2) types visible file entry.
3) accessions piece (unless orientalia's responsibility).
4) types references as necessary.
5) types preliminary master.
6) photocopies one copy of ms. sheet and 2 copies of cover and masthead and forwards to NSDP.
7) files ser rec entry before pieces are released (referring dups to cataloging section head).

Ms. sheet, prelim. master and piece to prelim. for duplication and forwarding to subj. cat. div.

Subject cataloger:
1) sends prelim. to PIF.
2) assigns class. no. and subj. headings.
3) completes "GAC", and boxes 11 and 12 on ms. sheet.
4) forwards to shelflisting.

Shelflisting:
1) completes LC call number and records it on at least 4 prelim. cards (one each for shelflist, ser rec, PIF, and custodial div.).
2) forwards to decimal classification div. for dewey no. [2]

Prelim. card with call. no. forwarded to custodial division; piece with surplus prelim. cards forwarded to photodup. [3]

Ms. sheet with 2 prelim. cards (1 with call no. for ser rec) sent to edit. sec., subj. cat. div.

MARC-S personnel pick up and log in ms. sheets by LC card no. and forward to NSDP

NSDP:
1) adds ISSN to ms. sheet as last note and to prelim. with call no. [4]
2) adds key title [4]
3) forwards all to MARC-S

MARC-S:
1) forwards prelim. with call no. and, if applicable, ISSN, to ed. and ref. unit for noting in visible file and discarding.
2) photocopies 2 copies of ms. sheet.

If roman alphabet [5]

If non-roman alphabet

Original retained for MARC-S input [6]

One copy to card div. for check against card no. control book

One copy (with NST prelim. card) to NST

Original to printer via card division

One copy retained for MARC-S input in romanized form [6]

One copy (with NST prelim. card) to NST

To card prep, cat mgmt div, (used for writing up the cards printed from the MARC-S tape for LC's catalogs)

Normal procedures

Normal routines for printing and filing into LC's catalogs

Normal procedures

[1] Does not include monographic series.
[2] Some titles bypass Decimal Classification Division.
[3] Photoduplication Service makes aperture cards for NSDP; those titles for which the Selection Officer has indicated "Acquire" are generally sent next to the Order Division or Exchange and Gift Division as applicable.
[4] Ms. sheets for non-U.S. imprints are forwarded to MARC-S without ISSN and Key Title; this information is sent later to MARC-S when supplied by the Paris Office.
[5] Until Card Division Phase II is operational, all titles are handled as if non-Roman alphabet.
[6] Card Division Phase II and NSDP receive copies of MARC-S tapes.

Fig. 17-6. Cataloging for printed cards — detailed procedures.

New serial titles if not to be cataloged for printed cards [1] · Normal procedures (See B1.1 for prior handling)

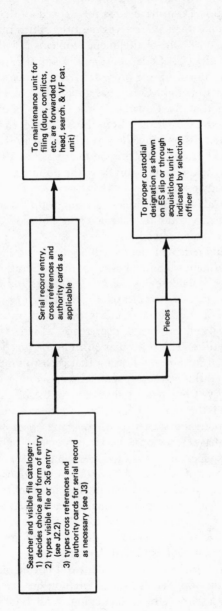

[1] "Discards," "Current issues only," "Review before binding," "Sample serials," and "Send to NLM/NAL."

Fig. 17-7. Cataloging, not for printed cards — detailed procedures.

Librarians involved with serials often wonder about LC's policies, and there are many questions in the backs of their minds. One that frequently comes up is "When can I expect LC to have cards for a specific title I have in mind?" Often this depends on when LC receives the title, which may be considerably later than other libraries. One of the major problems is with copyright items, which, according to the U.S. Code, must go through the Copyright Office for registry. This tends to hold up the process. Then LC chooses what it wants to keep from what the Copyright Office has gone through. The procedure may even be held up more if the Copyright Office has to request issues. Copy is bound to appear from LC later than from those libraries current on their first-issue cataloging, even discounting the possible delays in the cataloging maze just outlined. Because cards are not printed in order of cataloging, and because of the intricacies of the cataloging workflow, the public cannot predict if there will be LC cards for any given serial.

LC may not know about title changes back and forth because of the routines it follows. Such a change could be done as a "title of short duration," but LC very rarely goes back to redo something.

LC will go back and redo a monograph as a serial if it really turns out to be a serial or if serial treatment would be better for the publication. This latter type is what Osborn calls "pseudoserials." *Burke's peerage* and Cattell's *Directory of American scholars* are two examples of LC's recataloging.

The Library of Congress rarely catalogs exhibition catalogs as serials. It catalogs the principal publications of conferences as serials if the volumes do not bear distinctive titles. This is a variation from the practice under the ALA rules, which provided for notes indicating that each volume had a distinctive title. Serials cataloged this way are generally being recataloged as monographs under the new policy. Conference publications must be published for every meeting, and under the same title, to be considered serials. International conference publications are treated as monographs because there is such a possibility for language variations. Lesser conference publications such as abstracts or working papers are rarely cataloged serially. Libraries following LC's policies should be aware of LC's outlook on such publications.

Many questions tend to come up about monographic series. The decisions on series treatment are made by the subject cataloger as the piece comes through as a monograph. If the decision is to class together, following much the same subject guidelines as given in this book, the piece will go back to the Serial Record Division for treatment as a serial. Decision notes are made and filed in the Official Catalog so that double treatment will not be made for the series. The note also says that the Serials Record Division has the book. The serials cataloging is sent back to the Subject Cataloging Division for subject cataloging and shelflisting. The call number is added to the series treatment card. A series treatment card is also sent back to be filed in the Descriptive Cataloging

Division to await more issues of that series. This slows down series treatment considerably. Serials cataloging then follows the same routines already outlined. Decision is always made on subject content, never on frequency or other criteria. Here is a copy of the series treatment card. (This one is a blue card for a collected set, traced).

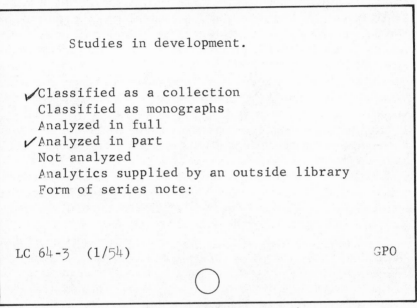

Fig. 17-8. Blue series treatment card.

Some titles were never permanently cataloged as series because of old form card cataloging practices. This is why a cataloger may search the LC book catalogs and find lots of analytic cards, but no cover card for the serial, even though the classification would indicate that the item was cataloged serially. An individual library will have to make its own serial card.

Notes are made for unanalyzable pieces of a series that is usually analyzed, if the Library decides to keep them. If a trend appears to be developing, LC may opt to change the decision on the series. An example of such a decision can be seen in Fig. 6-42 in this book, w1th appropriate LC notes.

There are probably many questions rising during this discussion of LC's practices. This has only attempted to be a brief overview, and any specific issues or titles should be addressed to the appropriate officers at LC. They encourage mail and have always proved to be helpful and informative when queried by grass-roots librarians.

The year 1951 saw the first issue of a new monthly publication entitled *Serial titles newly received*. It was prepared from the punched card records of serials at LC, at first, but there was hope of expansion. The Librarian of Congress said in his 1951 *Report:*

> It is hoped that the publication of this list [*Serial titles newly received*] will be a first step toward the development of. . .a union catalog of serials and toward the publication of bibliographical controls to provide maximum accessibility to the information contained in the serial resources of American libraries.[8]

His hopes have definitely been realized, for this fledgling publication became *New serial titles.*

New serial titles, colloquially called *NST,* is the serials bibliography and union list published at LC by an office located in the Serials Record Division. Its introduction describes it thus:

> The titles listed in this publication are serials that, so far as can be determined, began publication after December 31, 1949. They have been supplied by the Library of Congress and cooperating libraries. Serials not in the Roman alphabet are included under a transliterated or romanized entry if a standard transliteration or romanization scheme has been accepted by the American Library Association. Entries in all languages are filed according to the order of letters in the English alphabet. Diacritical marks and accents used to distinguish characters or letters not included in the Roman alphabet are not printed because of typographical limitations. Newspapers, looseleaf publications, books in parts, municipal government serial documents, publishers' series, motion pictures, filmstrips, and phonorecords are excluded. . . .[9]

Entries, using either ALA or AACR rules, are sent in by libraries, using the report slip shown in the section on cataloging routines of this book, or are derived from LC cataloging through the routines already described. Brief description is given, including issuing body in parentheses, numbering and dates of the title, frequency, publisher's address, price and bibliographic notes. Dewey numbers are given for subject information (There is also an *NST* publication arranged by these numbers.). Holdings are given briefly, using *NUC* symbols for reporting libraries.

NST has always been a little off-to-the-side in LC's activities, but attempts are being made to bring it more to the forefront, where it should be. LC's participation in CONSER (see next chapter) should do a great deal to expand, update and streamline activities both in the cataloging and *NST* aspects of the Division. Hopefully, *NST* will be automated as an offshoot of CONSER. Further involvement in automated projects involving serials cataloging data should hurl LC out of the Dark Ages of serials control, where it was such a few short decades ago, to the front, as a leader in automation and standardization projects that are the keystone of the future.

FOOTNOTES

1. Library of Congress. *Processing Department* (February, 1974) p. 9.

2. C. Sumner Spalding. *The cataloging of serials at the Library of Congress: a report with recommendations* (Washington: Library of Congress, Serials Record Division, February 20, 1956, retyped August 17, 1956), p. 6.

3. Ibid.

4. Library of Congress. *Annual report of the Librarian of Congress . . .* (1971):12.

5. Library of Congress. Processing Department. *Department memorandum* 111 (May 31, 1971):1-2.

6. *Cataloging service bulletin* 100 (June, 1971):1-2.

7. *Cataloging service bulletin* 114 (Summer, 1975):5.

8. Library of Congress. *Annual report of the Librarian of Congress . . .* (1951):81-82.

9. William J. Welsh, "Introduction," *New serial titles; a union list of serials. . .1950-1970 cumulative,* (Washington: Library of Congress. New York: R.R. Bowker 1973)

Chapter XVIII

Automation and Standardization

When dealing with serials, the issues of standardization are very important. Serials are elusive creatures, not easily standardized, and yet they are curiously among the first things automated in a library. Libraries join together to form systems and consortia and one of the first endeavours is a union list of serials. Without some kind of standardizing factors, such projects usually end up as disasters. There is a great need for uniformity in the cataloging of serial publications.

> Periodical entries are in themselves often so complicated and the methods employed by different libraries in their catalogues vary to such an extent, that some acknowledged uniform method of listing, both as to form and order of entry is most desirable.[1]

Since Mr. Bonser made this remark, many things have happened to promote standardization of library treatment of these elusive publications. For example, when he was writing there were several approaches to the treatment of changed titles. These have been explored already and the result is printed in the AACR: successive entry. There is, however, all of that retrospective material a poor harried union list editor has to cope with. And not all libraries went along with the new decision anyway, as LC didn't at first. Corporate entries may vary considerably according to the rule being used. Perhaps the Library of Congress' decision to drop superimposition toward the end of the decade may alleviate some of this problem, but this is at present an unknown factor. Not all libraries follow the lead of LC anyway.

Although there has always been the need for some kind of standardization, and various librarians have made remarks concerning this need from time to time, it has only been in the last decade-and-a-half that anything has been done, spurred on primarily by the dawn of the age of the computer in the library.

> Although cataloging has already reached a very high level of standardization in the United States, primarily through the services of the Library of Congress, any consideration of automation in relation to the desemination of cataloging data makes it obvious we have much to gain from even further standardization. . .[2]

So wrote Lucile Morsch in 1964. The feeling is still there and the Library of Congress and the world of libraries are trying to do something about it now that the computer is becoming a necessary and valuable tool in the library.

The age of automation has hit serials cataloging now and hit it hard, although the impact is slow in reaching the grass-roots. Serials processing and control records have always been among the first to be automated, although they represent the most difficult and least understood of library operations. Even libraries experimenting with automation on a very elementary level have serials catalogs in the form of holdings lists. These may be very elementary or extremely sophisticated. There are also attempts, some very successful, to automate claiming and predict receipt. The system at the University of California at San Diego has received acclaim as one of the great successes in this area of library automation. UCLA has also had success in its Biomedical Library. The University of Minnesota has another success. OCLC (Ohio College Library Center) hopes to have all of its check-in for serials operational in the near future. This will allow the automated system to produce purchase orders, send them out, and keep track of funding. Check-in, claim and bindery functions will also be maintained. OCLC is, of course, one of the pioneers in on-line shared cataloging. Other systems are very adequately chronicled in Mr. Bosseau's fine article on the computer in serials processing and control.[3] Now, as systems work develops even more in the library, serials cataloging records are coming more under the scrutiny of systems experts. This is involving serials people on a national and even international level. The wave of the future is upon us!

> Perhaps the least affected in any automated serial system, regardless of its simplicity or complexity, is the area of cataloging. The lack of standardization, especially in the area of corporate entries, is evident when comparing forms of entries for serials publications as used in different libraries. The new Anglo-American Rules are adding to the confusion at this time, partly due to their inherent flexibility, but also due to the variations in interpretation and degree of acceptance of the rules. Even with the LC MARC Serials Record Format now available (Library of Congress, 1969),[4] there has been little activity in the

area of utilizing computers to solve any of the serials cataloging problems. It is unlikely that major changes will be observed in the near future, even as libraries begin to use the record format in their own serials systems applications. The individuality in serials cataloging continues, so that, even as machine-readable data bases for serials become more readily available, cataloging of serials makes little use of them and has yet to feel any real impact from the computer.[5]

It is hard to know what Mr. Bosseau means by "the near future," but it would seem that three years after his article came out serials catalogers and systems people all around the world are trying to prove him wrong. Perhaps serials cataloging has taken a long time to hear the computer's call, and perhaps not all involved are listening (after all, they didn't all rally to the AACR either), and perhaps not all the "bugs" are worked out yet, but at least one can no longer say that serials cataloging has not felt the impact of the computer.

Automation can do a number of good things with cataloging data. There is great flexibility in manipulating the data, which facilitates search and retrieval. Given appropriate hard- and software, the horizons are limited only by the user's imagination.

Computerization of cataloging data gives an added dimension to bibliographic control. There is complete access to everything in the record from all possible angles. Changes can be made effortlessly and updating is a comparative breeze. The switching-over to new headings caused by "desuperimposition" could be done easily in the machine. (LC has decided to wait for this until all of its current cataloging is in the computer, sometime at the end of the decade, for just this reason.) Subject headings could be changed over wherever they occur en masse in the automated record.

Searching could be done on a few important words as in the OCLC system or Stanford's BALLOTS (Bibliographic Automation of Large Library Operations using a Time-Sharing System). Order and catalog copy could be printed out, with desired changes. The computer record can even be accessed by patrons desiring on-order or cataloging information through special programs and terminals in public areas.

Other cataloging by-products could be produced: book cards, pockets, spine labels — all preparatory for an automated circulation system. Lists could be generated for bindery preparation forms, and receipt and claim records. Special lists, such as subject lists, location lists and key word (KWIC or KWOC) lists could be run on the machine file. The computer could pull out such information as language, country of origin, price, vendor and other management data, depending on the information contained within the file itself. List possibilities are endless.

Libraries are finding that their serial subscriptions are taking over the major part of their book budgets with the current rampant inflation. In attempts to stop this before it gets too far out-of-hand, many are taking a long hard look at their serial commitments in terms of their real needs. Some academic libraries are finding it easier to distribute printouts of shelflist-ordered serials for the faculties in the various disciplines they support to evaluate. A number of printouts can be produced so that some titles may be duplicated and distributed to several faculties with overlapping interests. The professors are not overwhelmed by huge listings of material outside their areas, yet get to have their say on what should interest them. Evaluations can be keyed back into the computer and "deselection" lists generated. This cannot be done easily without a classed collection, however.

The most obvious use of automation in the individual library for serials cataloging records is the holdings list, mentioned earlier. In some libraries this serves as the only public record of serials in the library. In others, it serves as an addition to the catalog for holdings information — a more efficient updating than writing on the catalog cards, as of yore. It is, in other words, the "now" version of the old serials catalog. Costs can be cut by putting the list on computer-generated microfiche or film, called COM (Computer Output Microform).

The demise of the book catalog was caused by the lack of a rapid method of updating. Cataloging is coming full circle with the advent of the computer-produced catalog or serials list in book form. This book catalog, unlike its predecessor, can be rapidly updated and superseded. Andrew Osborn[6] feels that automated cataloging in a library should supersede card cataloging for serials publications. At least until things are more stabilized and several hurdles are successfully jumped, many catalogers and serials librarians are reserving judgment on this aspect of automation. However, cataloging methods, including form and content, will be affected greatly by the computer. Vestiges of card cataloging practices, such as the addition of place names to corporate authors, can be eliminated, for example. Computer lists and check-in records can also utilize a lot of abbreviations, formerly an unacceptable practice in cataloging circles.

In this age of ever-shrinking budgets, the accent is on the sharing of resources. Libraries are depending more on the holdings of wealthier neighbors as their own funds diminish. Some libraries are becoming more specialized. Libraries are forming systems. Consortia are becoming a fact of library life right now. The era of splendid isolation of each library unto itself is over. With the boom in technology and the explosion in publishing, no library can hope to control under its own roof all the materials a serious researcher would need. Catalog records input into an automated system would facilitate circulation, reference and interlibrary loan functions. The world would become our own library, except in physical terms. Perhaps someday those can be improved upon too.

Union lists of periodical holdings in the various cooperating libraries are essential for smooth operation of these sharing plans. In 1930, Edna Goss[7] chronicled a small number of union lists of interest and assistance to the serials cataloger. She lamented that there were not more, and then went on to describe the good and bad points of each. She had observed that there were few (6) helps for serials catalogers listed in Cannon's *Bibliography of library economy, 1876-1920,* and even since 1920 there had been few advances. Since then the advances have been geometric in increase so that now the numbers are staggering. *New serials titles* is, of course, the biggest one. The twenty-one year cumulation issued by Bowker in 1972 is the largest machine-readable data base, composed of over 220,000 records. The State of California has three large union lists, put out by the State Library, the State College and University System, and the nine campuses of the University of California through its University-wide Library Automation Program (ULAP). Perhaps one day these will merge into a state union list. The Minnesota Union List of Serials (MULS) is just such a state list. There are union lists in various subject areas too, such as the Union Catalog of Medical Periodicals (UCMP) developed at the Medical Library Center of New York. The list could go on and on. The problems of an editor of such a union list are monumental, for one is confronted with an alarming number of variables.

It is to combat these variables that many standardizing methods are in effect. This creates a veritable alphabet soup of acronyms and initialisms that is hard for the serials cataloger to swallow at first. ISDS, ISSN, NSDP, CONSER, MARC-S and ISBD(S) are just a few of the big ones cluttering the air around serials people as they speak to each other in hotel lobbies at conventions. Of course, each of these collections of letters have many other attendant ones, amounting to a revolution in serials cataloging. Let us see what the future holds in store for us.

The growing impact of electronic automation has given new impetus to the efforts for standardization of cataloging. This is level three of a three-level viewpoint on the mechanized exchangeability of bibliographic information. These three levels can be stated as follows:

1. the physical-technical conditions, which may be created without difficulty,

2. conditions concerning the formal and logical structure of data, and

3. conditions concerning the content of data categories (e.g., cataloging rules).[8]

The second point of view is important. It relates both to individual bibliographic data elements and their mode of interchange in machine-readable form. This is where most of the alphabet soup comes in.

The first acronym will be ISDS. This stands for International Serials Data System. ISDS grew out of resolutions passed at the 1966 and 1968 general conferences of UNESCO. These resolutions initiated a feasibility study into the establishment of a world scientific information system (UNISIST). The International Council of Scientific Unions (ICSU) assisted in this inquiry. One of the recommendations of this study was that "an international registry of scientific periodicals should be established as a basis of a system for the normalization of the citations of the journal literature of science and technology."[9] Eventually this worldwide registration system would form the basis on which future systems for the unique identification of individual bibliographic units of serials would be built.

The French Government and UNESCO provided funding for the establishment of ISDS and the International Centre for the Registration of Serials in Paris. "Serial" is defined by ISDS basically with the *Anglo-American cataloging rules* definition, slightly revised to include either publications in print or nonprint forms. It also allows for the inclusion of unnumbered series.

The objectives of ISDS are:

a   To develop and maintain an international register of serial publications containing all the necessary information for the identification of the serials.

b   To define and promote the use of a standard code (ISSN) for the unique identification of each serial.

c   To facilitate retrieval of scientific and technical information in serials.

d   To make this information currently available to all countries, organizations, or individual users.

e   To establish a network of communications between libraries, secondary information services, publishers of serial literature and international organizations.

f   To promote international standards for bibliographic description, communication formats, and information exchange in the area of serials publications.[10]

The International Centre is responsible for developing a basic international field of serials in machine-readable form; publishing an international register of serial publications; promoting the establishment of a worldwide network of national and regional centers; registering serials published in countries which cannot or do not choose to establish national centers; managing the ISSN; and establishing close coordination between ISDS and other international organizations.[11] The national centers will have the following functions as elements of the international network:

a   Registration of serials published in their respective countries. Each National Centre will receive from the International Centre a block of ISSN for the registration and numbering of serials published after January 1971.

Retrospective numbering will be possible as soon as the basic international file is completed.

b   Contribution to the International Register. The international file will be a cumulation of the base file. . .

c   Relationship with publishers. The National Centres will carry the main responsibility for the establishment of links between ISDS and the publishers of serial literature.

d   Relationship with users. Organizations of individual users of ISDS will, as a rule, deal with their respective National Centres. This does not exclude direct contacts between users and the International Centre.[12]

National centers may also have other duties as well, as NSDP, the national center in the United States, does. Centers will communicate with each other and cooperate closely. They will use already established ISO (International Standardization Organization) standards, and will agree on temporary standards if an ISO international standard does not exist. The format to be used is a list of minimum data elements, which is a subset of MARC for serials. The data elements are as follows:

* 1. Date of entry or most recent amendment
* 2. Centre code
* 3. ISSN
  4. Coden[1]
  5. Publication status (currently published, discontinued, unknown)
  6. Type of publication
* 7. Start date
  8. End date
  9. Frequency[1]
*10. Country of publication
*11. Alphabet of original title
  12. Language of publication[1]
  13. UDC, DC, or LC classification[2]
*14. Key title
  15. Abbreviated title[3]
*16. Variant title (any other form of title appearing on the piece)
  17. Former title(s)[4]
  18. Successor title(s)
  19. Other language edition of
  20. Has other language edition
  21. Inset to or supplement to

22. Has inset or supplement
23. Related title
*24. Imprint
25. Coverage by abstracting services[1]

* Essential elements.
[1]To be supplied when readily available.
[2]UDC or DC are preferable. LC classification may be provided if UDC or DC are not available.
[3]Journal title as provided by the "International List of Periodical Title Word Abbreviations."
[4]Elements 17 to 23 should be represented by their respective ISSN.[13]

Sources for information should be title-page, cover, summary and other sources. Key title is derived from the title information appearing on the piece-in-hand.

ISDS regional centers are springing up all over the world. The Canadian one is housed in the National Library of Canada, the Australian one has been integrated into the *Australian national bibliography*. The United Kingdom, France, Federal Republic of Germany, Argentina, Japan, Sweden and Finland are also designated for national centers. The Soviet Union will represent the COMECON (Council for Mutual Economic Assistance) countries with a regional center. In the United States, ISDS is represented by NSDP; the National Serials Data Program. It is housed in the Library of Congress.

Various products could be derived from the ISDS: Title Index, ISSN Index, ISDS register of periodicals ("Register"), Classified Title Index ("CTI"), New and Amended Titles Index ("N&AT"), Cumulated New Titles ("CNT"), Permuted Index, and Microform Reference File ("MRF").[14] ISDS also

. . .has the potential of providing to the bibliographic data handling community internationally acceptable standards for the identification of serial publications. It offers a solution to problems inherent in the difficult identification conventions of libraries, abstracting or indexing services, and publishers or distributors.[15]

The editing staff at the International Centre (ISDS/IC) in Paris spent 1974 concentrating on the creation of a single file from the contents of CASSI (Chemical Abstracts Service Source Index), CNRS (Centre National de la Recherch. Scientifique), INSPEC (Information Service for Physics, Electrotechnology, and Control of the IEEE), BIOSIS (Biological Science Service of *Biological abstracts*). and *Geological abstracts*. This will result in a file of about 30,000 titles.[16] This will be used to create a basic world list for the national centers to upgrade. It will also be used to test ISDS rules and formats. ISSN and key titles will be supplied to this list. The ISDS/IC has assumed the responsibility for maintaining the world list of journal title abbreviations formerly under the auspices of the Chemical Abstracts Service. The base file will also provide input for this project. The National Clearinghouse for Periodical Title Word Abbreviations (NCPTWA) was superseded also by this amplification of the International Centre's responsibilities. The monumental world undertaking has begun. The year 1975 saw the beginning of a bimonthly publication, *Bulletin de l'ISDS*. The information is in ISSN order, with data elements and punctuation following ISBD(S) [q.v.].

The major project for ISDS, however, is the ISSN (International Standard Serial Number). After the ISBN (International Standard Book Number) came out, it became obvious that something similar was needed for serial publications. The American draft standard for Standard Serial Numbers (SSN's), entitled *Identification numbers for serials publications*, emanating from a subcommittee of the American National Standards Institute (ANSI) Committee Z-39 was placed before the International Standardization Organization Technical Committee 46, the same group that was instrumental in the discussions regarding the ISBN. At the same time it was being considered by the British Standards Institution. In due time, an ISO draft standard for International Standard Serial Numbers was issued for ratification in mid-1974. Numbers were picked as an identification designator because numbers are more international than any single alphabet. "Serial," for purposes of the ISSN, is defined by the AACR definition.

The ISSN is an eight-digit number, presented in two groups of four, separated by a hyphen. The eighth digit is a check digit, which is effective in detecting transposition errors. (The methodology for creating ISSN is discussed in the literature, but, since it will not affect catalogers at the local level, is not reproduced here. One authoritative source is the *Guidelines for ISDS.* See also p. xv of the twenty-one year cumulation of *NST*.) The number is accompanied by a country code and is preceded by the letters "ISSN." For example, the ISSN for *American libraries* is US ISSN 0002-9769. The number is an "idiot number" in that it cannot be broken down into meaningful digits like the ISBN can. The number is by no means idiotic, however. This number is a standard, unique and unambiguous code for the identification of a given serial publication, the only one to which it is assigned. It can be used whenever there is interchange of information about serials, either in a manual or automated system. The number is inseparably associated with the key title it is assigned to, and any change in the key title demands a new ISSN. The new number will bear no meaningful relationship to the one for the old title, however. Any serial can be identified by the number without problems of entry variation, spelling errors, etc.

Investigation showed six cases in which the libraries vary in the choice of main entry (principally serials) when they establish new headings, and six exceptions in determinining the form heading. . .[17]

The use of numbers would collapse the different versions of entry under the one number, thus providing some standardization of identification.

The ISSN code must be applied nationally and implemented internationally for it to be effective. Therefore, the International Serials Data System will provide the International Centre and the network of national and regional centers to implement the ISSN. A printed ISSN listing is planned. The ISSN is different, then, from the ISBN, which is a number tied to a specific piece of bibliographic material, a monograph in a certain format, and is controlled by the book trade itself.

The largest computerized data base equipped with ISSN was created with the publication of *New serials titles, 1950-1970* by the R. R. Bowker Company. When LC announced its intent to publish a ten-year cumulation (1961-70), Bowker proposed to convert the entire file to machine-readable form. At the same time, the first serials listing with ISSN was being published. This was the index to the second edition of *Irregular serials and annuals,* which also included titles listed in the fourteenth edition of *Ulrich's international periodicals directory,* published by Bowker. Bowker was given a block of numbers to assign while ISDS was getting on its feet and getting ready to assume the responsibility. The twenty-one year cumulation of *NST* was published with ISSN. Although pains were taken to avoid pitfalls, some were fallen into anyway. Because of duplication between the serials bibliographies and *NST,* some titles unfortunately got two ISSN. This will ultimately be cleaned up by NSDP and one of the ISSN will be retired and not reused. Also, Bowker did not necessarily assign numbers to key titles. This will also be revised and corrected by NSDP as time permits. But even with all of the errors, the *NST* cumulation is a remarkable file of tremendous import. ISSN are identified for the first time in an important and relevant way. ISSN are being incorporated into the International Standard Bibliographic Description for Serials and already have been incorporated into the new Chapter 6 of AACR in relation to monographic series. Publishers are printing ISSN in their periodicals and NSDP is strongly urging them to do so. More importantly, libraries, dealers and others are using the standard numbers as part of their bibliographic control devices, which further strengthens the system and encourages its wholesale utilization as a method of unique identification of serial titles. This should promote faster and more accurate transmission of information relative to serial publications.

The ISSN is uniquely and inseparably tied to something called "key title."

It is established by the ISDS center responsible for registration of the serial and is derived from the title information appearing on the publication, exclusive of subtitles. Title-page titles receive preference and others are treated as variants. The ISDS concepts that follow will be important to the future of serials cataloging.

If the title as it appears on the piece is *distinctive* it will be used as the key-title. . . .

If the title as it appears on the piece begins with or contains *the name of the issuing body,* and the name of the issuing body is grammatically inseparable from the rest of the title, then the title, beginning with or including the name of the issuing body is the key-title. . . .

If the title information on the piece contains a *generic word,*[1] and that word is not grammatically linked to the name of the issuing body, the key-title is to begin with the generic word, followed by the name of the issuing body.

The name of the issuing body will be transcribed in the sequence and form given in the piece. It will be linked to the generic word by a dash (space dash space). . . .

It is to be noted that a comma or other punctuation marks are not considered to constitute grammatical links.

If the name of the issuing body is the only title present, this name will be used as key-title, and transcribed in the sequence and form given in the piece.

[1]A generic word in a serial title is one which indicates the kind and/or periodicity of a publication such as: Abhandlungen, Annales, Berichte, Bulletin, Cahiers, Comptes rendus, Yearbook, etc.[18]

The *Guidelines for ISDS* (pp. 24-31) go on to be more specific regarding other aspects of titles. Initial articles are omitted unless they are part of place names, such as *Los* Angeles. Numbers are written as Arabic ciphers, with a variant title note having the word spelled out in the appropriate language. Numbers are included if part of the title, but excluded if part of a numbering sequence such as for conferences or chronological series. Subject series designated by numbers retain their numbers. The key title for a section of the *Bulletin signalétique* would be as follows:

Bulletin signalétique. Section 101. Information scientifique et technique.

Punctuation is added. Diacritics and capitalization will conform to national usage. Parallel titles will be used as variant titles, with the most prominent title, or the first if typographic prominence is not accorded one of the titles, becoming the key title. Identical titles will be distinguished by places of publication and dates in parentheses. (If a key title is input without qualifiers, and it is later determined that qualifiers would be necessary, the key title originally input will not be changed. The title with qualifiers will become a variant title, however.) Special key titles will be devised for different language editions of a work and also for different formats, such as microforms or Braille. Continuing supplements will receive their own ISSN as will serials within serials and subseries.

All of this means that the following will be considered key titles by ISDS:

Journal of creative behavior [distinctive title]
Quarterly journal of the Library of Congress [title with corporate body]
Annual report - New Jersey Development Disabilities Council [generic words with issuing body added]
List and Index Society [no title given on the piece]
Life (Chicago) ⎱ [Two identical titles with additional qualifiers added -
Life (New York) ⎰   probably one of these would be the base one, just called
                     Life]

Due to the change in rule 162B, already mentioned, the second and third key title examples here will agree with the cataloging title according to AACR.

A very interesting problem, mentioned in the chapter on entry, may well be solved by the ISDS guidelines for key title. This refers to acronyms and initialisms appearing as part of the title. Section 4.2.2 of the *Guidelines* says that:

> If the acronym is inseparable from the rest of the title, it should be retained as part of the key-title, as it appears on the piece.[19]

One of the examples given is *A.L.A. bulletin.* "American Library Association bulletin" would be entered as a variant form.

> If the title consists of a set of initials prominently displayed, and the expanded form is also present, the key-title will begin with the acronym, followed by the expanded form. The expanded form will also be entered as a variant title.[20]

The example given is "BLM Bonniers Literary Magazine." "Bonniers Literary Magazine" is the variant title.

> If the acronym and the expanded form do not match, the same procedure should be followed.

> If the acronym is the only title given in the piece, it should be considered a distinctive title. . . .The expanded form should be entered as a variant title whenever possible.[21]

This isn't much of an answer to our aforementioned problem, but it does give us a little something to go on.

One of the problems serials catalogers learn a lot about in their careers is title changes. What constitutes a title change for the ISDS and NSDP people? The simplest answer is:

> Any change in one or more words or characters in a work, or the addition or deletion of any word, constitute a valid title change.[22]

However, realizing that this would result in an inordinate number of changes, exceptions have been made.

Changes that would result in new key titles (and ISSN) can be enumerated as follows:

a) different or deleted or additional nouns, names or adjectives, except added subtitles. . . .

b) different order of the words. . . .

c) a change in the name of an issuing body which is part of the key-title. . . .

d) where the name of the issuing body is grammatically linked to the rest of the title, a change in the form of the name, for example from full words to an abbreviation, set of initials or acronym. . . .

e) changes in spellings of existing words, if the change occurs with the initial letter of the word or changes the meaning of the word; any change in an acronym or set of initials. . .[23]

Changes that would not result in new key titles and ISSN would be as follows:

a) different, additional or deleted articles, prepositions and conjunctions, or different order thereof that have no effect on the order of the significant words [i.e., addition or loss of "of the"]. . . .

b) minor changes in the names of the issuing body which is part of the key-title, particularly if the acronym used by the body is not affected by the change [i.e., ASTM's change to American Society for Testing and Materials by adding the "and."]. . . .

c) substitutions of conjunctions with a plus sign (+) or an ampersand (&). . . .

d) additions of words, previously added to the key-title to make it distinctive [i.e., Economic bulletin (Accra) becoming Economic bulletin of Accra]. . . .

e) changes in spelling, other than in first letters that do not affect the meaning of the words. . . .

f) changes in typographic prominence and similar changes which do not alter the nature of the publication. . . .

Minor title changes will become variant titles. If a title merges or splits into new titles, new key titles and ISSN will be assigned. Titles continuing will keep the same key title and ISSN. Titles which resume publication under an older name, after some interval under a different name, will receive new key titles, qualified by date. Facsimiles and reprints will receive new key titles, qualified by such terms as "(Reprint)" and new ISSN.[24]

It is almost certain that these guidelines will become fixed as criteria for title changes as we move forward with our automated projects and NSDP becomes functional and instrumental in serials cataloging ventures such as CONSER. Already these guidelines have shown an impact on our cataloging, and this impact will continue.

The ISSN has all but superseded another form of serials control worthy of brief mention. This is CODEN, published by the American Society for Testing and Materials. This is a short mnemonic system relating to titles. Examples are PWEE-A for *Publishers' weekly* and JACS-AT for *Journal of the American Chemical Society*. "JACS" refers to the title proper. The "A" is a further identifying factor, used when the first four digits could be another title, and the "T" is a check character, like the final digit of the ISSN. Osborn puts great stock in CODEN as a simplification of entry for check-in purposes.[25] CODEN codes can be found on many periodical covers, perhaps also suggesting a move toward title main entry, as the use of ISSN has. Its future is perhaps a little uncertain, however. There are tables being devised to translate CODEN into ISSN for titles already indexed using this system. Perhaps the fact that CODEN has worked so well in the past, and has been accepted by so many, will pave the way for the ISSN.

The Committee on Scientific and Technical Information (COSATI) created a special task force in April, 1964, to study ways to improve the processing and utilization of journal literature. Its work caused the National Science Foundation to award a study contract to IDC in April, 1965. This study was to cover serials in the fields of science and technology. The farseeing writers of the report on the Serials Data Program saw this initial effort as one that might serve as a "prototype and nucleus for a broader Serials Data Program concerned with all serials. . . ."[26] The report analyzed the data to be covered. It recommended primary examination of the physical pieces as the method for achieving most accurate data, but did not cover other possibilities for obtaining records. There was some concern about getting publications for new data collections on a voluntary or semivoluntary basis. In the light of future developments in the area, this sentence becomes a most interesting one:

> For example, if the Serials Data Program assumed a serials registration function and assigned registration numbers to all serials, publishers and other handlers of serials might have sufficient motivation to report voluntarily requested serials data to the program.[27]

This study prompted further discussions among the three national libraries. In June, 1966, the Association of Research Libraries (ARL) appointed an ad hoc committee to explore the problem. This committee became the Subcommittee on the World List of Serials of the JCULS (Joint Committee on the Union List of Serials). This subcommittee discussed plans for the three national libraries to undertake a cooperative serials data program.

The directors of the national libraries established the National Libraries Task Force on Automation and Other Cooperative Activities in the summer of 1967. It was charged with the planning, development and implementation of a National Serials Data Program.

January, 1969, saw the beginning of Phase I, under the Library of Congress Information Systems Office, employing the firm of Thomas Nelson Associates. The objectives were to define serials, identify the data elements needed to control them, and develop a content format for serials. This resulted in the MARC serials format [q.v.]. A user study was also undertaken. The report came out in 1969 recommending a pilot project as soon as possible.[28]

The Association of Research Libraries administered the National Serials Pilot Project on behalf of the three national libraries and at their request. This was Phase II of the National Serials Data Program. Its objectives were:

1) to create a machine-readable file containing live serials in the fields of science and technology held by the three national libraries;

2) to produce a number of preliminary listings, including a union list and other lists of interest to management; and

3) to produce one or more written reports relating to problems, solutions, information regarding the universe of serials, and recommendations.[29]

Among its conclusions and recommendations were:

1) a national serials data bank in machine-readable form is both technically and economically feasible;

2) such a data bank should have its own machine-readable authority file for corporate names;

3) input and output in upper case only would be more satisfactory from both the systems viewpoint and the cost viewpoint, but probably would not be accepted by the library community; and

4) serious consideration should be given to the question of applicability of existing cataloging rules in the determination of "main entry" in a machine-readable file.[30]

For serials catalogers numbers 2 and 4 are probably of the most interest. It was suggested that the next project which was mounted should use its own machine-readable authority file. This should be built out of AACR-established headings and should not relate to any previously-established file. The NSPP had used the LC files, and LC's policy of superimposition had proved to be a great stumbling block. It was also suggested that there should be tie-ins from this file to the master file records in various places, including non-main entries.

It was also suggested that a committee of experts in both cataloging and automation be set up to evaluate the applicability of present cataloging rules to machine-readable format. Rules should be added and modified to exploit the capabilities of the computer. There were problems with terminology. There were other problems because, while some of the limitations of the card catalog disappeared, other problems arose in an automated context. "Main entry" becomes a redundant phrase in a computerized file because there is only one entry. It may not be *the* main entry from the cataloger's point of view. There was also unnecessary repetition of bibliographic records. Systems designers felt that the system needed revamping, but that users of the output would not be concerned about the precise methods used, as long as the records could be printed or displayed in the desired manner.

Even the MARC format was considered limiting because it was designed primarily for catalog card production and the problems mentioned above were built into it. Some innovations were made as the project went along and it was recommended that these changes be made permanent.

The suggestions and predictions made at the end of the project seem to be playing a major role in what is happening now — namely, the current revolution in cataloging and the controversy over rule 6.

In January, 1970, NSPP experimented with SSN's, the proposed standard from ANSI Z-39. However, since it had no authority for permanent assignment of the numbers, these were only employed in the local system. However, this heralded the beginning of NSDP's involvement with what became the ISSN.

Phase I set the stage. Phase II did feasibility studies and set up the charge and a hierarchy. A national system of bibliographic control on all serials was discussed with the National Advisory Committee to the Program, which represents libraries, subscription agencies, abstracting and indexing services and publishers. Phase III began in early 1972, funded by the national libraries in an agreed-upon ratio. It became fully operational at the beginning of 1973. It was originally part of the Processing Department of LC, but since January 3, 1975, it has been part of the Serial Record Division. This is the National Serials Data Program, NSDP.

The third phase of the program will provide the three national libraries, and other research libraries as well, with an authoritative automated bibliographic resource upon which serials processing systems can be built; provide a base record of serial titles to which the International Standard Serial Number can be permanently affixed, thus ending the confusion about precise identification of serials; provide a machine-readable bibliographic resource for serials which will supply important cataloging information to libraries and at the same time permit the uniform transfer of data on serials among libraries; provide a base from which several kinds of library tools can be developed; and provide a serial system which will constitute the U.S. segment of the developing International Serials Data System.[31]

NSDP gets input from a variety of sources: magnetic tapes from NLM, NAL, and LC; worksheets from *NST,* NLM, and NAL; and aperture cards from NLM. These aperture cards are computer tab cards with microfilm of the serial covers and mastheads mounted in them giving the necessary bibliographic data. NSDP also gets MARC serials records, tagged and edited. NSDP may also receive corporate authority holdings information. NSDP assigns ISSN and key titles to all American serial publications which pass through its hands from one of these sources.

NSDP is maintaining an authority file for corporate entry according to AACR. This authority file shows all forms used by the national libraries, as well as the NSDP form. This authority file is designed to:

1) document the form used by NSDP

2) ensure accuracy and uniformity in the use of any name added to the NSDP data base

3) give variant forms of author's names, tracing the necessary cross references and indicating the sources used for this information

4) record the necessary history of reorganizations and changes of name for an author, tracing the appropriate cross references and citing the sources for this information

5) list the form of name used by any of the three national libraries, when different from that chosen by NSDP

6) register the ISSN for those titles with which an author is associated.[32]

Holdings are included in the NSDP file, identified by *NUC* library codes. These holdings statements indicate completeness of file in short verbal qualifications, such as: "Complete, or substantially complete" or "Substantially incomplete (scattered issues)." They are in no way specific.

The NSDP record includes, in field 245, a cataloging title constructed according to AACR specifications. Thus, a traditional cataloging approach can be made to the record as well as the key title approach. Steps may be taken to include ISBD(S) elements. NSDP had been instrumental in desiring the changes in AACR, previously mentioned. See Fig. 18-1 for a typical NSDP entry.

```
NSDP    Library of Congress
        National Agricultural Library
        National Library of Medicine
```

National Serials Data Program*

ESSENTIAL ISDS DATA ELEMENTS

DATE OF ENTRY:	731031
CENTRE CODE:	1
ISSN:	0031-806X
KEY TITLE:	Philosophical forum
ABBREVIATED TITLE:	PHILOS FORUM
VARIANT TITLE:	
START DATE:	1968
COUNTRY:	usa
ALPHABET OF TITLE:	a
IMPRINT:	Boston, Dept. of Philosophy, Boston University

NATIONAL DATA ELEMENTS

AUTHOR ENTRIES:	Boston University. Dept. of Philosophy.
CATALOGING TITLE:	The Philosophical forum. MAIN ENTRY

OTHER ISDS DATA ELEMENTS

CODEN:	
PUBLICATION STATUS:	c
TYPE OF PUBLICATION:	p
END DATE:	
FREQUENCY:	q
LANGUAGE:	eng
DDC NUMBER:	105
LC CALL NUMBER:	B1.P475
FORMER TITLE(S):	
SUCCESSOR TITLE(S):	
OTHER LANG ED OF:	
HAS OTHER LANG ED:	
INSET OR SUPPL TO:	
HAS INSET OR SUPPL:	
RELATED TITLE:	
ABSTRACTING SERVICE:	

OTHER NATIONAL DATA ELEMENTS

DATE AND VOLUME:	Began with fall 1968 issue. Cf. New serial titles.
LC CARD NUMBER:	73-644158
US SUPT DOC NUMBER:	
TITLE ON PIECE:	
NOTES:	

Fig. 18-1. NSDP entry.

*Appendix A, p. 7 of *Notes on special developments in the program,* January 1974.

NSDP is also involved in the establishment of an economically feasible system of handling serials and providing a central machine-readable source of serial cataloging information, as set forth in its goals. This is the CONSER project [q.v.]. NSDP also has funding from the National Science Foundation for generation of a data base for science and technology, which will be done in conjunction with CONSER.

NSDP is the American National Center for the ISDS network. Many of the projects it has undertaken, as just chronicled, are in connection with this function, such as the registry activities. NSDP also provides the communication channels and cooperative functions required of a national center. NSDP will update ISDS/IC and the other national centers with aperture cards like those it now receives as input.

NSDP plans to keep those interested in what it is doing up-to-date by an irregular serial entitled *Notes on special developments in the program.*

An informal meeting was held at the ALA Convention in Las Vegas on June 26, 1973. The people in attendance expressed concern about the following points:

1) The lack of communication among the generators of machine-readable serials files.

2) The incompatibility of format and/or bibliographic data among existing files.

3) The apparent confusion about the existing and proposed bibliographic description and format "standards."[33]

This group, styled the Ad Hoc Discussion Group on Serials Data Bases, agreed that something should be done. Groundwork for solving the problems should be worked out and set down and proposals should be presented as keys to solutions, guidelines for new projects, or revisions of existing ones. The existing serials programs, NSDP and MARC-S were not proceeding fast enough. A position paper was written by Richard Anable, leader of the Group, and others.

A steering committee was selected and the Council on Library Resources (CLR) agreed to fund its meeting in Toronto at York University. The Toronto Group consisted of representatives from CLR, Northwestern University, the Canadian Union Catalog Taskgroup and its subgroup on the serials Union List, SUNY (State University of New York), the Association of Research Libraries, JCULS, University of California Librarywide Automation Program (ULAP), OCLC, NSDP, LC, NLC, Université Laval, ISDS-Canada, and an observer from the British Library Association. The purpose of the meeting was:

1) To establish a mechanism for creating a set of "agreed-upon practices for converting and communicating machine-readable serials data."

2) To establish a mechanism for cooperatively converting a comprehensive retrospective bibliographic data base of serials.[34]

Four subcommittees were established to work toward these goals. On October 10th, three of the subcommittees met at the Library of Congress and recommended that a proposal for a cooperative conversion effort be prepared as soon as possible, using OCLC facilities as the conversion vehicle. ARL indicated interest when this project came up for discussion later that month and the group began to discuss the project in earnest.

Richard Anable has stated that the primary objective of the Cooperative Conversion Project is "to establish a relatively comprehensive bibliographic data base of serials titles within a time frame which would eliminate the necessity for redundant and costly efforts." He goes on to describe the secondary objectives as the following:

1) To assist the national libraries of both countries (Canada and the United States) in the establishment of a computer-maintained (and hopefully remotely accessible) serials data system. This will be accomplished partly by the very existence of the resulting data base, and partly by the experience gained in its establishment.

2) To assist in the definition of the roles of the regional or resource centers in such enterprises.

3) To provide a source data base for use within the International Serials Data System, and to seek the active participation of the Canadian and United States National Centers.[35]

The prime use of the data base that results from this effort will be in the production of a union list of serials.

The Group looked for an existing list that might fit the specifications it saw were important for a base list upon which to build. Finally it found one. The *Minnesota union list of serials* (MULS) has a different data base from most of the union lists. It is a union serials catalog using MARC serials format as its formal structure. It grew out of a project at the University of Minnesota and was expanded to include holdings of the Minneapolis Public Library, the State agency libraries, including the State Historical Society, and the libraries of eight private colleges. It has been growing by leaps and bounds to include eventually all academic, large public, and selected special libraries in the State of Minnesota. Because it is such a MARC-like list (for deviations, see an article by Audrey N. Grosch in the *Journal of library automation* for September, 1973), and because it is such a large rich list, it has been chosen as the base list for the project. It will be converted by computer, with manual edit, to NSDP specifications. Titles cataloged under latest entry will be eradicated. Multiple entries will be collapsed under one tag, pulled out, and worked on by the participating libraries. Information will be manipulated to conform to international standards. ISSN and key titles will be assigned by NSDP and the national center at NLC. MULS will become the beginnings of a national serials data base. It will be merged with LC's MARC serials records, OCLC records and Canadian MARC serials, and upgraded during the project.

The conversion of the MULS list will give the participants an opportunity to reconcile the conflicts that exist between MARC-S, NSDP and ISDS, Canadian MARC-S, AACR, and ISBD(S) formats and structures. One of these that has already come up is incompatibility of AACR, ISDS and ISBD(S) in the matter of title recording, which is causing upheaval and discussion at the present time. It was felt that the MARC serials format offered the best hope for machine compatibility, although it needs modification, largely by extension. There is, for example, the problem that NSDP requires a key title, which had no place in MARC-S. This was corrected by agreement, and the MARC Development Office now designates field 222 for key title. All proposed changes will be brought up before the appropriate committees of ALA and the library community before implementation. This is, of course, what is happening now with rule 6.

The Ad Hoc Discussion Group has dissolved, to be replaced by the group organizing the conversion project. This group, and its associated project, is called CONSER (Conversion of Serials or Consolidation of Serials, depending on who is discussing it; the former is now correct). The goal of the project is to convert 2,000,000 records in a two-year period.[36] Mr. Anable is still in charge of the operation. The initial participants are: LC, NLC, NLM, NAL, SUNY and the New York State Library, University of Minnesota, Yale, Cornell, and the University of California (through ULAP). An April 11, 1975 meeting at LC brought in the University of Florida, and the Florida Union List of Serials, and Boston Theological Institute. The National Federation of Abstracting and Indexing Services (NFAIS) has a cooperative agreement with CONSER and it will supply up to 25,000 scientific and technical serial surrogates (photocopies of covers, title-pages, and mastheads) to NSDP for the project. The Council on Library Resources is managing and supporting the effort, although the participating institutions are absorbing as much of the costs as possible. OCLC has agreed to be the conversion and storage mechanism for the project. There have been some troubles getting started, but CONSER hopes to be underway before 1975 comes to a close.

The following chart (Fig. 18-2) and explanation show CONSER's interrelationships.[37]

1. The interim responsibility for the management of the CONSER Project rests with the Council on Library Resources. The Council also provides partial

funding for the project. During the project, a more permanent arrangement will be made.

2. There is a two-way communication between the CONSER Advisory Group and the CONSER management staff at the Council on Library Resources.

3. It is the responsibility of the CONSER Advisory Group to inform the U.S. and Canadian library communities, as well as the publishers and the abstracting and indexing communities in both countries. The Advisory Group is also responsible for informing CONSER management of the reactions to CONSER from these communities.

4. The Ohio College Library Center's system is the interim host site for the CONSER data base. OCLC's staff and management work closely with the CONSER management, Centers of Responsibility, and the advisory group to implement the project.

5. The initial files are loaded from magnetic tape in a batch mode. Shown are the Minnesota Union List of Serials, the LC MARC serials, and the Canadian MARC serials. There may be other initial files.

6. After the initial files are loaded from the tape, the CONSER participants shown in the left semicircle begin their input on-line.

7. Periodically, on prior arrangement with OCLC, each user institution may get tapes of its own records from OCLC. These may differ from other CONSER records in that they contain local data.

8. This shows that Yale is also a member of the Research Library Group and the New England Library Information Network. Cornell University is a CONSER representative of the Five Associated University Libraries system.

9. Other OCLC users who are not CONSER participants also input serials records to the data base and have on-line access to these records.

10. After the initial files are loaded, there is a constant interaction between, on the one hand, OCLC and, on the other, the Library of Congress and the National Library of Canada. These two libraries input their own serials records; they receive separate tapes of their MARC serials records for MARC distribution. They also act as Centers of Responsibility for certain bibliographic content of the records.

11. Periodically during the project and at its end, the Library of Congress and the National Library of Canada will receive the CONSER files and distribute them as they do their MARC serials.

12. The National Serials Data Program (NDSP) within the Library of Congress and the ISDS/Canada within the National Library of Canada provide records from CONSER to the International Serials Data System (ISDS) International Center in Paris. In addition, these two activities receive from the ISDS records prepared by other national centers and by the ISDS Center itself. These

records become part of CONSER. The NSDP and the ISDS/Canada have the responsibility for providing the International Standards [sic] Serial Number (ISSN) and Key Titles to CONSER records for serials published in the two countries, and for authenticating and locking these data elements. These two centers also provide to the CONSER records additional data elements required by the international system.

13. The National Federation of Abstracting and Indexing Services provides input to CONSER by way of the National Serials Data Program, and receives CONSER records in the national distribution system.

14. The Library of Congress and the National Federation of Abstracting and Indexing Services inform the U.S. publishers concerning CONSER and request their assistance in using the International Standards [sic] Serial Number. The National Library of Canada has the same relationship with Canadian publishers. The International Serials Data System in Paris and other National Centers perform this function for foreign publishers.

15. The National Science Foundation provides some of the funds and guidance for the National Serials Data Program so that it may satisfy the requirements of the abstracting and indexing services primarily and of the scientific and technical comnunity generally.

16. The ISDS Center in Paris is responsible for communication with the international library and abstracting and indexing communities. It has other functions not related to CONSER.

[This is all keyed to the illustration (Fig. 18-2) which follows.]

All new serials cataloging from the participating libraries will be input into the on-line shared cataloging system at OCLC. LC will authenticate all non-Canadian names in the data base and will authenticate the complete cataloging record if previously cataloged by LC. The National Library of Canada will provide authentication functions for Canadian publications. LC will switch over to NLC-established headings for all Canadian corporate bodies due to CONSER. LC will also maintain an authority file of AACR-based headings and the older ALA ones, already in the LC files, so that someday a button can be pushed and desuperimposition can happen "as if by magic!" This will happen only when all of LC's current cataloging is mechanized, however. (Probably at the end of the decade.) The New York Public Library's machine-readable authority file will be the base of an authority file for CONSER, but this has low priority at present.

During the CONSER Project, LC will input on a CRT to OCLC. OCLC will return these records to LC in LC's internal processing format so that the MARC records can be produced. There will be two stages of LC input. The first will be after NSDP has added its information to the base record, so that ISSN data will be disseminated as rapidly as possible, and then, later, when LC is done with its

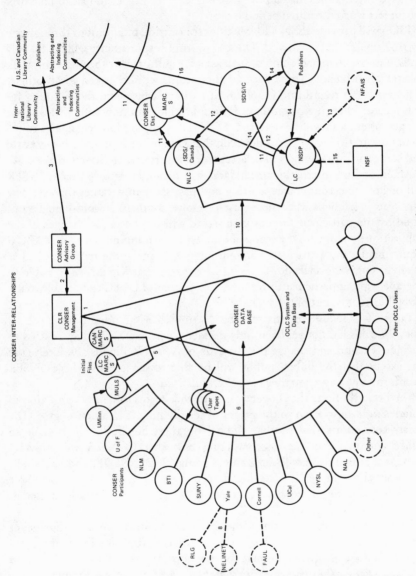

Fig. 18-2. CONSER interrelationships.

339

full cataloging process, LC may build records on a CONSER base or postedit non-CONSER records. There is even hope that, toward the end of the project, participating libraries may input on-line directly to LC. LC hopes to take over the project when the initial period is over.

ISDS will provide ISSN and key titles for outside publications through the two national centers involved. These centers of responsibility will be the only ones who can change elements, such as name authority or ISSN, within their spheres of influence. These parts of the records will be locked to all others. Whoever gets a record into CONSER first will be considered the authority for that record. There are possibilities for duplication, but hopefully this will not happen often, and will be detected. CONSER is hoping for a change in rule 6 going toward title entry to cut down on that kind of confusion. Both successive and latest entry cataloging will be accepted, but successive is preferred.

American and international standards will be adhered to so that CONSER will be able to accommodate existing and past standards, rather than set new ones, except perhaps when necessary to resolve conflicts. Records will be updated by the participants to ensure a record which reflects the changes in the publication it represents. Records are based on a minumum set of MARC-S requirements, but participants are encouraged to make the records as full as possible. Once the shakedown period is over, one participant will be able to upgrade another participant's record. Regular users of OCLC will be able to use CONSER records, but not change them.

Tapes of CONSER records may be distributed as an adjunct to MARC-S tapes, but this has not yet been fully decided upon. CONSER may be used to upgrade, expand and change the character of *NST*. Nothing is absolutely sure yet, except that the library public will be able to see and use the CONSER records in some way when they have been finalized.

The project reflects the cooperative spirit that seems to be in the air around libraries right now, even to the extent of heightening it to a new degree. The library community, led by the national libraries, hopefully will be able to utilize and maintain the good working base that CONSER will provide. Perhaps the prediction will come true, through ISDS, NSDP, and CONSER, that a serial would be ". . .cataloged once in the U.S. — once in the whole world — and never be cataloged again."[38] A truly international serials bibliography is under way.

One of the characters figuring somewhat prominently in previous discussions has been MARC-S. MARC-S is a machine-readable cataloging format for serial publications. The MARC formats are an implementation of the *American national standard format for bibliographic interchange on magnetic tape* (ANSI Z-39.2-1971). For the use of MARC-S, the AACR definition of "serial" is used, although the definition of newspapers is limited to those on newsprint and containing general news coverage. MARC follows Library of Congress cataloging patterns since it is a creation of LC.

Computers aren't really all bad, catalogers, for they helped to nudge LC into accepting AACR as written instead of the latest entry concept it had clung to. The main impetus for this was *Serials: a MARC format*.

MARC-S relates to main entry while NSDP and ISDS use key title as a benchmark. MARC-S did expand slightly to accommodate the key title, however. MARC-S has the ability to accommodate both ALA and AACR cataloging, with both the latest title and successive titles concepts and superimposition. This does not interface well with the other automated programs, unfortunately.

It sets forth bibliographic content in a structured format using special "content designators" (tags, indicators, and subfield codes) for each bibliographic item. If the information described in the variable fields of any of the formats (for books, serials, maps, etc.) is the same, the same tags are used. In the fixed fields, identical information in different formats is found in the same character position.[39] The organization of records accords with library practices.

When MARC-S was being developed, there were two schools of thought on the subject: one, that serials should be treated as much as possible like monographs, and the other, that serials should be treated as a world unto themselves. It was very difficult to come up with an adequate MARC format for serials.

The format is basically the MARC II bibliographic data format, with slight modification and extension. All programs based on accessing the MARC II type of file would be able to access serial records in MARC-S with only some modification, primarily in tag names, which need to be changed slightly to accommodate serials rather than monographs, like tag 850. The basic field for holdings is tag 850. This includes four subfields: (1) *NUC* symbol for reporting library, (2) holdings statement, (3) inclusive dates, (4) retention statement. Other adaptations can be seen by comparing the formats for monographs and serials.

LC is thinking about expanding the format to make it a processing format as well as an information exchange and recordkeeping format. Further data elements would then be required. It is questionable if this is really going to be efficient since so much information would be repeated from week to week in terms of a printout. We shall see what LC will do.

MARC will also work with CONSER, since adaptations of MARC are not desired.

MARC-S input is made by batch process from the cataloging workflow at LC. After the cataloging worksheet travels with the issue to Shelflisting or Dewey Classification (if such is desired) it goes to the MARC Office for edition and keypunching.

In November of 1966, LC began distributing machine-readable cataloging as part of the MARC Pilot Project. In March, 1969, this became fully blown as the

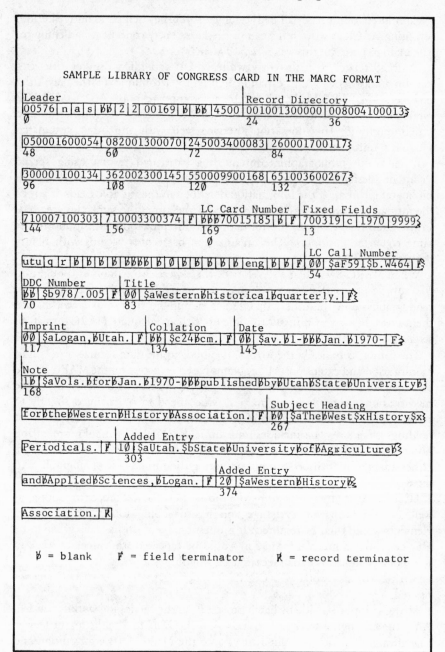

SAMPLE LIBRARY OF CONGRESS CARD IN THE MARC FORMAT

Leader Record Directory
| 00576 | n | a | s | ƀƀ | 2 | 2 | 00169 | ƀ | ƀƀ | 4500 | 001001300000 | 008004100013 |
Ø 24 36

| 050001600054 | 082001300070 | 245003400083 | 260001700117 |
48 60 72 84

| 300001100134 | 362002300145 | 550009900168 | 651003600267 |
96 108 120 132

LC Card Number Fixed Fields
| 710007100303 | 710003300374 | Ŧ | ƀƀƀ70015185 | ƀ | Ŧ | 700319 | c | 1970 | 9999 |
144 156 169 13
Ø

LC Call Number
| utu | q | r | ƀ | ƀ | ƀ | ƀ | ƀƀƀƀ | ƀ | Ø | ƀ | ƀ | ƀ | ƀ | ƀ | eng | ƀ | ƀ | Ŧ | ØØ | $aF591$b.W464 | Ŧ |
54

DDC Number Title
| ƀƀ | $b978/.005 | Ŧ | ØØ | $aWesternƀhistoricalƀquarterly. | Ŧ |
70 83

Imprint Collation Date
| ØØ | $aLogan,ƀUtah. | Ŧ | ƀƀ | $c24ƀcm. | Ŧ | Øƀ | $av.ƀ1-ƀƀƀJan.ƀ1970- | Ŧ |
117 134 145

Note
| 1ƀ | $aVols.ƀforƀJan.ƀ1970-ƀƀƀpublishedƀbyƀUtahƀStateƀUniversityƀ |
168

Subject Heading
| forƀtheƀWesternƀHistoryƀAssociation. | Ŧ | ƀØ | $aTheƀWest$xHistory$x |
267

Added Entry
| Periodicals. | Ŧ | 1Ø | $aUtah.$bStateƀUniversityƀofƀAgricultureƀ |
303

Added Entry
| andƀAppliedƀSciences,ƀLogan. | Ŧ | 2Ø | $aWesternƀHistoryƀ |
374

| Association. | Ʞ |

ƀ = blank   Ŧ = field terminator   Ʞ = record terminator

Fig. 18-3. MARC-S record[41]

MARC Distribution Service. The MARC Development Office was established in the Processing Department in June, 1970, to explore, develop and implement automation in technical processing at LC.

The first serials format was issued in 1969. It was revised by addendum in 1971. The second edition came out in July of 1974.

> The goal of MARC-S is the creation of multi-purpose machine-readable serial records, with standard catalog data in the MARC serials format, for LC's own data base and for dissemination in libraries and related communities.[40]

In February, 1973, LC began to convert catalog records for newly-cataloged serials to machine-readable form. All Roman alphabet languages have been included. Cyrillic, Greek and Hebrew will be added later. All serials cataloged for printed cards starting in 1973, as well as older serials for which cards are being reprinted, are included. The first MARC-S tapes came out in June, 1973. These records on magnetic tapes are available on subscription through the MARC Distribution Service.

The MARC Distribution Service for Serials costs $400.00 and:

> covers serials in all roman-alphabet languages and nonroman-alphabet languages with the latter being transcribed in romanized form, that are currently received and cataloged or currently recataloged at the Library of Congress. Tapes are mailed every four weeks and contain approximately 800 records per tape.[42]

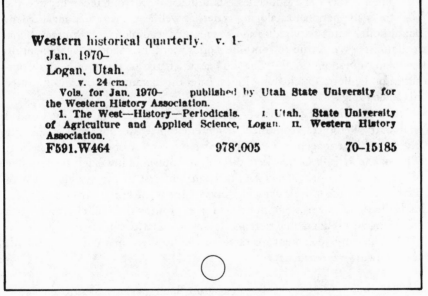

Fig. 18-4. Catalog card for record shown in Fig. 18-3.

A pilot project was mounted in 1974 to input into MARC-S some retrospective serial records. This project will continue as part of CONSER.

Hundreds of serials lists are now being created from machine-readable data bases, but very few are compatible with each other. Thus, the sharing of data and the production of union lists has suffered. With the arrival of the new format, first issued in 1969 and then again in 1974, this will change. Libraries will discover the need for sharing of data. In this age of budget crunches all over, libraries will discover the need to cooperate and produce union lists to share resources and MARC-S will provide the vehicle for this. "It is the essential step in convergence toward common standards in machine-readable cataloging.[43]

The primary activity within the UNISIST programme has been the establishment of ISDS; however, UNISIST has also organized a Working Group on Bibliographic Data Interchange (WGBDI). The Director of NSDP is a member of this group. It is looking into the areas of compatibility between data bases and systems, existing or being developed. It was felt early on that there was need for a revision of the ISO standard 2709, *Documentation format for bibliographic interchange on magnetic tape.* This is being worked on now. It is unknown whether this will affect the American Standard and MARC-S.

To trace the history of the International Standard Bibliographic Description, it is necessary to trace briefly fourteen years of cataloging history. In 1961, the International Conference on Cataloguing Principles was held in Paris, as mentioned earlier. The principles established at this conference became the basis for many national cataloging codes, as well as the international AACR. But although some standardization was reached, complete uniformity was not. A committee was set up to continue work toward international agreement on cataloging questions. A. H. Chaplin was in charge of this group, the Committee on Uniform Cataloguing Rules. Later this became the IFLA Committee on Cataloguing.

The International Federation of Library Associations, funded by the Council on Library Resources, convened an International Meeting of Cataloguing Experts in Copenhagen in 1969. There were several reasons for this meeting. Some of the Paris Principles were difficult to apply and it was felt they needed further consideration. There was increasing interest in the establishment of principles for descriptive cataloging, outside the scope of the Paris Conference. And there was increasing interest in the growing use of electronic data processing in bibliographic systems. It was felt that there was need for principles of descriptive content for cataloging entries, an international standard. The following was decided:

1. . . .that there should be a standard bibliographical description for publications, and that this should consist of a comprehensive statement of

the data likely to be useful in library catalogues and for other bibliographical purposes.

2. The items should be given in a fixed order, and, except for the title of the publication, need not be transcribed exactly from the titlepage.

3. It was agreed that where a uniform title is required as a filing device, this title is not considered to be part of the standard bibliographical description.

4. The principal items should be, in the following order:
   title
   subtitle
   author statement
   subsidiary author statement relating to the work
   edition statement
   subsidiary author statement relating to the edition
   imprint statement (consisting or place, publisher, and, if of importance, place of printing and printer, date)
   collation
   series statement
   notes (including any other title for the same work which is useful to mention).

5. It was agreed that the original title must always form part of the standard bibliographical description.

6. The Meeting welcomed the introduction of the International Standard Book Number and was emphatic that the ISBN should be included in the standard bibliographical description.

7. It was agreed that a working party should be set up to make detailed recommendations for the composition, form and order of the items listed above and for any other items which should be included in the standard bibliographical description.[44]

At the meeting the emphasis moved from cataloging in libraries, of more interest in Paris, to the recording of publications in national bibliographies. Shared cataloging was becoming more important. The adjusting to individual differences in a manual system is much easier than in an automated one. A standard for bibliographies was needed, especially as more were becoming automated. The framework for bibliographic description should be written to serve both the needs of catalogs and bibliographies. At the meeting it was also decided that:

1. Each country should have a national bibliography or cataloging service which would be responsible for cataloging all publications of that country for the libraries in that country and for export for use in other countries.

2. All countries should agree to a standard style of making bibliographic descriptions.

3. Each national cataloging service should avail itself of the product of the others in providing catalog entries for foreign books for libraries in its own country.

4. Since exchange of this data would eventually be in machine-readable form, the potentiality of standardized punctuation as a device to make possible automatic tagging of fields in the description (thereby cutting input costs) should be explored.[45]

Many of these decisions were based on a paper presented by Michael Gorman of the *British National Bibliography* entitled "Bibliographical data in national bibliography entries: a report on descriptive cataloguing made for UNESCO and IFLA." A Working Group on the International Standard Bibliographic Description was set up with Jack Wells of the *BNB* as chairman and Michael Gorman as secretary.

Henriette Avram of LC was the American delegate on the Committee. She consulted with librarians at LC and with the American Library Association, through its spokesgroup on such cataloging matters, the Descriptive Cataloging Committee of the Cataloging and Classification Section. The Committee and the Library of Congress approved the 1971 preliminary edition in principle. It was sent back for some final rewrites, however. It was felt it was too general and ambiguous and gave no real solution to some of the problems. Some national bibliographies tried it out: *BNB, Bibliographie de la France,* and *Deutsche Bibliographie.* The entries were examined and found to be uniform. A certain victory had been achieved.

Meanwhile, ISBD received a lot of negative reaction on the home front when it became known to American librarians. There was an uproar. Reference librarians would have to spend hours explaining the symbols to confused patrons! Those with computer-based systems would require costly modifications in programs! Radical changes in descriptive cataloging would take place! Catalogers would have to learn how to catalog all over again! It went on and on. There was chagrin that the entire library community was not let in on the "secret." However, these arguments did not hold water, as far as LC and the ALA Committee were concerned. The United States did not back out of the international venture, as some had hoped. LC did stop producing cards using the ISBD symbols for awhile, however, while the standard was being revised. ISBD(M), as it came to be called, was finally revised at the meeting in Grenoble, August 23-24, 1973. It was simplified, with greater detail; more examples and additional languages were used. It was published in 1974. Chapter 6 of the AACR, description for monographs, was rewritten to incorporate all the changes and was made available just before ALA's annual convention in New York, where it proved to be a best-seller. LC adopted the ISBD(M) on September 3, 1974. Large research libraries have followed its lead.

So far these international developments have been primarily monographic. Serials are always secondary in the general scheme of things, it would seem, and eventually the monographic rules are extended to encompass serials as well. As far as the ISBD was concerned, this occurred in 1971.

The IFLA Committee on Serial Publications had tried to find a common basis for the cataloging of serials by distributing a questionnaire to national cataloging committees, national libraries, and others with an interest in serials. The results were the basis of discussion at a session of the Committee at the IFLA General Council in Liverpool. A Joint Working Group of the Committees on Cataloguing and on Serial Publications was set up to draft an international standard bibliographic description for serials. Marie-Louise Bossuat, of France, was chairman of the group and Monique Pelletier, also of France, was secretary. These two ladies are chairman and secretary, respectively, of the Committee on Serial Publications.

Since this discussion was at about the same time as the establishment of the ISDS and the discussions of the draft of the ISSN document, two serial experts closely involved with these developments were also included in the Working Group.

The first draft was prepared in February, 1972, and circulated among the members of the Working Group. It was patterned on ISBD(M), as the monograph standard had come to be called. But it became obvious very soon that the basic differences between serials and monographs required different approaches. The "title proper" defined for a monograph in ISBD(M) would be interpreted by serials catalogers in many different ways. It was obvious the document needed to be reworked. There needed to be a reconstruction of "author" and "title" when speaking of serials. In April, 1972, at the second meeting on ISDS, the term "key title" came to the fore. This is the distinguishing feature of the ISDS, that to which the ISSN is assigned. All of the ISO people felt that this should also be part of the ISBD(S), so there would not be two systems of cataloging for serials in each country, one for the national bibliography and one for the national center in the ISDS. This was taken into consideration in the second draft, distributed during the IFLA General Council in Budapest and to other interested parties in June of 1972. At the discussion in Budapest there were objections to having the artificial key title included in a description of the serial as it really is. The Group met in Paris in November and considered a new working paper based on these discussions. Here came the real departures from the ISBD(M).

The most important element of the ISBD(S) became the "distinctive title." This is the title as it appears on the piece. It is in most cases the same as the key title, except in those cases where a title needs to be further identified by place of publication or dates to differentiate it from another which is identical. These added qualifiers are part of the key title but not part of the distinctive title. For ISBD(S) purposes this information appears in the imprint area. ISBD(S) does not provide for unique identification of a title. Its distinctive title will have to be further amplified to merge with union lists.

In early 1973, the fourth and final draft was approved by the Working Group and ISDS. It was not published, however, until mid-1974 because it was held back until the ISBD(M) revision meeting in Grenoble in August, 1973, to insure uniformity in those areas where this could be reached.

Three important studies were set up at the Grenoble meeting as offshoots of ISBD(S) discussions. These will be done by the Committee on Serial Publications with the Committee on Cataloguing and the Committee on Official Publications. They are: (1) a multilingual vocabulary list of terms used to indicate bibliographic relationships between serials, including a synthetic table of those terms; (2) a study of the problems that arise from the filing of serial titles; and (3) a study of the function of corporate bodies in a serials catalog.

The primary purpose of the ISBD(S) is to aid the international communication of bibliographic information. It does this by (i) making records from different sources interchangeable, (ii) assisting the interpretation of records across language barriers, and (iii) assisting in the conversion of bibliographic records to machine readable form.

[It] specifies requirements for the description and identification of printed serial publications. . .assigns an order to the elements of description, and specifies a system of punctuation for that description.

The ISBD(S) is primarily concerned with current publications, but it does make provision for recording serials in retrospective catalogues.

[It] is intended to provide all the descriptive information required in a range of bibliographic activities. . . .

The description provided by the ISBD(S) is complete and can be used as such in a library catalogue or in a bibliography in which the entries are under title. . .Problems relating to the choice of heading (personal author or corporate body) and its use (main entry or added entry) have not been examined in the ISBD(S).[46]

The following is the outline order of the elements:

1. Title and statement of authorship area
   1.1 Distinctive title
   1.2 Parallel titles, sub-titles and other titles
   1.3 Statement of authorship

2. Imprint area
   2.1 Place of publication
   2.2 Name of publisher
   2.3 Dates and numbering
   2.4 Place of printing (optional)
   2.5 Name of printer (optional)
3. Collation area
   3.1 Illustration statement (optional)
   3.2 Size
   3.3 Accompanying material
4. Series area
5. Notes area
6. International Standard Serial Number and price area
   6.1 ISSN
   6.2 Price (optional)[47]

There are prescribed marks of punctuation that act as delimiters between the elements in an area and between area and area. This has been one of the major bones of contention in the monographic standard, which is in effect at this time in many libraries in the United States, including LC.

Like the monographic standard, the serials standard opens up prime sources of information considerably. The following chart is given in the standard:

Area	Prime source of information
1. Title and statement of authorship	Title-page or that part of the issue or volume of the serial which takes the place of the title-page (e.g., cover, caption, masthead, editorial pages)
2. Imprint	Anywhere in the serial
3. Collation	The serial itself
4. Series	Anywhere in the serial
5. Notes	Anywhere
6. ISSN, price	Anywhere[48]

The use of brackets will be reduced drastically.

This is not the place to go into lengthy descriptions of the standard itself, particularly since Chapter 7 of AACR, the chapter immediately and intimately affected by the new standard, has not been rewritten. (LC is using some of the innovations and abbreviations already, as indicated by recent *Cataloging service bulletins,* and these are incorporated into the chapter on description in this book.) However, it would be apropos to give some examples as they appear in the standard. (These are set up for bibliographies so the spacing and a few other positional factors are wrong for catalog cards. The format can be changed to accommodate traditional card formatting, but this would be to "jump the gun" on the new Chapter 7, which would not be a good idea.) Note also that there are no headings for entries that AACR6 would put under corporate authors. ISBD(S) does not concern itself at all with entry.

Stockholm studies in theatrical history.—Stockholm : Stockholm Universitets, 1967 (no. 1)- .
—24cm
(Acta Universitatis Stockholmiensis, ISSN 0000-0000)
ISSN 0000-0000

[Note that both series, the serial and the larger monographic series it is part of, got ISSN.]

Archives européenes de sociologie = European journal of sociology = Europäisches Archiv für
Soziologie /publ. avec le concours de la Sixième section de
l'Ecole pratique des hautes études; réd. Raymond Aron, Thomas
Bottomore, Michel Crozier. . .—Paris : Plon, 1960 (no. 1)—.—24cm
Bi-annuel
ISSN 0000-0000: Le no. FF9: Le t. FF 18

[The equals signs denote parallel titles.]

Australian trading news. Canada edition.—[S.l.] : [s.n.], Sept. 1972 ([no. 1])-
— Ill. ; 28cm
Bimonthly
Common sub-title: journal of the Australian Trade Commissioner
Incorporates: Australian products for export, ISSN 0000-0000, and: Austral news, ISSN 0000-0000 and other Australian trade journals: "Under the name 'Australian Trading News,' the journals will appear in 43 different editions in more than 100 countries. They will be printed in 12 languages. . ." Obtainable from Australian Trade Commissioner, Montreal, Toronto, Vancouver
ISSN 0000-0000

[[S.1.] is the ISBD equivalent of [n.p.] It means "sine loco."
[S.n.] means "sine nomine" — the publisher is not named. Note too the "Ill." in the collation, which refers to illustrations (the former "illus.").]

R.L.C.'s Museum gazette / compiled and edited by Richard L. Coulton. — Longview, Alta (Box 127) : [s.n.], Apr. 1966 (no. 1)— . —36cm
Irregular
ISSN 0000-0000: Free

[Note recording of author statement. This is like the ISBD(M).]

Journal of the Institution of General Technician Engineers. — London (33 Ovington Square, SW3) : Institution of General

Technician Engineers, Feb. 1971 (vol. 82, no. 1)— . — 30cm
Monthly. — Continuation of: Journal and record of transactions - Junior In-
stitution of Engineers, ISSN 0000-0000
ISSN 0000–0000: £0.50 per issue[49]

[Note both methods of title recording of generic titles, a la the new rule 162B.
Notes like "Continuation of:" are being used by LC now.]

Because ISBD(S) does not concern itself with entry, this fits right in with the
movement afoot to do away with the rules of corporate and personal authorship
for serials. All serials would be put under title and ISBD(S) would not need to
be embellished upon by the cataloger. This all goes back to the "current
controversy" mentioned in Chapter 4.

Now the ISBD(S) awaits worldwide approval and incorporation into national
cataloging practices. The *Bibliographie de la France (Publications en série)* has
already started using the new serial standard. Its impact is, of course, felt
already with the recording of titles of series in the monographic standard. LC
and a few other libraries are using the new title recording for serials prescribed
by the dropping of rule 162B and the provisions for generic title which are part
of this new standard too. The real dress review and revision will come at the
October, 1975, revision meeting and the IFLA meeting in 1976, with input
from various countries. The United States put in its "two cents worth" in early
1975 with the North American position paper, and we'll see if anybody
listened.

A North American position paper on the ISBD(S) has been written by the
CCRC in conjunction with the Canadian Committee on Cataloguing and the
Library of Congress. Much of the document is aimed at clarification,
elaboration, better examples, more logic and more compatibility with the
ISBD(M) in matters common to both types of material. However, there are
some major changes that the paper advocates. The ISBD(S) as it exists now is
not really adequate for more than single-issue description, as might appear in a
national bibliography. The authors of the paper propose that the function of
ISBD(S) be twofold: both for the description of a single issue, as now, and the
run of many such issues. To this end they make many excellent proposals for
achieving stability in the entry and a more appropriate pattern of description.
One of the recommendations is that the serial standard adopt the "title
proper,' of the monographic standard — that is, without the need to construct
a generic title followed by a statement of authorship in order to be distinctive, a
term they ask to be changed to "identifying title" or "principle title" due to
its confusion with the old-fashioned definition of distinctive title (as opposed
to generic). The argument is that authorship and title are two different things
that should not be combined in such a fashion as the standard now advocates.
The generic title proper would become the key title for ISDS by being joined to

a statement of authorship by a space-slash-space, as in the ISBD(M). The paper also points out the problems of initial articles in the statement of authorship, multiple statements of authorship, and the fullness of hierarchy of corporate bodies in statements of authorship, and urges the revisers of ISBD(S) and the ISDS people to get together and work out a solution. One solution was discussed by the CCRC at the ALA annual meeting, in San Francisco in 1975, which covered at least two of these points. It was decided that initial articles should be dropped in statements of authorship, along with linking words, and that corporate hierarchies should be given in full, as on the piece, going from bottom to top. This was communicated to the people working on the ISBD(S) in another document. By resolving such problems in this fashion, more stability is retained in the entry. Minor variations can be noted or ignored, depending upon the magnitude thereof. Amplified forms of titles recorded as initials should appear as part of the title element, enclosed in brackets if not on the title-page or its substitute, to be consistent with the ISDS.

The paper also asks that a new area be created, to be called the "Numerical/Chronological Extent Area," and to come after the first area in the bibliographic record, due to the fact that such information is properly an extension of the title, not of the imprint. The source for this information should be "anywhere in the publication," and it should be mandatory that it be included. The paper included a draft for this proposed section, and rewording and numbering of other sections to accommodate it were suggested. It was suggested that items like frequency and accompanying material should be made optional, and there was some juggling of data to make a more logical sequence of bits of information.

All in all, the document is carefully thought-out, showing that its authors really did their homework. If the ISBD(S) is revised to include the provisions called for in these *Recommendations,* the ISBD(S) will be a much better and easier standard to apply to the description of living and everchanging serial publications.

C. Sumner Spalding summed up the present trends when he said: "The interface of cataloging with the computer has become explicit with the ISBD."[50]

All of the automated projects are working toward standardization. However, each has a different goal, operates within different constraints and is, to some degree, in conflict with the others, although steps are being made to reconcile these problems. Entry has already been mentioned as a problem. MARC-S uses AACR entry rules, with superimposition. In the light of CONSER and other developments, LC will drop superimposition (eventually), and this problem will disappear. The AACR, however, provides for corporate and personal author entry, which the others do not, except, of course, MARC-S. The ISDS/NSDP concept for "entry" is that of key title. There is no name entry, although NSDP has added "author entries" as an essential national data element, along with a means of indicating AACR main entry. NSDP maintains an authority file of corporate authors. ISBD(S) is not concerned with entry, for it is a self-sufficient description that does not need entry for identification. However, its main point of access is the distinctive title, if it does not have an entry superimposed upon it. The ISBD(S) and ISDS agree now as far as generic titles are concerned: for the corporate author is added if not linked grammatically with the generic term by means of a space-hyphen-space; and if the author is grammatically inseparable from the generic term, this becomes the key/distinctive title. AACR has been brought into agreement with this concept. Still to be resolved is the problem of identical titles, which receive qualifiers in ISDS practice, but not in ISBD(S). AACR rules of entry require qualifiers when the entry is an added entry, but this is not generally practiced in cataloging main entries or in the ISBD(S). For title changes, ISDS/NSDP use the key title as a benchmark. If this changed, as listed earlier, a new ISSN and key title must be assigned to the new publication. Under AACR, which MARC-S follows, this would only account for half of the changes. AACR also calls for new entries under new forms of corporate names. According to ISDS guidelines, this is not a new title. This discrepancy needs to be resolved. It has been suggested that title main entry should be used, which means essentially that rule 6 would have to be rewritten to conform to the ISDS guidelines. Something would have to be done to bring ISBD(S) into line where it deviates. The Catalog Code Revision Committee has discussed the matter and voted for title main entry in the light of future advances.

> Many cataloging decisions in the past have been based on the necessity of economy in the creation, operation, and maintenance of large dictionary catalogs. The introduction of the computer into cataloging has reduced the need for this kind of economy and will permit greater attention to the needs of users of the catalogs and indexes by allowing an increase in the number of access points with increased depth of indexing.[51]

It is also to be hoped, however, that the effectiveness of existing practices, which may exist in many libraries for many years to come, will not suffer as a result. As John Thornton said in 1938:

> It is unnecessary to stress the value of standardised rules for the cataloguing of periodicals, for the formation of union catalogues accentuates the importance of collecting together information on this material. To incorporate entries catalogued according to different codes is extremely difficult, but should any officially recognised code devoted to periodicals be published, its primary objective must be the service of those who use the catalogues and not the formation of a bibliographical tool.[52]

In any discussion of standardization, it would not be fair to overlook certain attempts made to influence publishers to make it a little easier for us serials people to live. Such advice was made at the Fifth-third Annual Conference of the American Library Association at New Haven in 1931; and all through the literature serials people have been saying, "Oh, if we could only tell them to do such-and-such." K.I. Porter tells us of the fine work of the British Standards Institution in this regard in "Standards for the presentation of information, with particular reference to serial publications."[53]

In the United States there are also standards, emanating from the ANSI Z-39 Committee: *USA standard for periodicals: format and arrangement.* These standards existed in 1935 and they have been subsequently revised and updated, the last update being 1967. This proposes that location and form of bibliographic information be standardized on periodical issues. This would do a great deal to lessen the costly handling periodicals get from both libraries and dealers who work with them. But this standard is virtually unknown by scores of publishers. It has been proposed that it be publicized and enforced by the Post Office as a rider to second- and third-class mailing privileges.

Huibert Paul, in an excellent exposé[54] of the chaos caused by non-standardization among publishers, sees the above mentioned standard as the beginning step in a set of steps leading to the much needed uniformity automation demands. He goes on to a short discussion of its implementation.

Mr. Paul feels that titles should be unique to each serial. Duplicate titles like *Challenge,* of which there are reputed to be over forty, can cause many check-in problems. Publishers should be proud of the title they choose and not change them willy-nilly. He goes into the chronicling of the long and round-about procedure a library may take to determine a title change, including misrouting of mail, checking of various files, writing letters, and general time-consuming running-around. He feels that initialisms in titles should not exist because they can cause problems. He complains about variations in numbering and the skipping or nonpublishing of some numbers. Volume years that are not the same as calendar years produce confused records. Roman numerals, although they are dignified looking, tend to be inefficient, complex and confusing, often causing misnumbering. The variety of numbering systems used causes additional headaches. The numbers are often hidden, too.

Mr. Paul is one of the more recent people to complain about serial chaos, along with the staff, contributors and subscribers of *Title varies,* mentioned previously. In the past, others have suggested that publishers state clearly where the main office of publication of a journal is. When a title is absorbed by another title, the numbering of the continuing one, not the dead one, should be used. The sequence and uniformity of style should be maintained in numbering. Numbering should not be skipped. Frequency should be changed at the end of a volume, not in the middle. Size should be changed with a new volume, too. The same title should be used in all places, like title-page, caption, cover, etc. Indexes and title-pages should be issued uniformly. They should always be sent to libraries so binding isn't delayed while letters are being written. Publisher-bound serials should always include original front covers because much information of value to libraries appears on covers.

Perhaps most of the problems stem from the fact that publishers think mostly in terms of individual subscribers who do not keep records, rather than libraries who do. Perhaps, someday, it will come to pass that the standards will be followed by publishers, perhaps under postal enforcement. After all, a lot of publishers are rallying to the use of identifying numbers, ISSN and ISBN, for their publications. Maybe publishers, under the influence of "Worst Title Change of the Year Awards" and other notoriety, as well as discovery that some uniformity in their procedures might be beneficial to them, as the numbering systems are, will have a change of heart. (They might even get tired of having to change ISSN!) Who knows, maybe publishers aren't as incorrigible as librarians have always thought! (Then again, read *Title varies*!) And think how deathly dull and boring all of our serial-inspired lives would be!

Seriously, though, uniformity and standardization are the bywords of the day. Under the impact of automated systems and cooperation on an ever-widening base, all of us will have to look forward to the building of systems within the framework of new technology and cooperative ventures. The new frontier of serials control is at hand.

FOOTNOTES

1. W. Bonser, "The necessity for uniformity in the cataloguing of periodicals," Association of Special Libraries and Information Bureaux. *Report of proceedings* 4 (1927):45.

2. Lucile M. Morsch, "Cataloging at the Library of Congress: a look into the future," *Southeastern librarian* 14 (Winter, 1964):246.

3. Don L. Bosseau, "The computer in serials processing and control," *Advances in librarianship* 2 (1971):103-164.

4. Updated in 1974 (Author's note).

5. Bosseau, "The computer," p. 123.

6. Andrew D. Osborn, *Serial publications: their place and treatment in libraries,* 2d. ed., rev. (Chicago: American Library Association, 1973), p. 410.

7. Edna L. Goss, "The cataloging of serials," *Catalogers' and classifiers' yearbook* 2 (1930):73-92.

8. Otto Lohmann, "Efforts for international standardization in libraries," *Library trends* 2 (October, 1972):342.

9. G. J. Koster, "International standard serial numbers and the International Serials Data System," *Libri* 23 (1973):71.

10. "UNISIST International Serials Data System," *LARC newsletter* 5 (May, 1973):1.

11. M. Rosenbaum, "International Serials Data System," *International cataloguing* 1 (October/December 1972):5.

12. *Ibid.*

13. *Ibid.* Also in UNISIST, *Guidelines for ISDS* (Paris: UNESCO, May, 1973), p. 39.

14. "UNISIST International Serials Data System," p. 1.

15. UNISIST, *Guidelines*, p. 1.

16. National Serials Data Program, *Notes on special developments in the program* 3 (January, 1974):5.

17. D. D. Gull, "Convergence toward common standards in machine-readable cataloging," *Bulletin of the Medical Library Association* 57 (January, 1969):33.

18. UNISIST, *Guidelines* pp. 22–23.

19. *Ibid.*, p. 24.

20. *Ibid.*, p. 25.

21. *Ibid.*

22. *Ibid.*, p. 32.

23. *Ibid.*, p. 32-34.

24. *Ibid.*, p. 34-37.

25. Osborn, *Serial publications*, 2d. ed. rev. p. 132.

26. Information Dynamics Corporation, *A serials data program for science and technology* (Reading, Massachusetts, 1965), p. 10.

27. *Ibid.*, p. 35.

28. Donald W. Johnson, *Toward a National Serials Data Project; Final report of the National Serials Pilot Project* (Washington: Association of Research Libraries, 1972), p. 1.

29. *Ibid.*, p. 2.

30. *Ibid.*, p. xiii.

31. "National Serials Data Program enters a new phase," *Information — part 1: new sources/profiles* 4 (May–June, 1972): 137. Also in Daisy Ashford, "Serials in Review: 1972," *Library resources and technical services* 17 (Spring, 1973):169.

32. Library of Congress, *Annual report of the Librarian of Congress . . .* (1973):13.

33. Richard Anable, "The Ad Hoc Discussion Group on Serials Data Bases: its history, current position and future," *Journal of library automation* 6 (December, 1973):207.

34. *Ibid.*, p. 208.

35. *Ibid.*, p. 210.

36. Lois Upham, "Conser; cooperative conversion of serials project," *Library of Congress information bulletin* 33 (November 29, 1974):A-246.

37. "Meeting of the Cooperative Conversion of Serials (CONSER) Project Advisory Group," *Library of Congress information bulletin* 34 (May 30, 1975):A-87-89.

38. "Cooperative conversion of serials," *American libraries* 6 (January, 1975):10.

39. Library of Congress. MARC Development Office, *Serials: a MARC format*, 2d. ed. (Washington: Library of Congress, 1974), p. 1.

40. *Serials: a MARC format.* Quoted in Josephine S. Pulsifer "Comparison of MARC serials, NSDP and ISBDS," *Journal of library automation* 6 (December, 1973):194.

41. Library of Congress. MARC Development Office, *Serials: a MARC format*, p. 97.

42. Library of Congress. MARC Development Office, *Information on the MARC system*, 4th ed. (Washington: Library of Congress, 1974), pp. 28-29.

43. Gull, "Convergence," p. 28.

44. A. H. Chaplin, "International Meeting of cataloguing experts, Copenhagen, 1969, report," *I.F.L.A. annual* (1969):81.

45. C. Sumner Spalding, "ISBD; its origin rationale and implications," *Library journal* 98 (January 15, 1973):122.

46. International Federation of Library Associations. Joint Working Group on the International Standard Bibliographic Description for Serials, *ISBD(S); International standard bibliographic description for serials*, (London: I.F.L.A. Committee on Cataloguing, 1974), p. 1.

47. *Ibid.*, p. 3.

48. *Ibid.*, p. 5.

49. *Ibid.*, pp. 27-32.

50. Spalding, "ISBD," p. 123.

51. Gull, "Convergence," p. 34.

52. John L. Thornton, *Cataloguing in special libraries — a survey of methods* (London: Grafton and Co., 1938), p. 226.

53. K. I. Porter, "Standards for the presentation of information with particular reference to serial publications," in *Standardization for documentation*, edited by Bernard Houghton (London: Archon Books and Clive Bingley, 1969), pp. [27]-43.

54. Huibert Paul, "Serials: chaos and standardization," *Library resources and technical services* 14 (Winter, 1970):19-30.

Appendix A

Acronyms and Initialisms Used in this Book

Librarianship today has become a veritable maze of acronyms and initialisms. Trying to wade through them all is beyond most human endeavour, although librarians are supposed to manage, somehow. In order to help comprehend this book, most of the alphabet soup is listed here, as well as described in the text, if necessary. Here goes:

AACR
Anglo-American cataloging rules (NA refers to North American text, BT refers to British text)

ALA
American Library Association. May also refer to the *A.L.A. cataloging rules for author and little entries*

ANSI
American National Standards Institute

ANSI Z-39
Committee of ANSI devoted to library-related matters

ARL
Association of Research Libraries

BALLOTS
Bibliographic Automation of Large Library Operations using a Time-sharing System (Stanford University's automated system)

BNB
British national bibliography

CCRC
Catalog Code Revision Committee (of ALA)

CLR	Council on Library Research
CODEN	Mnemonic code for periodical titles developed by the American Society for Testing and Materials
COM	Computer Output Microform
CONSER	CONversion of SERials (sometimes called CONsolidation of SERials)
COSATI	Committee on Scientific And Technical Information
DC	Dewey Classification (also DDC)
ICCP	International Conference on Cataloguing Principles
ICSU	International Council of Scientific Unions
IDC	Information Dynamics Corporation, publishers of the MCRS
IFLA	International Federation of Library Associations
IMCE	International Meeting of Cataloguing Experts
ISBD	International Standard Bibliographic Description
ISBD(M)	ISBD for Monographs
ISBD(S)	ISBD for Serials
ISBN	International Standard Book Number
ISDS	International Serials Data System
ISDS/IC	the International Centre of ISDS (in Paris)
ISO	International Standardization Organization
ISSN	International Standard Serials Number
JCULS	Joint Committee on the Union List of Serials

KWIC	Key Word in Context
KWOC	Key Work Out of Context
LC	Library of Congress. May also refer to its catalogs, subject headings, or classification scheme, depending on the context.
LCSH	Library of Congress Subject Headings
LUTFCSUSTC	Librarians United to Flight Costly, Silly, Unnecessary Serial Title Changes
MARC	MAchine-Readable Cataloging
MARC-S	MARC for Serials
MCRS	Micrographic Catalog Retrieval Service (also called "IDC microfiche")
MULS	*Minnesota union list of serials*
NAL	National Agricultural Library
NFAIS	National Federation of Abstracting and Indexing Services
NLC	National Library of Canada
NLM	National Library of Medicine
NSDP	National Serials Data Program
NSPP	National Serials Pilot Project
NST	*New serial titles*
NUC	*National union catalog*
OCLC	Ohio College Library Center
PRECIS	Preserved Context Indexing System
RDC	*Rules for descriptive cataloging*
RTSD	Resources and Technical Services Division (of ALA)
SSN	Standard Serial Number
UCLA	University of California at Los Angeles
ULAP	University-wide Library Automation Program (University of California)

ULS	*Union list of serials*
UNESCO	United Nations Educational, Scientific and Cultural Organization
UNISIST	World science information system

Appendix B

Card Formats and Other Typing Instructions

A serial card for a serial entered under title has a hanging indention. This means that the top line is started at the first indention and the rest of the material in the body of the entry is at the second indention. If the title is incomplete, it has an open entry.

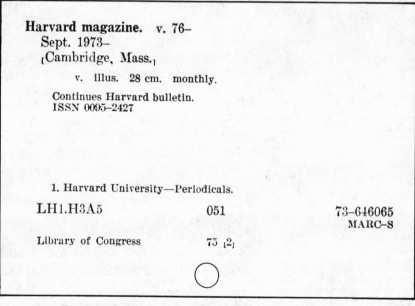

Fig. B-1. Open entry serial card with hanging indention.

The following is a schematic of how such cards should be typed.

```
Call     Title.............................................
No.      .................................................
         Volume and date information...............
         .................................................
         Imprint.......................................
         Collation          Frequency

         Note..........................................
.................................................
         Note..........................................
.................................................

         Tracings......................................
.................               .................

                         ◯
```

Fig. B-2. Schematic for open entry card.

The next page shows a card for a title cataloged under corporate author. Note that three indentions are to be observed on such a card, as shown by the schematic in Figure B-3. This form is also used by the Library of Congress for serials entered under a personal author.

Some libraries do not use the three indentions shown above, but prefer to have only two. In this case, they type the volume and date information on the same indention as the title. Notes are all given paragraph indention.

Some libraries use upper case to indicate corporate authors or the surnames of personal authors in main entries. This does make the card easier to read, particularly if there is a lot of information on the card; it tends to look less crowded with type variations. Some also capitalize the entire word of serial titles, or perhaps all of the serial title, when the entry is under title. One should be careful, however, in giving appropriate directions for filing, or perhaps not capitalizing on the occasion when there might be question as to whether the first word is an initialism and should be filed as such, not as a word, or an acronym with the reverse policy. Filers may be unsure and should have adequate directives, preferably on the cards themselves.

Normal capitalization, — that is, not for ease in reading, as mentioned above — should be restricted to proper names and derivatives of proper names,

Pioneer America Society.
　　Proceedings.　v. 1–
　　1972–
　　[Falls Church, Va.]

　　　　v. 28 cm. annual.

　　　　Vols. 1–　include papers for the fifth–　　annual meeting of
　　　　the Pioneer America Society.

　　　　1. Pioneer America Society.

　　　　E172.P5615　　　　　　　973′.06′273　　　　　74–640020
　　　　ISSN 0092–6582　　　　　　　　　　　　　　　　　MARC–S

　　　　Library of Congress　　　　　74 [2]

Fig. B-3. Serial card with corporate author heading.

```
Call    Corporate Heading.............................
No.         Title.....................................
        Volume and date information..................
        Imprint......................................
            Collation       Frequency

            Note.....................................
            Note.....................................
        .............................................

        Tracings.....................................
        .............................................
```

Fig. B-4. Schematic for serial card with author entry.

such as adjectives. The definition of "proper name" should include names of countries, administrative divisions, regions, localities, geographic features, names of persons, national, racial, cultural, or tribal groups, and names of corporate bodies. Names of months and other calendar divisions may be capitalized if this is normal for the language involved. Usually the first word of a serial title is capitalized, even if it is an article.

If a title is derived from the merger of two titles, the second title is not normally capitalized. For example:

Illinois mining gazette and railway age.

The frequency in the collation is not capitalized. "Series" and other words in the statement of "holdings" are not normally capitalized, unless the usage of the language requires it, as in German. For other capitalization rules, see Appendix II of the AACR.

It is standard cataloging punctuation that the colon [:] should be followed by an explanatory title. Generally the semicolon [;] is used after the main title to introduce the subtitle. More than one can be confusing in a single entry, however, and a comma [,] should be used in place of the second one. The period [.] comes at the end of a title (or subtitle). It may be followed by (an)other title(s) of a parallel nature, as in the case of a serial with a title in one or more additional languages. Brackets [[ ]] indicate information not found on the title page, and ellipses [. . .] indicate that something has been omitted. The former is not used very much in serial cataloging, except in imprints, and the latter is rarely, if ever, used in cataloging at all anymore. For punctuation of numbering, see rule 163D. Double punctuation generally should be avoided, except when prescribed by the ISBD(S).

The spellings of the title-page should be used. Current usage should be followed. Misspellings can be noted by [!] or [sic] in brackets, as with monographic cataloging. This is not normally done, however, for cute typographical oddities of serials like the *Artbibliographies.*

In serials cataloging it is important to leave space for additions. The numbering and dates should have the greater part of a line, or even two, depending upon the length of the title which precedes it. Then the card can simply be added to, rather than having to retype the entire card from scratch for closing dates or indicating a new series or change of numbering. Space should be left to close the number of volumes in the collation, as in the previous examples. As much space as possible should be left for notes. If an index is received, it should be entered a few lines down so that notes may be entered above it, if needed. If the tracings will take up an extraordinarily large amount of room on the card, they should be typed on the back or on an extension card. Same for contents. All precautions should be taken that the card will not have to be retyped for additions. If holdings are listed, or stamps are used, sufficient space should be left for these, too. For other directions, see LC cards for models, the appendices to AACR, and any local typing manuals.

Appendix C

Generic Titles

The following list of generic titles is given to alleviate in part the confusion brought on by the expression "generic title." A generic title is one which describes a type of material, a kind of publication. It may also denote frequency. This should not be confused with a "common title," which may be just as nondistinctive, but which is not a description of genera, such as *Anthropological papers* or *Studies in communication*. Note also that these titles are only generic when standing by themselves or in conjunction with a corporate body:

Journal of the American Catch Society
Transactions of the American Philosophical Society
Bulletin of the American Schools of Oriental Research.

Although some of the same terms appear in the following titles, these titles are distinctive:

Journal of secondary education
Newsletter on intellectual freedom
Bulletin of the atomic scientists.

The list which follows should only be considered a guideline, for it makes no claim of being complete. (Hopefully, a more complete one will be forthcoming in the near future so that catalogers can better interpret the rules.)

Abhandlungen	Acta
Abstract of accounts	Actas
Abstracts	Actes
Abteilungen	Activities report
Accession list	Acts

Advance sheet
Agenda
Almanac[k]
Almanach
Almanaque
Anais
Analecta
Analele
Anales
Anleitung
Annalen
Annales
Annali
Annals
Annalyi
Annotated bibliography
Annuaire
Annual
Annual budget
Annual conference minutes
Annual conference proceedings
Annual conference report
Annual financial report
Annual meeting
Annual plan
Annual plan of work
Annual progress report
Annual report
Annual report and accounts
Annual report and balance sheet
Annual report and statement
    of accounts
Annual report statistics
Annual research report
Annual review
Annual roster
Annual seminar
Annual statistical report
Annual statistical summary
Annual technical report
Annuario
Annuarium

Anuário
Anuário estatístico
Appendix
Arbeiten
Arbeten
Arbog
Arbok
Archiv
Archive(s)
Archivio
Archivium
Archivo
Archivos
Arkhiv
Arkiv
Arsbok
Arskrit
Arsskrift
Atti
Audit report
Avdelning
Avulso
Beihefte
Beiträge
Beretning
Bericht
Bibliografia
Bibliographia
Bibliographical contributions
Bibliographie
Bibliographies
Bibliography
Biblioteca
Bibliotheca
Bibliothek
Bibliotheque
Biennial report
Biennial reviews
Bi-monthly
Biographical directory
Biuletyn
Biulleten'

Blätter
Boletim
Boletim informativo
Boletin
Boletin de información
Boletines y trabajos
Bollettino
Booklet
Brochure
Budget
Budget in brief
Budget summary
Bulletin
Bulletino
By-Laws
Byulleten
Cadernos
Cahiers
Calendar
Cases
Catalog
Catalogo
Catalogue
Chapbook
Checklist
Circulaire
Circular
Circular of information
Collected papers
Collected reprints
Collection
Collections
Colloque
Colloquia
Communications
Compte(s) rendu(s)
Contributions
Crônica
Cuadernos
Decisions
Denkschriften
Digest

Directory
Documents
Doklady
Dokumenty
Essais
Essays
Estimates
Etudes
Executive reports
Extension bulletin
Extension circular
Extracts
Ezhegodnik
Fact sheets
Final report
Förhandlingar
Folder
Folletos
Forschung
Forschungen
Fortschritte
Gaceta
Gazetta
Gazette
General bulletin
General report
Giornale
Glasnik
Godishnik
Godish'jak
Godovoi obzor
Godovi otchet
Guidebook
Handbook
Handbook and directory
Handbuch
Handlingar
Highlights
Index
Informaciones
Information actualités
Information bulletin

Information circular
Information pamphlet
Information series
Information sheet
Informator
Informe
Informe anual
Interim report
Investigations
Izdaniia
Izvestiia
Jaarboek
Jaarverslag
Jahrbuch
Jahresbericht
Jahresschrift
Jahresverzeichnis
Jornal
Journal
Katalog
Leaflet
Lecture series
Lectures
Letopis'
Letter
Lietopisi
List
Listok
Magazine
Manual
Materialy
Matrikel
Meddelanden
Meddelelsen
Mededelingen
Mélanges
Membership directory
Mémories
Memoirs
Memoranda
Memoria y balance general
Memorials

Memorias
Memorie
Minutes
Miscellaneous papers
Miscellaneous publications
Miscellaneous reports
Miscellaneous series
Mitteilungen
Mitteilungsblatt
Mitteilungsdienst
Monatsbericht
Monatsheft
Monatsschrift
Monografias
Monographien
Monographies
Monograph series
Monographs
Monthly bulletin
Monthly journal
Monthly report
Monthly review
Nabliudeniia
Nachrichten
National conference
Nauchnye trudy
Naukovi zapysky
News
News bulletin
News letter
Newsletter
Notas
Notes
Notes de recherches
Notices
Noticias
Observations
Occasional newsletter
Occasional papers
Official minutes
Official proceedings
Official publications

Official reports
Operations
Opinions
Pamphlet
Papers
Periodical
Portfolio
Prace
Preliminary report
President's report
Proceedings
Proceedings of the annual conference
Proceedings of the annual convention
Proceedings of the annual meeting
Proceedings of the conference
Procès-verbaux
Professional papers
Program
Program de trabalho
Progress report
Protokll
Protokoly
Publicaciones
Pubblicazioni
Publicaçãos
Publications
Publikationen
Publikationer
Obzor
Occasional publications
Otchet
Otchet o diatel'nosti
Quarterly
Quarterly bulletin
Quarterly bulletin of statistics
Quarterly digest
Quarterly journal
Quarterly newsletter
Quarterly report
Quarterly review
Quarterly statistical review
Raccotta

Rapport annuel
Rapport d'activité
Rassegna
Record
Recueil
Recueil des travaux
Register
Relatório anual
Rendiconti
Report
Report of activities
Report of investigations
Report series
Reporter
Reprint
Research bulletin
Research notes
Research papers
Research publications
Research report
Research report series
Research reporter
Research series
Research summary
Review
Revista
Revue
Rivista
Rocznik(i)
Roster
Sammlung
Sbornik
Sbornik nauchnykh rabot
Sbornik nauchnykh trudov
Sbornik rabot
Sbornik trudov
Schriften
Schriftenreihe
Semiannual report
Seminaires
Seminars
Série

Serie trabajos técnicos
Series
Seriia
Sitzungsberichte
Skrifter
Sobranie
Soobshcheniia
Special bulletin
Special publications
Special report
Special report series
Spisok
Statement
Statistical analysis
Statistical data
Statistical handbook
Statistical report
Statistical summary
Statistical yearbook
Statisticheskii ezhegodnik
Statistics
Studi
Studia
Studien
Studies
Summary
Supplement
Supplementary series
Survey
Svod
Svodka
Symposia
Technical bulletin
Technical notes
Technical papers
Technical publications
Technical report
Technical report series

Textes
Textos
Texts
Tidskrift
Tidsskrift
Tijdschrift
Toimituksia
Trabajos
Tracts
Transactions
Translations
Travaux
Trudy
Tsirkuliary
Uchenyi trudy
Uchenyi zapiski
Uspekhi
Verhandlingen
Verhandlungen
Veröffentlichung
Vestnik
Visnyk
Voprosy
Vorträge
Vremennik
Wissenschaftliche Abhandlungen
Wochenblatt
Yahrbuch
Yearbook
Yearly report
Zapiski
Zbirnyk
Zeitschrift
Zeitung
Zentralblatt
Zhurnal
Zpravy

Appendix D

Holdings Reference Notes

Following are variations of notes used on public catalog cards giving information on holdings (and sometimes location as well). Some are typed-on notes, some are stamps, perhaps with attendant arrows penciled on the cards. The list is representational and makes no attempt to be complete. For the most part, the directives are clear to serials staff, although it is questionable whether patrons understand such technical terms as "main entry" or "Kardex." Such directives should always be made as clear as possible for the patron. Each library, however, must make its own decision, knowing its own situation. The examples here should be self-evident.

A COMPLETE RECORD OF ALL VOLUMES OR NUMBERS IN THE LIBRARY WILL BE FOUND IN THIS CATALOG UNDER THE ABOVE TITLE

A COMPLETE RECORD OF ALL VOLUMES OR NUMBERS IN THE LIBRARY WILL BE FOUND IN THIS CATALOGUE UNDER THE ABOVE MAIN ENTRY

APPLY FOR VOLUME DESIRED

COMPLETE RECORD IN SERIAL CATALOG

CURRENT NUMBERS IN PERIODICAL ALCOVE

CURRENT NUMBERS IN PERIODICAL ROOM

FOR A FULL RECORD OF THE LIBRARY'S HOLDINGS APPLY TO THE REFERENCE DESK OR THE SERIALS DIVISION

FOR A FULL STATEMENT AS TO VOLUMES POSSESSED BY THE LIBRARY, SEE MAIN CARD

FOR ADDITIONS SEE SERIAL RECORD
FOR COMPLETE INFORMATION SEE SERIAL CATALOGUE
FOR COMPLETE LIST OF VOLUMES IN LIBRARY SEE CARD BEGINNING
[main entry]
FOR COMPLETE LIST OF VOLUMES IN THE LIBRARY, SEE CON-
TINUATION CHECKLIST IN CATALOG ROOM
FOR COMPLETE RECORD, SEE CHECKLIST
FOR COMPLETE RECORD SEE CHECKLIST IN PERIODICAL DIVISION
FOR CURRENT NUMBERS SEE BINDER'S RECORD
FOR CURRENT NUMBERS SEE PERIODICAL FILE
FOR DETAILS AND LOCATION OF SETS SEE BINDING REGISTER
FOR FULL INFORMATION AND HOLDINGS SEE UNDER [ARROW ON
UNIT CARD TO MAIN ENTRY[
FOR FULL INFORMATION SEE CARD UNDER [main entry]
FOR FULL INFORMATION SEE MAIN ENTRY
FOR FULL INFORMATION SEE TITLE
FOR FULL STATEMENT OF HOLDINGS SEE MAIN AUTHOR ENTRY
FOR FULL STATEMENT OF VOLUMES IN LIBRARY SEE CARD BEGIN-
NING: [main entry]
FOR FULLER INFORMATION SEE [arrow to main entry]
FOR FURTHER INFORMATION CONSULT THE SERIAL RECORD IN THE
PERIODICAL ROOM
FOR HOLDINGS INFORMATION INQUIRE AT [name of information desk]
FOR HOLDINGS SEE AUTHOR ENTRY
FOR HOLDINGS SEE LOCATION FILE
FOR HOLDINGS SEE MAIN ENTRY
FOR HOLDINGS SEE OFFICIAL SERIALS CHECKLIST
FOR HOLDINGS SEE PUBLIC SERIALS LIST
FOR HOLDINGS SEE SERIALS CHECKING FILE
FOR HOLDING SEE SERIALS RECORD
FOR HOLDINGS SEE SERIALS REGISTER
FOR HOLDINGS SEE SHELFLIST
FOR ISSUES NOT RECORDED HERE INQUIRE AT PERIODICAL DESK
FOR LIBRARY HOLDINGS SEE SERIAL RECORD
FOR LIST OF VOLUMES IN THIS LIBRARY SEE NEXT CARD
FOR LOCATION OF UNBOUND NUMBERS INQUIRE AT REFERENCE
DESK
FOR RECORD OF HOLDINGS SEE SHELFLIST AND SERIAL RECORDS
FOR SERIALS HOLDING SEE SERIAL RECORD
FOR STATEMENT OF HOLDINGS IN THIS LIBRARY, SEE CARD UNDER
TITLE
FOR VOLUMES IN LIBRARY SEE MAIN CARD

FOR VOLUMES IN LIBRARY SEE PERIODICALS SHELFLIST
FOR VOLUMES RECEIVED SEE CARD BEGINNING: [main entry]
FULL RECORD IN [location]
FULL RECORD OF HOLDINGS IN CENTRAL SERIAL RECORD
HOLDINGS AND BIBLIOGRAPHICAL HISTORY IN SERIAL RECORD
IN PROGRESS. ADDITIONS ON SHELFLIST
IN PROGRESS. FOR NUMBERS IN LIBRARY SEE PERIODICALS
  CATALOG
INCOMPLETE. ADDITIONS ON SHELFLIST
INFORMATION REGARDING ISSUES RECEIVED IS AVAILABLE AT THE
  DESK IN THE PERIODICAL ROOM
LIBRARY HAS A COMPLETE SET OF THIS PERIODICAL BEGINNING
  WITH VOLUME 1, 1935
OTHER NUMBERS UNBOUND IN PERIODICALS DIVISION
RECORD OF HOLDINGS AT PERIODICAL DESK
RECORD OF HOLDINGS UNDER MAIN ENTRY ONLY
SEE KARDEX
SEE SERIAL RECORD
SEE SERIALS CATALOG
SEE SERIALS DEPARTMENT FOR HOLDINGS
SEE SERIALS OR PERIODICAL FILE FOR HOLDINGS

Appendix E

The Serials Department, General Library, University of California, Riverside

The point of this book is definitely not "how we do it good at UCR"; however, it may help to know the atmosphere in which it was conceived. The General Library Serials Department at UCR is somewhat unique and has elicited some interest and favorable comments in the past. It is in this spirit that it is described here as a prototype of an integrated serials department.

The Library system at this, one of the smaller campuses of the University of California's nine-campus system, is composed of three libraries, each housed in a separate building. The Physical Sciences Library and the Bio-Agricultural Library are located near the disciplines which they serve and are really special libraries. The Bio-Agricultural Library, descended from the library of the Citrus Experiment Station which predates the campus, houses most of the technical processes for "Phys Sci" as well — "Phys Sci" being primarily a public service unit with some housekeeping functions. The Library Administration manages all three library buildings as one and resides in the General Library. The General Library houses the general collection that serves the social sciences, humanities and fine arts faculties. The working staff is divided into: Circulation Services (including the Reserve Book Room), Reference Services (including Government Publications, Interlibrary Loan, Education Services [the curriculum collection], and Special Collections, as well as General Reference), Monographs (Acquisitions, Bibliographic Searching, Typing, Bindery and Marking for monographic materials, and Catalog Maintenance) and Serials.

The Serials Department is composed of five sections which comprise a "mini-library" of serials experts. Serials remain under the aegis of this Department except for the shelving, inventory, and circulation of bound holdings, which comes under the jurisdiction of the Circulation Department. All other functions are concentrated and centralized in the Serials Department. There are 7,900 current subscriptions and a total of 13,400 serials controlled by this department. The Serials Department has an administrative staff of two: the Serials Librarian and an Administrative Assistant. (See Table of Organization which follows.)

The *Public Service Section* provides circulation and reference services for unbound serials and maintains a current reading room of about 3,500 titles. The current issues do not circulate, but the older issues do for three days. These are paged from closed backfile stacks. The Department is open almost all of the hours the library is, including nights and weekends. This section also assists patrons with the General Library's microform collection (all of the General Library's microforms except those in the Government Publications Department are housed in Serials). Most of the Department's staff has reference duty in Public Services, usually on nights and weekends. This benefits the Department, the person involved, and the patron immeasurably. (This Department firmly believes in the sharing of staff, as the Table of Organization will show.)

The *Acquisitions Section* has two subsections. The Ordering/Invoicing Subsection covers pre-order searching, claiming, gifts and exchanges, and invoicing. There is sharing of staff here among the several functions. Public Service staff also have some respite from the "firing line" by trading jobs with some of the Acquisitions people so that they can help out in invoicing, claiming, or other areas where they might have expertise or interest. This is also of benefit to all concerned.

The Processing Subsection covers standing orders processing, receipt, and record maintenance. Mail check-in functions are under the jurisdiction of this section. Staff members and some student help come from all sections for the checking-in of the daily mail. Due to this set-up, people involved in mail check-in only do it for one to three times a week, which cuts down on fatigue and errors. The Kardex is the central serial record used by all sections. It is adjacent to the Public Service area for ease in answering patron requests.

The *Automation Section* maintains the serials union list, which is updated on a quarterly basis. The section is also involved in providing data for the TRIP list (see Appendix G), which is a management information file. The Section is also looking at further expansion of its functions as the Library gets more involved in automated systems.

The *Cataloging Section* performs the role of bibliographic authority for the Department, as described in the text. It is involved in precataloging searching for both serials and analytics. Members of this section catalog both serials and analytics, either with copy or originally. This was not always true and many of

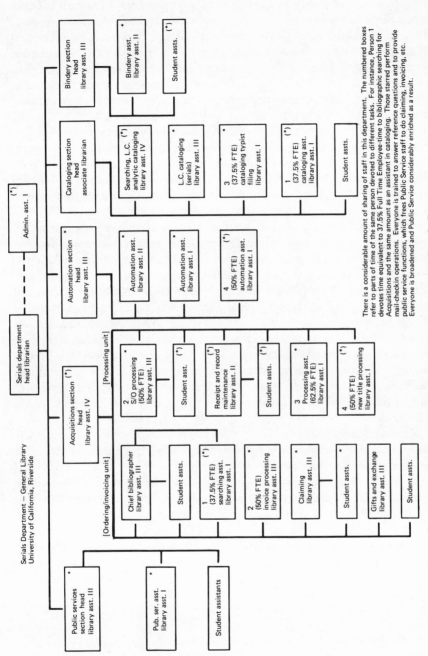

Fig. E-1. Table of Organization – UCR Serials Dept.

the dire predictions made in the text come from the "school of hard knocks" here. The serials catalogers are also involved with card production, typing, filing and shelflisting of bound volumes. The Cataloging Section also is in charge of marking the bound volumes, a function which also grew out of great need. Our experience at UCR has proved the need for the cataloger to be "right there" for resolution of the constant everyday problems. The Department interfaces with the Monographs Department on the general problems involving acquisitions and cataloging, but the real "nitty gritty" is kept within the bounds of the Department, which is the most satisfactory arrangement.

The binding for all units in the campus system is under the administrative jurisdiction of the head of the Serials *Bindery Section*. The Bindery Assistant does only serials. Shipments are sent to the University of California southern campus bindery in Santa Monica and turnaround time on most items is two weeks, giving optimum patron access to the collection.

Staff is shared back and forth so that communication is at its maximum. There is a great deal of sharing outside the Department on a library-wide basis, as well. The Serials Librarian is involved in a task force on problems relating to selection, duplication, etc., of serials on a campus-wide basis. This person is also member of a "super" task force of department heads who share ideas and provide policy-making input to the University Librarian. The Head of Serials Public Service sits on a Circulation Task Force. The Serials Cataloger is a charter member of a task force to discuss cataloging problems and methods of standardization. Other sections meet with their counterparts as time permits and need dictates. In this manner, Serials has ceased to be a stepchild of the library, always the "last to know," and has stepped into the mainstream of administrative functions as indeed the importance of its function should dictate.

Having all services in one Department allows one to adjust and control the work flow. Seeing how records and procedures affect the public causes one to try to make them easier to cope with and they are adjusted accordingly. All records in the Department become a continuation of the Kardex. Having the materials always in the department gives us the ease of putting our hands on it at any time. Administrative headaches are cut down. The esprit de corps is built up, for each staff member sees the fruits of his labors and his place in the Library's mission to its clientele. Public service colors the attitude of the whole department.

Appendix F

Charts of Serials Cataloging Workflow

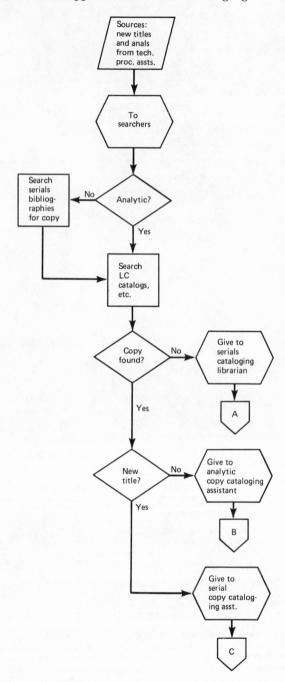

Fig. F-1. Flow chart of serials cataloging.

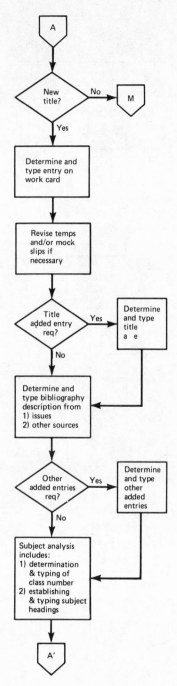

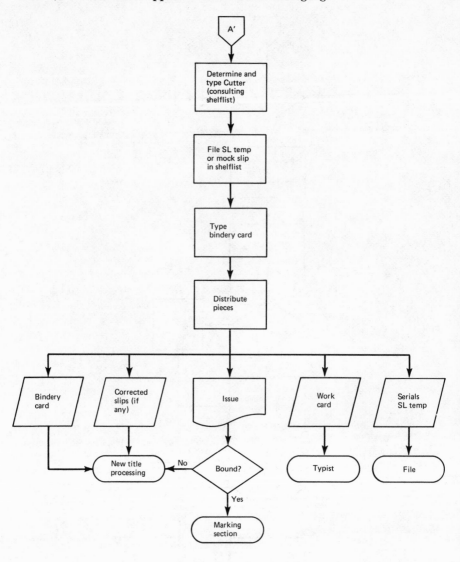

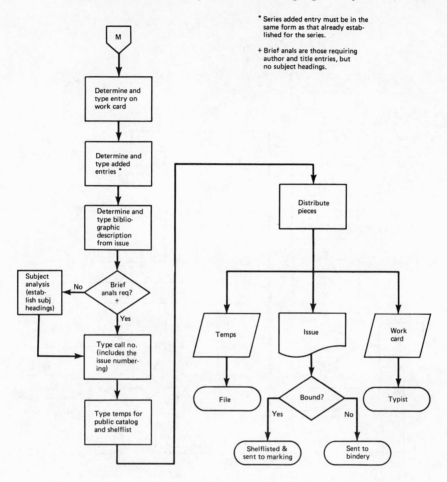

* Series added entry must be in the same form as that already established for the series.

+ Brief anals are those requiring author and title entries, but no subject headings.

M

Determine and type entry on work card

Determine and type added entries *

Determine and type bibliographic description from issue

Brief anals req? +

No → Subject analysis (establish subj headings)

Yes

Type call no. (includes the issue numbering)

Type temps for public catalog and shelflist

Distribute pieces

Temps → File

Issue → Bound?

Yes → Shelflisted & sent to marking

No → Sent to bindery

Work card → Typist

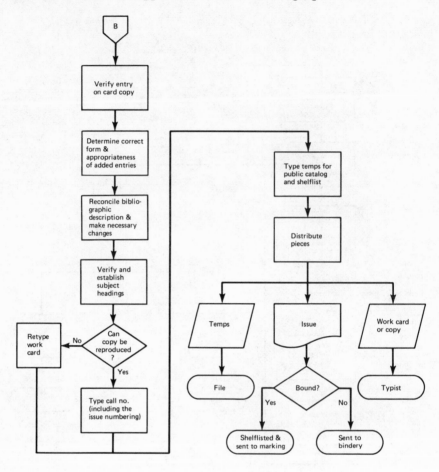

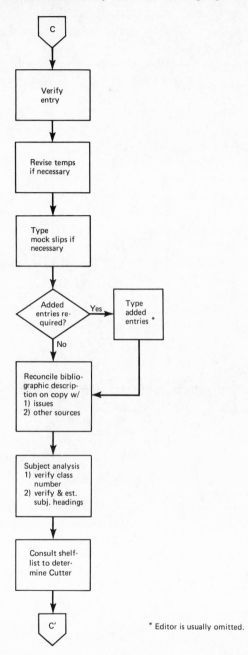

* Editor is usually omitted.

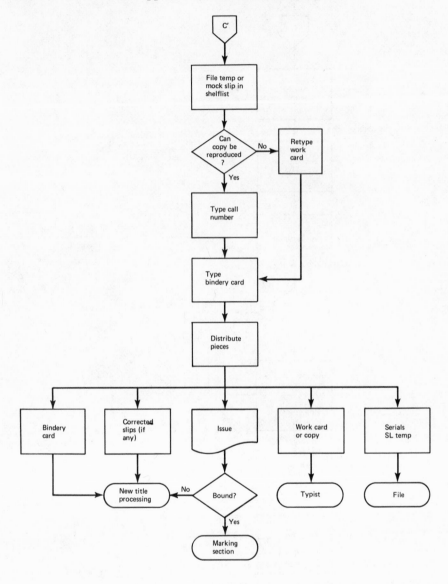

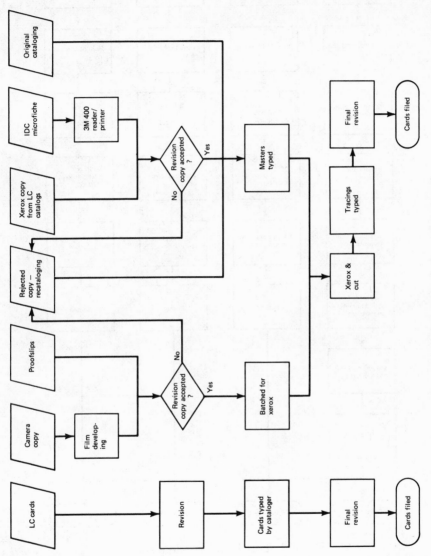

Fig. F-2. Serials cataloging card production.

387

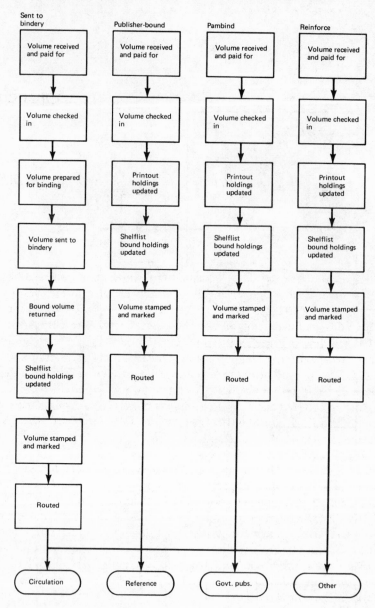

Fig. F-3. Serials added volume flow.

Appendix G

Explanation Of The UCR Change Memo

Some of the terms on the Change Memo form, which appear as Fig. 16-6, may be self-evident even to one not involved with its use or with the files at UCR. Many librarians who have worked with serials will recognize some of the files, although different names might have been used. Others, like TRIP, are unique to UCR and deserve some clarification. The top part is pretty straightforward, but the "record affected" might not be, so here are some clarifications.

Serials Cataloging: The entire section is circled if any records need a change. Because the staff knows which cataloging records are affected, these are not particularized on the memo. Changes appear on all cards in the set (except the Reference shelflist, which is changed by the Reference staff, see "Notify Reference").

{ *Pulled*   bd. vols.:
{ *Nothing bound:* The Cataloging Section is responsible for the bound volumes, but Processing keeps statistics for inventory so the Change Memo provides a mechanism whereby this information is passed on. If Processing has already pulled the volumes, a number in the blank indicates to Cataloging that the volumes have already been pulled. If nothing is bound, the staff is notified so that trips won't be made to the stacks in vain.

Public Catalog only: For "uncataloged collection" titles which have cards only in the main card catalog.

Kardex: The central serial record.

Problem Box: The snag file giving disposition of unwanted titles, explanation of mail coming in as solicited samples, records of material sent for review, and other problems. Also lists transfers and withdrawals (necessary because of odd issues "wandering in" or requests for titles which bibliographies such as *NST* list us as having which we no longer do).

389

Statistics form: Processing statistics, such as titles or volumes withdrawn, generated by a change.

On order/in process file: Order card and three copies of order (filed alphabetically). Kept until issue arrives. If title is new to this library, order card (with searching) and two copies of order are sent to Serials Cataloging with the issue. These become the Shelflist and Serials Shelflist temporary cards. The third copy is a control copy which indicates where the issues are located in the Department.

Printout: Computer-generated union list of serials for the campus.

TRIP: Computer-generated list of current titles with vendor codes, analytics notations, bindery priorities, and a binding calendar indicating when issues should be prepared for bindery. At present, it is for the General Library Serials Department only. There are plans to enlarge it to include other data, such as price information, language, country of origin, etc. and to expand it to include the current serial titles in the other libraries on campus. It is hooked up to the Printout via identification numbers. The acronym means "Titles Requiring Incessant Processing," an apt name.

Newspaper list: List of newspaper titles held by the Library, also a "spinoff" from the Printout.

Bindery priority: Self-evident.

Bindery/file of indexes: This is the bindery card illustrated in the text. The Bindery Section has a file of indexes awaiting binding with their volumes when they are complete or thick enough.

Pull issues for Bindery: Self-evident. Used, for example, if the title has ceased and is complete and may be bound.

Notify Reference: Reference is appraised of changes to titles shelved there.

Notify Music: The Music Department library is notified of changes to its titles. (Some current issues of music serials are housed in the School of Music.)

RR Label/Issues: Changes affecting the current serials reading room issues and labels, such as pulling for a canceled, ceased, or withdrawn title or changes in classification or entry for serials located in the reading room.

Backfile label/issues: Same as above for the closed backfile of noncurrent unbound issues.

Outside Serials Department: Record changes affecting some other area of the Library where serials are shelved: Reserve, Special Collections, Government Publications (for nongovernmental serials with "Govt. Pubs. Ref." as a location), Monographs Department, etc.

Payment record card: Self-evident.

Control file: One copy of each order, filed by date, until invoice is paid.

Fund slip: Copy of order sent to Accounting, at the time of order, to place a lien on funds. Purpose on change memo is to notify Accounting to cancel the lien if the order is canceled.

Claim record: Self-evident.

Replacement file: File of missing or mutilated issues which need to be ordered on replacement funds.

Cancellation letter sent: Self-evident.

Public Catalog: For on-order slips filed in the Public Catalog (see text) which are canceled.

Deselection list: The Library is trying to cut down on subscriptions so that serial subscriptions will not take over the static book budget in the next few years. The Library is weeding out titles no longer relevant to its collection. This is discussed somewhat in the text.

Exchange file: Files of titles that we are supposed to send and titles that we are supposed to receive on exchange.

Reorder with: Self-evident.

The term "Location Directive" in the middle of the memo refers to locations within the Department or outside the Department but not reflected in the call number, such as "Current edition is Reference copy" (a stamp which appears on the catalog cards). This does not appear in the call number because it does not refer to the entire set. Within the Department, it usually means reading-room location, which is set up according to an abbreviated Library of Congress scheme. It may also refer to an area of compact shelving called "Bind as received," which is a small current backlog of single issues of annuals, irregulars, and analytics awaiting bindery preparation and which, due to the type of material they are, do not receive backfile status.

Appendix H

Serial Record Division Manual

M12
(Revised August 1973)

Instructions Regarding Manuscript Sheet for Serials

[An LC manuscript sheet for serials appears in the text as Fig. 17-4.]

(Note: In addition to normal elements supplied for printed card cataloging, printed elements in non-Roman alphabets are to be romanized. The romanization is to be typed in red and should follow to the right of or appear below the information for the printed card within the same box. If any word (or words) in a field needs to be romanized, then the entire field should normally be repeated in red. It is not necessary to romanize in red a title which will be romanized completely in black in either uniform title position or in a title romanized note.)

Front of manuscript sheet:

Box		*Information to be Included*
1.	Classified as a collection; Call Number	To be checked and call number provided (if available) by Descriptive Cataloger for monographic series. Information available in the Official Catalog.
2.	Classified separately	To be checked by the Descriptive Cataloger for monographic series. Information available in the Official Catalog.

3.	Blank box in upper right hand corner under "Serials"	Priority number; also such terms as "Reprint," "New Copy," etc., if applicable.
4.	ME (Main Entry)	Main entry unless main entry is title (see no. 6 below).
5.	UTI (Uniform Title)	Uniform title for a work entered under an author, whether to be printed or to be given in corner mark position. If it is to be printed on the card, e.g., Law and Music cards, it is to be enclosed in brackets. If it is to be given in corner mark position, no brackets are used.
6.	TIL (Title)	Full title of the work (information from the title up to the edition statement).
7.	EDN (Edition Statement)	Edition statement.
8.	DAT (Dates of Publication)	Beginning and/or ending dates of publication (and other LC holdings). (Such information, when presented in a note, will be input in the note area — see no. 14 below.)
9.	IMP (Imprint)	Imprint.
10.	COL (Collation)	Collation.
11.	FRQ (Frequency)	Frequency, when it can be described by a single adjective or a brief phrase. (Such information, when presented in a note, will be input in the note area — see no. 14 below.)
12.	SE (Series statement)	Series statement.
13.	OAN (Overseas Acquisition Number)	Overseas acquisition number, i.e., LACAP.
14.	Large unmarked box	Notes, subject headings, and added entires.

15.	CAL (C͟al͟l Number)	To be completed by MARC-S editors.
16.	Class	Class number.
17.	Date	Date, when part of the class number.
18.	Cutter	Cutter number.
19.	Other	Date, when part of the book number. Alternate class numbers.
20.	COP (C͟op͟y Statement)	A different call number when assigned to 2d copies or sets.
21.	DCC (D͟ewey D͟ecimal C͟lassification Number)	Dewey classification number.
22.	CRD (LC C͟ar͟d Number)	Card number.
23.	L-shaped box in the lower right of the sheet	Reserved for the Estimating Unit, Card Division.
24.	MARC-S legend	This legend informs one that the cataloging data will be input into machine-readable form.

25. Boxes on the right side of the manuscript sheet. (Fixed field and variable field information *not* to be printed.

LAN (Languages)
FF
  1 (Encoding level)
  2 (Conference publication)
  3 (Type of serial)   (LAN and FF boxes 1, 15, 26,
  8 (Publication status) and 34 filled in, if applicable,
  9 (Frequency) by Descriptive Catalogers)
10 (Regularity)
11 (Type of material)
12 (Nature of Contents)
15 (Language)
20 (Type of cataloging used)
21 (Beginning date of publication)
22 (Ending date of publication)
23 (Country of publication)

25 (Form of reproduction)
26 (Physical medium designator)
28 (Modified record)   (FF boxes 11 and 12 and GAC
31 (Priority by to)   filled in, if applicable,
32 (Major/ minor change)   by Subject Catalogers)
33 (Nondistribution indicator)
34 (Government publication)
GAC (Geographic Area Code)

Verso of Manuscript Sheet:

Box		*Information to be included*
1.	Blank box to the left of the abbreviation "Cds."	To be used by the serials descriptive cataloger to indicate whether or not the main entry is established in the Official Catalog.
2.	Blank box to the left of the word "Series."	To be used by the serials descriptive cataloger to indicate whether or not the series is established in the Official Catalog.
3.	Series	To be left as is or to be crossed through by the serials descriptive cataloger to indicate whether or not the series is being traced.
4.	Cataloger's Notes	Serials descriptive cataloger's notes; Serial record file stamp. If shelflisting should send holdings for Serial Record, the notation "Send holdings" is to be written by the cataloger in this box.
5.	Large box in the upper right hand corner	To be filled in by the appropriate person at each stage of the processing flow.
6.	Class x-ref.	Notations (i.e., LAW, Juv) added by Subject Catalogers to indicate certain types of materials for which special card catalogs are maintained in the Library.
7.	Uniform Title x-ref.	Uniform title cross-references.

8. Cont. of p. 1

Any cataloging data to appear on the printed card which could not fit on the front of the manuscript sheet.

9. KEY (Key Title)

Key title information supplied by the National Serials Data Program.

10. ABB (Abbreviated Title)

Abbreviated title information supplied by the National Serials Data Program.

11. Local Info.

LC kept set and custody information. 901 tags refer to those copies being kept by the Library; 911 tags refer to x-copies being received by the Library. Custody refers to the last place where each copy is to be routed. (Such information is to be taken from the new serial routing slip and is to be filled in by the typist in the Maintenance Unit, Serial Record Division at the time the Serial Record entry is typed.)

12. ADD (Subscription Address)

The place to which one must write to place a subscription or order the publication in romanized form. (Filled in, when applicable, by serials descriptive catalogers.)

13. PRI (Subscription Price)

The subscription price of a serial when it is mentioned in the publication. (Filled in, when applicable, by serials descriptive catalogers.)

14. Blank box in lower right hand corner

Information which is to appear in the lower right hand corner of the preliminary master, i.e., a designation indicating whether the serial is bound or unbound and such designations as LL, MCL, etc. (Filled in by serials descriptive catalogers.)

References

PRIMARY SOURCES
[All citations given with cataloging entry.]

Ad Hoc Discussion Group on Serials Data Bases. Working Communications Subcommittee. *Memorandum*, 14 December, 1973.

Adams, Scott, "Progress toward a National Serials Data System," *Library trends* 18 (April 1970):520–536.

_____. *Proposal for a National Serials Data System*, Washington, D.C.: National Library of Medicine, 1969.

American Library Association. Catalog Code Division Committee, with the collaboration of a Committee of the (British) Library Association, *A.L.A. catalog rules: author and title entries*. Preliminary American 2nd edition, Chicago: American Library Association 1941.

_____. *Recommendations for the revision of the "International Standard Bibliographic Description for Serials."* Submitted by the ALA/RTSD Catalog Code Revision Committee, the Canadian Committee on Cataloging and the Library of Congress. (Typewritten.)

_____. Committee on Descriptive Cataloging. *Final report on the rules for descriptive cataloging in the Library of Congress.* Washington, D.C. : Library of Congress, 1948.

_____. Division of Cataloging and Classification. *A.L.A. cataloging rules for author and title entry.* 2nd edition, edited by Clara Beetle. Chicago: American Library Association, 1949.

Anable, Richard, "The Ad Hoc Discussion Group on Serials Data Bases: its history, current position, and future," *Journal of library automation* 6 (December, 1973):207-214.

_____. "CONSER: an update," *Journal of library automation* 8 (March, 1975):26-30.

Anglo-American cataloging rules, prepared by the American Library Association, the Library of Congress, the Library Association and the

Canadian Library Association, North American text, general editor: C. Sumner Spalding, Chicago: American Library Association, 1967.

Anglo-American cataloging rules, North American text, Chapter 6 separately published monographs, incorporating Chapter 9, "Photographic and other reproductions," and revised to accord with the "International Bibliographic Description Monographs," prepared by the American Library Association, the Library of Congress, the Library Association and the Canadian Library Association, Chicago: American Library Association, 1974.

Anglo-American cataloguing rules, prepared by the American Library Association, the Library of Congress, the Library Association and the Canadian Library Association, British text, London: Library Association, 1967.

Ashley, M. H. G., "Title entries: entry of serial publications whose titles have changed," Working Paper No. 5 in Canadian Institute on Cataloguing Principles and Rules, St. Andrews, New Brunswick, June 17, 1961, *Summary of proceedings and working papers,* Canadian Library Association Occasional Papers, No. 33, Ottawa: Canadian Library Association, 1961.

Bennett, Fleming, "A multipurpose serials record," *College and research libraries* 9 (July, 1948): 231–237.

Berry, Paul L., "Library of Congress serial record techniques," *Serial slants* 3 (July, 1952): 14-18.

Bidlack, Russell, *Typewritten catalog cards; a manual of procedure and form with 25 sample cards,* Ann Arbor, Mich. : Ann Arbor Publishers, 1959.

Bird, Nancy, "Title cataloging of periodicals at Florida State University," *Serial slants* 4 (January, 1953): 19-20.

Bonser, W., "The necessity for uniformity in the cataloguing of periodicals," Association of Special Libraries and Information Bureaux. *Report of proceedings* 4 (1927): 44-48.

Borden, Elizabeth C., "Revision of cataloging rules for serial entries proposed in the Lubetzky report," *Serial slants* 5 (April, 1954): 95-100.

Borden, Joseph C., "The advantages and disadvantages of a classified periodicals collection," *Library resources and technical services* 9 (Winter, 1965): 122–126.

Bosseau, Don L., "The computer in serial processing and control," *Advances in librarianship* 2 (1971): 103-164.

Bradford, S. C., "The cataloging of publications of societies and corporate bodies," *I.I.D. communications* 3 (1936): columns Br. 1-10.

Brynteson, Susan, "Change in rule 6?" *Title varies* 1 (June, 1974): 21, 23.

Cannan, Judith Proctor, "The impact of international standardization on the rules of entry for serials," *Library resources and technical services* 19 (Spring, 1975):164-169.

_____. "Serials cataloging: successive entry," *Library resources and technical services* 17 (Winter,1973): 73-81.

_____. "Successive entry at CUL," Cornell University. Libraries. *Bulletin* 179 (September, 1972): 7-11.

"Catalog code revision; get your headgear out of bed dear and write to Edgar," *Title varies* 2 (March, 1975): 5, 7.

"Cataloged serials converted into a MARC format," *Library of Congress information bulletin* 32 (January 26, 1973): 33.

"Cataloging rules," *Library resources and technical services* 8 (Summer, 1964): 299.

"Change in form of entry for the serial record," *Library of Congress information bulletin* 11 (January 7, 1952): 6-7. Also in American Library Association. *Division of Cataloging and Classification. Journal* 8 (March, 1952): 11.

Chaplin, A. H., "International Meeting of Cataloguing Experts, Copenhagen, 1969, report," *IFLA annual* (1969):78-83.

Clark, Pearl Holland, *The problem presented by periodicals in college and university libraries,* Chicago : The University of Chicago, 1930.

Clitheroe, Edith, "Serials in a university library," *Library resources and technical services* 1 (Winter, 1962): 89-92.

Colloquium on the Anglo-American Cataloging Rules. *The code and the cataloger; proceedings. . .held at the School of Library Service, University of Toronto on March 31 and April 1, 1967,* Toronto : University of Toronto Press, 1969.

Columbia University. School of Library Service. *Sample catalog cards for use in connection with courses in technical services in libraries and organization of materials,* 4th. edition, New York: Columbia University School of Library Service, 1967.

Comins, Dorothy, "Catalog code revision for serial publications," *Library resources and technical services* 5 (Summer, 1961): 220-224.

"Cooperative conversion of serials," *American libraries* 6 (January, 1975): 10-11.

Corbin, John B., "Centralized vs. decentralized serials handling; a review," *Library resources and technical services* 7 (Winter, 1963): 96-99.

Cornell University. Libraries. *Manual of cataloging procedures,* 2d edition, Ithaca, N.Y. : Cornell University Libraries, 1969.

Croghan, Antony, *A short code of rules for author, title and descriptive cataloguing; with explanations and examples,* London:Coburgh Publications, 1971.

Cutter, Charles A., *Rules for a dictionary catalog,* 4th edition, Washington, D.C. : Government Printing Office, 1904.

Daniels, Mary Kay, "Automated serials control: national and international considerations," *Journal of library automation* 8 (June, 1975):127-146.

Danielson, Rosamund H., "Serials holdings information service in research libraries," *Library resources and technical services* 10 (Summer, 1960):261-283.

Dewey, Harry, "Handling monographs in series," *College and research libraries* 15 (July, 1954):271-276.

_____., *Specialized cataloging and classification theory and technique*, Madison, Wisc. : College Typing and Printing Co., 1963.

Dickinson, Sarah S., "Idiosyncrasies of periodicals," *Catalogers' and classifiers' yearbook* 2 (1931):93-98.

Duffy, Lucille, "The Lubetzky report approved and disapproved," *Serial slants* 6 (April, 1955):63-71.

Dunkin, Paul S., "Problems in the cataloguing of serial publications," Working Paper No. 8 in International Conference on Cataloging Principles, Paris, 1961. *Report.* London : Organizing Committee of the International Conference on Cataloguing Principles, 1963.

Edgar, Neal, "CCRC Report," *Title varies* 2 (July, 1975):23, 27.

Escreet, P. K., *Introduction to the Anglo-American cataloguing rules*, with a foreword by N. F. Sharp, London : Andre Deutsch, 1971.

Ewald, Alice E., "Peculiarities, perplexities, and perversities of periodicals, with illustrations," *ALA bulletin* 30 (August, 1936):730-736.

Falconer, Helen M., "Function of the main entry in the alphabetical catalog," Working Paper No. 1 in Canadian Institute on Cataloguing Principles and Rules, St. Andrews, New Brunswick, June 17, 1961. *Summary of proceedings and working papers.* Canadian Library Association Occasional papers, No. 33, Ottawa: Canadian Library Association, 1961.

Fasana, Paul J., "Impact of national developments on library technical services and public services," *Journal of library automation* 7 (December, 1974):249-262.

Ferrer, Maxima M., "Guide to the cataloging of serial publications," Association of Special Libraries of the Philippines. *Bulletin* 1 (February 1, 1954):33-36.

Field, F. Bernice, "Comments on papers relating to the application of the Lubetzky principles to serials at the Armed Forces Medical and the New York Public Libraries," *Serial slants* 8 (July, 1956):125-132.

_____. "The new catalog code: the general principles and the major changes," *Library resources and technical services* 10 (Fall, 1966):421-436.

_____. "Serial entry," Paper No. 3 in Institute on Cataloging Code Revision, Stanford University, July 9-12, 1958. *Working Papers*, Stanford, Calif., 1958.

Gable, J. Harris, *Manual of serials work*, Chicago:American Library Association, 1937.

_____. "The new serials department," *Library journal* 60 (November 15, 1935):867-871.

Gemmell, Hortensia Tyler, *A study of the methods used in the cataloging of serial publications of societies and institutions in small college libraries*,

M.S. in L.S. thesis, Columbia University, 1940. Also abstracted in *Catalogers' and classifiers' yearbook* 9 (1940):115-116.

Goss, Edna L., "The cataloging of serials," *Catalogers' and classifiers' yearbook* 2 (1930):73-92.

Gravell, F. W., "The cataloguing of periodicals with special reference to the 'World List of Scientific Periodicals' and the 'Union List of Serials'," *State librarian* 2 (May, 1949):pages unnumbered.

Grenfell, David. *Periodicals and serials; their treatment in special libraries*, London : Aslib, 1965.

Grosch, Audrey N., "Minnesota Union List of Serials," *Journal of library automation* 6 (September, 1973):167-181.

Gull, C. D., "Convergence toward common standards in machine-readable cataloging," *Bulletin of the Medical Library Association* 57 (January, 1969):28-35.

Hamdy, M. Nabil. *The concept of main entry as represented in the Anglo-American cataloging rules; a critical appraisal with some suggestions: author main entry vs. title main entry*, Littleton, Colo.: Libraries Unlimited, 1973.

Hamilton, G. E., "Chapter 7: Serials (rules 160-168)" in Seminar on the Anglo-American cataloguing rules (1967), Nottingham, Eng., 1968, *Proceedings of the seminar,* organized by the Cataloguing and Indexing Group of the Library Association. . ., London : Library Association, 1969.

Hammer, Donald P., "Serial publication in large libraries: machine applications," in *Serial publications in large libraries,* edited by Walter C. Allen, London : Clive Bingley, 1971.

Hanson, Matilda F., "Use of the 'traveling card' in cataloging serials," *District of Columbia libraries* 11(January, 1940):23-24.

Harmon, Marian, "Policies for analyzing monograph series, part II: university libraries," *Serial slants* 4 (July, 1954):129-134.

Hartje, George N., *Centralized serial records in university libraries,* M.S. in L.S. thesis, University of Illinois, 1950. Also abstracted in *Serial slants* 1 (January, 1951):14-22.

_____. *Serial practices in public libraries.* University of Illinois. Library School Occasional papers, No. 45. Urbana: University of Illinois Library School, 1956.

Henderson, Katherine Luther, "Serial cataloging revisited — a long search for a little theory and a lot of cooperation," *Serial publications in large libraries,* edited by Walter C. Allen. London: Clive Bingley, 1971.

Hitchcock, Jennette E., "Works entered under title," Working paper VIII in Institute of Catalog Code Revision, McGill University, June 13-17, 1960. *Working papers,* Chicago, 1960.

Hitt, Sam W., "Evolution of the serials department at the University of Missouri library," *Serial slants* 6 (April, 1955):85-88.

Howard, Joseph H., "Main entry for serials," *Library of Congress information bulletin* 33 (November 22, 1974):A-232-A-236.

Hunter, Eric J.. *Examples illustrating Anglo-American cataloguing rules, British text 1967*, London: Library Association, 1973.

Information Dynamics Corporation. *A serials data program for science and technology; results of a feasibility study*, by William A. Creager, et. al, Reading, Mass., 1965.

International cataloguing, Vol. 1– January/March 1972– . London: IFLA Committee on Cataloguing.

International Conference on Cataloguing Principles, Paris, 1961. *Report*, London: Organizing Committee of the International Conference on Cataloguing Principles, 1961.

_____. *Statement of principles. . .*, Annotated edition with commentary and examples by Eva Verona, assisted by Franz Georg Kaltwasser, P. R. Lewis, Roger Pierrot, London : IFLA Committee on Cataloguing, 1971.

International Federation of Library Associations. *ISBD(M) — International standard bibliographic description for monographic publications*, 1st standard edition, London: IFLA Committee on Cataloguing, 1974.

_____. *ISBD(S) — International standard bibliographic description for serials*, recommended by the Joint Working Group in the International Standard Bibliographic Description for Serials set up by the IFLA Committee on Cataloguing and the IFLA Committee on Serial Publications. London: IFLA Committee on Cataloguing, 1974.

"International Serials Data guidelines," *Information retrieval and library automation* 9 (August, 1973):1-2.

Iskenderian, Yuchanik. *The extent and possibilities for co-operation in the cataloging of serial publications, based on a survey of libraries of over 350,000 volumes*, M.S. in L.S. thesis, Columbia University, 1941.

Johnson, Donald W. *Toward a National Serials Data Project: final report of the National Serials Pilot Project*, Washington, D.C.: Association of Research Libraries, 1972.

Kebabian, Paul B. "Application of the Lubetzky principles to serials at the New York Public Library," *Serial slants* 8 (July, 1956):118-124.

_____. "The Chaplin report: a symposium; large public libraries and the Paris Conference," *Library resources and technical services* 8 (Summer, 1964):213-218.

Kilpatrick, Norman L., "Serials records in a university library," *Journal of cataloging and classification* 6 (Spring, 1950):33-35.

Koltay, Emery I., "International standard serial numbering," *Bowker annual of library and book trade information* 17th (1972):197-200.

_____. "New serials titles 1950-1970, an international retrospective base for

ISSN," *Bowker annual of library and book trade information* 19th (1974):116-121.

Koster, C. M., "International standard serial numbers and the International Serials Data System," *Libri* 23 (1973):70-72.

Kuhlman, A. F., "Administration of serial and document acquisition and preparation," in *The acquisition and cataloging of books; papers presented before the Library Institute at the University of Chicago, July 29 to August 9, 1940,* edited by William M. Randall, Chicago: University of Chicago Press, 1940.

Lehnus, D. J.. *A manual of form and procedure for typewritten catalog cards and Anglo-American descriptive cataloging, a compilation of 200 exemplary cards indexed by rule number,* Kalamazoo, Mich., 1969.

Library of Congress. *Annual report of the Librarian of Congress,* 1866- Washington, D.C.: Library of Congress.

_____. *Guide to the cataloguing of periodicals,* prepared by Mary Wilson MacNair. 3d edition. Washington, D.C. : Government Printing Office, Library Branch. 1925, Reprinted in 1931.

_____. *Guide to the cataloguing of the serial publications of societies and institutions.* 2nd edition, compiled and edited by Harriet Wheeler Pierson, with a special section on the treatment of the publications of Masonic bodies by George M. Churchhill, Washington, D.C. : Government Printing Office, 1931.

_____. *Instructions for reporting serials for inclusion in the New serial titles,* Washington, D.C. : Library of Congress, revised March 1959.

_____. *New serial titles; a union list of serials commencing publication after December 31, 1949, 1950-1970 cumulative,* Washington, D.C.: Library of Congress; New York: Bowker, 1973.

_____. *Processing Department,* Washington, D.C.: Library of Congress, February, 1974.

Library of Congress. Descriptive Catalog Division, *Descriptive cataloging manual,* Washington, D.C.: Library of Congress, n.d.

_____. *Rules for descriptive cataloging in the Library of Congress adopted by the American Library Association.* Washington, D.C.: Library of Congress, 1949.

Library of Congress. MARC Development Office. *Information on the MARC system.* 4th edition. Washington, D.C.: Library of Congress, 1974.

_____. *Serials: a MARC format.* 2d edition. Washington, D.C.: Library of Congress, 1974.

Library of Congress. Processing Department. *Cataloging service bulletin.* Washington, D.C.: Library of Congress, 1– June 1945– .

_____. *Department memorandum* 111 (May 31, 1971).

———. *Department memorandum* 114 (August 1, 1972).

Library of Congress. Serial Record Division. *Serial Record Division manual,* Washington, D.C.: Library of Congress, n.d.

Livingston, Lawrence G., "A composite effort to build an on-line national serials data base," *Library of Congress information bulletin* 33 (February 1, 1974):A-35-A38.

———. "The Conser Project: current status and plans," *Library of Congress information bulletin* 34 (February 14, 1975):A-38-A42.

———. "International Standard Bibliographic Description for Serials," *Library resources and technical services* 17 (Summer, 1973):293–298.

Lohmann, Otto, "Efforts for international standardization in libraries," *Library trends* 21 (October, 1972):330-353.

Lubetzky, Seymour. *Cataloging rules and principles: a critique of the A.L.A. Rules for Entry and a proposed design for their revision,* prepared for the Board on Cataloging Policy and Research of the A.L.A. Division of Cataloging and Classification. Washington, D.C.: Library of Congress Processing Department, 1953. Reprinted, 1954.

———. *Code of cataloging rules, a partial and tentative draft for a new edition of bibliographic cataloging rules prepared for the Catalog Code Revision Committee,* [n.p.] June 1958.

———. "Fundamentals of Cataloging," Working paper II in Institute of Catalog Code Revision, McGill University, June 13-17, 1960. *Working papers,* Chicago, 1960.

———. *Principles of cataloging. Final report, phase I: descriptive cataloging.* Los Angeles: Institute of Library Research, University of California, July, 1969.

MacDonald, M. Ruth, "Application of Lubetzky['s] principles to serials at the Armed Forces Medical Library," *Serial slants* 7 (July, 1956):114-117, 145-148.

———. "Cataloging at the Armed Forces Medical Library, 1945-1952," American Library Association. Division of Cataloging and Classification. *Journal* 9 (June, 1953):58-78.

———. "Entry of corporate bodies under successive names," paper IV in Institute on Catalog Code Revision, Stanford University, July 9-12, 1958. *Working papers,* Stanford, Calif., 1958.

McMillen, Carolyn, "AACR revision," *Title varies* 1 (June, 1974):21, 23.

Mann, Margaret. *Introduction to cataloging and the classification of books.* Chicago: American Library Association, 1930.

"Meeting of the Cooperative Conversion of Serials (CONSER) Project Advisory Group, Washington, D.C., April 11, 1975," *Library of Congress information bulletin* 34 (May 30, 1975):A-87-A89.

Moriarty, John H. "Let's tell each other about our serial problems," *Serial slants* 1 (July, 1950):1-4.

Morsch, Lucile M., "Cataloging at the Library of Congress: a look into the future," *Southeastern librarian* 14 (Winter, 1964):245-251.

Mudge, Isadore G., "Present day economies in cataloging as seen by the reference librarian of a large university library," *Catalogers' and classifiers' yearbook* 4 (1939):9-23.

Muller, Hans, "Why classify periodicals?" *Wilson library bulletin* 14 (July, 1940):758-759.

"National Serials Data Program," *Library of Congress information bulletin* 33 (January 11, 1974):A-15-A-16.

National Serials Data Program. *Notes on special developments in the program,* Vol. 1- August, 1972- . Washington, D.C.: Library of Congress.

"National Serials Data Program enters new phase," *Information part 1: new sources/profiles* 4 (May-June, 1972):137.

"National Serials Data Program progress report is given," *Library of Congress information bulletin* 31 (December 1, 1972):513-514.

New rules for an old game; proceedings of a workshop on the 1967 Anglo-American Cataloguing Code, held by the School of Librarianship, the University of British Columbia, April 13 and 14, 1967 edited by Thelma E. Allen and Daryl Ann Dickman. Vancouver: Publications Centre, University of British Columbia, 1967.

Nitecki, Joseph Z., "Simplified classification and cataloging of microforms," *Library resources and technical services* 13 (Winter, 1969):79-85.

Osborn, Andrew D., "The crisis in cataloging," *Library quarterly* 11 (October, 1941):393-411.

_____. *Descriptive cataloging.* (Preliminary edition.) Pittsburgh: University of Pittsburgh, Graduate Library School, 1969.

_____. "International aspects of code revision; the long-standing desire for standardization of cataloging rules," Paper No. XI in Institute on Catalog Code Revision, Stanford University, July 9-12, 1958. *Working papers,* Stanford, Calif., 1958

_____. *Serial publications; their place and treatment in libraries,* Chicago: American Library Association, 1955.

_____. *Serial publications; their place and treatment in libraries.* 2d edition, revised. Chicago: American Library Association, 1973.

Osborn, Jeanne, "Multiple editions and serial cataloging," *Library resources and technical services* 13 (Fall, 1969):484-492.

Paul, Huibert, "Serials: chaos and standardization," *Library resources and technical services* 14 (Winter, 1970):19-30.

Pearson, J. D. "The analytical cataloguing of periodicals in a specialized field," *Library Association record* 57 (January, 1955):1-7.

Pierson, Robert M., "Where shall we shelve bound periodicals? Further notes," *Library resources and technical services* 10 (Summer, 1966):290-294.

Porter, K. I. "Standards for the presentation of information, with particular reference to serial publications," *Standardization for documentation*, edited by Bernard Houghton, pp. 27-43, London: Archon books and Clive Bingley, 1969.

Prevost, Marie Louise, "The Lubetzky report: harbinger of hope," *Journal of cataloging and classification* 10 (April, 1954):73-76.

_____. "Why classify periodicals?" *Wilson library bulletin* 15 (September, 1940):85.

"Progress on code revision," *Library resources and technical services* 19 (Summer, 1975):279-282.

Pulsifer, Josephine S., "Comparison of MARC serials, NSDP and ISBDS," *Journal of library automation* 6 (December, 1973):193-200.

Quartz, Beatrice M., "Policies for analyzing monograph series; Part I, college libraries," *Serial slants* 4 (July, 1953):124-128.

Rajan, T. N. and Guha, B., "The Anglo-American Cataloging Rules with emphasis on rule 6 (Serials)," *Annals of library science and documentation* 14 (December, 1967):206-211.

Rift, Leo R., "The girl they left behind. . .serials and the new catalog code," *M.L.A. quarterly* 13 (June and September, 1957):51-56, 83-86.

Rogers, Joseph W., "Miscellaneous rules, including the entries for congresses, conferences, etc.," Paper No. 8 in Institute on Cataloging Code Revision, Stanford University, July 9-12, 1958. *Working papers.* Stanford, Calif., 1958.

Rosenbaum, M., "International Serials Data System," *International cataloguing* 1 (October/December, 1972):4-6.

Rothman, Fred B., "Pooh-Bah of the serials division," *Library journal* 62 (June 1, 1937):457-459.

Rothman, Fred B., and Ditzion, Sidney, "Prevailing practices in handling serials," *College and research libraries* 1 (March, 1940):165-169.

Sample catalogue cards exemplifying the anglo-American Cataloguing Rules, compiled by K. L. Ball, *et. al.*, Toronto : University of Toronto Press, 1963.

Sauer, Mary, "Catalog Code Revision Committee serials meeting," *Library of Congress information bulletin* 34 (March 7, 1975):A-67-A-70.

_____. "RTSD CCS Serials Section program meeting," *Library of Congress information bulletin* 33 (August 16, 1974):A-186-A189.

Sayre, John L., and Hamburger, Roberta. *An illustrated guide to the Anglo-American cataloging rules.* Enid, Okla.: Seminary Press, 1971.

Schley, Ruth and Davies, Jane B. *Serials notes compiled from Library of Congress cards issued 1947 - April 1951.* New York : Columbia University Libraries, 1952.

Schlipp, Emily C., "Short cuts in serials cataloging?" *Serial slants* 1 (April, 1951):2-9. Also in *Journal of cataloging and classification* 7 (Spring, 1951):42-46.

"Semiannual report on developments at the Library of Congress, June 1975," *Library of Congress information bulletin* 34 (June 20, 1975):A-97-A-122.

"Serials: projects and publications," *International cataloguing* 4 (April/June, 1975)4: 6-8.

Shachtman, Bella E., "Simplification of serials records work," *Serial slants* 3 (July, 1952):6-13.

Sharp, Henry A., *Cataloguing; a textbook for use in libraries.* 4th edition. London: Grafton and Co., 1944.

Shores, Louis, "Serials in the library school curriculum," *Serial slants* 1 (October, 1950):4-14.

Simon, Beatrice V., "Cataloguing of periodicals," *Ontario library review* 33 (August, 1949):237-245.

_____. "Let's consider serials realistically," *Library journal* 71 (October 1, 1946):1302-1308.

Simpkins, Edgar G., *A study of serials processing,* M.S. in L.S. thesis, Western Reserve University, 1951. Also abstracted in *Serial slants* 2 (January, 1952):6-17.

Skipper, James E., "Organizing serial records at the Ohio State University Libraries," *College and research libraries* 14 (January, 1953):39-45.

Slocum, Robert B., and Hacker, Lois. *Sample cataloging forms; illustrations of solutions to problems in descriptive cataloging, 2nd revised edition of "Sample catalog cards," with a section on the "Anglo-American Cataloging Rules" and the "A.L.A. Cataloguing Rules,"* Metuchen, N.J.: Scarecrow Press, 1968.

Smith, Esther Anne, "Form cards," *Catalogers' and classifiers' yearbook* 5 (1936):55-62.

Smith, Lynn S., "The great serials department change memo and how it works," *U*N*A*B*A*S*H*E*D librarian* 8 (Summer, 1973):10-11.

_____. "A method of briefly cataloging newspapers," *U*N*A*B*A*S*H*E*D librarian* 9 (Fall, 1973):12.

Spalding, C. Sumner. *The cataloging of serials at the Library of Congress; a report with recommendations.* Washington, D.C.: Library of Congress. Serial Record Division, February 20, 1956, Retyped August 17, 1956.

_____. "I.S.B.D.: Its Origin, Rationale, and Implications," *Library journal* 98 (January 15, 1973):121-123.

_____. "ISBD(S) and title main entry for serials," *International cataloguing* 3 (July/September 1974):A-229-A-232.

_____. "Keeping serials cataloging costs in check," *Library resources and technical services* 1 (Winter, 1957):13-20.

_____. "Main entry: principles and counter-principles," *Library resources and technical services* 11 (Fall, 1964):389-396.

Swanson, Gerald, "ISBD, standard or secret?" *Library journal* 98 (January 15, 1973):124-130.

Tait, James A. *Authors and titles; an analytical study of the author concept in codes of cataloguing rules in the English language, from that of the British Museum in 1871 to the Anglo-American Cataloguing Rules 1967*, London: Clive Bingley, 1969.

_____. "Paper 1: editor's introduction and chapter 1: entry (rules 1-33)," in Seminar on the Anglo-American Cataloguing Rules (1967), Nottingham, Eng., 1968. *Proceedings of the Seminar organised by the Cataloguing and Indexing Group of the Library Association. . .*, London: The Library Association, *(1969)*.

Tauber, Maurice F., "Cataloging and classifying microfilm," *Journal of documentary reproduction* 3 (March, 1940):1-25.

Tauber, Maurice F. and Associates. *Technical services in libraries; acquisitions, cataloging, classification, photographic reproduction, and circulation operations*, New York: Columbia University Press, 1954.

Taylor, David C., "LUTFCSUSTC," *Michigan librarian* 39 (Winter, 1973):13-14.

Texas. Agricultural and Mechanical College, College Station. Library. *Rules for making title added entries*, compiled by Clara M. McFrancis, College Station, Texas: the Library, 1957.

Thornton, John L. *Cataloguing in special libraries — a survey of methods.* London: Grafton and Co., 1938.

Trotier, Arnold H. "The draft code and problems of corporate authorship," *Library resources and technical services* 6 (Summer, 1962):223-227.

_____. "Economies in the cataloging of continuations," *Catalogers' and classifiers' yearbook* 4 (1934):29-38.

_____. "Organization and administration of cataloging processes," *Library trends* 2 (October, 1953):264-276.

_____. "Organization of the catalog department in a university library," *Catalogers' and classifiers' yearbook* 5 (1936):9-18.

_____. "Some persistent problems in technical processes," *Serial slants* 1 (January, 1951):5-13.

Truelson, Stanley D., "The need to standardize descriptive cataloging," *Bulletin of the Medical Library Association* 57 (January, 1969):21-27.

UNISIST. *Guidelines for ISDS* Paris: UNESCO, "UNISIST International Serials Data System," *LARC newsletter* 5 (May, 1973):1-2.

Upham, Lois, "CONSER; cooperative conversion of serials project," *Library of Congress information bulletin* 33 (November 29, 1974):A-245-A-248.

Vassallo, Paul, "Introducing the National Serials Data Program," in Conference on Management Problems in Serials Work, Florida Atlantic University, 1973. *Management problems in serials work,* edited by Peter Spyers-Duran, and Daniel Gore. Westport, Conn.:Greenwood Press, 1974.

Walker, Elaine, "Serials in a college library," *Library resources and technical services* 6 (Winter, 1962):79-82.

Welsh, William J., "The Processing Department of the Library of Congress in 1968," *Library resources and technical services* 13 (Spring, 1969):175-197.

Whetstone, Gloria, "Serial practices in selected college and university libraries," *Library resources and technical services* 5 (Fall, 1961):284-290.

Wimersberger, Evelyn G. Methods of indicating seria holdings in the catalogs of college and university libraries. M.S. in L.S. thesis, Columbia University, 1939. Abstracted in *Catalogers' and Classifiers' yearbook* 8 (1939):133–134.

Wulfkoetter, Gertrude, "The organization of a periodical department," *Library journal* 55 (May 15, 1930):448-450.

SECONDARY SOURCES

Akers, Susan Grey. *Simple library cataloging.* 5th edition. Metuchen, N.J.: Scarecrow Press, 1969.

American Library Association. Catalog Code Revision Committee. "Report of progress addressed to Council on January 31 by the Committee's chairman," *A.L.A. bulletin* 42 (April, 1948):176-178.

Ashford, Daisy, "Serials in review: 1972," *Library resources and technical services* 17 (Spring, 1973):168-174.

Bakewell, K. G. B. *A manual of cataloguing practice,* Oxford, New York: Pergamon Press, 1972.

Ball, Katharine L., "International Conference on Cataloguing Principles, Paris, October 9th-18th, 1961," *Canadian library bulletin* 18 (January, 1962):147-155.

Bradford, S. C., "The cataloging of publications of societies and corporate bodies," *I.I.D. communications* 3 (1936): columns Br. 1-10.

Cabeen, Violet Abbott, and Cook, C. Donald, "Organization of serials and documents," *Library trends* 2 (October, 1953):199-216.

Casford, E. Lenore, "Periodicals, their use and preservation," *Wilson bulletin for libraries* 13 (May, 1939):593-596.

"Cataloging rules," *Library resources and technical services* 8 (Summer, 1964):299.

Chaplin, A. H., "Report of the International Meeting of Cataloguing Experts, Copenhagen, 1969," *Libri* 20 (1970):105-118.

Cockshutt, Margaret, E., "The Lubetzky report — its nature and significance," *Ontario library review* 38 (August, 1954):243-251.

Davinson, E. E., *The periodicals collection; its purpose and uses in libraries,* London: Andre Deutsch, 1969.

Dawson, John Minto, "A history of centralized cataloging," *Library resources and technical services* 11 (Winter, 1967):28-32.

Dean, Hazel, *Cataloging manual to supplement the A.L.A. Catalog Rules, 2nd edition, 1949, and the Library of Congress Rules for Descriptive Cataloging, 1949, for use in connection with the Library Science 394 and 505.* Los Angeles: School of Library Science, University of Southern California, n.d.

Desmond, Robert D., "1968: a summary treatment of the year in serials," *Library resources and technical services* 13 (Summer, 1969):387-390.

Dewey, Harry. *An introduction to library cataloging and classification,* 4th edition, rev. and enl. Madison, Wisc.: Capitol Press, 1957.

_____. "Serials clearinghouse number 4: cataloging," *Serial slants* 7 (April, 1956):96-97.

Dix, William S., "Recent developments in centralized cataloging," *Library resources and technical services* 11 (Winter, 1967):32-35.

Domanovsky, Akos, "Codemaking: a criticism and a proposal," *Vjesnik bibliotekara hrvatske* 14 (1969):58-67.

Dunkin, Paul S. *Cataloging U.S.A.* Chicago: American Library Association, 1969.

Elrod, J. McRee, "Applying the principle of dealing with exceptions," *Library resources and technical services* 16 (Summer, 1972):331-337.

_____. *Choice of main and added entries,* Chicago; educational Methods, 1969.

_____. "Year's work in cataloging and classification," *Library resources and technical services* 17 (Spring, 1973):175-200.

Fellows, Dorcas. *Cataloging rules with explanations and illustrations,* New York: Wilson, 1922.

Franck, Marga, "Some international differences in the cataloging and bibliographical listing of serial publications," American Library Association. Division of Cataloging and Classification. *Journal.* 8 (March, 1952):6-11. Also in *Serial slants* 2 (October, 1951):1-10.

Gjelness, Rudolph, "Research in cataloging and classification," *Library trends* 6 (October, 1957):171-186.

Gocher, Mary, "Periodical consultation," *Library journal* 65 (March 15, 1940):218-219.

Hall, H. W., "Serials '74: a review," *Library resources and technical services* 19 (Summer, 1975):197-205.

Hanson, J. C. M., "Corporate authorship versus title entry," *Library quarterly* 5 (October, 1935):457-466.

Harrod, Leonard Monague. *The librarians' glossary of terms used in librarianship and the book crafts and reference work.* Grafton library science series. London: Seminar Press, 1971.

Haykin, David Judson. *Subject headings; a practical guide,* Washington, D.C.: Government Printing Office, 1951.

Hill, Barbara M., "Serials in a special library," *Library resources and technical services* 6 (Winter, 1963):82-85.

Hill, Dorothy Jeanne, "Monograph series: their classification and their catalog records," *A.L.A. bulletin* 31 (October 15, 1937):735-736.

Hoodless, Jean, "National Research Council publications: a cataloging problem," *Serial slants* 7 (April, 1956):87-93.

Hopkins, Judith, "The Ohio College Library Center," *Library resources and technical services* 17 (Summer, 1973):308-319.

Horner, John. *Cataloguing,* London: Association of Assistant Librarians, 1970.

Huff, William H., "Serial observations — 1967," *Library resources and technical services* 12 (Spring, 1968):189–220.

_____. "A summary of some serial activities, 1942-1966," *Library resources and technical services* 11 (Summer, 1967):301-321.

"I.F.L.A. Committee on Cataloguing, 1954-1975," *International cataloguing* 3 (January-March, 1974):5-8.

"Institute on catalog code revision: a composite report," *Library resources and technical services* 3 (Spring, 1959):123-140.

Jolley, L., "Anglo-American Cataloguing Rules," *Journal of documentation* 23 (December, 1967):343-349.

_____. "International Conference on Cataloguing Principles II. Thoughts after Paris," *Journal of documentation* 19 (June, 1963):47-62.

Kapsner, Oliver L., "A.L.A. code revision progress," *Catholic library world* 33 (October, 1961):85-87.

Lazerow, Samuel, "Serial records: a mechanism for control," *Serial publications in large libraries,* edited by Walter C. Allen. London: Clive Bingley, 1971.

Lehnus, Donald J. *How to determine author and title entries according to AACR; an interpretive guide with card samples.* Dobbs Ferry, N.Y.: Oreona Publications, Inc., 1971.

Leigh, Charles W. E., "On the cataloguing of serial publications with special reference to the compilation of union lists of periodicals," *Library Association record* 3 (January, 1933):1-11.

Lyle, Guy R. *The administration of the college library.* 3rd edition. New York: Wilson, 1961.

Massoneau, Suzanne, "The year's work in cataloging and classification," *Library resources and technical services* 16 (Spring, 1972):155-164.

Merrill, William Stetson, "Report on standardization of publications," *A.L.A. bulletin* 25 (September, 1931):571-573.

Musiker, Reuben, "The new Anglo-American Cataloguing Code 1967: a review," *South African librarian* 35 (January, 1968):81-90.

Needham, C. D. *Organising knowledge in libraries; an introduction to information retrieval,* London: Andre Deutsch, 1971.

Nicholson, Natalia N., and Thurston, William, "Serials and journals in the M.I.T. library," *American documentation* 9 (October, 1958):304-307.

Olson, Kenneth D., "Union lists and the public record of serials," *Special libraries* 61 (January, 1970):15-20.

Pan, Elizabeth. *Library serials control systems: a literature review and bibliography* Washington, D.C.: E.R.I.C. Clearinghouse on Library and Informational Science and the American Society for Information Science, December, 1970.

Peddie, Robert A., "Cataloguing of periodicals," *Library* ser. 1, vol. 3 (1891):119-120.

Pettee, Julia, "The development of authorship entry and the formulation of authorship rules as found in the Anglo-American Code," in *The catalog and cataloging,* edited by Arthur Ray Rowland. Hamden, Conn.: Shoestring Press, 1965.

Piercy, Esther J. *Commonsense cataloging; a manual for the organization of books and other materials in school and small public libraries.* New York: Wilson, 1965.

_____. "Policies for analyzing monograph series; Part III: public libraries," *Serial slants* 4 (July, 1953):135-140.

Quigg, Patrick. *Theory of cataloguing; an examination guidebook.* 2nd edition. London: Archon Books and Clive Bingley, n.d.

Rather, John, "Tradition-bound demands on the catalog," *Journal of cataloging and classification* 11 (October, 1955):175-180.

"Reports on the Institute on Catalog Code Revision, held in Montreal, June 13-17, 1960, prior to the Joint Conference of the American Library Associaiton and the Association Canadiennes des Bibliothéques," *Library of Congress information bulletin* 19 (June 20, 1960):317-326.

Rescoe, A. Stan. *Cataloging made easy.* New York: Scarecrow Press, 1962.

_____. *Technical processes simplified.* Nashville: George Peabody College, Peabody Library School, 1956.

Sawyers, Elizabeth J., "Union list development: control of the serial literature," *Bulletin of the Medical Library Association* 60 (July, 1972):427-431.

Seely, Pauline A., "A.L.A. to A.A. — an obstacle race," *Library resources and technical services* 13 (Winter, 1969):7-25.

Skadlerup, Harry R., "Phonograph records in serials," *Library resources and technical services* 7 (Spring, 1963):216-218.

Spalding, C. Sumner, "Building, controlling and cataloging the serials collection," in A.A.L.L. Institute for Law Librarians, Grossinger, New York, 1959. *Cutting costs in acquisitions and cataloging.* A.A.L.L. publications series 1. Hackensack, N. J.: Fred B. Rothman and Co., 1960.

Tate, Elizabeth L., "Main entries and citations: one test of the revised cataloging code," *Library quarterly* 33 (April, 1963):172-191.

Tee, Edward Lim Huck, "Cataloguing of serial publications," *Malayan library journal* 2 (October, 1961):59-64.

Thompson, Elizabeth H. "Recent cataloging activities in American libraries, 1934-39," *Catalogers' and classifiers' yearbook* 8 (1939):102-120.

Trimmingham, Harriet Lawson, "Serial cataloging in the John Crerar Library," *Serial slants* 7 (April, 1956):68-70.

University of Utah. Libraries. Cataloging Department. *Manual,* by Roberta Purdy, and edited by Tom Landikusic. new edition. Salt Lake City, 1971.

Viswanathan, C. G. *Cataloguing theory and practice,* New York: Asia Publishing House, 1965.

Weber, Hans H., "Serials '73 — review and trends," *Library resources and technical services* 18 (Spring, 1974):140-150.

Wilde, Alice B., "Practical variations from Library of Congress methods of cataloging continuations," American Library Association. *Bulletin* 31 (October 15, 1957):827-830.

Wilkins, Eleanore E., "Solving the 'serial record' problem," *Special libraries* 53 (May-June, 1962):258-261.

Wilson, Louis Round, and Tauber, Maurice F. *The university library; the organization, administration, and function of academic libraries.* 2nd edition. New York: Columbia University Press, 1956.

Wright, Wyllis E., "General philosophy and structure of the code," in Arthur Ray Rowland, *The catalog and cataloging.* Contributions to library literature. Hamden, Conn.:Shoestring Press, 1969.

_____. "Some fundamental principles in cataloging," *Catalogers' and classifiers' yearbook* 8 (1939):133-134.

_____. "A report of progress on catalog code revision in the United States," *Library quarterly* 26 (October, 1956):331-336.

INDEX

415

Index of Rules/Rule Interpretations Quoted or Referred to

(Starred page numbers indicate quoted material)